CHURCH DOGMATICS

KARL BARTH
CHURCH DOGMATICS

VOLUME IV

THE DOCTRINE
OF RECONCILIATION

§ 61–63

JESUS CHRIST, THE LORD AS SERVANT III

EDITED BY
G. W. BROMILEY
T. F. TORRANCE

t&t clark

Published by T&T Clark
A Continuum Imprint
The Tower Building, 11 York Road, London, SE1 7NX
80 Maiden Lane, Suite 704, New York, NY 10038

www.continuumbooks.com

Translated by G. W. Bromiley

Copyright © T&T Clark, 2010

Authorised translation of Karl Barth, *Die Kirchliche Dogmatik IV*
Copyright © Theologischer Verlag Zürich, 1953–1967
All revisions to the original English translation and all translations of Greek, Latin and French
© Princeton Theological Seminary, 2009

All rights reserved. No part of this publication may be reproduced or transmitted in any form or by any means, electronic or mechanical, including photocopying, recording or any information storage or retrieval system, without permission in writing from the publishers.

British Library Cataloguing-in-Publication Data
A catalogue record for this book is available from the British Library

ISBN13: 978-0-567-26718-4

Typeset by Interactive Sciences Ltd, Gloucester, and Newgen Imaging Systems Pvt Ltd, Chennai

For further resources, including the forewords to the original 14-volume edition of the *Church Dogmatics*, log on to our website and sign up for the resources webpage: http://www.continuumbooks.com/dogmatics/

PUBLISHER'S PREFACE TO THE STUDY EDITION

Since the publication of the first English translation of *Church Dogmatics I.1* by Professor Thomson in 1936, T&T Clark has been closely linked with Karl Barth. An authorised translation of the whole of the *Kirchliche Dogmatik* was begun in the 1950s under the editorship of G. W. Bromiley and T. F. Torrance, a work which eventually replaced Professor Thomson's initial translation of *CD I.1*.

T&T Clark is now happy to present to the academic community this new *Study Edition* of the *Church Dogmatics*. Its aim is mainly to make this major work available to a generation of students and scholars with less familiarity with Latin, Greek, and French. For the first time this edition therefore presents the classic text of the translation edited by G. W. Bromiley and T. F. Torrance incorporating translations of the foreign language passages in Editorial Notes on each page.

The main body of the text remains unchanged. Only minor corrections with regard to grammar or spelling have been introduced. The text is presented in a new reader friendly format. We hope that the breakdown of the *Church Dogmatics* into 31 shorter fascicles will make this edition easier to use than its predecessors.

Completely new indexes of names, subjects and scriptural indexes have been created for the individual volumes of the *Study Edition*.

The publishers would like to thank the Center for Barth Studies at Princeton Theological Seminary for supplying a digital edition of the text of the *Church Dogmatics* and translations of the Greek and Latin quotations in the original T&T Clark edition made by Simon Gathercole and Ian McFarland.

London, April 2010

HOW TO USE THIS
STUDY EDITION

The *Study Edition* follows Barth's original volume structure. Individual paragraphs and sections should be easy to locate. A synopsis of the old and new edition can be found on the back cover of each fascicle.

All secondary literature on the *Church Dogmatics* currently refers to the classic 14-volume set (e.g. II.2 p. 520). In order to avoid confusion, we recommend that this practice should be kept for references to this *Study Edition*. The page numbers of the old edition can be found in the margins of this edition.

CONTENTS

§ 61–63

§ 61. THE JUSTIFICATION OF MAN
    1. The Problem of the Doctrine of Justification 1
    2. The Judgment of God 16
    3. The Pardon of Man 54
    4. Justification by Faith Alone 94

§ 62. THE HOLY SPIRIT AND THE GATHERING OF THE CHRISTIAN COMMUNITY
    1. The Work of the Holy Spirit 130
    2. The Being of the Community 137
    3. The Time of the Community 214

§ 63. THE HOLY SPIRIT AND CHRISTIAN FAITH
    1. Faith and its Object 229
    2. The Act of Faith 246

INDEX OF SCRIPTURE REFERENCES 269
INDEX OF SUBJECTS 274
INDEX OF NAMES 280

§ 61

THE JUSTIFICATION OF MAN

The right of God established in the death of Jesus Christ, and proclaimed in His resurrection in defiance of the wrong of man, is as such the basis of the new and corresponding right of man. Promised to man in Jesus Christ, hidden in Him and only to be revealed in Him, it cannot be attained by any thought or effort or achievement on the part of man. But the reality of it calls for faith in every man as a suitable acknowledgment and appropriation and application.

1. THE PROBLEM OF THE DOCTRINE OF JUSTIFICATION

The event of the death of Jesus Christ is the execution of the judgment of God, of the gracious God who in the giving of His Son in our place, and the lowly obedience of the Son in our place, reconciled the world with Himself, genuinely and definitely affirmed man as His creature in spite of his sin which cried to heaven, confirmed His faithfulness towards him and carried through His covenant with him. And the event of the resurrection is the revelation of the sentence of God which is executed in this judgment; of the free resolve of His love, and therefore of the righteousness of this judgment, the righteousness of the Father in the giving of His Son, the righteousness of the Son in His lowly obedience, the righteousness which has come to man too, and especially to man, in this judgment.

But the judgment of God executed in the death of Jesus Christ, and the sentence of God revealed in His resurrection and executed in that judgment, have both of them a twofold sense. They have a negative sense in so far as they are the judgment and sentence of the God who is gracious to man, the burning, the consuming fire, the blinding light of His wrath on the corrupt and sinful man who is unfaithful to Him and therefore to himself. They have a positive sense in so far as they are the judgment and sentence of the God who has turned to man in goodness, mercy and grace; His decision and pronouncement in man's favour, for man; the work of His redemption, His Word of power: "Rise up and walk." We can also say that they have a negative sense in so far as in that judgment and sentence God remains, and therefore confesses Himself to be, true to Himself (to the salvation of man); and a positive sense in so far as in the same judgment and sentence (to His own glory) He remains, and pronounces Himself to be, true to man. Or we can say that they have a negative sense in so far as His judgment and sentence are related to the being and activity and attitude of man, in so far as they have to do with the man of sin

§ 61. *The Justification of Man*

and his pride and fall; and a positive sense in so far as God looks back to the fact that as His creature and elect covenant-partner man is from all eternity and therefore unchangeably His own possession: looking back to His own will and plan and purpose, and looking forward to the goal which, in spite of man's being and activity and attitude as the man of sin, is still unchangeably set for him, since God Himself has set it. We can and must say these two things concerning the judgment of God executed in the death of Jesus Christ and the sentence of God revealed in His resurrection, because in both events we are dealing with the execution and revelation of the divine rejection of elected man and the divine election of rejected man. It was in the indissoluble unity and irreversible sequence of these happenings that the reconciliation of the world with God took place in Jesus Christ.

We have already spoken of the execution of the divine judgment in the humiliation and obedience of the Son of God to death, and of the Easter revelation of the sentence carried out in Him, in the first and—in the narrower sense of the term—christological part of our exposition (§ 59). And we have just completed (§ 60) our development of the negative sense of the divine sentence carried out in the death of Jesus Christ. In the mirror of Jesus Christ who was offered up for us and who was obedient in this offering it is made clear who we ourselves are, the ones for whom He was offered up, for whom He obediently offered Himself up. In the light of the humility in demonstration of which He acted as very God for us, suffering and dying for us, we are exposed and made known and have to acknowledge ourselves as the proud creatures who ourselves want to be god and lord and redeemer and helper, who have as such turned aside from God, who are therefore sinners: the enemies of God, because our disposition to Him is hostile; those who choose and have fallen a prey to nothingness; debtors who cannot clear themselves; rejected therefore, and because rejected perishing. The sentence which was executed as the divine judgment in the death of Jesus Christ is that we are these proud creatures, that I am the man of sin, and that this man of sin and therefore I myself am nailed to the cross and crucified (in the power of the sacrifice and obedience of Jesus Christ in my place), that I am therefore destroyed and replaced, that as the one who has turned to nothingness I am done away in the death of Jesus Christ. This is—to put it rather more precisely—the negative side of the divine sentence executed in that judgment.

We must not lose sight of this negative side even when it is our task to develop the positive. In virtue of the resurrection of Jesus Christ from the dead it is just as much a valid truth of revelation as the positive. Jesus Christ rose again from the dead and lives and reigns to all eternity as the One who was crucified and died for us. The fact that this being destroyed and done away and replaced came on Him in our place—and in Him as our Substitute on us—is something which because it happened once and for all never ceases to be true for Him and therefore for us. By suffering death—our death—for us, He did for us that which is the basis of our life from the dead. Therefore we

1. *The Problem of the Doctrine of Justification*

cannot be the ones for whom He has done this without being the ones for whom He has suffered. In God's eternal counsel the election of rejected man did not take place without the rejection of elected man: the election of Jesus Christ as our Head and Representative, and therefore our election as those who are represented by Him. Therefore the positive sense of the sentence executed in that judgment belongs together with the negative. It is the consequence of it and is related to it. If Jesus the Crucified lives, and we live in Him and with Him, the sentence of God revealed in His resurrection is valid in Him and therefore for us in that negative sense. Therefore the knowledge of the grace of God and the comfort which flows from it in this sentence, the knowledge, therefore, of its positive sense, is bound up with the fact that in it we do not cease to see ourselves as those who are condemned.

In turning now to the positive sense, we enter the particular sphere of the doctrine of justification. What we have to say here is that in the same judgment in which God accuses and condemns us as sinners and gives us up to death, He pardons us and places us in a new life before Him and with Him. And what we have to show is that this is possible, that the two belong together: our real sin and our real freedom from sin; our real death and our real life beyond death; the real wrath of God against us and His real grace and mercy towards us; the fulfilment of our real rejection and also of our real election. We are dealing with the history in which man is both rejected and elected, both under the wrath of God and accepted by Him in grace, both put to death and alive: existing in a state of transition, not here only, but from here to *there*; not there only, but from *here* to there; the No of God behind and the Yes of God before, but the Yes of God only before as the No of God is behind. This history, the existence of man in this transition, and therefore in this twofold form, is the judgment of God in its positive character as the justification of man.

The doctrine of justification not only narrates but explains this history. It is the attempt to see and understand in its positive sense the sentence of God which is executed in His judgment and revealed in the resurrection of Jesus Christ.

> The concept of right is the formal principle for the explanation given. It cannot be more than a formal principle. And what it means can be deduced only from the matter in question, from the history which has to be explained. The matter in question is the divine sentence as executed in the divine judgment and revealed by God. It is from this that we learn what "right" means. But the fact that we are dealing with God's sentence and judgment means that we have to use the concept. The Bible itself gives it to us in this connexion, and the Church has always accepted it in its proclamation and theology concerning this matter, sometimes with more and sometimes with less caution in respect of meanings foreign to the matter itself, sometimes with more and sometimes with less attachment to the meaning which it necessarily acquires and has as applied to this matter.

[517]

It is a question of explaining the fact and the extent to which in this history, or in the divine sentence on man which underlies this history, we are dealing with that which is just and right. It is a question of showing the right of God

§ 61. The Justification of Man

which gives right to man, and of the right which is given by God to man. The highly problematical point in the history is obviously the notorious wrong of man. In relation to God he is in the wrong, and therefore he is accused and condemned and judged by God. He is *homo peccator*[EN1], and in this history he never ceases to be *homo peccator*. How, then, in the same sentence of God, and therefore in the same history, can he be *homo iustus*?[EN2] How can he be seriously in the wrong before God and in the divine sentence and judgment, and yet also before the same God and in the same sentence and judgment come to be and be seriously in the right? How can he be *simul peccator et iustus*?[EN3] And how can God for His part (the omniscient and righteous Judge of good and evil) give right to man when man is obviously in the wrong before Him, and God Himself has put him in the wrong? To what extent does God act and speak and prove and show Himself in the justification of man—this man—as God the Father, Son and Holy Spirit, in whom there is no contradiction or caprice or disorder, no paradox or obscurity, but only light? To what extent does He demonstrate and maintain in this remarkable justification His righteousness as the Creator confronting the creature and as the Lord of His covenant with man? To what extent is the opposition which man has taken up in relation to God taken seriously and seriously overcome in this justification which is given to Him by God? To what extent is this justification not a mere overlooking or hiding of the pride and fall of man, a nominalistic "as if"—which is quite incompatible with the truthfulness of God and cannot be of any real help to man—but God's serious opposition and mighty resistance to the pride of man and therefore the real redemption of fallen man? How in this justification can God be effectively true to Himself and therefore to man—to man and therefore primarily to Himself? How can He judge man in truth and even in that judgment be gracious to Him? How can He be truly gracious to him even in the fact that He judges him? This is the problem of the doctrine of justification which we now have to develop.

[518] Even an outline of the question which we have to answer is enough to show the particular importance of it. It is a matter of the genuineness of the presupposition, the inner possibility, of the reconciliation of the world with God, in so far as this consists of a complete alteration of the human situation, a conversion of sinful man to Himself as willed and accomplished by God. The Christian community as the community which proclaims this alteration to the world, because it knows and believes in it, derives from this presupposition, as does also the faith of every individual Christian. Therefore the Christian community and Christian faith stand or fall with the reality of the fact that in confirmation and restoration of the covenant broken by man the holy God has set up a new fellowship between Himself and sinful man, instituting a new coven-

---

[EN1] sinful man
[EN2] righteous man
[EN3] simultaneously righteous and sinful

1. *The Problem of the Doctrine of Justification*

ant which cannot be destroyed or even disturbed by any transgression on the part of man. The community rests and acts on this basis. Faith lives by the certainty and actuality of the reconciliation of the world with God accomplished in Jesus Christ. There can be a basis for the community and certainty for faith only if this actuality is true, and true with a divine and unconditional clarity. What is not divinely true cannot be actual, and therefore cannot be basic and certain. But whether we are dealing with a divinely true actuality depends upon whether in this alteration of the human situation in the atonement—as the work of the grace and mercy of God—we are dealing with that which is just and right. It depends upon whether—however strange it may seem to us—there is a genuine justification: that is, whether the right of God which gives right to man and the right of man which is given by God to man is a true and indisputable right. If we do not have an indisputable divine right, and (for all its difference) an indisputable human right, how can the conversion of man to God be true, and how then can it be actual? The Christian community would then be based merely on the hypothesis that this new conversion and therefore peace between God and man might be true and actual, and the certainty of faith on the suspicion that the hypothesis might be more than a hypothesis. And if there is no knowledge of the over-ruling righteousness of God, or knowledge only in the form of a mistaken apprehension distorted by partial or total misunderstandings, how can the community escape error and decay, how can faith be kept from doubt and dissolution into all kinds of unbeliefs and superstitions? The task of the doctrine of justification is to demonstrate the righteousness of God which over-rules in the reconciling grace of God, and the grace of God which truly and actually over-rules in the righteousness of God. It is the task of finding a reliable answer to the question: What is God for sinful man? and what is sinful man before the God who is for him? The basis of the community and the certainty of faith stands or falls with the answer to this question. The doctrine of justification undertakes to answer the question of this presupposition. Hence its importance and theological necessity.

But even a cursory glance at the problem reveals the particular difficulty of the doctrine. The sweet fruit is here found in a shell which is unusually hard and bitter. In whichever direction the theologian tries to move he is unusually hampered. Where is he to begin to think and where to cease? Can we take both the basic concepts, grace and right, in all their strictness? Can we relate them with sufficient strictness to one another, seeking the explanation of the one strictly in the other? Which aspects have to be brought to the forefront, and which necessarily pushed into the background? How can we prevent the whole falling apart like a heap of skittles stood up on end? Yet in a sense these are only technical matters which we might overcome were it not that they represent the much more pressing question: How are we going to think and say not merely anything at all, but the right thing, that which corresponds to the matter itself? Do we really know this presupposition, and therefore that which we have in some way to define and formulate? Do we really know what is the basis [519]

§ 61. *The Justification of Man*

of the community and the certainty of faith, the grace and righteousness of God in their unity, and therefore that which we have to demonstrate? Do we really know God in the one and twofold mystery of His activity as we have to narrate and explain it? Where are we going to find the light which is necessary for this knowledge? And do we really know ourselves as the men who stand over against God in the mystery of this activity? What heavy responsibilities we undertake when we make this statement, what temptations we have to recognise and guard against on the right hand and the left, what misunderstandings we have to avoid, what obligation and freedom is necessary, what attention to the binding counsel of those who have preceded us in the consideration of this matter, what attention to the even more binding Word of God in the witness of the prophets and apostles, what determination to stick to that which is actually told us concerning the justification of man and to repeat it undisturbed by all the obvious doubts and objections! Which of us has any real knowledge of this matter? And if we have not, what is the value of all our repetition of ecclesiastical or even biblical theology, or our ever so original theorising? In the first and final instance the problem of justification is, for those whom it occupies, the problem of the fact of their own justification. Even when we have done our best, which of us can think that we have even approximately mastered the subject, or spoken even a penultimate word in explanation of it?

Certainly Martin Luther did not think so, and he was perhaps the man who worked and suffered and prayed more in relation to this matter than any man before or after him in the post-apostolic period. Even Paul himself did not think so. We remember the pregnant and almost too bold saying in Rom. 11[32] in which he stated the mystery of sin and the mystery of grace in their connexion and sequence in the sentence and judgment of God: "For God hath concluded them all in disobedience, that he might have mercy upon all." And he adds at once in v. 33 f.: "O the depth of the riches both of the wisdom and knowledge of God! How unsearchable are his judgments, and his ways past finding out! For who hath known the mind of the Lord? or who hath been his counsellor?" Obviously this is not rejoicing in his own knowledge which has taken him so far, but adoration in face of the incommensurable height of the matter, and therefore modesty in respect of even the best of his own knowledge, as in 1 Cor. 13[9f.], when he expressly spoke of it as a knowing in part, as the speaking and understanding and thinking of a child, as seeing through a mirror. But let us listen to what Luther has to say. *Non est jocandum cum articulo iustificationis*[EN4], he warns us: the example of Peter at Antioch shows us what dreadful havoc (*ingentes ruinas*[EN5]) can be caused by a single slip or mistake in this matter (on Gal. 2[12], 1535, W.A. 40[1], 201, 26). The *causa iustificationis*[EN6] is *lubrica*[EN7] (i.e., there is something slippery and therefore unsafe and dangerous about it), not in and for itself, *per se enim est firmissima et certissima, sed quoad nos*[EN8], for us who try to grasp it and have to speak of it. Luther knows very well the hours of darkness when it seems as though the rays of the Gospel and grace are about to disappear behind thick clouds, and he knows other proved and hardy warriors who have the same experience.

[EN4] The doctrine of justification is no laughing matter!
[EN5] immense ruins
[EN6] cause of justification
[EN7] slippery
[EN8] for in itself it is most firm and sure, but as it is toward us

1. *The Problem of the Doctrine of Justification*

It is a good sign if we know this doctrine and can state it. But it is another thing to be able to use it *in praesenti agone*^{EN9}, when the Law as a word of wrath and sorrow and death, or perhaps only a single passage threatening us with perdition, strikes us and shakes us to the very core and takes away all our comfort, when even reason speaks against the Gospel and the flesh cannot and will not lay hold of the truth of it. It is then necessary to fight with all our power for a right understanding, *et ad hoc utatur humili oratione coram Deo et assiduo studio ac meditatione verbi*^{EN10}. *Et quanquam vehementissime decertaverimus, adhuc satis tamen sudabimus*^{EN11}, for we are not dealing with contemptible foes but with the strongest and most tenacious of all, which may include amongst others even the rest of the Church (on Gal. 1^{12}, *loc. cit.*, 128 f.). And in another word of warning: *Haec dictu sunt facilia, sed beatus, qui ista probe nosset in certamine conscientiae*^{EN12} (on *Gal.* 2^{19}, *l.c.*, 271, 21). And again right at the beginning of the *praefatio*^{EN13} to the commentary on Galatians: *nec tamen comprehendisse me experior de tantae altitudinis, latitudinis, profunditatis sapientia, nisi infirmas et pauperes quasdam primitias et veluti fragmenta*^{EN14} (*l.c.*, 33, 11).

There is no doubt that the unusual difficulty of the doctrine of justification is an indication of its special function. In it we have to do with the turning, the movement, the transition of the existence of man without God and dead into the existence of man living for God, and therefore before Him and with Him and for Him. We will have to speak explicitly of this transition more than once in the whole doctrine of reconciliation. We will be dealing with it in the doctrines of sanctification and calling which we shall have to discuss in the second and third main parts of the doctrine of reconciliation. And where do we not have to do indirectly with this transition in the whole of the doctrine of reconciliation and indeed in dogmatics generally? Where do we not in some measure stand before this same difficulty and have to listen to the impressive warning of Luther? There is no part of dogmatics, no *locus*, where we can treat it lightly. At every point we are dealing with the one high Gospel. What we can and must say is that in the doctrine of justification we are dealing with the most pronounced and puzzling form of this transition because we are dealing specifically with the question of its final possibility. As we have seen already, how can it be that peace is concluded between a holy God and sinful man—by grace, but in a way which is completely and adequately right? Later on, in the doctrines of sanctification and calling we shall have to speak of the crisis of this relationship and of the decision which is made in it. And the crisis of this relationship and the decision which is made in it are, as it were, the red thread which we can follow through all the *loci*^{EN15} of the doctrine of reconciliation

[521]

EN 9 in the present struggle
EN10 and to this end, one must employ humble prayer before God and constant study and meditation in the Word
EN11 And although we have struggled most energetically, yet we will still continue to sweat
EN12 These things are easy to say, but blessed is the one who knows these things rightly in the struggle of the conscience
EN13 preface
EN14 But I know that I have not understood with wisdom of such great height, breadth and depth, but only some weak and poor first-fruits – fragments, so to speak
EN15 doctrines

§ 61. The Justification of Man

and dogmatics generally, the thread which makes all our knowledge in some sense dramatic and exciting and dangerous, which makes it the kind of knowledge which, as Luther rightly perceived, cannot either arise or continue without humble prayer and constant attention to the Word of God. But in the doctrine of justification we have to do with the original centre of this crisis, and to that extent with its sharpest form, with what we can describe provisionally as the crisis which underlies the whole. If we find it running through the whole with all kinds of repetitions and variations, at this point where we grapple with the peculiar difficulty of it, it has to be seen and handled as the main theme—the question: How am I to lay hold of a gracious God? And it is from here, and along the line which runs from here, that in different ways it works out everywhere.

It is, therefore, understandable that in at any rate some forms of Christian theology the doctrine of justification has had the function of a basic and central dogma in relation to which everything else will be either presupposition or consequence, either prologue or epilogue; that its significance has been that of *the* Word of Gospel.

The discussion of this point brings us into implicit controversy with Ernst Wolf, "Die Rechtfertigungslehre als Mitte und Grenze reformatorischer Theologie" (*Evang. Theol.*, 1949-1950, 298 f.).

It was again Luther, above all others, who obviously regarded and described the doctrine of justification as *the* Word of the Gospel. To him it was not merely the decisive point, the hub, as it were, of the whole of Evangelical theology in controversy with the Romanists. It was this, in the sense of the *Schmalkaldic Articles* of 1537 (*Bek.-Schr. der ev.-luth. Kirche*, 415 f.)—in which it is called the *primus et principalis articulus*[EN16] in this special sense: "In relation to this article we cannot doubt or yield an inch, though heaven and earth or all things passing may fall.... On this article stands all that we teach and live against the Papacy, the devil and the world. Therefore we must be sure and not doubt. Otherwise all is lost, and the Papacy and the devil and all will prevail against us." The fact that Luther linked together the Papacy, the devil and the world shows us, however, that Luther was not thinking merely in terms of the polemic against Rome. In the *praefatio*[EN17] to the 1535 Galatians we are told immediately before the passage quoted earlier: *In corde meo iste unus regnat articulus, sc. fides Christi, ex quo, per quem et in quem omnes meae diu noctuque fluunt et refluunt theological cogitationes. Ea (doctrina) florente florent omnia bona, religio, verus cultus, gloria Dei, certa cognitio omnium statuum et rerum*[EN18] (*l.c.*, 39). Then in the *argumentum*[EN19] of the same commentary we read (*l.c.*, 48, 28): *Amisso articulo iustificationis amissa est simul tota doctrina Christiana*[EN20]. And on Gal. 1³ (*l.c.*, 72, 20): *Iacente articulo iustificationis iacent omnia. Necesse igitur est, ut quotidie acuamus (quemadmodum Moses de sua lege dicit) et inculcemus eum. Nam satis vel nimium non potest concipi et*

[EN16] first and principal article
[EN17] preface
[EN18] That one article reigns in my heart, namely the article of faith in Christ, by which, in which, and through which all my theological reflections flow back and forth by day and by night. If that doctrine is flourishing, then will flourish all good things, religion, true worship, the glory of God, and assured knowledge of all conditions and matters
[EN19] argument
[EN20] If the article of justification is lost, then the whole of Christian doctrine is lost at the same time

1. The Problem of the Doctrine of Justification

teneri[EN21]. According to Luther's exposition of Gal. 2²⁰ (*l.c.*, 296, 23) this article and this article alone has the power to refute all sects, anabaptists and sacramentarians, etc., seeing they are all at error in relation to it. Moreover it is by the *sententia de iustificatione*[EN22] that Christianity is distinguished from all other religions: *soli enim christiani hinc locum credunt et* [522] *sunt iusti non quia ipsi operantur, sed quia alterius opera apprehendunt, nempe passionem Christi*[EN23] (*Schol. on Is.* 53²ᶠ, 1534, *W.A.* 25, 329, 15; 330, 8). And in the same context (*l.c.*, 332): this *Locus*[EN24] is the *fundamentum Novi Testamenti, ex quo tanquam ex patenti fonte omnes thesauri divinae sapientiae profluunt*[EN25]. Similarly in 1537 Luther could open a disputation (*W.A.* 39¹, 205, 2) with the words: *Articulus iustificationis est magister et princeps, dominus, rector et iudex super omnia genera doctrinarum, qui conservat et gubernat omnem doctrinam ecclesiasticam*[EN26]. If it does not know and consider this article, the human reason is defenceless against the vainest errors. But a mind which is strengthened by it will stand against all their assaults. The dominating role which Luther assigned to the matter in his own sermons and other works corresponds to these declarations of principle. The well-known description of the doctrine as the *articulus stantis et cadentis ecclesiae*[EN27] does not seem to derive from Luther himself, but it is an exact statement of his view. He found in it the one point which involved the whole.

Orthodox Lutheranism in the 16th and 17th centuries handed down his doctrine of justification from generation to generation—it is not our present business to inquire whether they understood it or not—and with a respectful loyalty tried to reproduce it exactly. Neither Melanchthon nor those who followed him tried to draw out the logical consequences, as, for example, in the order of dogmatics, of what Luther said concerning its primacy. They can hardly have understood that for Luther it was more than an indispensable point of controversy, that in it Luther saw that everything was at stake and not merely the opposition to Rome. We must not overlook the fact that there have been men (not confessional Lutherans) like Zinzendorf and the Bernese Samuel Lucius and John Wesley who followed Luther in this matter, but whose activity and expression did not lie in the narrower theological field. But it certainly betrays a lessening of interest in the subject, and would undoubtedly have earned the censure of Luther himself, when in the dogmatic works of later Lutheran orthodoxy, as in the much read *Camp. Theol. pos.* of W. Baier (1686, *Prol.* 1, 33), and also in the corresponding passages in Hollaz and Buddeus, the doctrine was reckoned among the *articuli fundamentals secundarii*[EN28], on the ground that a Christian can believe and therefore attain forgiveness by faith without ever having reflected on *iustificatio per solam fidem et non per opera*[EN29]. And when the tide of the moralistic Enlightenment of the 18th century had run its course, was it really a re-discovery of the meaning and intention of Luther, or was it a questionable discovery of the modern spirit, that in German theology in the 19th century the doctrine was again appealed to as the material principle of Protestantism? At any rate, an influential contribution was made on the one side by a romantic historicism which was less

---

[EN21] If the article of justification lies in ruins, then all lies in ruins. Therefore, it is necessary that we sharpen it (in the manner in which Moses spoke of his Law) and cram it in. For it cannot be understood and held enough or too much
[EN22] position on justification
[EN23] For only Christians believe this doctrine and are righteous not because of what they themselves do, but because they receive the works of another, that is, the passion of Christ
[EN24] doctrine
[EN25] basis of the New Testament, from which, as from an open fountain, all the treasures of the divine wisdom flow
[EN26] The article of justification is master and emperor, Lord, ruler and judge over all kinds of doctrines, and it preserves and steers all the church's doctrine
[EN27] article by which the church stands or falls
[EN28] fundamental, secondary articles
[EN29] justification through faith alone and not through works

§ 61. *The Justification of Man*

concerned with theology than morphology, and on the other by a desire for speculative systematics kindled by idealistic philosophy. We cannot deny an actual parallelism between this neo-Lutheran emphasis and the statements of Luther himself. The only thing is that with the possible exception of M. Kähler, no one dared actually to plan and organise Evangelical dogmatics around the doctrine of justification as a centre. It is a matter for reflection that neither in the older nor more recent Lutheranism has this ever been done.

[523] There can be no question of disputing the particular function of the doctrine of justification. And it is also in order that at certain periods and in certain situations, in face of definite opposition and obscuration, this particular function has been brought out in a particular way, that it has been asserted as *the* Word of the Gospel, that both offensively and defensively it has been adopted as *the* theological truth. There have been times when this has been not merely legitimate but necessary, when attention has had to be focused on the theology of Galatians and Romans (or, more accurately, Rom. 1–8).

One such time was when Augustine had to take up arms because the, in a sense, innocent righteousness of works of the first centuries had obviously ceased to be innocent in the teaching of Pelagius and his followers and now threatened actually to obscure the Gospel as the message of the free grace of God. Another such time was that of the Reformation when Luther recognised that the sacramentalistic and moralistic misunderstanding of the much cited "grace" was the abuse which underlay all the other abuses of the mediaeval Church, and he set out to overcome it. Another such time was the awakening at the beginning of the 19th century, with its very necessary reaction against the secularisation of the understanding of salvation in the Enlightenment, in face of which post-Reformation orthodoxy—which had gone a good way along the same road—had shown itself to be powerless. Another such time may well be our own day, when in face of the notable humanistic religiosity which is our heritage from the 19th century, and in face of all ecclesiasticism, sacramentalism, liturgism and even existentialism, we have been glad enough, and still are, to find in the doctrine of justification a fully developed weapon with which to meet all these things.

But in theology it is good to look beyond the needs and necessities of the moment, to exercise restraint in a reaction however justified, to be constantly aware of the limits of the ruling trend (however true and well-founded it may be). And since our present business is with Church dogmatics, which is ecumenical at least in prospect, this must be our attitude in relation to the doctrine of justification, not because we deny but because we maintain our Evangelical position.

In the Church of Jesus Christ this doctrine has not always been *the* Word of the Gospel, and it would be an act of narrowing and unjust exclusiveness to proclaim and treat it as such. We have to express and assert it with its particular importance and difficulty and function. But we have also to remember that it relates only to one aspect of the Christian message of reconciliation. We have to understand this aspect with others. Neither explicitly nor implicitly have we to overlook this aspect. There never was and there never can be any true Christian Church without the doctrine of justification. In this sense it is indeed the

1. The Problem of the Doctrine of Justification

articulus stantis et cadentis ecclesiae[EN30]. There is no Christian Church without the truth of what God has done and does for man in virtue of its witness, without the manifestation of this truth in some form in its life and doctrine. But in the true Church of Jesus Christ the formulated recognition and attestation of this truth may withdraw, it may indeed be more or less hidden behind other aspects of the Christian message, without it being right and necessary to draw attention to its absence, to believe that its truth is denied and the unity of the Church is broken. When we come across actual cases of this we have to remind ourselves and others of something which has perhaps been forgotten or mistaken. But we for our part have to remain open to aspects of the Christian message which are perhaps new to us. It is the justification of man itself, and our very confidence in the objective truth of the doctrine of justification, which forbids us to postulate that in the true Church its theological outworking must *semper, ubique et ab omnibus*[EN31] be regarded and treated as the *unum necessarium*[EN32], the centre or culminating point of the Christian message or Christian doctrine. [524]

The view of A. Schweitzer and W. Wrede is probably exaggerated that in Paul's doctrine of the δικαιοσύνη θεοῦ[EN33] or πίστεως[EN34], we have to do only with a "subsidiary crater," i.e., a controversial doctrine in his conflict with the Judaisers. But so, too, was the doctrine of Luther and the younger Melanchthon that Paul is only the great apostolic teacher of justification. The Christology of Paul is more than simply an argument for his doctrine of justification. And his view of the corporate and individual fellowship of Christians with Christ, his view of the relationship between the Church and Israel as developed in Rom. 9–11, his ethics too, all have their own roots and heads, although they cannot, of course, be separated from this doctrine. In 1 Cor. 1^{30} we read that Christ Jesus is made unto us wisdom, righteousness, sanctification and redemption, and this obviously means that we are pointed in at least three other directions. And the Epistles of Paul are not the whole of the New Testament. If caution is necessary in relation to the view that the Pauline doctrine of justification is disputed in the Epistle of James, there can be no doubt that the message of James and the Synoptics and the Johannine writings and the other parts of the New Testament witness cannot be simply equated with this doctrine, even though it is not excluded by but included in them.

As already mentioned, the Church of the first centuries lived in a naive Pelagianism (as also in a naive Adoptionism or Sabellianism). It did not know any explicit doctrine of justification—*per nefas*[EN35] and to its shame, we might say. But if we are tempted to blame or accuse the early Church for it, we must never forget that we are dealing with the Church and theology of the Christendom of the martyr-centuries, which obviously knew without the doctrine of justification what their faith was all about, and for which the truth of the doctrine was not in question, although they did not clearly understand it. The same can be said of the later Greek Church and of the Eastern Church generally. The development of the doctrine of justification which began with Augustine was something which belonged specifically to the Western Church. The East was much less interested in the contrast between sin and

---

[EN30] article by which the church stands or falls
[EN31] 'always, everywhere, and by all'
[EN32] single necessity
[EN33] righteousness of God
[EN34] of faith
[EN35] wrongly

§ 61. *The Justification of Man*

grace than in that between death and life, between mortality and immortality. It had no great concern for the problem of law—the question of the possibility and basis of a positive relationship between God and man. Therefore in this matter of justification (and this was no doubt a limitation) it contented itself with the bare minimum.

In the West it was only at the time of the Reformation that the doctrine of justification became a burning issue, or, to put it more exactly, it was only in the questing German spirit of Luther. But then this doctrine—although not only this doctrine—impressed itself upon the face of Protestantism in its relation to the ancient Church. Not only this doctrine: note the place and function of the doctrine in Calvin's *Institutio*. He saw its basic, critical importance. He developed it (III, 11–18) broadly and carefully, marking off both the Romanist errors on the one hand and the Protestant, like those of A. Osiander, on the other. But in the obvious modern dispute amongst Calvin scholars concerning his central doctrine no one would ever dream of maintaining that it is to be found in his doctrine of justification. In many passages of his masterpiece, and in other writings as well, he asserts that there are two main gifts which the Christian owes to Christ or the Holy Spirit, *iustificatio*[EN36] (or *remissio peccatorum*[EN37]) on the one hand, and indissolubly connected with it *sanctificatio*[EN38] (or *renovatio*[EN39] or *regeneratio*[EN40]) on the other. And if we consider as a whole his doctrine *De modo percipiendae gratiae*[EN41] in the third book of the *Institutes*, it seems more obvious to see in the second of these, the question of the development and formation of the Christian life and therefore of sanctification, the problem which controls and organises his thinking. This is in accordance with the tendency already found in Zwingli and in the reconstruction of the Church in Switzerland and other non-German territories which derives from him. In Calvin the doctrine of justification offered the necessary basis and critical certainty for the answering of this question, although not without being itself caught up in and rather overshadowed by the doctrine of predestination, which was raised later (*c.* 21–24) and which plumbed the matter even further. Or is the starting-point the *insitio*[EN42] of the Christian into Christ which is described at the very beginning of the third book (*c.* 1) and which is accomplished by the Holy Spirit? Or do we have to seek the basic teaching in the doctrine of faith as such which we find developed in *c.* 2? One thing at least is certain—that if the theology of Calvin has a centre at all, it does not lie in the doctrine of justification. The doctrine of the older Reformed Church which followed him usually kept to the *schema* justification and sanctification so often laid down by him. By separating the two and pursuing them along different paths, it was more able to give the proper emphasis and therefore to take seriously the second question (that of sanctification, of the Christian's obedience of faith, of good works) than were the Lutherans. It was also less susceptible to the temptation which threatened from the very first to weaken and obscure the answer to the question of justification by mixing it with the question of sanctification (which could not be avoided). That this actually happened in Neo-Lutheran theology (including Ritschl and his followers) is the charge levelled against them rather violently but not unjustly by a Reformed teacher in Vienna, Edward Böhl (*Dogmatik* 1887, *Van der Rechtfertigung durch den Glauben* 1890). The only trouble is that the first and positive concern of the Calvinistic distinction seems to be concealed from Böhl himself. We might almost describe him as a Reformed hyper-Lutheran like his teacher and father-in-law, Hermann Kohlbrügge, for he thought that he could appeal to

---

[EN36] justification
[EN37] forgiveness of sins
[EN38] sanctification
[EN39] renewal
[EN40] regeneration
[EN41] On the Means of Obtaining Grace
[EN42] ingrafting

1. The Problem of the Doctrine of Justification

the doctrine of justification as the cardinal dogma of Protestantism (something which no Lutheran either old or new had ever dared to do).

But it is worth noting that in Luther himself—although we might easily miss it under the overpowering impression of his doctrine of justification and what he has to say concerning it—we can trace a pervasive and not by any means a thin line in which he did not speak with the one-sidedness that we should expect from his talk of the *unicus articulus*[EN43], but with an obvious two-sidedness, with the same kind of two-sidedness as later characterises the thought of Calvin. He could speak (*Enarr. on Is.* 53^8, 1544, W.A. 40^{111}, 726, 24) of a twofold *sanatio*[EN44] of man proceeding from the exalted Christ: the one the forgiveness of sins by virtue of His substitutionary death; the other the gracious gift of a holy life purifying itself from sins. Or, again (*Pred. üb. Act.* $2^{1f.}$, W.A. 52, 317, 22), of a twofold sanctification, the first perfect, the other imperfect but, in its own way, no less real. Or, again (*Pred. üb. Kor.* 1 $5^{6f.}$, W.A. 21, 16), of a twofold purification, the first having taken place once and for all in Christ, the second to be accomplished day by day in us. Or, again (*Pred. üb. Luk.* $16^{1f.}$, E.A. 13, 238), of a twofold justification, inwardly in the spirit and before God only by faith, outwardly and publicly, before men and according to the judgment of men by works. Or, again (*Pred. üb. Matth.* $22^{34ff.}$, 1537, W.A. 45, 34), of a twofold help of Christ, the first consisting in the fact that He represented us before God, spreading out His wings over us against the devil like a hen over her chickens, the second that He feeds and nourishes us with the Holy Spirit as a hen does her chickens, so that we begin to love God and keep His commandments. Or, again (*zu Gal.* 3^{13}, W.A. 40^1, 408, 24), of a twofold fulfilling of the Law, the first by the imputation of the righteousness of Jesus Christ, the second by the gift of the Holy Spirit which begets a new life. In substance the distinction is one and the same. Luther connected the two elements of the atoning activity of God in Christ with the relationship between eternity and time, between the present and the future life of man, between heaven and earth, or (*zu Gal.* 2^{12}, W.A. 40^1, 427, 11) between the divine and the human nature of Jesus Christ. Many things have to be noted. As the parallels show, and in accordance with his basic view, (1) he never hesitates to assert the priority of the first of the two elements over the other: the one is the main part (*Pred. üb.* 1 *Petr.* $2^{20f.}$, W.A. 21, 313, 22), the other is secondary. Again (2) on every available opportunity he shows the great difference between them. He describes them separately (with particular emphasis on the first) and therefore refrains from doing the very thing which was so often attempted under his name, the merging of the first into the second, or the second into the first, the interpretation of justification in terms of sanctification or of sanctification in terms of justification. But (3) he insists that both these parts have always to be properly maintained. If either of them is forgotten or neglected in favour of the other, this will inevitably involve the corruption either of faith or of its power and fruit. And (4) he perceives and confesses that the origin and unity of the two elements, the source and object of a necessarily complete Christian faith and the measure of a necessarily incomplete Christian obedience, is in Jesus Christ acting for us as very God and very man. It is clear—and this is our present concern—that side by side with the doctrine of justification and distinct from it, directly confronting and connected with it, but seen and asserted with the same clarity, he also knew and taught this second article, which Calvin was everywhere to present as that of *sanctificatio*[EN45]. All these statements are, of course, drawn from the theology of the older Luther. More recent research (cf. Axel Gyllenkrok, *Rechtfertigung und Heiligung in der frühen ev. Theologie Luthers*, 1952) has shown that at first Luther did not dialectically equate justification and sanctification merely with one another, but also with Christology, and the three

[526]

[EN43] single article
[EN44] healing
[EN45] sanctification

§ 61. *The Justification of Man*

together with the Word of God, and the Word of God understood in this way and man's faith in the promised grace of God with the grace itself, and this again with the humble acknowledgment of sin. In this original and tremendously profound enterprise of Luther there is no end to the parallels and coincidences of subject and object, of God and man, of giving and receiving, of passion and action. It was a *theologia crucis*[EN46] which had strangely enough all the marks of a *theologia gloriae*[EN47]: a theology which saw everything together from the standpoint of God (which will also be that of the believer). In his own life-time Luther himself did not deny that this was his original enterprise, and we are always coming upon traces of it, blinding flashes and confusing uncertainties which we can explain only in the light of it. We do not have to decide here whether we prefer the younger Luther to the older. What is certain is that in that first stage of his thinking and teaching he did not manage to say plainly what he meant by the one thing or what he meant by the other, so that he could not establish with any theological clarity either a certainty of salvation or a Christian ethics. If we prefer the more violent dialectic of the younger Luther we must see to it that we are more successful than Luther himself in these two respects. It is also certain that, at the very latest in the early twenties—Gyllenkrok traces the beginning of the movement—Luther himself turned from this theology of parallels to a less interesting but more articulated theology of dissimilarities and distinctions—it was still exciting enough. If in his earlier period he had spoken almost suspiciously much of *humilitas*[EN48], he now began to practise it. His theology now became—I am almost bold to say for the first time—a *theologia viatorum*[EN49]. It was reforming from the very first. In this new form it was effectively so for the edification of the Church. And the change is perhaps explicable from within if we can accept that it went hand in hand with a developing isolation of his Christology from the Christian anthropology which almost completely dominated his early thinking. At any rate we are forced to say that in the last resort Lutheranism old and new followed the direction of Luther—or at least the older Luther—when, like Calvin and Calvinism, it refused to centre its theology upon the one article of justification.

We have already drawn attention to the independent importance and function of the problem of sanctification side by side with that of justification not only in the older Protestantism but also in Calvin, and even Luther himself. But we have to remember that in this problem, from the historical standpoint, we have to do with the particular problem of Pietism and Methodism. Whatever reservations we may have with regard to this movement, an attempt to do justice to it is something which no Church dogmatics can evade.

But in conclusion we have also to remember that there is a third element in the reconciling work of God in Jesus Christ which, like sanctification, cannot be subsumed under the concept of justification, or can be so only very artificially and to the great detriment of the matter: The office of Jesus Christ is that of the priest who sacrifices himself and the king who rules, but it is also that of the prophet. And the reconciling grace of God has a dimension and form which cannot simply be equated with justification or sanctification, the form and dimension of the calling of man, his teleological setting in the kingdom of God which comes and is present in Jesus Christ, the form of mission in relation to the community and in relation to the individual Christian the form of hope. There are many things that we can say against the theology of the last few centuries but they were not *saecula obscura*[EN50] in this respect, that they brought out this aspect of the Christian message with a much greater

---
[EN46] theology of the cross
[EN47] theology of glory
[EN48] humility
[EN49] theology of pilgrims
[EN50] dark ages

1. The Problem of the Doctrine of Justification

clarity than it had for the great Christians of the 16th century. This was the time when the world-wide mission of the Church was taken up in earnest, the time of a new vision and expectation of the kingdom of God as coming and already come, the time of a new awakening of Christianity to its responsibility to state and society, the time of a new consciousness of its ecumenical existence and mission. These are actualities of Church history which a Church dogmatics cannot overlook. And here, as in the doctrine of sanctification, we shall have to adopt as far as we can the concern of the Eastern Church, which is so very remote from the tradition of the West, but is still genuinely grounded in the New Testament. One good reason for doing so is that in it we have to do with at least one of the roots of the secularised political and social Chiliasm of the Eastern world which, for all the horror and repugnance which it feels at its perversion, the Christian West has not so long outgrown that it can try to close its eyes to the *particula veri*^{EN51} perverted in this way. Now without justification there is certainly no calling, no mission, no hope, no responsibility to the world. We still have every reason to go very carefully into the great question of the Reformation and of Luther in particular. The modern movements and enterprises of which we have to think in this connexion have neglected this to their own hurt. It would not really harm the Eastern Church to try to understand seriously the doctrine of the justification of the sinner by faith alone—and certainly not the contemporary Eastern world. But, again, if we are going to consider properly what we have to consider in connexion with the prophetic office of Christ, we need a rather greater freedom than that which is allowed us if we move only within the framework of the Reformation doctrine of justification. All honour to the question: How can I find a gracious God? But for too long it has been for Protestantism—at any rate European and especially German Protestantism—the occasion and temptation to a certain narcissism, and a consequent delay in moving in the direction we have just indicated.

The *articulus stantis et cadentis ecclesiae*^{EN52} is not the doctrine of justification as such, but its basis and culmination: the confession of Jesus Christ, in whom are hid all the treasures of wisdom and knowledge (Col. 2³); the knowledge of His being and activity for us and to us and with us. It could probably be shown that this was also the opinion of Luther. If here, as everywhere, we allow Christ to be the centre, the starting-point and the finishing point, we have no reason to fear that there will be any lack of unity and cohesion, and therefore of systematics in the best sense of the word. [528]

The problem of justification does not need artificially to be absolutised and given a monopoly. It has its own dignity and necessity to which we do more and not less justice if we do not ascribe to it a totalitarian claim which is not proper to it, or allow all other questions to culminate or merge into it, or reject them altogether with an appeal to it, but if we accept it with all its limitations as this problem and try to answer it as such. Its very confusion and fusion with the problem of sanctification has only been to the detriment of its proper treatment. The general significance and reach of the doctrine of justification will themselves be better brought out if we accept it with all its limitations as this problem. And although other questions are all connected with it, and the answering of this question has for them the decisive significance of a leaven, they will then have their own particular place side by side with it. The doctrine

---

^{EN51} grain of truth
^{EN52} article by which the church stands or falls

§ 61. *The Justification of Man*

of justification will then further the free development of the riches of Christian knowledge instead of hindering it. It can then be recalled with a good conscience as a warning where the importance of its particular truth is not recognised or where in the preoccupation with other interests it is far too rashly and unthinkingly assumed that it can be ignored. With a good conscience—for the inculcation of it will not be a compulsion, a Caudine yoke, a disqualification or artificial transmutation of that which at other times and places has rightly been important for others in the same knowledge of the one Jesus Christ. With a good conscience—for we can be open to the viewpoints of these others, and communication (and not simply tolerance) is then rightly possible in the Church. In its own place—in the context in which it has to be put and answered—the problem of justification does arise with a pitiless seriousness, and it has to be answered with the same seriousness: the problem of the presupposition and the possibility and the truth of the positive relationship of God with man, of the peace of man with God.

2. THE JUDGMENT OF GOD

By sin man puts himself in the wrong in relation to God. He makes himself impossible as the creature and covenant-partner of God. He desecrates the good nature which has been given and forfeits the grace which is addressed to him. He compromises his existence. For he has no right as sinner. He is only in the wrong.

[529] The presupposition, the possibility and the truth of a positive relationship between God and man and the peace of man with God consists (1) in there being a right which is superior, absolutely superior to the wrong of which man is guilty and in which he now finds himself, (2) in this right not merely being transcendent but worked out in man and (3) in the wrong of man being set aside and a new human right being established and set up in the working out of this higher right. This higher right is the right of God, and its outworking, the setting aside of the wrong of man and the restoration of his right, is the judgment of God. The justification of man takes place in the eventuation of this judgment.

We must first speak of the right of God which is absolutely superior to the wrong of man. What kind of a right is this? We cannot see it except in the judgment of God. But to understand this and the justification of man, we must first lay down that it is right, the right of God, which is worked out and executed in it. Where do we see the freedom of God more clearly than in the justification of sinful man? But nowhere do we see more clearly that it is true freedom and not the false freedom of an arbitrary whim. The fact that God acts as He does in the justification of man proves conclusively that He could not act in this way just as well as any other but that what we have here is not whim and caprice but right, the supreme right of all. Not, of course, that God

2. *The Judgment of God*

is determined and bound and limited by some law which is different from Himself and therefore is forced to act in this way. God does not stand under any alien law, any general truth and possibility and presupposition embracing and conditioning and limiting both Himself and the world and man. It would be a futile undertaking to try to measure Him by any such law when answering the question of His right. What we know or think we know as law, truth, possibility and presupposition are hypotheses which (consciously or unconsciously) we venture to hold because the world and man actually derive from and are ruled by the One who is not merely the supreme but the true and primary Law-giver, not *exlex*[EN53] but Himself *lex*[EN54], and therefore the source and norm and limit of all *leges*[EN55]. There can be no point in equating the essence of our laws and hypotheses of right with the maxim on the basis of which God is our Creator and Lord, and therefore trying to measure Him by one such principle of order and to understand His activity in accordance with it. In the justification of man God is in the right. Therefore any such path will be a hopeless failure. The exposition of the doctrine of justification has always suffered from the fact that attempts have been made to determine the right of God in the activity which has to be explained here by a hypothesis which is rashly held to be the same as His own maxim, by a natural or moral law which is thought to be recognisable as such. God—who is not a God "of confusion, but of peace" (1 Cor. 14^{33})—is Himself (with supreme and inflexible strictness) law, maxim and order: in perfect and unshakable harmony with Himself, in complete loyalty to Himself, and, in distinction to the stars of the firmament and all the phenomena of the nature and history of the created cosmos (although not at the expense of the richness of His inward being and outward activity), "without variableness or shadow of turning" (Jas. 1^{17}). It is in this harmony with Himself that He very clearly acts in the justification of sinful man. This harmony with Himself is the right of God—the reliable anchor which is the basis of the community and the assurance of its faith. Nothing else could happen than that which does happen when God causes righteousness, His righteousness, to come to sinful man. If anything else could happen, if there were even the shadow of a well-founded doubt in relation to the presupposition and possibility and truth of justification, that would mean that God Himself is not law, that His harmony with Himself is discord, His freedom is whim and caprice, He Himself is *exlex*[EN56], in short, He is not God. Or, to put it the other way round, to doubt the truth of justification is to doubt God Himself. To reckon with any other possibility than that which is actualised in it is to reckon with the non-existence of God. To deny its actuality is to deny God. Or, again, to know God is to know the right of God in this matter. And, conversely, to know the right of God in this matter is to know God.

[530]

[EN53] not bound by the law
[EN54] law
[EN55] laws
[EN56] not bound by the law

§ 61. *The Justification of Man*

Hence the peculiar urgency of the problem of justification. It has its root in this problem of the right of God in His grace as addressed again and this time truly to sinful man. Therefore it brings us face to face with the whole, that is to say, the knowledge of God Himself. Of all the superficial catchwords of our age, surely one of the most superficial is that, whereas 16th century man was occupied with the grace of God, modern man is much more radically concerned about God Himself and as such. As though there were such a thing as God Himself and as such, or any point in seeking Him! As though grace were a quality of God which we could set aside while we leisurely ask concerning His existence! As though the Christian community and Christian faith had any interest in the existence or non-existence of this God Himself and as such! As though 16th century man with His concern for the grace of God and the right of His grace were not asking about God Himself and His existence with a radicalness compared with which the questioning of modern man is empty frivolity! As though that which seems to be lacking to modern man—and all the Christian Churches are very much to blame—were not that he has not learned to ask concerning God with this reality compared with which there is no other; that he asks concerning the existence of God without knowing for what he asks; that he maintains it perhaps without knowing what he is maintaining, or denies it without knowing what he is denying; that his asking and answering is necessarily frivolous because it is irrelevant! Obviously we cannot even begin to discuss with him until the discussion is lifted on to quite other ground by the proclamation of the Church, i.e., until the subject is put before him which alone gives any sense to the question about God—the one and only God who is gracious to man and who in His grace is in the right, faithful to Himself and in harmony with Himself.

The God who is present and active in the justification of man, and therefore as the gracious God, has right and is in the right. Not subject to any alien law, but Himself the origin and basis and revealer of all true law, He is just in Himself. This is the backbone of the event of justification.

It is the backbone of the relationship with God even in the Old Testament. Why does the Old Testament saint rest on the election of his people and the covenant which God made with it when its history is a continuous series of transgressions and consequent divine judgments? Why does he rest on the faithfulness and forbearance and mercy and grace of God when it is not concealed from him that he has not shown himself to be worthy of it and when it is revealed constantly by the triumph of his enemies that he has forfeited his right to appeal to that faithfulness? He plainly rests on God because he does not see in the election of Israel and God's covenant with it a happy chance or in the free loving-kindness of God a fortuitous favouritism, but the supreme and inflexible right of God; because His God is to Him One who is just in Himself, and not a being who one time can will and act in one way and another time in quite a different way. No, "thy right hand is full of righteousness" (Ps. 48^{10}), "thy righteousness is like the great mountains" (Ps. 36^6), it is "an everlasting righteousness" (Ps. 119^{142}). "For the righteous Lord loveth righteousness" (Ps. 11^7): this is to him an ontological statement and therefore one which is indisputable and unchangeably valid. God is just in Himself. Because this is true for the Old Testament saint he does not merely think or believe but knows that God will be faithful to His election, that He will keep his covenant, that He will fulfil His promise. He therefore rests on his God, finding in Him his place of defence, his stronghold, his rock, in spite of everything which might cause him not to rest on Him. It is therefore in the election and covenant and loving-kindness of God that he sees this inward and therefore authentic and trustworthy justice of God.

But the same is true of the New Testament, and especially of the New Testament. How can Paul dare to pronounce himself and Christians both Jews and Gentiles free from the obser-

2. The Judgment of God

vance of the Law in view of the end of the Law as reached in Jesus Christ (Rom. 10⁴), referring them only and altogether to the Gospel of this One, to the ἀπολύτρωσις^EN57 which has already taken place in Him (Rom. 3²⁴), to the love of God shed abroad in their hearts by the Holy Spirit (Rom. 5⁵), to the free obedience of the children of God impelled by the Spirit of God (Rom. 8¹⁴)? And all this in spite of the fact that the flesh and sin and death are still present realities both for him and for them. It was hardly *disputationis causa*^EN58 that in his answer to this question he seized on the term δικαιοσύνη^EN59, nor was it by accident that in the first instance he always called it the δικαιοσύνη θεοῦ^EN60 (and then as such the δικαιοσύνη πίστεως^EN61). This is the backbone of his Gospel, of his own faith and of the faith to which he summons men as an apostle. This is what makes possible and necessary the astonishing boldness of his message, and in practice of his way from the Synagogue to the (ἐκκλησία^EN62, and out into the world as an ambassador of Jesus Christ. It is a matter of God and the righteousness of God. The grace of Jesus Christ deserves and demands faith and obedience and all confidence and all sacrifice and its relentless proclamation on the right hand and the left, both to Jews and Gentiles; its revelation and promulgation is the irruption of the last day, and the free word of its proclamation can anticipate the end of the last day and be pronounced as the final word even in a present which is still characterised by the flesh and sin and death, just because the grace of God as such is the outworking and fulfilment of the right of God, His righteous judgment. Why does Paul deny and reject the δικαιοσύνη διὰ νόμου^EN63 (Gal. 2²¹), or ἐκ νόμου^EN64 (Gal. 3²¹, Rom. 10⁵)? Why does he deny and reject all ἰδία δικαιοσύνη^EN65 (Rom. 10³, Phil. 3⁹)? Because they do not work out in practice? Yes. Because they are opposed to the grace of Jesus Christ? Yes. But first and finally because being in opposition to grace they are opposed to the δικαιοσύνη θεοῦ^EN66 because in spite of their claims and appearance they do not rest on right but wrong, because [532] they are not δικαιοσύνη^EN67 but ἀδικία^EN68. In the revelation and efficacy (ἔνδειξις^EN69) of the grace of Jesus Christ proclaimed in the Gospel what comes first is not the justification of the believer in Jesus Christ but the basis of it—that God shows Himself to be just: εἰς τὸ εἶναι αὐτὸν δίκαιον^EN70, and only then and for that reason: καὶ δικαιοῦντα τὸν ἐκ πίστεως Ἰησοῦ^EN71 (Rom. 3²⁶). In it God Himself is right. He is at one with Himself. He is faithful to Himself. That is its basic ontological content. And the corresponding content of the knowledge of God's own right in this matter—and therefore of the inflexibility of its goodness and necessity—is the mystery which marks off Paul's advocacy of this matter from an insubstantial and therefore equivocal assumption. He knows the point of departure in this matter, his own point of departure as an apostle of Jesus Christ. His feet are set on a rock. The

---

EN57 redemption
EN58 for the sake of argument
EN59 righteousness
EN60 righteousness of God
EN61 righteousness of faith
EN62 church
EN63 righteousness through the law
EN64 from the law
EN65 own righteousness
EN66 righteousness of God
EN67 righteousness
EN68 unrighteousness
EN69 demonstration
EN70 'so that he might be just'
EN71 'and the one who justifies by faith in Christ'

§ 61. *The Justification of Man*

faithfulness of God Himself, the πίστις τοῦ θεοῦ, which cannot be destroyed by any unfaithfulness of man (Rom. 3³), is the foundation of the πίστις[EN72] in which he himself lives and which he proclaims. And the recognition of the πιστὸς ὁ θεός ("But God is true": 2 Cor. 1¹⁸, cf. also 1 Cor. 1⁹) is the pledge and guarantee that His Word to the communities and the world is not an unreliable Yes and No. But how does he know that God is true to Himself? The continuation (2 Cor. 1¹⁹) tells us that it is by the fact that in the Jesus Christ, the Son of God, proclaimed by Him what is revealed and active is not a Yes and No but the plain Yes of God.

This is the right of God which is maintained in the justification of sinful man, which marks it off even as a free act of grace from the caprice and arbitrariness of a destiny that apportions blindfold its favour and disfavour, which clothes it with majesty and dignity, which gives to the knowledge of faith an infallible certainty—that in the first instance God affirms Himself in this action, that in it He lives His own divine life in His unity as Father, Son and Holy Spirit. But in it He also maintains Himself as the God of man, as the One who has bound Himself to man from all eternity, as the One who has elected Himself for man and man for Himself. In the action of His grace He executes that which He willed and determined when to man as this creature He gave actuality and his human nature. In executing it He does not surrender anything. And in His relationship to man He does not transgress but fulfils His own law, beside which there is no other and above which there is no higher, the law which is Himself. In this respect, too, the grace which He exercises in justification is not one which is foreign to Him. It is not an act in the performance of which He has to alter or correct Himself, in which He has in part at least to cease to be God and therefore true to Himself. If it were otherwise, how could there be a confidence in His grace which corresponds to the deity of God? How could the revelation of it be the solid basis of the community, the durable certainty of faith? How could the confession of it be distinguished from a mere value-judgment of religion, dependent for its truth upon the power of the human religiosity expressed in it? And beyond that, how could God have given up His own Son to execute it and His own Holy Spirit to reveal it? In that He has done and does do this, He shows Himself to be the One who as the gracious God is righteous and as the righteous God gracious. It is not at the expense but in the exercise of His Godhead that for the sake of all flesh His Word becomes flesh (Jn. 1¹⁴). It is not a denial but a confirmation of His Godhead that He causes His Holy Spirit to dwell and work as the witness of His grace in those who are still threatened by sin and the flesh and death.

As the God who in all this was true to Himself, in the power of this His right, He encountered man in justification, the man who is in the wrong before Him. What is this wrong of man? We know it as the outrage of his pride in which in direct contrast to the nature and way of the God who is righteous in His grace he strives for a dignity which is not his. We know it as the movement in which

---

[EN72] faith

2. The Judgment of God

man undoubtedly alienates himself from God, making God his enemy and bringing upon himself the wrath of God. We know it as the movement in which man can only wither, in which he can only corrupt and destroy himself and therefore the work of God. We know it as man's impossible and senseless alliance with the darkness which God the Creator has marked off from light and rejected, as the great and inconceivable, but for all its inconceivability very real, invasion of that which is, because God has willed and created it, by that which in itself is not. We know it as the fate which man deserves, which comes upon man, which man has to suffer, but which is an offence to God because it is contrary to His will, the greatness of which can be measured only by the fact that in His Son God has Himself risen up to meet it, and destroy it, becoming the Saviour of man in His encounter with it, and restoring His own offended honour. We have every reason to be horrified at the actuality of it. In nature and form and operation it belongs to a dimension which does not in any sense allow us even theoretically to ignore or overlook it, to understand it in terms of category, and to that extent to relativise and control it. We are at once forced to relinquish any attempts in this direction when we consider that we are no more able to control it in practice than we are to jump over our own shadow. And the decisive ground of this impossibility is that God Himself has risen up to control it, taking the matter once and for all into His own hands.

But whatever may be the wrong of man, there can be no doubt that it does not belong to the same dimension as the right of God and cannot stand against it. It does not alter in the slightest the seriousness with which we have to consider it, but we still have to remember that it is absolutely subordinate to the right of God, that for all its greatness it is infinitely small in relation to it. It is a matter of man's rebellion against God, of the invasion of God's good creation by chaos. God Himself—and first of all—takes it in all seriousness. He takes it so seriously that He encounters it in His own person. It grieves Him for our sake, His creatures and covenant-partners. It offends His glory that in committing it we turn against Him and therefore have to be without Him. But there can be no question whatever of its being His equal. If it is great before Him because it is wrong against *Him*, it is also small before Him because it is wrong, and therefore cannot either be or posit another right to compete with His right. It can say only No and not a corresponding Yes. It does not found any new being or new man or new world. It would like to do so. We cannot deny to it the reality of a desire for this. But no more. It is only its aim to found a kingdom. From the very first it has no power to do so. It is not in any way comparable with God the Creator, nor is its work in any way comparable with the creation of God. The wrong of man cannot in any way alter the right of God.

It cannot alter it especially to the extent that as the right of the Creator and the Lord of the covenant it is His right over man and to man. If man puts Himself in the wrong that means that as the creature and covenant-partner of God, man is unworthy of the right held out to him, that he forfeits that right,

[534]

§ 61. *The Justification of Man*

that he corrupts and destroys his existence. His concurrence with the right of God, to which he is determined by his election and calling and for which he is prepared by the good nature with which he is endowed, is the presupposition of his very existence. In conflict with God he can only wither and fade and perish and die and be lost. By the fact that he sets himself in the wrong he cannot take away the right which God has over Him and to Him. He cannot even break it or limit it. In face of his wrong, God is still God, and He is unchanged in His right, the right of the One who has elected and made Himself the Creator and the Lord of the covenant. Whatever man may do in the folly of his pride, he cannot disrupt this self-determination of God, nor can he make for himself a place or status or being in which to have what he obviously aims to have, an independent existence, a genuine freedom in face of God. Not even in hell can he have and enjoy this freedom. Every kind of demon possession is possible, but it is not possible to make the nature and existence of man devilish. Man may fall. Indeed he necessarily falls, and into the abyss, when he sets himself in the wrong against God. But in this fall into the abyss he cannot fall out of the sphere of God and therefore out of the right which God has over him and to him. Even in his most shameful thoughts and words and deeds, even in the most terrible denial and perversion of his good nature, even in the complete forfeiture of his rights and dignity as a man, even in the lowest depths of hell, whatever that may mean for him, he is still the man whom God has elected and created, and as such he is in the hand of God. He has not escaped the right of God over him and to him, but is still subjected to it, utterly and completely. He is still in the sphere of God's jurisdiction.

[535] But God does exercise this jurisdiction. There can be no question, therefore, of His acquiescing in the fact that man puts himself in the wrong, of His consenting to man's wrong. He would not be God, the living God, if He could do that, let alone if He willed to do it and did it, if He were content to be in the right and true to Himself in face of man's wrong, to continue—although only, as it were, theoretically—to maintain His right over man and to man without exercising it, in such a way, therefore, that the hand is inactive in which He irresistibly holds man and by which man is inescapably held. His right is the right of the judgment which is executed by Him. It is not merely a valid right but one which is exercised. It is the right which God exercises for His own sake (because He is not a dead but the living God) and for the sake of the creature and covenant-partner man who even as a transgressor is still subject to His right, and therefore again, in this sense, for His own sake, because, in these two ways man is His and belongs to Him.

Man's wrong cannot be merely his own affair. It takes place in his relationship with God. In essence it is directed against God. It contradicts and opposes His right. Because of this it demands the judgment which is the application of His right and the exercise of His righteousness. It has fallen victim to its execution. Because God is in the right against it in these two ways, the wrong of man cannot be maintained or tolerated. Man cannot be allowed to put himself in

2. The Judgment of God

the wrong, to renounce the right which is set up for him by God, to execute in the sphere of the divine jurisdiction the movement in which he acts as though he were not subject to it and could in some way escape it. This movement is quite futile. It cannot attain its end. For with the man who executes it, it stands under the non-willing of God, under His superior contradiction and opposition, under the wrath of God. The fact that God applies and reveals His right means that between Him and the wrong of man, which is to say at once between Him and the man who puts himself in the wrong, there arises a conflict and crisis in which the man who puts himself in the wrong is not the judge of God, but in virtue of the unconditional superiority of His right God is the judge of man. Man's wrong, i.e., man himself as a wrongdoer cannot stand in the judgment of God. The righteousness of God means God's negating and overcoming and taking away and destroying wrong and man as the doer of it.

"The mighty God, even the Lord, hath spoken, and called the earth from the rising of the sun unto the going down thereof. Out of Zion, the perfection of beauty, God hath shined. Our God shall come, and shall not keep silence: a fire shall devour before him, and it shall be very tempestuous round about him. He shall call to the heavens from above, and to the earth, that he may judge his people. Gather my saints together unto me, those that have made a covenant with me by sacrifice. And the heavens shall declare his righteousness: for God is judge himself" (Ps. 50^{1-6}). "For thou art not a God that hath pleasure in wickedness: neither shall evil dwell with thee" (Ps. 5^4). "Therefore the ungodly shall not stand in the judgment, nor sinners in the congregation of the righteous. For the Lord knoweth the way of the righteous; but the way of the ungodly shall perish" (Ps. $1^{5f.}$). "The face of the Lord is against them that do evil, to cut off the remembrance of them from the earth" (Ps. 34^{16}). "The enemies of the Lord shall be as the fat of lambs: they shall consume; into smoke shall they consume away" (Ps. 37^{20}). "For thine arrows stick fast in me, and thy hand presseth me sore. There is no soundness in my flesh because of thine anger; neither is there any rest in my bones because of my sin. For mine iniquities are gone over my head: as an heavy burden they are too heavy for me" (Ps. $38^{2f.}$). "For we are consumed by thine anger, and by thy wrath we are troubled. Thou hast set our iniquities before thee, our secret sins in the light of thy countenance. For all our days are passed away in thy wrath: we spend our years as a tale that is told" (Ps. $90^{7f.}$). These are only a few voices singled out from the great Old Testament chorus of witnesses to the crisis in which God is the Judge of sinful man. And the New Testament confirms this witness—on the basis of a quite different outlook from that which was possible for the Israelites in consequence of the visitations which came upon them: "For what fellowship hath righteousness with unrighteousness? and what communion hath light with darkness?" (2 Cor. 6^{14}). And in the decisive passage: "The wrath of God is revealed from heaven against all ungodliness and unrighteousness of men, who hold the truth in unrighteousness" (Rom. 1^{18}).

[536]

Note that this also means, and primarily, that it is not too small a thing for God to defend and maintain His right, His lordship and His claim as Creator and Lord of the covenant against the wrong of man, and man as the doer of that wrong, even to the point of bringing about this crisis. His stake in man is so great. His right over man and to man is so much on His heart. He carries it through with such consistency. He will so little tolerate man's refusal to accept

§ 61. *The Justification of Man*

His divine right. He is so much a living God, and the rule of His righteousness is so necessary and complete.

But in saying this have we not indirectly and implicitly said something else, something which is apparently the very opposite of His non-willing and contradicting and opposing and wrath? Have we not said that the rule of His grace is so necessary and complete and that He is so much a gracious God? Yes, indirectly we have said this, too. For what kind of a will is it in which God willed from all eternity to co-exist with man? Seeing He is free, and it was not too small a thing for Him to will this, to will Himself in this co-existence in His eternal Son and Word, it is obviously His free and gracious will. And what kind of an eternal decree of God is it in which, conversely—and again in His eternal Son and Word—He elected man to this co-existence with Himself? Seeing He did not owe this to man, yet man was not too small to Him that He should make this decree concerning him, it is obviously the decree of His free election of grace. What kind of a divine act is the creation of man, his endowment and equipment with his human nature as appointed to serve God, the setting up of his existence with its reality which is different from His own reality and yet absolutely related to His own existence? Seeing that in it the planning and willing and capacity of man is nothing and the wisdom of the decision and act of God is everything, it is obviously the inconceivable work of the divine grace. If, then, the right of God over and to man is grounded in the inward right of His Godhead, if it is right in the strict and supreme sense, what other right can it be than that of His grace, and what else can the exercise and application of it be in His righteousness but in its very essence and at its very heart the realisation of His grace? Or as a work of the righteousness of God—whatever may happen in it, whatever we may have to think and say concerning it—is it not at the same time a work of His grace that it is not too small a thing for Him to enter into this conflict with the wrong of man and therefore with the man who does it? Do we not have to say that even in the non-willing, the wrath of God expressed in this conflict, even in the terrible "Away with thee" which is pronounced upon the wrong of man and therefore upon man as the doer of it, what rules finally and properly is grace, the divine Yes deeply buried under the divine No, in so far as God's free address to man is operative even in the No? At any rate God has not turned away His face from him. He has not withdrawn His hand. He does not cease to speak with him and act towards him. He continues to do so, even if it is in this way. He still regards him as His elect. In a way which is painful but intensive He still encounters him as his God, and He treats him as His man. Even in the hiddenness of this crisis He still holds fellowship with him, and because in all its forms, and therefore in this form, this fellowship rests on His divine right, because it is a work of righteousness, but because as the fellowship into which He has freely entered with man it cannot be otherwise understood than as grace, we cannot refuse to see that even in the judgment which comes upon man and his wrong God is gracious to man.

2. *The Judgment of God*

The crisis which comes upon man when he encounters the righteousness of God, but in which the grace of God is secretly present and operative, is frequently described in the Bible as chastisement. "Behold, happy is the man whom God correcteth: therefore despise not thou the chastening of the Almighty" (Job 5^{17}). For: "as many as I love, I rebuke and chasten" (Rev. 3^{19}). In an apparent paradox, Ps. 62^{12} grounds and recognises the mercy of God in the fact that He renders "to every man according to his work." The normative conception is that of the father who shows his fatherly love to the son by the strict exercise of his fatherly right. This is the thought in Prov. $3^{11f.}$, "My son, despise not thou the chastening of the Lord; neither be weary of his correction: For whom the Lord loveth he correcteth; even as a father the son in whom he delighteth." And again in Heb. $12^{7f.}$: "If ye endure chastening, God dealeth with you as with sons; for what son is he whom the father chasteneth not? But if ye be without chastisement ... then are ye bastards, and not sons." The original form of this conception, which plainly reveals its relation to the redemptive history, is perhaps in the promise given to David in 2 Sam. $7^{14f.}$ with respect to his son: "I will be his father, and he shall be my son. If he commit iniquity, I will chasten him ... but my grace shall not depart away from him." The wrath of God is purposeful, not purposeless and meaningless and unlimited. So little is it the latter than in contrast to the livelong and indeed eternal goodness of God its duration can be rather boldly described as only for a moment (Ps. 30^5, Is. 54^8). The men of the Bible do not fail to recognise its seriousness. But they boldly count upon its formal limitation: "Thou shalt arise, and have mercy upon Zion: for the time to favour her, yea, the set time, is come" (Ps. 102^{13}). And they always look back to its dominion: "The Lord hath chastened me sore: but he hath not given me over unto death" (Ps. 118^{18})—this was the [538] passage which Paul had in mind in 2 Cor. 6^9: "As dying, and behold, we live; as chastened, and not killed." "For thou, O God, hast proved us; thou hast tried us, as silver is tried. Thou broughtest us into the net; thou laidst affliction upon our loins. Thou hast caused men to ride over our heads; we went through fire and through water; but thou broughtest us out into a wealthy place" (Ps. $66^{10f.}$) "Now no chastening for the present seemeth to be joyous, but grievous: nevertheless afterward it yieldeth the peaceable fruit of righteousness unto them that are exercised thereby (τοῖς δἰ αὐτῆς γεγυμνασμένοις)" (Heb. 12^{11}). Where there is this fruit, there has obviously been the corresponding seed.

We must give the precedence over everything else to this statement concerning the grace of God in the rule of His righteousness. Its basis is plain in the goal of this event, where the grace of God is evident in the destruction of the wrong of man and the restoration of the right which he has squandered and lost. But the right perception of everything else depends upon the perception that the goal of this rule of the divine righteousness does not contradict but corresponds to its beginning, that from the very first it moves towards this goal. What God does in the gracious act of justifying the ungodly is not a sidestep or an act of juggling. He Himself in this act is not a *deus ex machina*, an unjust judge. He is the righteous Judge. From the very first His action in righteousness is the rule of His grace, and the action of His grace is the rule of His righteousness. How else could it be trustworthy and therefore credible and therefore the genuine redemption of sinful man? How else could the knowledge of it be the true consolation of sinful man which he can maintain in triumphant defiance of every temptation and doubt? How else could it be both legitimate and possible to confess: "Therefore being justified by faith, we have peace with God" (Rom. 5^1)? The subjective knowledge expressed in this

§ 61. *The Justification of Man*

Christian confession and rising far beyond any mere opinion or suspicion rests in the objective knowledge that the gracious justification of man is the work of God's eternal righteousness.

But this anticipation must not prevent us from facing without reservation the full seriousness of the crisis which comes on man in his encounter with the righteousness of God. We have been speaking of the grace of God which is hidden deep under the righteousness of God, which can disclose itself to us men who are wrongdoers only by the act of God, which is not simply disclosed and cannot be disclosed by us: as though we had only, as it were, to reverse the righteousness of God to find that its other side is grace; or as though we could see through the righteousness of God as through a veil, thus coming to the consoling conclusion that the true meaning and purpose of the judgment of God is His grace. For how do we know this? In itself, the grace of God is His free grace. And the knowledge of it (both ontic and noetic) is also free. It cannot be controlled by us. It cannot be comprehended even theoretically. God is indeed true to Himself and it is grounded in His divine right that He should be gracious in the rule of His righteousness. But that does not mean that of ourselves we can count on His grace, regarding it as our own, boasting of it, applying it to ourselves, claiming it. This has to happen. This is what faith does, as we often find it rather astonishingly in the Psalms. But faith does not do it in any impertinent way, with any arrogance, but in a freedom which can only be given to man, which has nothing whatever to do with his own capacity, which rests only on the fact that by the revelation of His grace, by the word of His promise, God has put it in a position to do it, to postulate grace. The believer is well aware that of himself he is not in a position and cannot put himself in a position to do this. He confesses that he is the man who is in the wrong before God and has therefore no right to do this. The man who is in the wrong before God has no insight into the grace hidden in the righteousness of God, let alone any claim to it, let alone any hold upon it. It is secretly present and at work for him, but that is nothing to him. In the act of his wrongdoing he protests against it; he exists (in flagrant contradiction to his being as the creature and covenant-partner of God) as one whom it does concern, who will not live by it, who will not be obedient to it, who rather flees and hates it. The pride of man which is his sin is that he will not know anything of the grace of God. And his fall is that he does not actually know anything of it, that having turned away from it he cannot take refuge in it or return to it. For how else can he have a gracious God?

He does not have a gracious God but a wrathful God. That is how he wants Him and that is how he has Him. The consequent crisis which comes upon him, that God will not accept his wrong, but exerts His right over him and to him, confronting him, therefore, in righteousness, is both total and inevitable. Setting himself in the wrong before God, he cannot and will not stand before Him. As this man he is completely impossible before God, without any hope of salvation. For wrong is an outrage and abomination to God. It has to perish.

2. *The Judgment of God*

The right of God confronts it with such majesty. It cannot exist before it. It is taken and burnt up and destroyed by the life of God like dry wood by the fire. This is the event of His righteousness. What takes place in it is the breaking of a catastrophe. And wrong does not exist merely *in abstracto*^{EN73} but in the act and therefore in the heart of man. Man gives to it the nature and form which it could not have of itself, since it is not the creation of God. He gives to it a place and actuality in the created world to which it does not belong, in which there is no category of its possibility. Man is the dark corner where wrong can settle and spread and flourish in all its nothingness as though by right. It is therefore man who evokes the wrath of God, who comes into conflict with the righteousness of God, upon whom it breaks as crisis, as catastrophe, as mortal sickness. He is the one who is impossible and intolerable before God, who cannot remain in His presence but can only disappear. It is his existence which is untenable. It is he who is confronted by the majestic right of God. It is he who must perish. "There is no peace, saith the Lord, unto the wicked" (Is. 48^{22}, 57^{21}). This applies to him. There is no escaping this judgment of God, this sentence and the execution of it, least of all by the consideration which is theologically quite true that at bottom the righteousness of God is that of the gracious God. This is true enough. But it means nothing to man as a wrongdoer. It has no significance for him. This man has to be repaid, and repaid according to his works. This man has to die. And it is, of course, the hidden grace of the righteousness of God which demands this retribution in virtue of which he cannot live but only die. God would not be gracious to him, and it would not be good for him—what would be the point?—if he could live and not die, if the judgment of God were not to fall upon him, and in all its inescapable fulness and strictness.

[540]

We are speaking of this man, man the wrongdoer, the man who has identified himself with wrong, and who in so doing has fallen victim to the divine negating and overcoming and setting aside and destruction. But is there any other man? Can the man who is this man also be quite a different man? Certainly even as this man he has not ceased to be the good creature and the elect of God. Even as a wrongdoer he cannot fall from the hand of God; he cannot, as it were, snatch himself out of the divine grasp. And that means that, even as he identifies himself with wrong, he cannot cease to be the man who is the divine work and possession. As God is still the same, so man is still the same even when that catastrophe breaks upon him, even in the consuming fire of the wrath of God, even in his mortal sickness, even when he has to perish, even in his dying and destruction. If he has no power to prevent this, this does not mean that he has the power to put an end to his existence as the good creature and the elect of God, which would mean that he has the power to escape the kingdom of God and effectively to oppose the will of God.

---

^{EN73} in the abstract

§ 61. *The Justification of Man*

That is what Jonah tried to do: "But Jonah rose up to flee unto Tarshish from the presence of the Lord, and went down to Joppa; and he found a ship going to Tarshish: so he paid the fare thereof, and went down unto it, to go with them unto Tarshish from the presence of the Lord" (Jon. 1³). But, of course, he failed. As God was still the same in relation to him, he was still the same before God, His commissioned prophet. He was this even when the terrible storm broke upon him and when he tried to sleep it out in the sides of the ship, as man so often likes to do when the judgment of God comes upon him. He was this even when he was to be cast into the sea, and actually was cast into the sea. He was this in the belly of the great fish and therefore in the final extremity of the divine judgment which overtook him. And his salvation was not a new thing, but the realisation of the inflexible divine purpose against which he had striven in vain.

[541] If it is the case, then, that as a wrongdoer man has fallen victim to the strict and radical and definitive judgment of God but still continues to belong to Him as the good creature and elect of God, this means that the righteousness of God comes upon him as a crisis in the sense that its realisation involves a separation which cuts his existence at the very root, severing it right across, dividing him into a right and a left. For who and what is he? On the left hand he determines himself as a doer of the wrong with which he has identified himself and in which he is caught up in the divine judgment. On the right hand he does not cease to be a wrongdoer and therefore under the divine judgment, but he determines himself as man, as the possession of God, in the kingdom of God, the object of His positive will and purpose, on the way to the goal which God has marked out for him. On the left hand, therefore, he is the man, who can only perish, who is overtaken by the wrath of God, who can only die, who has already been put to death and done away, and on the right hand he is the same man who even in this dying and perishing, even as the one who has been put away, is still the one who stands over against God, object of His purposes, surrounded and maintained by His life. To put it in another way, on the left hand man is the one who because of His wrong is condemned and rejected and abandoned by God, and on the right hand he is the same man as the one who even in his condemnation and rejection and abandonment is still pardoned and maintained by God, being kept for the fulfilment of His will and plan. We have to say at once that on both sides God acts righteously, because He acts in consequence of His right, of His faithfulness to Himself, and in execution of His right over and to man. On the left hand He acts righteously in His wrath which consumes the sinner, and on the right hand He acts righteously in the limitation, or more exactly in the interpretation of His wrath, in His holding fast to the man who even as a sinner that He can only chide is still His man. And God is righteous in this distinction as such: for satisfaction would not be done to His right if He could only chide on the left hand or only pardon on the right, if He accepted the identification of man with wrong, and was content simply to banish from the world both wrong and the wrongdoer, or if in spite of the wrong which man has done and his identification with it He allowed him to live at the price of not destroying the wrong which man has committed, of recognising *de facto* its right to exist. The righteousness of God

2. *The Judgment of God*

would not be God's righteousness and therefore it would not be true righteousness if it did not proceed on both sides, i.e., if its fulfilment did not involve this division which cuts right across the whole of man's existence.

We take up an earlier point when we interject at once that this righteousness would not be the righteousness of God if the distinction as such—and that which happens to man on the left hand as well as the right—were not the work of His grace. We have seen that even that which God does on the left hand is grace. It is not too small a thing for God actually to continue His fellowship with man in the form of the wrath which consumes man because of his wrong. [542] And we have seen that it would not in fact be good for man to continue to be as a wrongdoer, that it is therefore grace if he has to perish and die as such. But how much more the work of God on the right hand, in which He does not abandon man even in his fall into the abyss, in which He does not cast him out of His hand, in which He does not annul and extinguish his being as His creature and covenant-partner, in which He remains to him a home even in the far country into which he has wandered, in which even in death He surrounds and maintains him with His own life! If on both sides it is true that the final mystery of the righteousness of God is His grace, then it must be the case that man experiences both and therefore the totality of grace, wrath and destruction and death to the man of sin, pardon and preservation to the man who even as a sinner is the creature of God and elect. Necessarily, therefore, there is this separation in the execution of the right of God.

But now—at the risk of making the puzzle seem even harder—we must go on to add that the righteousness (and therefore the grace) of God would not be the righteousness (and grace) of God if its work were not carried right through on both sides, if as the work of God it were not a genuine and a perfect work. On the left hand, therefore, it is not at all the case that God condemns man only nominally and that only in appearance He destroys him with his wrong. And it is also not the case that He causes him only nearly or half to die and to perish. Again, on the right hand, it is not at all the case that He will only partly spare and preserve him, that He will allow or promise or grant him as His creature and elect only a partial right—a bare right to exist. On the contrary, on the left hand it is the case that God judges man and his wrong in all seriousness, that He destroys him genuinely and truly and altogether, that this man has actually to die, that the wrong with which he is identified has actually to be purged and consumed—a whole burnt offering in the flame of which both he and his sin are burnt up, disappearing in the smoke and savour, and ceasing to be. And on the right hand it is the case that God accepts His creature and elect genuinely and truly and altogether, that the faithfulness which He displays to him does not flicker like an exhausted lamp but shines out brightly like the sun. The words pardoning and preserving and maintaining which we have so far used to describe the activity of God on this side are far too weak, because here on this positive side we are dealing with the positive replacement of the wrong which has been set aside, with its crowding out by

§ 61. *The Justification of Man*

the new right of man, with the fact that to seal the passing of the dead and unrighteous man God introduces a new and righteous man in His place. In the one case as in the other therefore, in His No and also in His Yes, God does for man an honest and perfect work. In the one case, as in the other, He does not fashion a mere *quid pro quo*^{EN74}, a mere "as if," but actualities. He does not do a little pulling down here and a little building up there, but in both the pulling down and the building up He does a perfect work. The corresponding separation which comes to man in His judgment is also real and total. How can it be otherwise if it is the righteousness (and therefore the grace) of God which is at work in this judgment?

And now a final definition. Will it solve the puzzle, or will it make plain to us that it cannot be solved—and point us to the divine solution? Either way, we must add that the righteousness (and therefore the grace) of God would not be the righteousness (and therefore the grace) of God, if its dividing of man on the left hand and the right—man under the No of God on the one hand, and man under the Yes of God on the other—involved a state of dualism, that is to say, if the visible result of it was the static co-existence of two men, into whose divided being the one man is, as it were, torn apart and apportioned, in which he has either simultaneously or alternately to see himself, and in whose form and aspect he must understand himself: now coming partly or altogether under the one aspect, now under the other; now in a relative or absolute freedom choosing the one aspect, now the other. What has this division to do with either righteousness or grace if the result of it is this dual existence of man? if it involves this necessary or capricious vacillation between the two—mutually exclusive—forms of his being: the vacillation between extreme light and extreme darkness? For how then can both be real: the fact that God is against him and the fact that God is for him; the being of man on the left hand and his being on the right; his death and his life; the destroying of his wrong and the maintaining and establishing of his right? And what kind of a picture of God does this give us, indeed what kind of a God does this involve? What a hybrid being is the Almighty who—obviously in accordance with His own inward contradiction—has nothing better to offer to man than this dual existence! And what a self-understanding it is, and the human life grounded upon it, which can consist only in this see-saw or criss-cross movement! This state of dualism, this static co-existence of two quite different men, can only be the result of a misunderstanding, a caricature, of what we really have to see at this point. But if this is the case, then the only alternative is to understand the work of the dividing of man on the left hand and the right as the putting into effect of a history in which the man on the left hand is the Whence and the man on the right hand the Whither of the one man, the former being this man as he was and still is, the latter being this man as he will be and to that extent already is. The truth of human life under the control of the righteousness of God and

---

EN74 this for that

2. *The Judgment of God*

therefore of His grace is not a being divided into two, but something which it is impossible to consider, which can only be lived by the passive and active participant, the drama of the one human life in its dynamic sequence and co-relation. I was and still am the former man: man as a wrongdoer, whose wrong and whose being in identification with his wrong can only perish and has in fact perished when confronted with the righteousness of God, with the life of the One who is majestically and unconditionally in the right, falling a victim to death, and actually dying and being removed and erased and destroyed under the wrath of God. But I am already and will be the latter man: the man whom God has elected and created for himself, whose right he himself has squandered and spoiled, but God has protected and maintained and re-established in defiance of his wrong, in defiance of the catastrophe which necessarily overtook him as the doer of that wrong; the man who is not unrighteous but righteous before God, righteous, because he is in an accord which has been maintained and restored with the right of God Himself. It is in this way that God is in the right both against man and for him. It is in this way that He activates and lives out His righteousness in the encounter with man. And it is in this way that man lives before Him his true and genuine life as a man: one and the same man in spite of this division on the left hand and the right, in spite of the sequence, and the being in sequence, which is his life in this division; his being in the present of this yesterday and to-day, in the simultaneity of this past and this future. In this way, in this history, there is fulfilled the co-existence of the two, of God and of man. "This thy brother was dead, and is alive again; and was lost, and is found" (Lk. 15^{32}). That is man. No, that is the mystery of God's dealings with man, the mystery of His over-ruling of human existence. For here we find both the strict righteousness of God and in that righteousness His free grace. This history is God's justification of the godless, the *iustificatio impii*. [544]

But when we look at it in this way we come upon the real puzzle of it all.

For all the difficulty in carrying through the construction, it is at least conceivable, or at a pinch it can be made conceivable, and therefore it is no genuine puzzle, that I recognise and understand myself in this dualism, in this static co-existence of two diametrically opposed aspects. Here I am, on the one hand, in my empirical reality—unconsciously in error and consciously at fault. Here I am, supremely compromised in a way that I cannot overcome. Here I am, perishing, moving forward to a destruction which I can already foresee and which is to that extent already present. But here I am, on the other hand, in my ideal reality; my human nature which is quite unaffected by all this, my proper self in which I am in the right and therefore finally secure against myself and everything that speaks against me and the fall which I cannot deny. Why not? At some point, not on the surface perhaps, but in the depth of my being, I can appear to myself both as this empirical man and also as this ideal man. I can obviously learn to handle this antithesis between the empirical and the ideal. And in this way I can make the dualism conceivable. Many of us do, [545]

§ 61. *The Justification of Man*

in fact, conceive of it in this way, and in this alternation, this ebb and flow of the two pictures, which is so restless and and yet at bottom so peaceful, so disturbing and yet in the last resort so consoling, we can attain to a view of ourselves in which we actually live or think we live. We are speaking of the schema which underlies every natural religion and philosophy. If this schema is not known instinctively to every man, it can easily be known and its application learned. And if the understanding of self in this schema does involve a certain riddle, its solution can be described as attainable in theory and to some extent at least applicable in practice. The only trouble is that this schema, this picture, this riddle and the approximate solutions of this riddle have nothing whatever to do with the righteousness and grace of God, with what man is before God both on the left hand and on the right, with his justification by God. And conversely the divine justification of man has nothing whatever to do with the distinction and relationship of an empirical and an ideal picture of man.

The justification of man by God belongs neither to the empirical nor to the ideal world, for God who is at work in it is one God and the Creator of all the visible and invisible reality distinct from Himself which is beyond this contrast.

Nor is it possible to see how the man on the left hand is to be empirical man or the man on the right hand ideal man. To be sure, this corresponds to the well-known Platonic distinction, but this is not in any sense identical with the division which comes to man in the judgment of God. Is not the so-called ideal man the reflection of the pride of the man who is set on the left hand of God, and does not the poor empirical man have a certain similarity to the man to whom God says Yes, because even as he is he has not ceased to be the creature of God and His elect?

Again, the justification of man by God is an event between God and man, not the static relationship of their being, but the being of God and man in a definite movement which cannot be reproduced in two pictures which can be placed alongside and studied together. It takes place as the history of God with man. That which is twofold but one in it is the righteousness and grace of the one God above, condemning and pardoning, killing and making alive; and corresponding to this divine activity the dark Whence and the bright Whither of the one man below, experiencing His judgment—his transition and progress from that yesterday to this to-morrow, his coming out of the wrong which is removed and destroyed, his coming, therefore, out of his own death, and in that coming—this is his present—his going forward to his new right and therefore to his new life.

As this history the justification of man is a genuine puzzle, unlike that of the dualism which can be caught in that picture. The justification of man cannot be caught in any picture, not even in moving pictures. The reason for this is that the man who lives in this history of God with him is not in any sense perceptible to himself. We have described this history as a drama which cannot be seen by any spectators but can only be lived by those who participate in it.

2. *The Judgment of God*

But obviously—and we cannot put this too strongly—there can be no self-experience of this drama. The fact that it is our history which is in train, that we participate in this drama, is something which must be true and actual quite otherwise than in some depth of our own self, and recognisable as the truth quite otherwise than in the contemplation of one of the phenomena which meet us in these depths. Where and when do we find ourselves in that present, in the transition and progress from that yesterday to this to-morrow? In what past of this our time do we see our wrong actually removed and erased and extirpated, and ourselves actually put to death and buried and destroyed with it? And in what future of this our time do we see our right established and ourselves righteous and acquitted? When and where do we find ourselves in the distinction and unity of this past and coming to be? When and where can we think of ourselves as those who are justified by God?

> If justification is a happening which we experience in ourselves, if we can find ourselves in it, so that there is no puzzle, but it can all be readily conceived, then we must have made a mistake and we must retrace our steps at a most important point in our previous deliberations, for the judgment of God cannot be so total and comprehensive as we have supposed. Let us suppose for a moment that the wrong of man is not so great, that it is not the radical evil that we have assumed, that the conflict between it and the righteousness of God is not so bitter, the wrath of God not so consuming, the catastrophe which breaks on man not so serious, the perishing and dying not a real but a partial or perhaps only a symbolical perishing and dying. And let us suppose, on the other hand, that God's Yes to man is not so strong and unequivocal, that the new right of man is not so sure, that the obliteration of his wrong is not so clear and definitive and certain, that the activity of God on the right hand is not a perfect and complete activity. Let us suppose that on the left hand as on the right everything is relative and not absolute, that the antithesis is only quantitative and not qualitative, that the transition from the one to the other, from yesterday to to-morrow, is also relative and quantitative. It is true that in *this* transition, *this* coming out and going in, we shall be able at bottom to experience ourselves, we shall be perceptible and comprehensible to ourselves, however great may be the step involved. We know this kind of judgment in this kind of history, which may be very serious and meaningful both in its backward and also in its forward reach, but which is not entirely serious, and not entirely meaningful. Histories and crises and revolutions of this kind do exist. And in them it is not impossible to experience ourselves, to be perceptible and comprehensible to ourselves. But if this is the case, we are not dealing with the righteousness and grace of God, which does an honest and total work both on the left hand and on the right. We are not dealing with the revolution of God. And it is this revolution which is our present concern. We cannot, therefore, retrace our steps or make the matter easier than it is.

If we stand in His judgment, in the history which He has set in train, then this means that the antithesis between our yesterday and to-morrow is absolute and qualitative, that there are no half-measures, no possible mitigations either on the left hand or on the right, that our situation is entirely serious both in its backward and also in its forward reach, the situation of absolute decision. And in this entirely serious and decisive situation—"as dying, and, behold, we live"—we do not know ourselves, we never have and we never shall. That this history is my history, that I am the one who is so forcefully divided by the

[547]

§ 61. *The Justification of Man*

righteousness and grace of God, that I am caught up in this transition, that I am the man who participates in this drama, that that which is said of the prodigal is said of me—this is something which I do not see and therefore do not understand. There is no man who can try to maintain that he experiences and understands himself as the prodigal son, for it is said of the prodigal that he was dead and is alive again, and was lost, and is found. No one can try to maintain that this is an expression of his self-understanding. That man is, in fact, the prodigal son is the genuine riddle before which we stand at this point.

Of course, it is not a meaningless riddle. It is a genuine one to the extent that it is to us insoluble, that it cannot be solved on the basis of any subjective experience or with the development of any self-understanding. But it is a riddle which has been solved in quite a different way—and one which is not actually hidden from the knowledge of man (i.e., his knowledge of the revelation of God). It is all exactly as we have described it. It cannot be found in us or conceived by us. It is an absolute riddle. The dividing of the righteousness and grace of God as we have described it is an event: a dividing which is forcefully prefigured by the Creator's dividing of light and darkness, of the waters above the firmament and the waters below the firmament, of the sea and the land; a dividing to left and right which is comprehensive, total and definitive. And the absolutely serious situation created by this event is our situation. It is our wrong and death which is behind us, our right and life which is before us. The transition from that past to this future is our present. We are the participants in this great drama. That history is, in fact, our history. We have to say indeed that it is our true history, in an incomparably more direct and intimate way than anything which might present itself as our history in our own subjective experience, than anything which we might try to represent as our history in explanation of our own self-understanding. It is indeed a riddle. But in spite of the riddle of it, it is not a fairy-tale or a myth. Compared with it, measured by the reality of it all, the things which we think we know of ourselves—in the unriddling of riddles which are not genuine riddles—are a fairy-tale and a myth: our life-histories, and the sum of all life-histories; that which we usually call universal history; the way in which all this presents itself to us; the way in which we usually explain and construct our own existence and the existence of [548] the race; the way in which we experience and perceive and then conceive ourselves in the obvious relative and quantitative divisions and transitions of our life—not to speak of the picture in which we think we possess and recognise ourselves now in an empirical and now in an ideal form. Here in the sphere of our supposed or actual competence—we think and postulate and speculate. Here we brag. Here we spin and ramble and dream to our heart's content. Here our reason takes to phantasy and our modest poetic powers attempt to reason. Here we produce images of events and forms in face of which it may well be asked how they apply to us or what concern they are of ours. Here we are never truly alone, but we "exist" enthusiastically in some higher or lower

2. *The Judgment of God*

"transcendence." But what is demanded at this point is caution, reserve, scepticism. The one history in which we are all undoubtedly and absolutely and directly alone as in our own true history is the history of man's justification by God in the unmitigated antithesis of our transition from the yesterday which stands under the No of God to the to-morrow which stands under His Yes. For all that it is a riddle, it is our true and actual to-day, and very different from any fairy-tale or myth.

What is it that makes it so puzzling to us? It is necessarily puzzling. The reason is that we cannot experience and perceive and comprehend ourselves in this our real to-day. Our real to-day, the to-day of our true and actual transition from wrong to right, from death to life, and therefore the to-day of the judgment which falls upon us by the righteousness and grace of God, is always a strange to-day. We must now give it its name and utter the decisive word which we have so far withheld. It is the to-day of Jesus Christ. The day of the judgment of God which overtakes us, of the clash of the righteousness of God with our wrong, and therefore with ourselves, the day on which our wrong and death becomes to us the past and our right and life the future—that day is His day. It is as His day that it is our day. His history is as such our history. It is our true history (incomparably more direct and intimate than anything we think we know as our history). Jesus Christ comes to us. In Him we are quite alone, torn away originally and finally from the whole world of fairy-tale and myth, taken right beyond all our empirical and ideal pictures of ourselves, genuinely alone, and therefore the men who stand in that judgment and transition. In all our previous consideration we were looking tacitly at Him, not with the intention of looking past us men, but with the intention, as we look at this man, of looking at all us other men in a first and final reality and truth—with the intention of finding ourselves in Him, of finding in Him God's mighty and righteous and gracious contesting of our wrong, of finding in Him our justification. We could not have entertained our previous considerations at all except with reference to Him. What other source could there be for the statements we have made? How else could we know of that high right of God which is superior to our wrong, which is grounded in itself and the ground of all other right? How else of the nature and extent, the curse of human wrong? How else of the clash of the two, of the wrath of God which consumes man as the doer of wrong with the wrong itself? How else of the steadfast faithfulness of God to man as His creature and elect, the faithfulness which is the ultimate ground of his justification? How else of the dividing of man on the left hand and the right, of the condemnation and pardon in both of which God is both righteous and gracious? How else of the fact that on both sides the work of God is a complete and perfect work? How else that both apply to the one man, and that they are not the basis of any dualism, but the transition of the one man from his dark yesterday to his bright to-morrow, the history of man, his redemptive history? We have not invented all this. We have found it at the place where it is reality and truth, the reality and truth which applies to us and comprehends

[549]

§ 61. *The Justification of Man*

us, our own reality and truth. We have found it where we ourselves are and not merely appear to be. We have found it where we do not merely seek ourselves in opinions but find ourselves in knowledge. We have found it where we are not called upon to think and express things which are rambling and vacillating, but firm and definite. We speak of the proclamation of Jesus Christ, of the happening of His death on the cross, of the revelation of it in His resurrection from the dead, or, better and more exactly, of Jesus Christ Himself, who lives, who is present and active, who gives Himself to be known as the Crucified and Risen, not merely in the proclamation of Him, but by virtue of the proclamation of Him. It is all true and actual in Him and therefore in us. It cannot, therefore, be known to be valid and effective in us first, but in Him first, and because in Him in us. We are in Him and comprehended in Him, but we are still not He Himself. Therefore it is all true and actual in this Other first and not in us. That is why our justification is not a matter of subjective experience and understanding. That is why we cannot perceive and comprehend it. That is why it is so puzzling to us.

It is a matter of the knowledge of this Other, of His transition from the curse of death to the glory of life, of His to-day, which will always be to us a strange to-day, although it is ours. It is a matter of the knowledge of His history, which will always be to us a strange history although it is our history. It is a matter of the knowledge of this Other Himself, who will always be to us a stranger although He comprehends us and we are in Him. It is a matter of the rule of the righteousness of God in Him, which, although it rules over us and applies to us, is always a strange righteousness: *iustitia aliena*^{EN75}, because first and essentially it is *iustitia Christi*^{EN76}, and only as such *nostra, mea iustitia*^{EN77}.

In the final part of this section we must take up and explain the fact that as the righteousness of Jesus Christ, and therefore a strange righteousness, this righteousness is ours, mine. We shall be developing what has been our tacit presupposition from the very first—the righteousness of the divine judgment in its original and proper and typical character as the righteousness of Jesus Christ and therefore a righteousness which is strange to us.

By the righteousness of God we have meant the realisation of His right in its relation to the wrong of man, to man as a wrongdoer. It is, therefore, identical with the judgment of God. And in respect of the men concerned in that judgment it is identical with their justification. We have thought of it as the divine inauguration of the history in which one and the same man was in the wrong, and as a wrongdoer had to be negated by God and die, and has in fact died, only to be affirmed and maintained by God in that death, being carried through it to become the man who is in the right before Him and can live as such. But this righteousness, this judgment of God, this justification by God

---

^{EN75} alien righteousness
^{EN76} Christ's righteousness
^{EN77} our, my righteousness

2. The Judgment of God

which comes to man, is something which has taken place concretely in Jesus Christ. It had to take place in Him because in His person as the Son of the Father He is Himself both very God electing and creating man and very man elected by God and as such ordained from all eternity to fulfil all the righteousness of God. It could take place in Him, because as very God and very man He was competent and qualified to accomplish and suffer the contest between God and man, to be both the Judge and the judged in this conflict. It could take place only in Him because only He as this one person could be both subject and object in this history, uniting the antithesis of it in Himself: Himself the full end which is made in it; and Himself also the new beginning which is made in it; and both in the place and therefore in the name of all other men, for them and in their favour. It took place in Him in that He as the true Son of God became true man, and in this unity of His person became the Judge of all other men: their Judge as the One who was judged in their place—delivered up in His death, and reinstated in His resurrection from the dead. As it has taken place in Jesus Christ this is the justification of sinful man. We will now try to understand it in detail.

What has in fact taken place in Jesus Christ? We will first give the general answer that there has taken place in Him the effective self-substitution of God for us sinful men. The contest of God with the man of sin and of this man with God is inevitable. The right of God holds sway, and it has to be executed in righteousness. The judgment of God is inevitable. This is true in respect of man. If there is salvation for him, it is only as judgment is passed. But this judgment involves the destruction of wrong and of the man who does wrong. It also involves the defence and restoration and reinstatement of the right of the man elected and created by God, the life of man in this right before Him. But man is not at all adapted for this twofold way of dealing with wrong, either actively or passively, either as subject or object, either as a creature or as sinful man. As the man who has put himself in the wrong both before God and against Him, he is not suitable for participation in this happening. As a creature, where can he find the capacity, and, as the sinner that he is, where can he find the will, actively to co-operate in this process (perhaps with the help of divine grace), or even to suffer and experience and receive that which must come upon him in the course of it? Seeing that it is a matter of the replacement of his absolute wrong by his absolute right, of his death by his life from this death, it belongs to the very nature of the case that he cannot be considered, but falls short, as the divine partner in this happening. But it has to concern him. The righteousness of God has to overtake him, the judgment of God to fall on him. It must be his justification. Obviously both God and man belong to this happening. But if man is disqualified, if he is not present, and has no place, how can it be inaugurated and take place and attain its end? It does take place and it attains its end in the fact that God takes the matter out of the hands of man and conducts it as His own—even though it is the affair of sinful man. God does not merely confront him as God and Lord and Judge,

[551]

§ 61. *The Justification of Man*

but as such He effectively takes His place at the side of sinful man, indeed, He takes the place of sinful man, representing him against Himself. His eternal Word becomes flesh. He Himself in His Word becomes man. Why? In order that He may not only conduct His own case against all men, but take up and conduct the case of all men, which they themselves cannot conduct, in that process between Him and them. In order that He may be for them what they cannot be for themselves—an active subject and a passive object in that conflict. In order that He may take over on their behalf the suffering and activity for which they are not adapted, which is completely beyond their capacity and will. In order to carry through as their Representative the justification which cannot take place or be carried through if they fall short. Not from His own side. Not as God, Lord and Judge. But from their side. As the God, Lord and Judge who is man, servant and judged. In general terms, what has taken place in Jesus Christ is the divine participation in the situation of the man confronted by His right, encountering His righteousness and in need of His justification; the divine intervention for Him in virtue of which man can do all this and suffer all this, in virtue of which man can and will be the partner of God, at which the righteousness and judgment of God aims and does not aim in vain. It is as God identifies Himself with man—His participation and intervention is as direct and complete as that—it is as He becomes a man and as this man the Representative of all men, it is as He makes His own the cause of all men that justification can and does take place. To make it possible, God became man. This is the meaning of the existence of Jesus Christ. If there is a justification of sinful and proud man, the man who has fallen into the abyss in his pride, but from whom God has not withheld His hand, who cannot therefore fall from [552] the hand of God, then it is to be sought in Jesus Christ. It has actually taken place in Him, as there has taken place in Him God's participation in man, His identification with Him, His intervention for all men. We do not postulate this event. We derive its significance and necessity and scope from the simple fact that it has taken place. Jesus Christ lives, very God and very man. If we look at Him and see Him, then we find in Him the justification of man which has taken place in Him, and we know that we do not need to seek it elsewhere, that we shall seek it elsewhere in vain. We will now turn to two more detailed explanations.

On the one side the justification of man in Jesus Christ is the destruction of his wrong and his own setting aside as the doer of that wrong. The man of sin, proud man who has fallen in his pride, is destroyed in this justification. He becomes the man of yesterday. This is the first thing which we cannot find in any event in our own life, which we cannot, therefore, picture as a determination of our own existence. And for the good reason that it has not actually happened in our existence as such. Looking at ourselves we can only say that this fatal man of yesterday is still the man of to-day, and we have no prospect other than that he will also be the man of to-morrow. But in Jesus Christ, the very man in whom the very God has intervened for us, and acted in our place,

2. *The Judgment of God*

it is all quite different. That man has been set aside. He has perished. He is only to the extent that he was; that he is the same as the one who died as that man.

On this side we have to do with a definite action of the Son of God. It has been carried through by Him in His unity with the man Jesus of Nazareth, in our midst and as one of us, but it has been carried through also in the power of God and therefore effectively. And (because in this power it applies to all men) it is in force and effective for all men. This action of the Son of God and the man Jesus Christ is the act of obedience in which, very God in His willingness and capacity for this obedience, He chose and willed and did that which is humble, making Himself like the man who had fallen so deeply into the abyss in his pride, unreservedly placing Himself at his side, and indeed taking his place. Why? In order to accept his responsibility, in order in his place to enter and tread to the end the way which as the way of sinful man, in fulfilment of the right of God, could only be the way to death. He did not shrink from this intervention for man and its consequence. As the Brother and Representative of all men He was ready to give Himself as very God and very man to do away with that which is impossible and intolerable to God, the wrong of man and unrighteous man, to make a full end of it, to banish from the world both the offence and the one who had caused offence.

He has therefore suffered for all men what they had to suffer: their end as evil-doers; their overthrow as the enemies of God; their extirpation in virtue of the superiority of the divine right over their wrong. They had to suffer this, but they could not suffer it, not one of them.

[553]

For even if it had been, or were to be, laid upon one of them really to taste and experience in his suffering and death the judgment of God on himself and his wrong, how could he experience it for others, for all others? And even if it were laid on all men really to taste and experience the judgment of God, even if they were willing and able to do so, how could they who have given offence, suffering merely what they have deserved, banish the offence from the world by their death, even their eternal death? For the offence would still be there. It would not be as though it had never happened. It would not be made good. As something which had been it would remain as an unerased blot on the world of God's creation, an element in its history. And even if by their suffering of the divine judgment they were able to erase the blot, even if their suffering and death were costly enough for that, would not the will of God for elect and created man be given the lie by their destruction? To satisfy His righteousness they would have to perish genuinely and finally, to fall from His hand. But then God would not be the God who has sworn to be faithful to them. Or He for His part would not have kept His oath and covenant with them.

What we men must suffer—if it is to be suffered in accordance with the righteousness of God—can be suffered for us only by God Himself as man: if, that is to say, it is to take place validly and effectively for us all; if it is to be the one and total destruction of wrong and all wrongdoers; if it is to be the erasure of that blot from the world of God's creation; if at the same time it is to be the keeping of His faith, the carrying out of His covenant with man, not to man's destruction but to his salvation, to the justification of the unjust. And Jesus

§ 61. *The Justification of Man*

Christ was ready and gave Himself up to suffer and perish and die in that way—in accordance with the perfect righteousness of God. God judged the world in Him—and judged it in righteousness—by delivering Himself up in Him to be judged. To suffer validly and effectively for us His own judgment upon us, He condescended to us, He humbled Himself so profoundly, He was willing to be so lowly, and in our flesh the eternal Son, the man Jesus of Nazareth, rendered the obedience of humility to the eternal Father, thus fully satisfying the righteousness of God on its negative side, the side of wrath. God identified Himself with man in Jesus Christ. In the person of this one man He set a term, an end, He was Himself the end which must come upon us all. And because of that our wrong has in fact become a thing of the past. It is no longer there. It is extinguished. It is present only as something which has been eternally removed and destroyed. And we men as the doers of it, as those who willingly identified ourselves with it, are dead and buried. We, too, are in fact a thing of the past. We are present only to the extent that our existence as such has this past. In Him our sin and we ourselves have perished. In Him we all start at the divine No which has been spoken with such power and carried through with such effect; at the liberation which is an accomplished fact in this No because it is spoken and carried through in Jesus Christ. This liberation which has taken place in Him is the presupposition of our future. And the freedom given to us by this No is our present. In Him our wrong and we ourselves as the doers of it are behind us. He has taken it away from us. He has taken us away from it. He has set aside and cancelled our existence as the doers of it. In this respect it is of decisive importance to see that He has done this in the act of His humble obedience. He has done this deed by suffering. He was, of course, the subject of this happening. Taking our place and suffering for us, He did not do what we as wrongdoers are always doing, and He did what we do not do. He was lowly where we are proud. He condescended to us where we arrogantly try to rise up. He the Lord became a servant. He the Judge became the judged. He accepted what was laid upon Him by the Father. He let the will of the Father be His will. He drank the bitter cup instead of putting it from Him. He suffered the shame of the cross. And all this in freedom, in free obedience, in the obedience of humility. In this humility He expressed and revealed His deity, and in it, in the power of His deity, He made an end of sin and the old man of sin in His own person, speaking that liberating No. We do not therefore leave behind us a vacuum when we start at this No, when we have behind us sin and the sinner. That they are behind us, that it is all up with sin and the sinner, rests on the fact that that liberating No has been spoken in this way, in the lowly obedience of Jesus Christ. Our arrogant disobedience has been set aside once and for all in Him. He has not merely suffered for us, but suffering for us He has done the right for us, and therefore suffered effectively and redemptively for us. Judged in Him we cannot be to-morrow the proud men we were yesterday. Those men are no longer there, for yesterday we were delivered up to the divine judgment. As those who are freed from our past in Him, we no longer

2. *The Judgment of God*

have the freedom (the false freedom) to return to our old pride. Between us and our past there stands positively and divisively the act of right which is His death. That is the final and decisive thing that we have to see in order to realise that our wrong and we ourselves as the doers of it are really and truly at an end. That, then, is the righteousness of God in its concrete form as the righteousness of Jesus Christ, as our justification accomplished in Him, on its first and negative side; the gracious and redemptive work of God on the left hand.

On the other side, the justification of man in Jesus Christ is the establishment of his right, the introduction of the life of a new man who is righteous before God. This man, his life, is the future of man in Jesus Christ—the same in whom that first man is put to death and is therefore past. Man will live as this righteous man when he has died and therefore only *was* as that unrighteous man. But this second thing, too, we shall not find in any event of our life. That we live as righteous men is not an immanent determination of our existence and cannot therefore be conceived. It is not in our existence that man has acquired this future. Looking at ourselves we should have to regard this future as that of the man of to-morrow as just as unreal and impossible as the fact that that man of yesterday is our past. In Jesus Christ, the very man who as such is the eternal Son of the eternal Father, this future man, the new and righteous man, lives in an unassailable reality. In Him I am already the one who will be this righteous man and live as such, just as in Him I am still only the unrighteous man, to the extent that I once was this man. In this positive sense Jesus Christ lives in our place, for us, in our name. As our wrong and death are our past in His name, in Him, so our righteousness and life are our future.

[555]

On this second and positive side of our justification as it has taken place in Jesus Christ, we are dealing with something specific which has happened to Him, the Son of God, in His unity with our fellow-man Jesus of Nazareth. As the true Son of God and Son of Man, as our Lord and our Brother, He is not merely the subject but the object of the righteousness in which God vindicates and establishes His right amongst us. He received something which in what He did—it was the act of His lowly obedience and He carried it through to death—He neither would nor could take to Himself. He received to what He did the answer of the free omnipotent grace of God His Father. The hidden good will of God, to which He subjected Himself without reserve and was obedient even to death, was proclaimed to Him. God acknowledged the right of the One who gave Himself to judge the world by letting Himself be judged in its place. God confirmed the innocence of the One who allowed Himself to be accused and condemned and put to death for the guilty. God revealed the meaning and purpose of His wrath, His consuming love, to the One who had exposed Himself to it and borne it to the very end. The righteousness of God did not merely take place by Him, in the obedience of His Son acting in His passion for us, but when it had taken place by Him in the act of His death, it was also revealed in Him as the righteousness of the eternal faithfulness and grace of God, as the righteousness of His positive will, which was present from

§ 61. *The Justification of Man*

the very first, although only latent in His non-willing, His will to introduce the new and righteous man, His will that this man should live. This is something which Jesus Christ has not done, which has come to Him as the answer to what He has done, but just as real, just as concrete, just as visible, audible, perceptible, just as historical as the death which He took upon Himself and in which He acted passively. We speak of His resurrection from the dead by the glory of the Father (Rom. 6⁴).

As He was delivered up, as He delivered up Himself, for our offences, so this took place for our sake, for our justification (Rom. 4²⁵). It was for us that He received what He did receive in it. As He did what He has done in our place, for us, so the answer which God the Father gave Him in respect of His act of obedience applies to us. The good will of the Father, which was hidden in His dying for us and revealed to Him in His resurrection, was and is the good will of God with us. His right, which was acknowledged by God in His resurrection, the right of the Judge judged on our behalf, was and is our right. His innocence, the innocence in which He bore and bore away our sin, the innocence which was manifested in His resurrection, was and is our innocence. The consuming love which revealed itself in His resurrection as the meaning and goal of the divine wrath which He bore for us was and is the love in which God willed to seek us and to find us, to carry us and to embrace us. The righteousness revealed to Him, the Representative of the unrighteous, as the righteousness of the faithfulness and grace of God, was and is therefore the revelation of the promise made to us, that we should live before Him as the righteous. As He in His act of humility has carried through for all men the end to which we had all fallen victim, so for all men He has actually opened the gate of righteousness and life. His resurrection is the beginning from which we all come when we leave the past which He has concluded, going forward in Him to the future which is already present.

> We ourselves could not open this door. We could not make this beginning. We could not make this future our future. We could not do so even if we were in a position (which we are not) to make our wrong as though it had never been, to obliterate ourselves as the enemies of God that we are, and thus to suffer for ourselves what Jesus Christ has suffered for us; with our death to satisfy the righteousness of God on its negative side. Even if we had the power to do this, where should we find the power to raise ourselves from our wrong before God to our right, to move from the death to which we have fallen a prey to life? If the putting to death cannot be our own work, how much less our resurrection! Even Jesus Christ did not secure for Himself His resurrection from the dead. On this side He was a pure recipient. He was crowned, He did not crown Himself. How, then, can we act in this matter? We cannot even receive that which Jesus Christ has received from God for ourselves, on our own initiative, or otherwise than in Him. What He received was God's answer to the act of His lowly obedience, the confirmation of His innocence, the reward and revelation of the rightcousness which He maintained in bearing our wrong. That He received this answer, this confirmation, this reward for us, does not alter the fact but shows plainly that anything we could receive and only receive for ourselves, apart from Him, would be very different from the future and

2. The Judgment of God

hope of our right and life. Left to ourselves, the only thing that we can expect after our destruction as evil-doers is to have no future.

Negatively, the justification of sinful man before God means a basic turning away from his wrong and from himself as the doer of it. Positively, it means his basic turning to God. Neither as the one nor as the other can it be his own affair—neither as our work nor as our experience. It is our affair, of course, but on the negative side and more particularly on the positive it is our affair as it has been conducted and carried through by the one Jesus Christ—in His work and in that which happened to Him. By virtue of His resurrection from [557] the dead, by virtue of the righteousness revealed in His life, in Him and from Him we have a future and hope, the door has been opened, and we cross the threshold from wrong to right, and therefore from death to life. Risen with Him from the dead, we do this, or rather it takes place for us. What God has applied to Him, He has applied to us. We are the righteous and living men that we shall be. In Him our justification is a complete justification, fulfilled on the right hand as on the left.

We note that it takes place in Jesus Christ and in Him first with this clear and inextinguishable differentiation and unity. In relation to Him, to His death and resurrection, we are forced to speak of the twofold character of the divine judgment. But again in relation to Him we affirm that the divine judgment is a single act and therefore one which cannot be divided or separated, a strictly coherent history. In Him there takes place that transition of man from his wrong to his right, from death to life. It would not be the act of judgment of the one God if it were not this one complete act, beginning here and completed there, beginning in the death and completed in the resurrection of Jesus Christ, beginning with the destruction of human wrong, completed in the establishment of human right, beginning with the doing away of unrighteous man, completed in the life of the righteous—but a single act with this differentiation. And both have taken place on behalf of all men in the one Jesus Christ; in this indissoluble relationship, in this irreversible sequence.

We must take note of the indissoluble relationship. The life of the new and righteous man acquires a place only with the passing and death of the old man of unrighteousness. The one has to perish in order that the other may begin. There is no place for the new man alongside the old. He can only crowd him out and replace him. He can only have him behind him. His day can break only when the day of this other is over. This is what took place in the death of Jesus Christ. Jesus Christ lives as the One in whom this has taken place; as the Crucified, as the One who was delivered up for our transgressions, as the One who has taken the place of the man of unrighteousness, who has put him to death and destroyed him. He lives as the One in whose self-sacrifice the justification of man begins. The fact that there is no more place for the old man, that he has been put to death and has perished, shows itself to be true and actual in the fact that he is replaced by the new, that the day of the new has

§ 61. *The Justification of Man*

broken, that Jesus Christ has been made the Victor in His resurrection from the dead. Jesus Christ lives as the risen One, as the bearer of the right which God has given to man, as the recipient of His grace, completing the justification of man by His receiving of it.

A *theologia gloriae*[EN78], the magnifying of what Jesus Christ has received for us in His resurrection, of what He is for us as the risen One, can have no meaning unless it includes within itself a *theologia crucis*[EN79], the magnifying of what He has done for us in His death, of what He is for us as the Crucified. But an abstract *theologia crucis*[EN80] cannot have any meaning either. We cannot properly magnify the passion and death of Jesus Christ unless this magnifying includes within itself the *theologia gloriae*[EN81]—the magnifying of the One who in His resurrection is the recipient of our right and life, the One who has risen again from the dead for us. The magnifying in its unity of the transition which has taken place in Jesus Christ is the true confession of our justification. It can be a true confession only in this totality, in its application to the transition of the strictly coherent history which has taken place in Him.

But we must also take note of the irreversible sequence in this unity. How can it be the unity of this history, this transition, if it is reversible, if it can be thought of as a cycle? It is not for nothing that Jesus Christ called Himself "the Way" (Jn. 14⁶). A garden path may be circular. But a garden path is not a true way. A true way has a beginning and an end which is different from it, which lies somewhere else. The same applies to a true history—and to a true transition. That which has been in Jesus Christ is still present in Him as that which has been—the wrong which is blotted out, and the wrongdoer with it. This cannot and must not happen again. It must never again become the future. Rather the future will always be the past of human wrong and the human wrongdoer. This is something upon which in all our future we can only look back. Israel cannot again return to the depths of the Red Sea, where it was kept by the mighty hand of God, and the enemy was destroyed. What Jesus Christ has done to put our sin and death behind Him and, therefore, behind us, He has done once and for all. He cannot and must not do it again. It cannot become for us a fresh problem of our future, as though it had not been done. And what He has received as righteousness and life He has again received once and for all in our place and for us. In Him it is our future which cannot become the past. It is our hope which cannot be changed into care and uncertainty and doubt and sorrow. What He has done for us as the eternal Son of God He has done rightly, and what He has received for us from the eternal Father He has received rightly. In Him, therefore, there is set both a *terminus a quo*[EN82] and a *terminus ad quem*[EN83], between which we are now on the way, but which cannot for that reason be confounded or confused with one another. If

---

[EN78] theology of glory
[EN79] theology of the cross
[EN80] theology of the cross
[EN81] theology of glory
[EN82] starting point
[EN83] end point

2. The Judgment of God

we do confound or confuse them, if we try to return along the way upon which He has set us, we shall again be looking past Him, we shall again be holding to ourselves instead of to Him. Our justification, as it has taken place in Him, has given to God's history with us—notwithstanding its coherence and totality—a very definite direction. If we look at Him, we can look and go only in this direction, from here to there, but not in the reverse direction.

> The Western seriousness with which we emphasise the beginning of justification is a good and necessary thing. In it we insist on the fact that in relation to Jesus Christ we can look only from *here* to there, only from the death on the cross to the resurrection, only from the yesterday of our death as it was suffered by Him for us to the to-morrow of our life as He has received it for us. But we must see to it that this seriousness—there are examples of this both in Roman Catholic and also in Protestant circles—does not, at a certain point which is hard to define, become a pagan instead of a purely Christian seriousness, changing suddenly into a Nordic morbidity, losing the direction in which alone it can have any Christian meaning, suddenly beginning to look backwards instead of forwards, transforming itself into the tragedy of an abstract *theologia crucis*[EN84] which can have little and finally nothing whatever to do with the Christian knowledge of Jesus Christ. Certainly the self-sacrifice of Jesus Christ in death, and the death to which we are delivered up in His death, can never occupy us too much. But we miss what He has done for us in it if we understand it in isolation from what He has received for us in His resurrection, if we do not try to see it in its movement to what He has received for us. We will not inquire at this point whether there may not be the corresponding danger of the obscuring of the direction of the justification which has taken place for us in Jesus Christ by a far too ready forgetfulness of its *terminus a quo*[EN85], of the lowly obedience in which Jesus Christ undertook to withstand the wrath of God in our place on the cross. On the whole, the danger in the West is not in this direction. One of the things we have to learn from the Eastern Church is an unwearied looking forward from the *terminus a quo*[EN86] to the *terminus ad quem*[EN87] of our justification, the joy which is commanded us in relation to Jesus Christ who is the "Way," boundless joy in what He has received in our place, what we have received in Him. The knowledge of our justification as it has taken place in Him cannot possibly be genuinely serious except in this joy, the Easter joy, which looks in this direction.

[559]

Our conclusion brings us back to our starting-point with the question: What is the meaning of the judgment of God, and therefore of the justification of man (as it has taken place in Jesus Christ), for God Himself? The question is not an idle one. Let us suppose that it is an activity which is purely external, which is accomplished merely with reference to man, but which does not affect Himself and mean anything for Him. There are many views of God for which this possibility might seem to be worthy of consideration. The justification of man is perhaps worked out and presented to man in one of the many spheres within this world, perhaps one of the most important, perhaps the most central of all, but only as a process within the world which follows the law of a dialectic within the world; in such a way, therefore, that God has nothing

---

[EN84] theology of the cross
[EN85] starting point
[EN86] starting point
[EN87] end point

more to do with it than that He is the final mystery which embraces it, as it does everything that takes place in the world. It is evident that if this is the case there can be no question of any true or final certainty concerning its occurrence. It takes place with all the ambiguity of all world events, about the meaning of which, both in detail and as a whole, man may have his well-founded suspicions, but in face of which he must always accept—even in the light of his most notable hypotheses—a continuing doubt whether after all everything might not be quite otherwise. Nor can the justification of man have any true or final importance or urgency. There may be many important relations between God and the world, and also between God and man, and they may be ordered approximately according to the statement of the Christian doctrine of justification. But why should this doctrine be of any urgent concern to man—who does not always have religious, let alone specifically Christian, interests—if this relationship is only external for God, and does not mean anything to Him, or anything more than any other relationship? If this is the case, do I have to have an answer at all, an absolutely reliable answer, to the question how I am to find a gracious God? The urgency of the question, as a request for an absolutely reliable answer, obviously stands or falls with the fact that the justification of man has a meaning for God Himself, that it has for Him at least as much meaning as it has for us. Then, and only then, does the question touch us closely. Then, and only then, is there the prospect of an answer which is not merely pious but true, not merely notable but certain. Only if God Himself is involved can we be seriously and totally involved and count on it that we are not involved in vain. For that reason our final question is not by any means an idle one.

Now we have left far behind us the possibility that God Himself is not involved, that the justification of man before Him does not mean anything for Him, or anything more than any other event. That is has supreme significance for God is already decided by the fact that He allowed its fulfilment to cost Him no less than His own interposition, the incarnation of His eternal Word. The One who made Himself ours in Jesus Christ, in order that justified in this One we might be His, is obviously involved in this matter not merely externally and indirectly but with a supreme directness. For obviously it also and in the first instance (how could it be otherwise?) concerns Himself. Our question cannot, therefore, be whether it has a meaning for God. This is a fact which is already decided. But it is a fact which we cannot leave without clarification. In this respect, too, we must be able to proceed with a purer knowledge. We have to ask, therefore, what meaning it has for God.

Our starting-point is again the fact that what is executed in God's righteousness and therefore in His judgment and therefore in the justification of unrighteous man, in the *mortificatio*[EN88] and *vivificatio*[EN89] which have come to

---

[EN88] mortification
[EN89] vivification

2. *The Judgment of God*

man in Jesus Christ, is the right of God Himself which is, as such, the supreme and only true right. The right of God, the law which is Himself, rules and illuminates and is glorified in this His work. As we have seen, in the totality of it, in both its great dimensions, it is the work of the grace in which He has addressed man from all eternity, of the faithfulness which He has sworn to Him from all eternity. But fulfilled on this eternal basis, in its character as the work of His free mercy, it is from first to last the application of His supreme and only true right. In other words, it is the expression and therefore the self-affirmation of the One who is the essence and basis and source and guarantee and norm of all right. That this is the case we have already described as the backbone of the doctrine of justification. What the justification which has this [561] basis means for unrighteous man we have already seen in outline and we shall come to see in detail. That it means for God Himself, not merely something, but the supreme thing of all, rests on the fact that for its accomplishment His only Son and therefore He Himself in the person of His Son is not too big a price to pay. But what does this work mean for Him? We have already answered this question in the words of Rom. 3^{26}. It means for Him that He Himself is just (in this work), that in it He affirms His right and therefore Himself. We do not take too great a liberty if we paraphrase: In this work of the justification of unrighteous man God also and in the first instance justifies Himself. If this is true in a general and comprehensive way, then we are in a better position to see the hinge on which justification as the justification of man turns, the source from which it flows as man's justification, the original movement in which God sets this work in train as a work for man and to man. Its basic necessity is then quite clear, and with it the basic necessity of our knowledge of it and again the supreme degree of certainty of the true knowledge of it. If it is the case that in our justification God also and in the first instance justifies Himself, then in the knowledge of it we have to do with the knowledge of God Himself, who in the fact that He affirms His right proves that He is the One who neither can nor will deceive. But to what extent is it true that in our justification God does also and in the first instance justify Himself?

One thing is certain. It can be true only on the presupposition that God as God is in Himself the living God, that His eternal being of and by Himself has not to be understood as a being which is inactive because of its pure deity, but as a being which is supremely active in a positing of itself which is eternally new. His immutability is not a holy immobility and rigidity, a divine death, but the constancy of His faithfulness to Himself continually reaffirming itself in freedom. His unity and uniqueness are not the poverty of an exalted divine isolation, but the richness of the one eternal origin and basis and essence of all fellowship. The fact that according to His revelation God is the triune God means that He is in Himself the living God. In the light of God's revelation the idea of a God who is dead because of His pure deity is anthropomorphic. As against this, the statement that in and with the justification of man God also and in the first instance justifies Himself does not at any rate contain any

§ 61. *The Justification of Man*

anthropomorphism. It is not, therefore, a presumptuous statement, the kind of statement which encroaches on the divine glory. Quite the contrary. With its particular application it tells us that God is the living God. It tells us this with reference to the eternal right in which God Himself is law, in which He is faithful to Himself in His wholly sovereign freedom, in which He is in agreement with Himself. The activity of God in His righteousness, in His judgment, in the justification of unrighteous man, is the activity of the One who is God in this eternal right—its application and outworking. In this activity He affirms Himself in this His right. This is the meaning of justification for God Himself. In this sense it is true that in it God also and in the first instance justifies Himself.

We say "in the first instance" in order to bring out the precedence—the unconditional precedence—of the dignity and importance of this direction and reach of the divine activity. But it does not take place only within the framework of an external relation of God to man. It is not a contingent action which might never have taken place or might have had a quite different theme and content. Its basis is in the life of God Himself. In it we have to do with the living being of God as God. There can be no question of belittling it for that reason, as His action in relation to man. On the contrary, it is for that reason that it has its significance even in that relation; that it is the act of His true and concrete participation in man. And the fact that in the justification of man God in the first instance justifies Himself gives to the justification of man, to the judgment that kills and makes alive in which this is executed, its holiness, the true and divine seriousness which in contrast to all the immanent judgments and crises and catastrophes and revolutions and their relative and limited killing and making alive, with their relative and limited certainty, distinguishes it as His judgment, the revolution of God. But what does it mean and to what extent does it actually happen that in this occurrence God in the first instance justifies Himself?

We are simply pointing to the most obvious aspect when we say that in the justification of man we have to do with the expression of God's right as Creator; His right to man as His creature, a creature which does not belong to itself or to anyone else but to God, which as His exclusive handiwork is also His exclusive possession. This right of God is compromised by sin, by the existence of man as the man of sin, by the fact of his pride and fall. We have described this fact as the invasion by chaos of the cosmos of God's creating, as the blot on His creation. Is God the Creator and Lord in relation to this blot on the cosmos and man, or is He not? Is He the Creator and Lord if this invasion is possible or tolerable, if evil can sustain and make good its claim to actuality? The justification of man is plainly God's decision that this claim is empty, that this invasion and blot is impossible and intolerable, that it cannot be suffered. It is God's contradiction of the contradiction raised against Himself. For this reason it is an act of judgment, an act of judgment which aims to destroy the wrong of man and positively to re-establish the right of God. As that history,

2. *The Judgment of God*

that transition, that *mortificatio*^{EN90} and *vivificatio*^{EN91}, it proves that God takes sin seriously as the compromising of His right as Creator, that He is not willing by one hair's breadth to forgo His right in face of it. He said: "Let there be light," not: "Let there be darkness." Therefore He intervenes against darkness. He marks off light from darkness and darkness from light. He beats back and beats down the assault upon His right to man, the attempt upon His right and creation. He does so with all the radicalness and totality with which this is done in the justification of man. In so doing, He justifies in the first instance Himself as the Creator of man, the Creator of the heavens and the earth. [563]

But His right goes deeper than that. It is the right of the Creator, but it is also the right of His grace extended to man. Man is not merely His handiwork and possession. Beyond that—in answer to the call of God—he is His covenant-partner, who has not merely been given existence, but who is appointed for salvation, to whose existence He has given the end of eternal life, i.e., of fellowship with Himself in the form of service to Him. Man is the elect creature of God. God's right to him is therefore the right of His gracious election. The transgression of man compromises this right. It is man's attempt to break loose from His election, from the covenant with God. Has God stretched out His hand to him in vain? Is He going to accept the defection of His covenant-partner? Will He have to abandon the idea of attaining with him the appointed goal? Will the salvation promised to man, being lost by man, remain in the hand which God has stretched out in vain, or elsewhere in the clouds? Will it not be the salvation of the one for whom it is meant, who is elected to attain it? The justification of unrighteous man shows that God does not accept this rejecting and despising of His grace. It is the intervention of God against it in judgment, His intervention for the right of His grace. The man who sets Himself in the wrong against it must die as a wrongdoer, but He must rise again as the recipient of the right of the elect, of the covenant-partner of God, which is granted to Him. The one man must go, the other come. The right of God, with which man's wrong cannot compete, demands this. And this is what takes place in the justification of man, to man's own redemption and salvation, but obviously in the first instance to the glory and justification of the gracious God Himself, to the demonstration that He cannot be mocked as the gracious God. Hence His consuming wrath, whose consuming is that of His love, which will not in any sense accept that rejection. Hence the inconceivable crowning of unrighteous man with grace and mercy. If we are to understand this event, everything depends upon the exclusion of any idea of a weak overlooking and pardoning of human wrong. Such an idea has nothing whatever to do with the truth of the grace and mercy of God. What we have to see here is rather that God does not weakly submit. He does not renounce the grace of election and the covenant. He does not yield in His will to save. He does not surrender the

---

^{EN90} mortification
^{EN91} vivification

§ 61. *The Justification of Man*

right in which He is in this will towards man. This will has to be done, and it is done in the justification of sinful man. In this way God in the first instance justifies Himself.

[564] But we must look higher still, to the fulfilment of justification in Jesus Christ. As it has taken place in Him as our justification, the justification of man, it is the work of God, the divine action in the death of Jesus Christ, the divine receiving in His resurrection from the dead. It is the work of God in its unity with what the man Jesus of Nazareth, our fellow-man and brother, has done and received. But in its unity with His human doing and receiving it is the work of God. And as the work of God in Jesus Christ it is both our justification and also—here in a sense at its inward centre—the justification in which God justifies Himself.

Here in Jesus Christ it begins with the action of the Son of God, with the humble obedience in which He abases Himself, giving Himself, undertaking to become man, in order that in His holy person He may take the place of all men, making an end of their wrong and of themselves as wrongdoers in His own death, casting them out in His holy person into outer darkness. But in speaking this No and accomplishing this liberation in our place and for us, He has also—and in the first instance—proved Himself to be the Son of God, very God from all eternity. In this act which is fully free, fully humble, without any claims, an act of pure obedience, He has claimed and exercised and put into effect and revealed His divine right, the right of the Son of God. The obligation of this Son, the Son of God, is not one which is originally alien to Him. It is not one which is laid upon Him from without. It is not one which is accepted by Him merely as a necessary duty. On the contrary, it is His divine glory and right to act with this obligation, to be perfectly obedient to the Father in freedom and humility and without any claim. Yet the speaking of this No, the accomplishing of this liberation, is from first to last a divine work. In rendering obedience in this work, He acts in His own way as the Son in exactly the same conformity with the divine nature, with exactly the same divine glory and right, as the One who lays this obligation upon Him and demands this obedience from Him. And He does what He does in execution of the divine will and purpose which is His own. Recognising and executing the right of the Father, He exercises His own right which is specifically that of the Son. Therefore the specific obligation in which He acts in the justification of man is not a new or alien one, let alone one which is unworthy of Him, which He has undertaken only unwillingly. He is the One in whom God elected man as His man and Himself as the God of man from all eternity. Again, He is the One in whom, in relation to whom, according to whose image, God created the heavens and the earth and man. Again, He is the One in whose person God made the eternal covenant of grace with man. In undertaking to become man and to act as the Representative of all men in His death and passion, what He does is simply the fulfilling of the office which, according to the counsel of God (His own as well as that of the Father), is His own office, the office of the

2. *The Judgment of God*

Son from the very beginning, from all eternity. In His substitutionary death [565] and passion, in this act of humble obedience, on what other ground has He acted than on the ground and in expression and confirmation of His own divine right as Son? In willing to do this and doing it, He did what as the Son He ought to do, what He could do in virtue of His right as Son. And He did it concretely as the legitimate bearer and representative and executor of the divine right of creation and the covenant to man and over man. All this obviously means that in the act of His obedience, and therefore of His substitutionary death and passion, in the first instance He justified Himself. Before God the Father, before the angels, and men and all other creatures He conducted and represented Himself as the One who was in the beginning with God and was Himself God, as the One by whom all things came to be, as the Lord who is over all things and everything. As the Lamb which bears and bears away the sin of the world He has exercised and put into effect His divine right of rule, setting it on a candlestick. And the fact that He has done this makes what He has done for us as the same One, the justification of man, indisputably valid and irresistibly effective. To deny or doubt that the sin of the world has been borne by Him and borne away in Him is to deny or doubt His right as the Son and therefore the eternal right of God. We must not be guilty of any such doubt or denial.

Again, here in Jesus Christ our justification is accomplished in the receiving of the Son of God, in that which comes to Him, crucified, dead and buried—and all in His unity with the man Jesus of Nazareth—as the act of grace and power of the Father in His resurrection from the dead. This is His divine confirmation as our Representative and therefore our divine confirmation in the right which is restored and the new life which is given to us in Him. This is the revelation of the love in which God has sought and found us in His death and converted us to Himself. This is—primarily and above all—the glory of the divine right which is revealed in Jesus Christ, which shines upon us from Him, in the application and outworking of which we are loved and justified by God, being set on the way to our right and to eternal life. The one divine right is indeed the right of the Father who delivered up His Son for us, sending Him into the world and interposing Him as our Representative, the right of the obligation which was laid upon Him and accepted by Him, the right of the high command which He obeyed in that free and humble act in which He made no claim. The demand which He met was not meaningless or arbitrary. It was not the formal and therefore the empty demand of a categorical imperative. It rested on the supremely concrete right of God. And this right was the right of the Father, of the God who as the Father of Jesus Christ, and in Him, is the Father of us all, the Father *par excellence*, the one true Father. The demand which Jesus Christ obeyed was therefore the demand of the fatherly right of God. And this fatherly right is the right of the grace, the mercy of God, the right of the One who has loved and elected man from all eternity, appointing [566] him to His covenant with Him, making Himself his covenant-partner. We can

§ 61. *The Justification of Man*

and must add that it is the right of God who in His wisdom sees and perceives and measures what is the dimension of the wrong of man, how deep is the plight in which he has plunged himself as a wrongdoer, how great is the damage which he has done in creation in so doing, and beyond that, who and what alone can ward off disaster, and beyond that again, in what true and effective help and salvation consist. We have to say further that it is the right of the omnipotence of God, who lets evil do its evil work, as it has done in the death of Jesus Christ, to the very limit of its capacity, in order to reduce it *ad absurdum*[EN92] and bring it to shame by its own action, its attack upon Himself in the person of His Son. All this, His grace and wisdom and omnipotence, was the fatherly right of God in which He demanded the obedience which the Son—in execution of His own right as the Son—rendered even to death, even the death of the cross. And His resurrection from the dead by the glory of the Father is the demonstration of the fatherly, because gracious and wise and omnipotent, right of that demand. On the basis of the free and sovereign, not the blind or tyrannical but the fatherly, will and decree of God it all had to happen as it did happen in the suffering and death and burial of Jesus Christ. This necessity, this fatherly will and decree, could not be something alien to the Son. He did not have to make it His own. He could not refuse it the completely free obedience in which—as the acting subject of what took place—He put it into effect and accomplished it to the very end. But His resurrection from the dead is the expression and confirmation of the right of this necessity, of the right of the demand to which He was obedient, as a fatherly right. In it it is revealed as the right of the One who in His grace does not will the death of a sinner, but that he should be converted and live; as the right of the One who in His wisdom knows the sickness of man but also the means to heal him; as the right of the One who in His omnipotence can give power to death, but in order to give it a meaning, in order to set for it a positive goal, in order to limit and overcome it and to take away its power from it. What comes to Jesus Christ in His resurrection, what He receives in it, as the Representative of all men and therefore on their, on our behalf, is that the fatherly right of the divine demand fulfilled in Him is made manifest, visible, audible and perceptible in Him, just as He has made it manifest, visible, audible and perceptible as the divine demand in the act of obedience of His death (in execution of His right as the Son), even to the point of His cry and question: "My God, my God, why hast thou forsaken me?" (Mk. 15^{34}). "So let all thine enemies perish, O Lord: but let them that love thee be as the sun when he goeth forth in his might" (Jud. 5^{31}). For it happened to Him in His resurrection that by His necessary death God achieved His end with man. The man of sin was put to death in Him, so that in Him this man, freed from the burden of His past, which was that of His wrong and pride and fail, became free for His future as a righteous man, free to live as this righteous man, and more than that, free for His salva-

---

[EN92] to the point of absurdity

2. *The Judgment of God*

tion, for the eternal life accorded to him, that he should be God's, "and live under Him in His kingdom, and serve Him in eternal righteousness and innocence and felicity, as He has risen from the dead and lives and reigns to all eternity." He has indeed risen from the dead as the One who in His person receives this future for us. The demand to which He was obedient in His death and passion had this right of ours as its goal, because the right which underlay it was the fatherly right of God. This is what came to Him (and in Him to all of us) in His resurrection from the dead, the demonstration of the right of God chastising the Son because He loved Him, and loving Him even as He chastised Him. It was the self-demonstration of God as His and our gracious and wise and omnipotent and righteous Father. It was the fulfilment of our justification as the self-justification of God.

But did God need to justify Himself? we may ask as we survey in retrospect this whole discussion. It is clear that He did not need to do so. He does not need anything. God is completely free. God does not owe anyone anything—least of all an account of the righteousness of what He does or does not do. But as the living God—as distinct from all the godheads of philosophies and religions—is He not free and able to justify Himself? May it not be that of His own good-pleasure He did in fact (and in the first instance) will to justify Himself, and actually do so, in our justification (and supremely in the fact that it took place in Jesus Christ)? What, then, can we bring against it, especially if we appeal to His freedom or argue that He does not need anything of this nature? A quite unnecessary concern for His majesty? Certainly God is—and was and will be—righteous without having to prove Himself righteous. But seeing He willed to and did prove Himself righteous, it is only right to count on it that He did not do so in vain. That the knowledge of our own justification by Him may be clear and certain, is it not right that He should first will to be known by us as the God who is right and just and righteous in Himself? Is it not right that for our sake He should have willed to avail Himself, and actually did avail Himself, of His freedom to justify Himself? Is it not right that in practice He should have loved man supremely and drawn him to Himself most intimately by not allowing him, when He justifies him, to stand and wonder and gape in astonishment at His own right as at a closed door, but by demonstrating His own right—His right as Creator and covenant Lord, His divine right as Father and Son—causing it to shine forth and to be proclaimed, and therefore to be known to man? "The sun of righteousness with healing in his wings" (Mal. 4^2). Supposing we cannot truly and actually and firmly know our own justification, without any problems or doubts, apart from this—if the door is in fact closed? Supposing that in our own righteousness we have a complete and utter need to know Him and His righteousness on the basis of His self-demonstration, so that knowing Him we may participate in His own inner life? Well, the door is not in fact closed to us. In justifying us, God in the first instance shows Himself to be righteous. He is revealed and may be known by us as such. Therefore we are well advised to let drop this anxious questioning of Him and instead to ask

[568]

§ 61. *The Justification of Man*

ourselves what use we are going to make of the freedom which He obviously willed to give to us in that He willed to make, and actually did make, use of this freedom of His; what use we are going to make of the freedom to know in our own justification the One who is eternally righteous, and in so doing to know the light and the power and the indisputable validity and the irresistible efficacy of our own justification.

3. THE PARDON OF MAN

Pardon—by God and therefore unconditionally pronounced and unconditionally valid—that is man's justification. In the judgment of God, according to His election and rejection, there is made in the midst of time, and as the central event of all human history, referring to all the men who live both before and after, a decision, a divisive sentence. Its result—expressed in the death and resurrection of Jesus Christ—is the pardon of man. And this as such is man's justification, this alone, but with unconditional truth and efficacy, so that apart from it there is no justification, but in it there is the total justification of man. Whether man hears it, whether he accepts it and lives as one who is pardoned is another question. Where men do hear it and accept it and dare to live as those who are pardoned, it is realised that its power is total and not partial, and there will be no refusal to give to it a total and not a partial honour.

The sentence of God passed in His judgment is a divisive sentence. And it is in virtue of the division that its result is man's pardon. It divides between his wrong, himself as a wrongdoer, as the object of the divine rejection on the one hand, and himself as the elect of God, His creature and covenant-partner on the other. It tears away the latter man from the former, and the former from the latter. It opens up between the one and the other an unbridgeable gulf. It makes the one an old man whose time has run its course, who belongs to the past, in order to introduce a new man who can move forward into the future in which there is no place for a return of the first man. It makes the one a shadow, a ghost, in order to give breath and flesh and blood, a real existence, to the other. It locks up the one in order to free the other: to free him from his identification with the first man and his wrong; to free him for the right (his own right as a man) which is freely granted to him when he is parted from that first man and his wrong—his existence in identification with wrong—is renounced. When he is free for this right, he is free for life on the basis and under the protection of this right, as a righteous man. This is the divisive and pardoning sentence of God passed in God's judgment.

Three things are clear. This pardon (1) can only be God's sentence on man. The division between the man of sin and man himself, the opening up of a gulf between them, the separation of the past and the future, the locking up of the

3. *The Pardon of Man*

old man and free emergence of a new man, cannot be a human but only a divine work. It is creation—a new creation, but still like the first creation, which also involved at bottom a great division. Man would have to be able to put himself to death in order to make himself alive as a new man, to remove himself and then to rise up again, if it were his own affair to carry through and to put into effect this judgment and in this judgment this divisive sentence, to pardon himself. If he does in fact stand in this judgment and under this divisive sentence, it is because it is the sentence and judgment of God. If he is pardoned, then it is God who has done it—God who has made him a righteous instead of an unrighteous man. This is what God has done in Jesus Christ.

But this pardon (2) can be received and taken to heart and put into effect by him only as the sentence of God on him and therefore as the Word of God's revelation addressed to him. The fact that he is pardoned by God is not his truth but God's truth. He cannot, therefore, reveal and tell it to himself. He can only let himself be told it as it is revealed to him by God. His transition from his existence as the old man to his existence as the new, his coming out of his past and his going forward into his new and different future, can never be by virtue of his own capacity. He cannot accomplish it himself. He can only find it accomplished. In the same way, the knowledge of himself as the one who is caught up in this transition can take place only in the sphere of a human self-knowledge in which he repeats the knowledge with which God knows him in that sentence. How else could he come to it except on the presupposition that it has already been made known to him by God—which is what God does in His Word? Except on this presupposition he can never know himself as a sinner against God and before Him. In the same way, and more so, he can never know himself as one whose sin and sinful being are pardoned. To receive and take to heart and put into effect means in both respects to accept what is told us concerning ourselves by God Himself. Anything that we may try to tell ourselves in both respects can neither have the genuine content that we are sinners and that we are justified nor be seriously received and taken to heart and put into effect by us. The pardon effected in Jesus Christ is not our word but God's Word.

But if our pardon is God's sentence and the content of His Word to us, then (3) it has an authority and force and validity which are not partial but total, not relative but absolute. When this sentence was passed concerning us, something took place which cannot be reversed. This pardon does not mean only that something is said concerning us, or, as it were, pasted on us, but that a fact is created, a human situation which is basically altered. We are, in fact, those who are pardoned by God. We have peace with God. And our corresponding self-knowledge—if it is really a self-knowledge in which we repeat what is told us by His Word concerning us—cannot possibly be exposed to any legitimate doubt or genuine problems. The only legitimate and genuine answer to the unconditional Yes in which God pardons man is an equally unconditional human Yes, a confession in which there are no ifs or buts. Any question marks [570]

§ 61. *The Justification of Man*

which we may try to put—and reasons enough can be found for them—can only be a rejection of God's judgment and sentence and Word, a basically impudent and a correspondingly dangerous presumption, for all the subjectively well-founded and sincere humility with which we may put them. The divine pardon which has taken place in Jesus Christ has a binding force. It speaks of a being and possession of the man to whom it applies.

We cannot overlook the fact that in the Old Testament Psalter, side by side with the pure worship of God, His acts and glory and faithfulness, and side by side with all the complaint and sorrow and longing and above all the penitence—indeed together with these—we not infrequently hear a voice of extraordinary confidence, in which other writers, and sometimes the same, boast of their own righteousness before God and man, appealing to their innocence and the purity of their heart and purposes and ways, and formally undertaking to plead their case with God on that ground. I will give a few examples: "I was also upright before him, and I kept myself from mine iniquity. Therefore hath the Lord recompensed me according to my righteousness, according to the cleanness of my hands in his eyesight. With the merciful thou wilt shew thyself merciful; with an upright man thou wilt shew thyself upright; with the pure thou wilt shew thyself pure" (Ps. $18^{23f.}$). "For thou, Lord, wilt bless the righteous; with favour wilt thou compass him as with a shield" (Ps. 5^{12}). "For thou hast maintained my right and my cause; thou satest in the throne judging right" (Ps. 9^4). "The righteous shall flourish like the palm-tree; he shall grow like a cedar in Lebanon. Those that be planted in the house of the Lord shall flourish in the courts of our God. They shall still bring forth fruit in old age; they shall be fat and flourishing; to show that the Lord is upright; he is my rock, and there is no unrighteousness in Him" (Ps. $92^{12f.}$). "The righteous shall be glad in the Lord, and shall trust in him; and all the upright in heart shall glory" (Ps. 64^{10}). The man whose delight is in the Law of the Lord, and who meditates in it day and night, is "like a tree planted by the rivers of water, that bringeth forth his fruit in his season: his leaf also shall not wither; and whatsoever he doeth shall prosper" (Ps. 1^3). For that reason, when he is in need and oppression, he demands: "Judge me, O Lord, according to my righteousness, and according to mine integrity that is in me. Oh let the wickedness of the wicked come to an end; but establish the just: for the righteous God trieth the hearts and reins" (Ps. $7^{8f.}$). "Judge me, O Lord; for I have walked in mine integrity: I have trusted also in the Lord; therefore I shall not slide. Examine me, O Lord, and prove me; try my reins and my heart. For thy lovingkindness is before mine eyes: and I have walked in thy truth" (Ps. $26^{1f.}$). And on occasion the positive complaint: "Verily I have cleansed my heart in vain, and washed my hands in innocency. For all the day long have I been plagued, and chastened every morning" (Ps. $73^{13f.}$). And against this background, what considerations concerning the ungodly, the proud, the "enemies," their threatenings, their unmerited fortune, their power, what prayers not merely for deliverance from them—but also—much bewailed by inoffensive Christians—for their overthrow and destruction! What are we to say to all this? And to Job's persistent protesting of his good conscience in face of all the clever and strong entreaties of his friends; not only to them, but even to God Himself—a position which he surrenders only when God speaks to him "from the storm": "I have heard of thee by the hearing of the ear: but now mine eye seeth thee" (Job 42^5)? And what does it mean that twice ($42^{7f.}$) it was expressly granted in distinction to his prudent friends that he was right in his impetuous insistence upon his right? To a smaller degree, but with the same distinctive assertiveness, we find the same insistence in Paul: "Let a man so account of us, as of the ministers of Christ, and stewards of the mysteries of God. Moreover, it is required in stewards, that a man be found faithful. But with me it is a very small thing that I should be judged of you, or of man's judgment: yea, I judge not mine own self. For I know nothing by myself; yet am I not hereby

3. The Pardon of Man

justified: but he that judgeth me is the Lord" (1 Cor. $4^{2f.}$), concerning whom we are then told that when He comes and brings to light the hidden things of darkness and counsels of the hearts everyone will receive—Paul does not say recognition or condemnation but quite simply—praise of God. With a view to this he warned the Corinthians not to judge before the time. This is the apostle's opinion of a righteousness by faith only. And what of the famous passage in Rom. $8^{30f.}$, in which—this time to the highest possible degree—a straight line is drawn from the election of those who love God to their calling and justifying and glorifying, with the conclusion: "If God be for us, who can be against us? He that spared not his own Son, but delivered him up for us all, how shall he not with him also freely give us all things? Who shall lay anything to the charge of God's elect? It is God that justifieth. Who is he that condemneth? It is Christ that died, yea rather, that is risen again, who is even at the right hand of God, who also maketh intercession for us." We do not need to force upon the confident words of the Psalms and Job any other sense than that which they obviously have according to their exact wording and context. But we must not read them outside the context of the rest of the Old Testament. We must hear them together with the other voices which sound in the Psalms. And if we do we shall see that for all their strangeness they did not really say anything other than what Paul said. On the contrary, what we have to ask is whether what Paul said—and much less brokenly at any rate in Rom. 8—is not a direct each of the Old Testament voice. The fact that the "innocence-motif" is also found in Babylonian Psalms does not alter in the slightest the fact that in the Psalms of Israel it has its meaning and right and necessity only from Israel's gracious election, on the basis of which God willed to set up and maintain His covenant with Israel. Israel was a notorious failure as a partner in the covenant (cf. Pss. 78 and 106). Behind the words of the Psalms there stand the catastrophic judgments which were God's answer to the unfaithfulness of His people. Their sequence, Israel's pitiable condition amongst the nations, exposed to external pressure and internal influence, the painful continuance within it of the unfaithfulness which has brought it to this pass: all these are the present, the negative presupposition of the words. But their positive presupposition is the recollection which these things have not extinguished of the faithfulness of God which has not been shaken by these things, which is quite unmerited, but absolutely certain in itself, which cannot be denied by those who see it, but now for the first time—and not in half-tones but *fortissime*^{EN93}—attested. It is the pious, the [572] pure, the innocent, the blameless, the upright, who are confident of their righteousness in face of their enemies, and with a consciousness of their righteousness cry out for the righteousness of God; those who do not forget His covenant and faithfulness but have it before their eyes, and with it the light which in spite of all these things lies upon their lives, who cannot, therefore, cease to boast of their right. If all the other things which have to be said are said in the Psalms—and often in the same Psalms—then this has to be said too, and preferably more strongly and clearly than anything else: "Truly God is good to Israel, even to such as are of a clean heart" (Ps. 73^1). The man who is of a clean heart not only can but must appeal to God's goodness to Israel, and therefore to his own knowledge of that goodness, notwithstanding all that can be said against Israel and against himself as a member of this people. He does not now have to do with this, but with what God is for Israel and therefore for him. The man who clings to this is bound to find comfort. He is this man. He would be falling at once into impurity of heart and unrighteousness—he would, strangely enough, be making himself guilty of an impropriety against God—if he let go this calling, if he did not appeal or did not appeal unconditionally from this righteousness of his to the righteousness of God, if he did not regard God with a final seriousness as his rock, his fortress, and his shield, on which ultimately all his "enemies" could only dash themselves to pieces. If Job is

---

EN93 very loud

§ 61. *The Justification of Man*

found wanting ($42^{1f.}$) in that he doubted or rather murmured against the righteousness of God, repudiating it, insisting on his own right against God, as though he could deal with Him like an advocate who is sure of his case, if in this respect he has to withdraw and repent in sackcloth and ashes, yet the wrath of God ($42^{7f.}$) is not kindled against him but against his friends, who tried to make him err in that in which even in his wrong he was, in fact, right, in the fact that with doubt and murmuring and revolt—with a badly croaking voice, as it were—he still could and would and indeed had to hold fast to God, and as one who was righteous in this seek for himself righteousness with Him. In this very fact he was the servant of God, and in saying this concerning Him even in his protest, he spoke rightly. But what became of the three very excellent theologians with their very exact and accurate knowledge of the righteousness of God and the humility which is demanded of man? They were directed to bring a burnt-offering of seven bullocks and seven rams—not for Job but for themselves. For God was willing to accept the intercession of Job—the more audacious but more perspicacious Job—on their behalf, and to spare them the evil that they had deserved, which He did. But Job's fate is "turned" when he makes intercession for them. His brothers and sisters and former acquaintances come to him and eat with him in his house and give him excellent comfort: "every one also gave him a piece of money, and an earring of gold." Job himself—the sun of righteousness rises visibly and tangibly upon him—is blessed more than he had been before, acquiring 14,000 sheep, 6,000 camels, 1,000 yoke of oxen, 1,000 she asses, and 7 sons and 3 daughters into the bargain (the latter being called "little dove," "sweet savour" and "little rouge-pot"), "and in all the land were no women found so fair as the daughters of Job: and their father gave them inheritance among their brethren. After this lived Job 140 years, and saw his sons, and his sons' sons, even four generations, and died, being old and full of days." Whether or not this conclusion is the work of a later redactor of the Book of Job does not make the slightest difference. Whoever may be the author, it is as it should be. For (with or without this ending) the meaning of the Book of Job is that God acknowledges with a supreme reality the one who, even though he may do it all too humanly, dares indefatigably to acknowledge Him. He affirms the human self-affirmation without which this acknowledgment is not possible, which, if there is to be this acknowledgment, is not merely legitimate but required. If we accept that in the light of the covenant fulfilled in Jesus Christ the self-affirmation hazarded by Paul ("If God be for us, who can be against us?") is quite in order, being embraced and supported by the divine Yes to this most audacious enterprise, then we can and must reckon with the fact that in Job and the Psalmists too, in their time of the expectation and promise and prophecy of the fulfilment of the covenant, we are dealing with something quite other than a form of the righteousness of Law and works (in spite of appearances and all the justifiable arguments to the contrary). And this other with which we are dealing is the Yes of man to the divine sentence and pardon which is pronounced in the judgment of the faithful God. Where this pardon is accepted, there could and can be, both *ante*^{EN94} and *post Christum*^{EN95}, only an unconditional Yes—without any question marks.

But when we have said this, and said it once and for all, we have to add that the justification of man is something which takes place. The pardon of man is spoken. It is the living Word of the living God in the present of every man. When we speak of what this term describes, we are never speaking of a state but of a history, of the transition which does, of course, move in one direction and therefore not in another, but which has a *terminus a quo*^{EN96} and a *terminus*

EN94 before
EN95 after Christ
EN96 starting point

3. The Pardon of Man

ad quem[EN97], and therefore moves from here to there, in which there is a beginning and a completing, a coming and a going, in which man stands under a twofold determination to the extent that he goes forward from the "before" of his wrong and therefore his death to the "after" of his right and therefore his life. The work of the divine sentence—of the pardon which is unconditional because it is spoken by God and revealed to man in the Word of God—is that man is placed on this way, that he is in fact permitted to go forward in this impossible and incomprehensible way from here to there, that by the act of God he becomes the man of this history—the history of Jesus Christ. He becomes the man who in every present has both this past and this future; the one as past and the other as future; the one set aside behind him, the other as a promise before him; irreversible in the same sequence as the death and resurrection of Jesus Christ—but in this sequence not merely the one and the other but both at once, and in their specific and highly distinctive ways equally actual and equally serious; not intermingled in any present (as though at bottom they were not twofold) but both distinct in every present; not separated in any present, but—in that sequence, as moments in that history—indissolubly bound together in every present.

Looking backwards—this is the necessary statement with which we must begin—justification is therefore the divine pardon of sinful man. It is the sentence of God in virtue of which man is separated from that past and therefore the sentence of God on the man who can go forward from that past to quite a different future. In every present he is still the man he was, the man of sin, the man of pride, and as such fallen man. He is not this man to remain such, but to be so no longer, to become another man. But he still is this man. How can he be the man of this history, caught up in this transition, how can God's pardon be spoken to him as such, how can it apply to him, if he is not this man, if he is already free and therefore does not need this pardon? The man who is justified and therefore pardoned by God is the man in whom it comes to pass that he is separated from that past. This happens in every present in such a way that he is found by God in that past. God meets him as the doctor coming to the sick and not the whole, as the shepherd who leaves the ninety-nine sheep to seek the lost, as the father who stretches out his arms to the son who has gone into the far country and orders for him the fatted calf, as the Saviour who sits down to meat with publicans and sinners. Justification begins as man's acquittal from sin, from his being as a sinner. Only as it begins there can it and will it be completed in the re-establishment of his right, the renewal of his life. If man is without sin and therefore not a sinner, how can it apply to him? It does apply to him, it is God's righteous sentence on him, because he is still not righteous but unrighteous, because he is still the old man and not yet the new. It is *iustificatio impii*[EN98]. That is the secret of it. That is what makes it the work

[574]

[EN97] end point
[EN98] the justification of the godless

§ 61. *The Justification of Man*

which can only be the creative work of God, a *creatio ex nihilo*[EN99], or rather *ex contrario*[EN100]. That is what characterises it as a work of grace, as the basis of the work of reconciliation. It is needed by the man who has fallen away from God, who resists Him in his pride. It is this man that God has in mind, that God loves, because it is this man that He has elected and created. It is this man that God justifies. It is to this man that He maintains and demonstrates His faithfulness to this unfaithful man—beginning with the fact that He is in the right against him, that He asserts His right, and therefore that He is angry with this unfaithful man, that He condemns and kills and causes him to perish as such, but in so doing beginning his justification, aiming thereby to separate him completely from this unfaithful man, to lead him into freedom. This separation has to take place in him. Sinful man is the man in whom it must and will happen, but has not yet happened, whose self-identification with his wrong has not yet been reversed. It is this man to whom God's sentence applies. It is he who is pronounced free—free from himself—by this sentence.

No one has ever known his justification—or what justification is at all, and therefore what really takes place in this divine pardon, no one has ever found himself acquitted in this divine judgment, no one has ever tasted the surpassing glory of this event, no one has ever known how to make use of the freedom of the man acquitted by God, without having had to recognise himself as a sinner before God even as all this took place. The man who knows his own and man's justification in truth and clarity is the man who knows himself as the one who has this past and comes from it, who in the present must still confess that he is this man even in his transition to the future. If he is now found and knows it, he has still to recognise that he is lost apart from this being found. If grace comes to him and he knows it, he must lay hold of the fact that he does not deserve it, that he has forfeited it and will always forfeit it. If he is now the work of a new divine creation and knows it, he cannot hide the fact that he had fallen a victim to nothingness, and that apart from this work he would necessarily do so again and again. If the divine pardon avails for him and he hears the Word of God in which it is pronounced, he will still see that he would be imprisoned to all eternity, and that every moment he would be imprisoned afresh, if it were not that every moment as the hearer of this pardon he can be the one who is acquitted by God. The pardon of God directed to him is valid and effective for him, but not grounded in him. It has no basis at all in him. It is only heard and accepted and received by him, as the present and gift of God. As it comes to him, he finds himself set on this way. He has his past as an unrighteous man behind him and his future as a righteous man before him. But where would he be even for a single moment without it? What is he even now as the one to whom this comes in sovereign power, who is intended and addressed and forcefully set on this way by God in actualisation of His divine

---

[EN 99] creation out of nothing
[EN100] out of its opposite

3. *The Pardon of Man*

right but for that very reason in free grace? he to whom God is so incomprehensibly and incontestably and irresistibly good according to this pardon? he who now has to thank God and can never thank him enough for the fact that He willed to turn to him in this way, in this sentence? he to whom there is now given this *terminus a quo*^{EN101} which he could not make or procure for himself? Where, and breaking out from where, does he find himself in this *terminus a quo*^{EN102} and therefore at the beginning of this way? As who and what, even when sought and found by God, can he offer himself to God or place himself at His disposal? As what material for anything that God might do with him and make of him? Certainly not as the one he will become when he enters this way. Certainly not as the righteous man he will be at the end of this way. Only as the one who is not yet this man, who is still unrighteous. Only, in fact, as the one who, to his own amazement, can now break out and go this way, living in the apprehension of the promise of this end. Only, in fact, as the one who—not yet having attained to this end—is still the old man, sinful and proud, who can only be accused and deplored as such, who has every reason to confess himself to be such with serious penitence, to concede that God is in the right against him, who can live provisionally only in the apprehension of the promise of this end, of his right and therefore of his justified life. That he can be as such, on the way from that beginning to that goal, that he can apprehend God's promise, that he can cling to it, and that in so doing he can live provisionally—that is the beginning of his justification.

There is no present in which the justification of man is not still this beginning of justification, and where if it is recognised it does not have to be continually recognised as such. There is no man justified by God who does not [576] have to recognise and confess that he is still unrighteous, still the proud rebel before Him, who does not have to grant that God is always in the right against him and therefore that he is always in the wrong against God. If he is not willing to be this, that means necessarily that he does not wish to be pardoned, justified. If he wants to deny that he is this, that means that he denies the promise, that he does not know it, that he is not caught up in this breaking out of acquitted man. Where there is this breaking out, where the justification of man takes place, it is the justification of the unrighteous, and the one to whom it comes will not refuse to admit that he is still this one, that as such he finds himself in this breaking out, and that only as such can he do so. He can do so only as the one who can go forward from the midst of an evil past—not good, but bad—to a good future, who dares to go forward not because he himself but God has acquitted and authorised and empowered him. Daring to go forward, in accordance with the truth of the situation, he will give all the glory to God and to himself none at all, but only the corresponding dishonour and unworthiness and incapacity and unwillingness. The divine pardon does not

---
^{EN101} starting point
^{EN102} starting point

§ 61. *The Justification of Man*

burst into man's willingness but his unwillingness. Man will always be a miracle and a puzzle to himself as he breaks out in this way. He will never find in himself any reason for doing so. He will not be of the opinion that he has made even the slightest contribution to it. He will rather confess freely and frankly that his own contribution is only his own great corruption, in which without any co-operation or merit of his own he is found by the divine pardon—not in his self-judgment but in the judgment of God—reached and converted to God and set on the way to his right and life. The man who is pardoned by God, the righteous man, is always as such this man. To be sure, he is also another man, but even as this other he is still this man; even as he goes forward he is still the one who comes from this place. And let us say expressly, he is always this man totally and altogether, from top to toe, just as in the same present of the divine pardon he is always that other man totally and altogether, from top to toe, the man who goes forward to the goal of his righteousness, who has indeed already arrived, who is alive there as a righteous man. Neither in the one case nor in the other are we dealing with a quantum, rising here and dropping there like a fluid in two communicating tubes, but in both cases we are dealing with a single and a total human existence. He himself, as he is, in soul and body, in his person with all his thoughts and words and works, is already at the goal as the man who is pardoned by God, and he himself is also only at the beginning; already righteous before God and yet still only a sinner; called to a complete and unreserved and unconditional certainty and comfort and joy, but also to a complete and unreserved and unconditional humility and penitence, directed to pray with all possible seriousness: "Forgive us our trespasses," "God be merciful to me, a sinner." How can it be otherwise when his justification is this transition, when the man justified by God is the man of this history, when man's pardon is the living Word of the living God to living man, when the fact created by it is man transposed into this conversion to God and caught up in this conversion?

> To illustrate what we have called the beginning of justification—*N.B.* in its simultaneity with its completion—we will select from the seven so-called Penitential Psalms of the Old Testament the two which can be described as such with relatively the greatest clarity, Pss. 32 and 51.
> First of all, Ps. 32. We see from its opening, heart and conclusion that it has to do with justification in its unity and totality. "Blessed is he whose transgression is forgiven, whose sin is covered. Blessed is the man unto whom the Lord imputeth not iniquity, and in whose spirit there is no guile" (vv. 1–2). That is the opening. And the conclusion is the triumphant: "Many sorrows shall be to the wicked: but he that trusteth in the Lord, mercy shall compass him about. Be glad in the Lord, and rejoice, ye righteous; and shout for joy, all ye that are upright in heart" (vv. 10–11). But the central portion is as follows: "For this shall every one that is godly pray unto thee in a time when thou mayest be found: surely in the floods of great waters they shall not come nigh unto him. Thou art my hiding place; thou shalt preserve me from trouble; thou shalt compass me about with songs of deliverance" (vv. 6–7). The man who speaks in these three parts of the Psalm is obviously a man who has known the covenant faithfulness of the God of Israel, and in it the faithfulness of his God and therefore

3. *The Pardon of Man*

of His justifying sentence, and therefore himself as the one who is acquitted by this sentence, who in face of every threat is thus in a position to appeal to God as his helper, to live in that appeal with absolute comfort and cheerfulness and indeed joy, and to bear testimony to that joy. Note that within the framework of this presentation of justification as completed this Psalm is a penitential Psalm. But is this really only the framework and not the picture which the Psalm envisaged? the substance of its message? Does it not hang in the balance whether it would not be better described as a Psalm of thanksgiving?

Now in v. 2 we read of the guileless spirit and in v. 11 of the upright heart of those who are certain in this way and can and must confess as much. It obviously all depends on the condition of their heart—which in the Old Testament means themselves at the centre of their being and out to the periphery of their whole existence—whether their transgression is forgiven, their sin covered, and therefore out of sight, their iniquity not imputed and therefore past (vv. 1–2); whether they appeal to God and in so doing can have an absolute certainty that they will be kept in every emergency and need (vv. 6, 7, 10); whether they can and must rejoice and be glad and shout for joy because of it (v. 11). What is needed is a spirit without guile, an upright heart, if all this—and therefore a completed justification—is not to be empty presumption and imagination.

But what kind of a heart is this? To see what is meant our best plan is to look at the instructional passage strangely interposed between the middle of the Psalm and the end, a passage which reproduces the voice of God, which the Psalmist declares at a decisive point that he has already heard and is ready to hear again: "I will instruct thee and teach thee in the way which thou shalt go: I will direct mine eye upon thee. Be ye not as the horse, or as the mule, which have no understanding: whose mouth must be held in with bit and bridle, lest they come near unto thee" (vv. 8–9). The Psalmist has let God tell him that he was like a horse or mule, that his heart was an unruly heart, that he would not let himself be led where he ought to come and go.

In what did this opposition consist in which he was reached by the divine pardon and from which he was delivered by it? According to v. 3 it consisted decisively in the fact that he kept silence concerning "it," concerning his transgression, sin and guilt, that he would not accept it, that he would not admit it to God or man or even to himself, that he tried to live it down in a self-confident blustering. It is strange that the man who is justified, the sinner who can live strong and joyful before God as a righteous man, recognises in this silence the really sinful thing about his past. This silence was the seed of death in his existence in this past. In this silence he would not be what he was, a transgressor, a sinner, a debtor. And by this silence he was not doing himself any good as he thought and purposed, but only harm. He was making himself insufferable. In this silence he withstood God, and God withstood him. In it he could only be broken on God: "When I kept silence, my bones waxed old through my roaring all the day long. For day and night thy hand was heavy upon me: my moisture is turned into the drought of summer" (vv. 3–4). All obviously without any awareness that he was suffering in this way and on the point of perishing because of the falseness and insincerity of his heart, because of this conflict with God.

[578]

In this darkness he found the eye of God (v. 8), the eye of the Lord, directed upon him, as was the case with Peter (Lk. 22[61]) in the court of the high-priest, and he was shown the way which he must go (v. 8), and bound with bit and bridle (v. 9). In this darkness there took place the beginning of his justification. What did this mean for him? In what did it consist? "I acknowledged my sin unto thee, and mine iniquity have I not hid. I said, I will confess my transgressions unto the Lord" (v. 5a). The really sinful thing about the past, that silence, now falls away, according to the instruction, the direction of the Lord (v. 8). The horse or mule finds that it is bound. It has acquired understanding. Its unruliness is curbed. Man can and will let himself be led where he should come and go. With the fact that this had happened,

§ 61. *The Justification of Man*

that he could no longer conceal himself but had to confess, he did not in any sense conclude: "It is already forgiven" (G. Keller), but he could say and indeed had to say: "*Thou forgavest the iniquity of my sin*" (v. 5). Thou! Being bound in such a way that he had to confess himself a sinner, he encountered the God who established against his wrong His own right, who therefore made an end of his past, who was the justifying, pardoning God. He became the man of that history. Confessing his sin, giving God the right against him, he could seize with joyful certainty his own right, raising that song of praise—"Blessed is he"—to the life which had been given to him in the very midst of that consuming drought, moving forward directly to the completion of his justification, with a guileless spirit and an upright heart.

And then Ps. 51. It is easier to understand than Ps. 32 because it does not contain any of the confusing interchange of speaker and hearer which is so frequent in the Psalms, but is a simple prayer in I-Thou form. And it is predominantly and almost exclusively a prayer of confession (in the two different forms of a prayer for the forgiveness of sin and a confession of sin). To this there is, of course, added once again the forward-looking request for renewal. The only thing is—and this makes Ps. 51 outwardly much harder to survey than Ps. 32—that of these three complexes only that of the confession of sin (vv. 5–7) is expressed in any unified sequence. The two others inter-cross with one another and with a fourth, which is the most important of all (vv. 8 and 18–19), and which expresses to some extent the principle of the beginning of justification in penitence. The final verses 20–21 may have been added by a later writer, since they obviously cannot be reconciled with what is said about sacrifice in vv. 18–19.

[579] It is important and instructive that the Psalm does not begin, as we might logically have supposed, with a confession of sin, but with a request for the forgiveness of sin: "Have mercy upon me, O God, according to thy loving-kindness: according unto the multitude of thy tender mercies blot out my transgressions. Wash me throughly from mine iniquity, and cleanse me from my sin" (vv. 1–2). We have the same line of thought in v. 7: "Purge me with hyssop, and I shall be clean: wash me, and I shall be whiter than snow," and again in v. 9: "Hide thy face from my sins, and blot out all mine iniquities." These words express a fourfold knowledge. The speaker knows (1) that there is something intolerable in his life—his transgression, guilt, sin, impurity, misdeeds. He knows (2) that if he is to be helped this intolerable thing must not be merely alleviated or weakened but taken right away, blotted out, cleansed, washed away, removed from the presence of God, and that he himself must be purged. He knows (3) that the removal of this intolerable thing cannot be his work but only God's: a divine blotting out, cleansing, and washing away; not man's hiding of his sin but God's hiding of His face from his sin, and therefore its radical putting away. He knows finally (4) that he can turn to God with the request to do this because there is grace and great mercy with God. This last is decisive: he knows that he can ask God for it, that he is free to do so. And he makes use of this freedom. He does what he can do in this freedom. The Israelite has only to think seriously of the covenant and its Lord to know this freedom. And clearly this Israelite does think of the covenant and its Lord. He knows His grace and mercy. He therefore knows that even as the sinner he is he can approach Him with the request that his sin should be put away. And how is it that he knows the other things: the intolerable nature of his sin, the necessity of its radical putting away, God as the One who alone can do this? How else but in the knowledge of this freedom! Naturally not with a theoretical and dead knowledge, but with a knowledge which is alive because it is put into effect, in the use of this freedom, by doing what he can do in this freedom. As he does this he knows God and himself and what he needs. And what is this but the knowledge of his justification as it has certainly not been completed but has very definitely begun? How could he know all this if it were not that as a beginner, but in very truth, he is already the man of this history?

3. The Pardon of Man

Now obviously the confession of sin is not, as it were, a precondition of this history, and especially of the prayer for forgiveness which initiates it and for which the Israelite has this freedom. On the contrary, it is as he dares to make this request, and actually does make it, that he has the freedom to confess that he himself is a sinner and to confess his sin: "For I acknowledge my transgressions, and my sin is ever before me. Against thee, thee only have I sinned, and done this evil in thy sight: that thou mightest be justified when thou speakest, and be clear when thou judgest. Behold, I was shapen in iniquity; and in sin did my mother conceive me" (vv. 3–5). This obviously means that the request for forgiveness corresponds exactly to the situation of the one who makes it. He is the man who has sinned, who has sinned against God, who has done that which is displeasing to Him, against whom God is absolutely in the right, who is himself absolutely in the wrong against God and therefore guilty, not merely in individual thoughts and words and works, but, as expressed in these, in the very root of his existence (in what will later be called his heart). And, conversely, his situation corresponds exactly to his request for forgiveness. The request is not addressed to God incidentally. It does not simply express one disposition of man. It is not dispensable. For man himself, the whole man, just as he is, is expressed in it. This is what he is, the one who is with God and before Him, who has transgressed against Him, who can only displease Him, who is entirely in the wrong against Him, not merely on the surface but to the very core, not partially, but in the unity of his existence. What is the confession of sin other than the discovery of the true situation, not of man alone, but of man in relation to God, to the God of grace and tender mercy, to whom he can and does draw near with his request, and over against Him man who has no other possibility, who cannot utter anything else in the face of God but this request: "Be merciful to me, a sinner"? But what else is this situation except once again the justification which has certainly not been completed but has very definitely begun?

What the Psalmist has in mind as the subject-matter of his prayer—and obviously not only as the subject-matter but also as the presupposition—is, as the continuation shows, his justification as the history which moves irresistibly from its beginning to its completion, that transition in its inconceivable but absolutely irresistible totality. How else, having made that confession of sin, could he go on to say with such confidence—apparently as a supreme and final request: "Make me to hear joy and gladness; that the bones which thou hast broken may rejoice" (v. 8)? Joy, gladness, rejoicing? Can we already demand that? None of the *gradus ad Parnassum* in which we first emerge from the depths and painfully make our way upwards? No process of sanctification which has to come between our aversion from ourselves and our conversion to God? No: "whom he justified, them he also glorified" (Rom. 8^{30}). The man who asks for the forgiveness of his sins, and confesses his sins and enters into the light of the situation between God and man as it really is, can and should as such and at once (as this beginner) expect to be satisfied with joy and gladness, and he can and should therefore pray for it, for his new right before God, the new possibility of living before Him. How can he really be crying from the depths for the grace and tender mercy of God if he is not reaching for this supreme gift? Reaching! This is what is meant when he says: "Create in me a clean heart, O God; and renew a right spirit within me. Cast me not away from thy presence; and take not thy holy spirit from me. Restore unto me the joy of thy salvation; and uphold me with thy free spirit" (vv. 10–12). "Deliver me from blood-guiltiness, O God, thou God of my salvation" (v. 14a). Note that instead of any intervening and preparatory operations to make it possible we have at once the new creation of a clean heart, i.e., of the man who has already turned to God from himself and his sin; at once the gift of a new and right or constant spirit, the spirit with which man can only look forward and not backward, the willing spirit, by which man is protected and kept as set up in this way, in and by which the joy of God's salvation is created and continually renewed; at once man's redemption from death; at once

[580]

§ 61. *The Justification of Man*

life and salvation; at once the creation and gift of a human existence which is not hidden from the face of God, which can stand before it, because it is righteous before it and is therefore commended to its care, before that same face of God from which the sin of man is hidden (v. 9) and has perished. What is it that man has apprehended if not this promise when he has the freedom and makes use of the freedom to pray for the forgiveness of his sin? As the one who does this, how can he fail to reach out for the fulfilment of this promise? and therefore to pray for the continuance, the progress, the completion of this transition, that the Holy Spirit who has given him this freedom will not be taken from him, but continue His work within him, that the justification which He has begun will be completed by Him—for in its totality it can be only the work of God?

How bold and certain is this forward reach we can see from vv. 13 and 14b–15. They go beyond the problem which occupies us here, but for that very reason they show the breadth of the Psalmist's vision: "Then will I teach transgressors thy ways; and sinners shall be converted unto thee .... And my tongue shall sing aloud of thy righteousness. O Lord, open thou my lips; and my mouth shall shew forth thy praise." Compare this with the confession of sin in vv. 3–5. The same man expects already that he will not merely participate in that completion in his own person, but that in that completion he will be an instrument to glorify God, a witness, a teacher, a prophet to others, his fellow-sinners. Yes, the very same man. The completion of justification cannot and will not be a private matter, but as such his commissioning for the service for God among men. It will attain its end in his calling. In the calling of the same man. The man and only the man who starts there, the man who prays for the forgiveness of his sin—with the knowledge of his sin, will be the right man for this, for the service of God, for prophecy. And he will be that man.

[581] There still remain vv. 6 and 16–17, in which we have in a sense the key to the whole: "Behold, thou desirest truth in the inward parts, and in the hidden part thou shalt make me to know wisdom" (v. 6). The truth in the inward parts which is pleasing to God is obviously what we have called the true situation between God and man as revealed in the request for forgiveness and the confession of sin. When man is placed in this situation, when he realises it, God makes him to know wisdom. He instructs him concerning Himself as the God and man as the man of this history, of its beginning and its completion. The Psalmist prays for this divine instruction. He prays that this wisdom may be revealed to him. He would not pray for it if it were not already being revealed to him. We are told the same in vv. 16–17, the only verses in the Psalm which are not direct petition: "For thou desirest not sacrifice; else would I give it; thou delightest not in burnt offering. The sacrifices of God are a broken spirit: a broken and a contrite heart, O God, thou wilt not despise." What is it that He will not despise? What is it that is pleasing to Him? What is it that He demands? What is it that He also creates and accomplishes? Simply this, that the situation between Himself and God should be made clear, that man should stand before him as he is and deal with Him as He Himself is. But that means the broken spirit and contrite heart of man, for whom there is no other possibility but to ask for forgiveness and confess his sin. He despises the proud who will not do this. But the man who will He not only does not despise but has pleasure in him, desiring and exalting and glorifying him. He receives him, He gives him His promise, He is already on the way to its fulfilment for him. He will keep it to him. He can and will use him in His service. He sacrifices to Him the sacrifice to which all other sacrifices can only point and without which they are empty, the sacrifice which He has demanded and which is well pleasing to Him, the sacrifice of himself, that God may accomplish in him and with him that which is His purpose for him.

The beginning of justification—its beginning in the midst of human sin—is described much more strongly in a New Testament passage than in these or the other Penitential Psalms or anywhere else in the Old. This passage is the seventh chapter of Romans, a chapter

3. *The Pardon of Man*

which continually demands our attention and has always caused difficulty in interpretation. It is described much more strongly here because after all that has gone before in chapters 3–6 the reader is not prepared to be brought back so suddenly and violently to this situation from which the man who is justified by God starts. He is not prepared to be reminded of the character of justification as *creatio ex opposito*^{EN103}. It is also described much more strongly here because the astonishing and quite improbable nature of the fact that man's justification begins in the midst of his sin is brought out in this passage with such a complex and minute description of what sin means for man, and therefore in a much more penetrating way. Finally, it is described much more strongly here because this presentation is so terribly closed, almost reminding us of a prison cell in which there seems to be only a small and barred and inaccessible window to allow any light to enter. A situation from which to start? But where can we start? How is it possible in these circumstances to find ourselves in that transition? Certainly there can be no question of this New Testament passage making the mystery of the whole affair any the less difficult, although in contrast to the Old Testament texts it is written with a direct knowledge of the crucified and risen Jesus Christ. On the contrary, it is only as we look back from this passage that we can see how great the mystery really is in those two Psalms.

If we are to understand Rom. 7 we must not forget even for a single moment that we are in the sphere of the problem and proclamation of justification. The chapter does not interrupt the great sequence of Rom. 3–8, but with its apparently backward movement it brings it to its climax. The man who comes out into the light in Rom. 8—still sighing heavily enough, still conscious of his supreme daring and peril—is the same man as the one who in Rom. 7 looks in this direction from afar, still surrounded by darkness. And the man of Rom. 7 is concerned with the darkness which engulfs, or rather fills him, not for its own sake, but for the magnifying of the light which greets him from afar. There is, therefore, no more forceful presentation of justification as transition than the turning of Rom. 7^{24-25} with the cry: "O wretched man that I am! who shall deliver me from the body of this death?" followed by what is hazarded only as a cry: "Thanks be to God through Jesus Christ our Lord." But then the bolt is drawn again and Rom. 7 is briefly and mercilessly—we might almost think definitively—summed up: "So then with the mind I myself serve the law of God; but with the flesh the law of sin." Yet at once and without any link we move on to Rom. 8^{1-2}: "There is therefore now no condemnation to them which are in Christ Jesus, who walk not after the flesh, but after the Spirit. For the law of the Spirit of life in Christ Jesus hath made me free from the law of sin and death." The man who can know this without presumption or self-deception, and who can and must say it with such definiteness, is the same man who has before him and knows and says that which precedes it, the man who comes from the one to go forward to the other. Obviously he is the only one who can do this. But he can. The justified man speaks of his sin as in Rom. 7. And we must not overlook the fact that even the opening section of chapter 7 (vv. 1–6: a good third of the chapter) establishes this message of freedom in all its forms. The parable of the woman who is made legally free by the death of her husband, indisputably free for re-marriage, is developed and expounded in these verses. Her husband, or rather ours, has been put to death. That is to say, we ourselves in the lusts of our sins, our being in the flesh, the end of which can only be death (v. 5). It is all up with him. How did this come about? We read: διὰ τοῦ σώματος τοῦ Χριστοῦ^{EN104}, by virtue of our being in the unity of our existence with that of Jesus Christ. Our putting to death has taken place in His existence, in His putting to death (as we are shown in Rom. $6^{6\ 8\ 11}$). Our being in the flesh is destroyed in Him. But if we are dead to that in which we were held (ἐν ᾧ

[582]

---

^{EN103} creation out of its opposite
^{EN104} through the body of Christ

§ 61. *The Justification of Man*

κατειχόμεθα, v. 6), that is to say, our being in the flesh, if we are dead to the Law which controlled and bound and committed us as long as we lived as this man, as long as we were in the flesh, then we are free from this man (v. 6), free for another man, that is, free to bring forth fruit to God instead of to death (v. 4), free for service in the completely new possibility not of the letter but of the Spirit (v. 6). The continuation must not make us forget that this is how Rom. 7 opens. And there can be no doubt that we are in the middle of a description of justification. Already in Rom. 6—from the standpoint of the sanctification to be realised in obedience—we have had a comprehensive and penetrating and express study of the new thing which necessarily and at once follows the destruction of the old as it has taken place in Jesus Christ. The beginning of Rom. 7 has established the fact that we have to reckon with this new thing as a possibility created by God and the reason why we have to do so. Rom. 8 will introduce it as an actuality. We might think that there was nothing to prevent Paul from going straight on from Rom. 7^6 to Rom. 8^1.

But he knew well enough what he was about when he did not do so. In Rom. 6^{14}—at the very heart of his insistence upon the necessity of the new life in obedience—he had given as the reason for his bold statement: "Sin shall not have dominion over you," the even bolder one: "For ye are not under the law, but under grace." And then in Rom. 7^{1-6} he proclaimed explicitly, with man's liberation from the flesh, his liberation from the Law which controlled and engaged and committed man in and with his being in the flesh. If the ensuing description of the freedom created by it was to have a genuine ring, this could not be stated as a truth which is lightly uttered and easily accepted.

[583]

A first reason for this is that there is for Paul a Law, the continuance and validity of which he never thought to question. The Law is not against the promises (Gal. 3^{21}). "Do we then make void the law through faith? God forbid: yea, we establish the law" (Rom. 3^{31}). In the message of the δικαιοσύνη θεοῦ EN105 (Rom. 3^{21}) apprehended in faith in Jesus Christ we have to do with the righteousness attested by the Law and the prophets (Rom. 3^{21}). The demand of the Law (its δικαίωμα EN106) will be fulfilled in those who walk after the Spirit and not after the flesh (Rom. 8^4). According to Gal. 5^{14} and Rom. $13^{8\ 10}$ love, the love of the neighbour, is the fulfilling of the Law. As distinct from the Jew who boasts of the Law but actually breaks it, the heathen who are called to be the people of God by faith have the work of the Law written upon their heart, so that they are doers of it, and as such will show themselves to be justified (Rom. 2^{13-15}). In 1 Cor. 9^{21}, rejecting the claim or blame that he was ἄνομος EN107, Paul called himself an ἔννομος Χριστοῦ EN108. In Gal. 6^2 he spoke expressly of a "law of Christ," and in the present context in Rom. 8^2 he referred to a "law of the Spirit of life," remarkably enough describing it as the subject of man's liberation. There can be no question of any liberation from this Law or abrogation of it. This Law is itself the ἕτερος ἀνήρ EN109 for whom, according to Rom. 7^3, man has become free with the death of the first man. It has nothing whatever to do with sin (v. 7) and with death (v. 13). We ourselves in our relation to it have much to do with these but not the Law. According to v. 22 and v. 25 it is the Law of God. Its aim, according to v. 10, is the life of man. According to v. 12 it is holy, and "its commandment is holy, and just and good." According to v. 14 it is spiritual. As a spiritual man Paul can only confess that it is καλός EN110 (v. 16). "After the inward man" he can only delight in it (v. 22). In the νοῦς EN111 enlightened by it, rightly perceiving what is revealed to

---

EN105 righteousness of God
EN106 requirement
EN107 lawless
EN108 under the law of Christ
EN109 other man
EN110 good
EN111 mind

3. *The Pardon of Man*

him, he can only serve it (vv. 23 and 25). This must not be forgotten in relation to the statement that we are not under the Law but under grace, and that we are dead to the Law and freed from it. The Law of God is not affected by this statement. On the contrary, this statement is the most positive indication of the fulfilment of the Law. Rom. 7² is, at any rate, an assurance on this side. He could not proceed without introducing it.

But obviously something else lay more closely on his heart in the apparent digression of Rom. 7⁷⁻²⁵. The transition from the transgression to the fulfilment of this Law is not immediately self-evident. In the illustration at the beginning of the chapter Paul showed that the liberation of the wife for union with another would be adultery as long as the first husband was alive, and therefore an illegitimate and false liberation (v. 3). The problem of vv. 7–25 is the question of the actual death of the first husband and therefore of the legitimacy and truth of our liberation. Where will we have to look if we are going to find that things are as they are described in Rom. 7¹⁻⁶ and later in 8¹ᶠ·? We can at once rule out the negative answer of Rom. 7²ᶠ·. Yet with bitter words Paul explains that when he looks at himself and takes stock of himself he finds that that first man is very much alive, that his being in the flesh which (in v. 5 according to the whole tenor of chapter 6) he has put into the past is still the present. Note that in the decisive statements of vv. 14–25 he uses the present tense. We need not exclude from these statements some recollection of what Paul was before his conversion to Christ and calling as an apostle. But we cannot possibly limit them to this recollection of his earlier life. Even as a Christian and apostle Paul sees and judges the whole of his life as expressed in these statements. So seriously does he understand man's justification as God's new and concealed miraculous act that he not only saw it begin once in his earlier life at the very heart of the life of the first man, his own being and flesh, but he continually sees it begin again in this way. Every morning and every evening his situation is one of departure in the very midst of sin. And only as he sees this, only as he acknowledges that this is his situation even as a Christian and an apostle, only as he looks away from himself, dare he take the leap forward: "There is therefore now no condemnation to them which are in Christ Jesus" (Rom. 8¹). From this point the leap can and must be hazarded, in this most realistic and therefore genuinely spiritual self-knowledge. But it can be hazarded only from this point. The function of vv. 7–25 is therefore to retard. They show clearly the point of departure from which the way leads forward. In this way they safeguard the mystery of justification as the transition from wrong to right, from death to life. They prevent us from representing this transition as anything but an event and this event as anything but a miraculous act of God. They prevent us from trying to attain any knowledge of it except as the knowledge of God and therefore as the knowledge of faith in the strictest sense.

[584]

And the instrument used by Paul for this purpose is again the concept of law, but this time with a meaning and usage quite the opposite from that of the Law of God. In v. 23 he speaks expressly of a ἕτερος νόμος^EN112, and in the same verse (and again in v. 25) he calls it the νόμος τῆς ἁμαρτίας^EN113. In Rom. 8² it is more widely described as the νόμος τῆς ἁμαρτίας καὶ τοῦ θανάτου^EN114. It is obviously the νόμος τοῦ ἀνδρός^EN115 (v. 3), the law of the husband which binds the wife so that apart from the death of the husband she can be free for another only in adultery and therefore illegitimately and falsely. It is the νόμος^EN116 from which we are freed on the presupposition of the death of this husband, the destruction of our being in the flesh (v. 4 and v. 6). Διὰ τοῦ σώματος τοῦ Χριστοῦ^EN117 that first man,

---

EN112 another law
EN113 law of sin
EN114 law of sin and death
EN115 law of the husband
EN116 law
EN117 Through the body of Christ

§ 61. *The Justification of Man*

our being in the flesh, has died and been destroyed, and our liberation from that law has been achieved. But when Paul, the Christian and apostle, looks at himself and takes stock of himself, he finds that he is still one who is in the flesh (ἐν σαρκί, v. 25), that that first man is still alive, that his past is still his present, that that ἕτερος νόμος [EN118] is still in force. He is, he has his seat, and Paul is aware of him, ἐν τοῖς μέλεσίν μου [EN119] (twice in v. 23), obviously his whole physico-psychical existence so far as he can see and view and conceive this as his own. He reigns there in contrast to the νόμος τοῦ θεοῦ [EN120] in which as a Christian and apostle Paul delights after the inward man (v. 22), but in which he only delights "also," only in the knowledge of his νοῦς [EN121] (vv. 23 and 25) in which he does not see himself. In so far as he does not see himself he has to confess that another rules in his members, this law, the law of sin and death. The use of this concept to describe the matter, the same concept originally used to describe the holy and just and good order and expression of the will of God, is perhaps rather bold. But it is very illuminating in relation to what Paul wishes to say. His aim is to magnify sin as the situation in which justification begins, in order that justification itself may be shown to be truly great, because far greater. He therefore shows both to himself and to the Christians in Rome that sin is the determination of human existence from which he and they are liberated only by justification as the miraculous act of God, from which apart from that act they are not liberated. He calls upon faith in justification to be faith alone: not man's secret understanding and control of himself. He therefore speaks not only of a Law of God but also of a law of sin, and even as a Christian and apostle every morning and evening he can only see and confess that he is a doer of this law. Naturally this law of sin is only a reflection distorted out of all recognition. It is only a poor caricature, an aping of the Law of God. Naturally it is comparable with it only in the fact that it is a law. It is the law of anomaly, but of the anomaly of its peculiar finality and consistency once man has fallen a victim to it, of the authority, the power to command and control, which sinful man cannot outgrow or escape but only God. Sin is not something accidental which the man who engages in it can brush off again like a speck of dust from his clothes. Being directed against God, it has in it something of the nature of God to the extent that it acquires, and with it the life of the man who engages in it, a negative logic and necessity which neither it nor the man who engages in it can evade. Both it and sinful man exist with and under and by virtue of an evil, we might almost say a demonic, right of wrong, according to which sin can bring forth only further sin and the sinful man can move only in a circle. Justification is the breaking of this right of wrong, the liberation of man from it and therefore from this *circulus vitiosus* [EN122]. He does not imagine that he can accomplish it himself, even in the form of a grateful welcoming and acceptance of the restoring grace of God, which is, of course, within his capacity. He exists under the law of sin. And his transition from sin to righteousness presupposes the breaking of this law and man's liberation from it. But he will never find this liberation actualised in himself, in his members. In himself, in his members, he will always come up against this law, against the power and force of this law, against himself as the one who does not fail to do sin but does it, and does not do good but fails to do it. Where and how will he see this liberation as something which has happened to him, and himself as the man who is freed from this law, free for the fulfilment of the Law of God?

Certainly not—the answer is tempting—in the Law of God in so far as he knows this and works it out in the life which he sees, in so far as he sees himself as one who knows the Law,

---

[EN118] other law
[EN119] in my members
[EN120] law of God
[EN121] mind
[EN122] vicious circle

3. *The Pardon of Man*

and its outworking in his life. He does, of course, know and respect and value the Law of God. How could Paul say anything else as a Christian and an apostle? He would be denying himself if he did. Moreover, he can and must sincerely confess (v. 25) that in the knowledge of his νοῦς[EN123] he serves it and therefore that he does at least will to be obedient. Why should he question this? On the contrary, he is in a position to ascribe to himself as something positive this knowledge and the good which rests upon it. Can he not find his liberation in this element of his self-knowledge—notwithstanding that other element in which, like all other men, he finds himself subject to the law of sin? Can he not at least find himself in this knowledge, his transcendental ego, beyond the power of that other law and therefore liberated from it? That is how Kant viewed the justification of man. But Paul cut off this solution both for himself and for his readers. What agitated him especially in Rom. 7^{7-13} was the really frightful discovery that it is in his knowledge of the Law of God and his attempt to keep it that the sinful man experiences the fact that as a sinful man he does not have the freedom either to sin or not to sin, but rather that he will only sin and sin again, that as a sinner he stands under the law of sin, that he is irresistibly subject to it and that he does in fact obey it. That is the outworking of the Law of God which he sees in his own life. "I had not known sin (sin not only as aberration but as an aberration which controls me), but by the law (of God)" (v. 7a). I had not previously known myself to be incapable of amendment, to be under the compulsion of sin, but in the light of the Law of God I have found this to be so. How? "I had not known lust, except the law had said, Thou shalt not covet. But sin, taking occasion by the commandment, wrought in me all manner of concupiscence" (vv. 7b–8a). Because the Law called me to humility, it was revealed who I am and what I think in contrast to the Law of God; it was shown at every point what is in me, the pride in which I myself will to be Lord and God, to help myself, to justify myself. As the hearer of the commandment of God I awaken as the man of sin. The authority, the power of the law of sin, the aim of that law is this evil awakening of the sinner, the opening of this bud, the ripening of this fruit of sin, as it takes place only—but surely—in its confrontation with the Law of God, in the light of His revelation.

Is there, therefore, such a thing as latent sin? That is undoubtedly the meaning of Paul. But he puts it more strongly: "For without the law sin was dead. For I was alive without the law once" (vv. 8b–9a). I was therefore alive as a sinner, although I was dead in trespasses and sins, as is said of the Christians who once lived as heathens in Eph. 2^1. We have the same in Rom. 4^{15}: "For where no law is, there is no transgression," and in Rom. 5^{13}, which is most illuminating for the present passage: "But until the law sin was in the world: but sin is not imputed when there is no law," i.e., it is not alive, it is not manifest as such. It is committed, but without a knowledge of its character as sin. It has terrible consequences, but they have no obvious connexion with it. It reigns, but it does not stand out in concrete form in the being and activity of man. Sin emerges from its anonymous existence when man encounters the self-revealing God and therefore His Law. This process is described in Rom. 5^{20} in the words: "Moreover the law entered, that the offence might abound," πλεονάσῃ[EN124] (like water in a pot placed over the fire). Rom. 7^{9b-10}, following on from what is said in v. 8, speaks of it even more pregnantly as a formal resurrection of sin: "When the commandment came, sin revived," with terrible consequences for man: "and I died. And the commandment, which was ordained to life, I found to be unto death." As the sin of the man who receives the Law of God it acquires an aspect, and character, and form. It rejoices and triumphs—a regular Easter festival at the celebration of which the man who has received the commandment of God can only die and perish as the one who has committed it.

[586]

[EN123] mind
[EN124] increase

§ 61. *The Justification of Man*

What Paul has before him in these verses (as in Rom. 5¹³⁻¹⁴ ²⁰) can only be the experience of Israel as distinct from other peoples. In contrast to others it is the people of the election, the calling, the covenant, and therefore of the gracious will and commandment of God revealed to it, the people confronted with the Law of God. There is no doubt that it knows the Law. It does not reject it at root. It knows that its existence depends upon the covenant with God and therefore upon the Law of God. It continually returns to it. It is continually summoned to try to serve it, as Paul says of himself in v. 25. Its boast is to be the people of the divine Law. Not in spite but because of this, it takes place in its history that Israel shows itself to be—and obviously has to show itself to be—what (in that anonymity) all other peoples also are, but what is only revealed in Israel, a people of proud and covetous transgressors, flagrantly and drastically contradicting and resisting God as His partner in the covenant which He has concluded with it, a people which in the very light of His special turning to it walks in the darkness like no other people and for that reason suffers under the heavy hand of God like no other people. All men are sinners (Rom. 5¹²), but the only notorious sinners (with all that that involves) are those to whom the will of God is revealed and proclaimed and known.

Does it lie in the nature of the Law that this should be the case? That would mean the exculpation of these notorious sinners. And it might suit the men of whom Paul is speaking, by whom he means not only his fellow-Israelites but the Christians of Rome, who, whether they were Jews or Gentiles, were just as much confronted by the Law of God as he was. If only they could thrust back upon God the responsibility for the terrible conjunction of their knowledge of the commandment of God and their living and rejoicing and triumphant sin unambiguously declared as such! If only they could make God responsible for it and then enjoy themselves as notorious sinners! Paul is at great pains to guard against this in these verses. The commandment of God has nothing whatever to do with sin (v. 7). It is holy (v. 12). It has nothing whatever to do with the corruption and death which strike the sinner (v. 13a). In itself it is the ἀγαθόν^{EN125} (v. 16). The Law of God has no character or office or function in which it has made man a sinner qualified in this way, or delivered him up as such to death. No, sin takes occasion (ἀφορμὴν λαβοῦσα^{EN126}, vv. 8 and 11) by the encounter of man with the commandment of God in order that by its misuse it might make him the sinner qualified in this way. It deceives man when it does this (v. 11), when it causes him to sin with a high hand against God even in His presence. Sin shows itself in its true colours by deliberately delivering him up to death διὰ τοῦ ἀγαθοῦ, διὰ τῆς ἐντολῆς^{EN127}. In this perversion it shows itself to be καθ' ὑπερβολὴν ἁμαρτωλός^{EN128}. But it is quite capable of this taking occasion, this misuse, this perversion, this self-revelation of its sinister majesty. This is the working out of its law, the consequence of its opposition to God and His will. Only where this will is revealed can sin be revealed. But where this will is revealed—it is brought to light by the sun—is it, too, revealed, revealed as the power which is not superior to God but superior to man, as the lord to whom he has sold himself (v. 14) by committing it, as his lawgiver and commander, whom he cannot escape as sinful man, subjected to whom he is a debtor to the grace of God, grasping at life and running headlong to death. If he looks at himself with an eye and νοῦς enlightened by the Law of God, that is the state of affairs which he sees. He comes up against the law of sin as the law which he obeys, the copy of the Law of God which he actually lives to please. He comes up against the outworkings of his obligation to this Law in all his impulses and thoughts and words and works. It is not the heathen,

---

^{EN125} good
^{EN126} 'seizing the opportunity'
^{EN127} through what is good, through the commandment
^{EN128} exceedingly sinful

3. *The Pardon of Man*

secular, godless man who lives in this self-knowledge and is constantly forced back to it, but the man who is elected and called: Paul the Christian and the apostle interpreting the experience of Israel. It cannot, therefore, be the case that looking at his own perhaps very real relationship with God and His Law (as in the case of Paul) a man will find his freedom from the law of sin and regard himself as justified. On the contrary, when he looks at this relationship, and himself as he exists in this relationship, he will be forced to recognise his obligation to this quite different law—and he cannot possibly regard himself as justified.

Vv. 14–25—this is the decisive part of the chapter—describe the position of man in relation to the Law of God as one who is subject to the law of sin. V. 14 is a brief summary of the whole, as later gathered together in other words in v. 25b: "We know that the law (of God) is spiritual." Later, in Rom. 8^2, it is described as the Law of the Spirit. This means that as such it has the authority and power to overcome and destroy the law of sin and death, to free man at a stroke and altogether from its usurped authority and power. As such it comes to him with this promise. But the fulfilment of the promise is the completion of justification, not the beginning of which Paul is now speaking. The situation from which it starts is characterised by the fact that to the knowledge that the Law is spiritual there corresponds the confession: "But I am carnal, sold under sin." As I see and know myself in my confrontation by the Law of God, as the promise comes to me but only comes, I am not spiritual but $\sigma\alpha\rho\kappa\iota\nu\acute{o}s$, fleshly, which means (this is the definition of the term "carnal"): not free in relation to sin, but bound, just as much bound as a slave who is sold. Sin is my owner and lord. This is brought out in two short sequences, vv. 15–17 and 18–20.

Vv. 15–17 begin with the statement that I cannot recognise myself in what I accomplish, in my own actual achievements ($\kappa\alpha\tau\epsilon\rho\gamma\acute{a}\zeta\epsilon\sigma\theta\alpha\iota$ EN129), in the details and the totality of my life's work, more especially from that point where, enlightened by the Law of God, I am supposed to be able to understand and recognise myself and my achievement and to be at unity with myself. I cannot do this because I have to say: "For what I would, that do I not; but what I hate, that do I" (v. 15). My non-doing is in contradiction with my will, my doing with my non-will. I contradict myself in my achievements, in the results of my doing and non-doing. Certainly (v. 16) in this contradiction, to the extent that I myself and my will are opposed to my doing, I agree with the Law of God and call it good. But what is the value of this contradiction and agreement (v. 17) when my doing and non-doing, my achievements, do not have a share in it? To my shame, I have to admit that in the event of my achievements it is not I myself who am revealed at work, but the sin which dwells within me and lays its law upon me. How then can I recognise myself in this event—except as the house in which sin dwells and is master?

Vv. 18–20 belong—in the reverse sense—to the same picture: What does not dwell in me, in my flesh, is, unfortunately (v. 18), the $\dot{a}\gamma\alpha\theta\acute{o}\nu$ EN130, or (v. 22) the Law of God. If I am flesh, as admitted in v. 14, how can I be the house of the Law of God? And if this Law is spiritual, as again in v. 14, how can it dwell in this house? I and the $\dot{a}\gamma\alpha\theta\acute{o}\nu$ EN131 can only exclude each other like fire and water. What is present in me—this is possible in the flesh—is the good will, not the doing of good—for which I should have to be spiritual and not carnal. Is the latter really wanting? Yes (v. 19): "the good that I would I do not, but the evil which I would not, that I do." Is it really I? Have I really to admit to my shame that I am the doer of what I would not (v. 20)? It is not I who am at work, but unfortunately I am not the master of my own house—the sin which dwelleth in me. In the completed action I have to admit to

[588]

EN129 accomplishing
EN130 good
EN131 good

§ 61. *The Justification of Man*

myself that I am only a kind of agent and not the subject, that I am only a functioning object.

The chapter closes with vv. 21–25, which towards the end are interrupted by a short but remarkable conversation which the apostle has with himself (vv. 24–25a) and which calls for a separate appraisal. The subject of the verses was the self-contradiction of sinful man: his will or non-will on the one hand, his doing or non-doing and therefore his achievements on the other, this man here and that man there. There can be no question how Paul views and describes himself. He identifies himself with the first I, the willing or non-willing I. And the whole difficulty, the contradiction expanded in vv. 15–20 is simply this, that he cannot recognise himself in his actual doing or non-doing, in his achievements, that he cannot identify himself as the one who wills with the one who achieves, that he is a stranger to himself in what he attains and accomplishes. Twice he says that it is not I who am at work, but the sin which dwells in me (vv. 17 and 20). Here we have a direct proof that in this whole chapter Paul is speaking of himself as a Christian and an apostle and not placing himself in the situation either of an unbelieving Jew—perhaps his own before his conversion—or of an unbelieving Gentile. How could an unbeliever see himself from a distance in this way, confessing that he is a stranger to himself? No Jewish or Gentile unbeliever would be able or willing to see and confess that he is in this contradiction with himself. What would distinguish him from the Christian and the apostle Paul would be this, that in the last resort he would, in spite of everything, declare himself to be at unity and satisfied with himself. It is another matter that existence in this contradiction is his situation, too, although he does not know it. But the Christian and the apostle Paul does know this human situation. He sees the contradiction. He is involved in it himself in that distance from himself. He knows that he has to bear it, to live in it. He also knows—and this is what he goes on to speak about in v. 21 f.—that he cannot bear it or live in it. In this respect he is radically different from the unbeliever. The latter may be conscious of a certain inner unrest, tension or opposition. It is not for nothing that his situation is in truth the same as that of the Christian and apostle Paul. In what the latter knows concerning himself that situation is brought to light instead of remaining hidden. But is it not to be expected that even in its hiddenness it will from time to time be noticeable? Yet not in such a way that the unbeliever is not in a position, as he thinks, to come to terms with himself, and at least to bear the conflict, and to live in spite of it. What he knows as inner unrest is always within his own unity and satisfaction with himself. It can actually be borne and he can live. But Paul knows that this is impossible. He knows that the conflict in which he finds himself, which he has to bear and in which he has to live, is the conflict between Law and law, the conflict between the Law of God which he knows with his νοῦς[EN132], which he is ready to serve in his willing and non-willing, by which he sees and judges himself, between this Law and (discovered by it) the law of sin, to which he finds himself obedient and subject in his doing and non-doing, his actual achievement. To be master in this conflict would mean to be obedient to the Law of God (which is what he wills), to overthrow and break the law of sin, to destroy it as a law which binds him, to bring his doing and non-doing, his achievement, into line with his willing and non-willing. But this is the very thing which he finds he cannot do.

Rather (v. 21)—behind and in his achievement, which unfortunately contradicts his willing and non-willing according to the Law of God—he finds the power of another law which is superior to him. By reason of this law it comes to pass that, although he not only wills the good but wills to do the good, yet when he translates his will into action evil is just as present (παράκειται[EN133]) in him as the willing (but unfortunately only the willing) of the good (v.

[EN132] mind
[EN133] lies near

3. *The Pardon of Man*

18). He finds (vv. 22-23) that all his sincere and earnest agreement with the Law of God, his best will to be righteous before it, the correspondingly determined attitude of the "inner man," does not alter in the slightest the fact that in his members, in the physico-psychical existence which he sees, this other law is in control. At the very point where he ought to accomplish what the Law of God demands and he himself wills in accordance with that Law, this other law is in victorious conflict ($ἀντιστρατευόμενος$ EN134) with what he himself recognises to be right and binding (the $νόμος\ τοῦ\ θεοῦ$ EN135), treating him as though he was already its prisoner ($αἰχμαλωτίζων$ EN136). In his achievement he does not obey the Law of God but this other law. It is not at all the case that in his doing and non-doing he overcomes it as he would like, breaking it and destroying it as the law which binds him. It is rather the case that in his doing and non-doing he confirms the authority and power of this other law. The fault is not with the Law of God. He has to acknowledge that the fault is with himself. It is no consolation to him to consider his better will and knowledge, just as this better will and knowledge cannot actually free him from his guilt.

V. 25b gathers together once more what has been said about his prison cell. It is obvious that he does not try to deduce any exculpation of himself or improvement of his situation from the fact that he sees himself at this distance. No: "So then I myself, the same man ($αὐτὸς\ ἐγώ$ EN137), the one who knows it ($νοΐ$ EN138) and wills it, serve the law of God; but with the flesh the law of sin." This is the meaning of the contradiction discovered in vv. 15-20, and this is the hopelessness of it. "No man can serve two masters" (Mt. 6^{24}). But the speaker here has to confess that he does in fact serve two masters. This is the plight of man, of Paul the Christian and apostle. He must exert himself to shake off this yoke, to escape.

His exposition is outstanding for the sober factuality of the presentation, but towards the end it is interrupted by a strange cry, or rather by two cries, the one answering the other (vv. 24-25a.). Here we have to do with the little window which does let at least a glimmer of light into the prison cell. And here again we have a direct proof that in this context Paul is not speaking in recollection—or only in recollection—of an earlier period in his life, or in the assumed role of a Jewish or Gentile unbeliever. "O wretched man that I am! who shall deliver me (tear me out) from the body of this death?" We make Paul extremely rhetorical if we take it that his complaint is only in recollection. And he drops the assumed role of a Jewish or Gentile unbeliever when—we might almost say from the outside—he answers his own complaint: "I thank God through Jesus Christ our Lord." The two sayings are very abrupt. And they come together very abruptly. But they are only meaningful together, the one pointing backwards, the other forwards. And together they fix the mathematical point at which the justification of man takes place as his transition from wrong to right, from death to life.

We will take the second of the two sayings first (v. 25a). It is simply an expression of thanks: "God be thanked for that which is true and actual and valid and effective by our Lord Jesus Christ as the decision which He has made, the act which He has accomplished." It is not stated what this is. In the preceding verses from 7 on we cannot see anything at all for which thanks might be given—not even for the fact that Paul can and must know the revelation and Law of God and think and will in the light of it. For, as we have seen, it is as one who knows and loves the Law of God that he is plunged into that contradiction, that he finds himself powerless in face of the law of sin in his members. The way from this point to the thankful

---

EN134 fighting against
EN135 law of God
EN136 taking captive
EN137 I myself
EN138 'in the mind'

§ 61. The Justification of Man

praise of God as we have it, for instance, in Ps. 119, is a necessary way but a far one. There can be little question that here Paul has in a sense placed himself at the end of that way. Hence in striking contrast to the baffled question: "Who shall deliver me?" thanks are actually ascribed to God, and to God in the light of His being and activity in Jesus Christ. The question itself is left unanswered, like the question of Jesus Christ on the cross: "My God, my God, why hast thou forsaken me?" (Mk. 15^{34}), or like the whole question of Job. In the boldest possible anticipation, but one which is obviously self-evident to Paul the Christian and apostle, he looks back upon the question and all that it implies from the far distance. The question and all that it implies have ceased to be. What was once true is true no longer. What was not true is now true. All at once there is cause simply to be thankful. Therefore he is thankful. Is not this the forward leap of the man who is justified by God, the attestation of Jesus Christ raised again from the dead? But note that he tells us explicitly only that he is thankful and to whom he is thankful, not for what. Or are we to conclude for what he is thankful from the fact that, after all that has gone before, he is thankful, and from the One to whom he is thankful? At any rate, the half-verse is enough to make it possible for us to say that in the second and third parts of Rom. 7 we have an exposition of the beginning of justification, as suggested by vv. 1–6 and the wider context.

But we must not forget that in the conclusion which follows this radiant half-verse—we now seem to hear the prison door closing to genuinely and finally—Paul takes up again the contrast of v. 14, confessing that he is the one man serving two lords, and therefore doing that which it is not possible to do, that he is therefore the "wretched" man of v. 24. Nor must we forget the baffled and unanswered question of this wretched man—this wretched Christian and apostle Paul: "Who shall deliver me from the body of this death?" (It does not seem possible to translate it in any other way, because τούτου^{EN139} cannot well refer to σώματος^{EN140} but only to θανάτου^{EN141}.) Paul is speaking of this, of a particular "body of death," or nexus of death, or kingdom of death. And his concern is for the redemption of man from the body of this death. In v. 4 he had spoken of another σῶμα^{EN142}, the σῶμα τοῦ Χριστοῦ^{EN143}, which can also be called a σῶμα τοῦ θανάτου^{EN144} to the extent that in it and by it there is a putting to death (a θανατοῦσθαι) of man, but a redemptive putting to death, a freeing of man from the law of sin and for life under the Law of God by the death of that "first man." To belong to that body, to the fellowship of that death, obviously means redemption, future, hope. Not so to belong to the body of death which is shown in vv. 7–23 to be the nexus or fellowship of all men under the law of sin. It is the body of the death which is absolutely without a future, hopeless and non-redemptive. It is the body from whose context and association man must be torn and delivered if he is to be able to live. The whole situation depicted in vv. 14–23 obviously has this character of death—the whole self-contradiction in which Paul sees himself entangled as one who knows and loves the Law of God on the one hand and is a slave of the law of sin on the other. But since this self-contradiction is a fact and cannot be resolved, since it cannot be resolved and is a fact, it can bring man only to corruption and death, to this utterly non-redemptive death. But, according to v. 4, this situation—man's incorporation in "the body of this death"—is already his past, thanks to the "body of Christ," in and with which he has been put to death as one who "is in the flesh," freed from this law of sin, taken out of this contradiction, torn out from "the body of this death." But, according to v. 24, it is still his present, in so far as all this has not

---

^{EN139} 'this'
^{EN140} 'body'
^{EN141} 'death'
^{EN142} body
^{EN143} body of Christ
^{EN144} body of death

3. The Pardon of Man

taken place in his own person, but validly and effectively for him in the person of Jesus Christ; for him, who in his own person, in so far as even as a Christian and apostle he is still this man Paul, he is still in the flesh and therefore is still subject to the law of sin and therefore still exists in this contradiction and therefore still belongs to "the body of this death." From this "still" even as a Christian and an apostle he can only cry daily as we hear him cry in the baffled question: "Who shall deliver me?" as though we had never read what is stated in v. 4 and he himself had never written it. Living already and altogether by the answer, living already and altogether in the deliverance which has already come to him, he still has to live in and with this question. He could not do the one if he tried to refuse the other, to be only the man of the answer, not to be wholly and utterly the wretched man of the question. He can only be both at once. But not in that unhappy contradiction (in which he lives only "also," which is only his past reaching into his present), but rather in the transition, the history of justification, in that transition as it is really both at once, as indicated in the relationship of the two sayings in v. 24 and v. 25a. If we read carefully the exposition in Rom. 8 we shall soon realise that even there the "also," and therefore the "both together," has not completely disappeared, nor has the "wretched man" of Rom. 7: the beginning of justification in the very midst of man's sin. [591]

If on this side, the left side, with reference to the *terminus a quo*^{EN145}, there is no place for human arrogance or frivolity, for the expunging or interpreting or adorning or explaining away of the past from which the justified man comes at every present, much less on the other side, the right side, with reference to the *terminus ad quem*^{EN146} of his way, is there any place for human uncertainty and half-heartedness, for the belittling and weakening and qualifying and questioning of the goal to which the justified man moves in every present. How much less! For if the knowledge that as a man justified by God he is a sinner is serious, the knowledge that as a sinner he is justified by God is even more serious. Simply because it is on this side and not the other that we have to do with the positive will of God to man, with his affirmation of man. As His affirmation of sinful man it includes his negation. The Yes cannot be heard unless the No is also heard. Hence the necessary recollection of the place from which we come, of the being which is still the being of man in all his forward movement—the being of the sinner who lives only by the grace of God. But although it includes the negation, it is still God's affirmation of man. This is what makes what we have to consider on the right hand so much more serious than that which on the left hand we can never consider too much with the seriousness appropriate to this sphere. What we have to say concerning the irreversible direction of the transition, the history in which the justification of man takes place, is relevant in this connexion. The new thing which comes from God has as such precedence over the old of man. The right which is ascribed to him by God has as such precedence over his own wrong. His life has precedence over his death. The goal, the *terminus ad quem*^{EN147} of his way,

---

^{EN145} starting point
^{EN146} end point
^{EN147} end point

§ 61. *The Justification of Man*

has precedence over its *terminus a quo*[EN148] and beginning. That which he already is in virtue of God's explicit pardon has precedence over what he still is in virtue of what is implicit in it. The completion of his justification has precedence over its commencement. If—without confusion or separation—we have to consider and emphasise both moments of this event, giving its due weight to the first as well, we have to do so in this order and sequence, in such a way that the direction of the whole stands steadily before us, in such a way therefore that the precedence finally rests with the second about which we must now speak. It is not at all the case that the two moments are related like the two ends of a scales or see-saw, both of which may rise or fall according to the accidental or arbitrary weighting of the one or the other. It is not at all the case that the justified sinner can alternately or with a turn of the wheel be wholly and utterly the sinner and wholly and utterly justified, so that alternately or with a turn of the wheel he has to see himself as the one and then as the other. The dialectic of justification is not that of a to and fro, or an up and down, but at every present it is that of a history in which the wrong of the justified man is (in all its reality) behind him and his right before him, in which, therefore, he can have his future only in the movement to his right and his past only in his wrong (in all its reality), in which he can be only on the way from there to here, because that and that alone corresponds to the positive will of God.

We will now proceed at once to the proposition which emphasises the positive will of God, that on its forward aspect justification is the divine pardon of sinful man. It is the sentence of God in virtue of which man has that past behind him and is turned to a new future which is no longer burdened with that past and determined by the good will of God with him. Who is man? According to the divine sentence which justifies him he is the man of the history in which there takes place both this turning away and this turning to. The one divine sentence which justifies man is wholly negation as we look backwards and wholly affirmation, promise, *promissio*, as we look forwards. In the same sentence in which the justifying divine sentence strikes him and confirms that he both was and still is a sinner standing under the divine No, he is already addressed and characterised as the one who will be under His Yes. As the object of His negation he is already the object of His affirmation and promise. And in virtue of this affirmation and promise he is already placed in His right, he is already made free for life. The sentence which justifies him is pardon, divine pardon, and as such valid and effective, as such God's mighty disposing concerning him, in virtue of which, even as the man he was and is, he is set on the way and in the movement from there to here, he already is the man he will be. He is still sick, but when this doctor comes he is already healed. The sheep is still lost, but when it is sought by this shepherd it is already found. The son is still lost, but this father looks for him and he is already at home. Those who are still publicans and sinners, when the Saviour sits down to meat with them, are

---

[EN148] starting point

3. *The Pardon of Man*

already the holy people of God. The man in the temple does not know what else to plead but that God should be merciful to him, a sinner, and he is already justified, and returns to his house as such. The justification of man as determined and accomplished and pronounced in the divine sentence is both at once in this order and sequence: it is *creatio ex contrario*[EN149], but *creatio*[EN150]; *iustificatio impii*[EN151], but *iustificatio*[EN152]. The grace of God, as it is addressed and comes to the sinful man who has fallen away from Him and resists Him in his pride, is free grace, sovereign, unmerited, miraculous, but valid and effective. In the sentence of God as His repudiation and promise the old man is already the new man, the unfaithful covenant-partner the faithful, the one who has set himself in the wrong the one who is set in the right, the dead raised again and alive. This is the divine pardon as God's affirmation and promise. And as directed to man it is His powerful summons. As the man he was and still is, man can and should look forward and go forward to what he will be, to what, now that he is free for it, he already is. It is of this "already" that we must now speak.

[593]

First, we can and must regard it as a test of the genuineness of the knowledge and confession of sin whether the man who is willing and ready to accuse himself of corruption and transgression, and therefore to bewail the fact that he is lost, can with the same or an even greater willingness and readiness accept and affirm the sentence of God on this other side, so that as the sinner he has seen and confessed himself to be, as the man who must give himself up for lost, he can grasp the promise of God and look and go forward and not backward; whether he really can do this; whether he can accept and affirm the fact that God is gracious to him the sinner, that He is his redeemer, the redeemer of the lost; whether he will hold to the right which God ascribes to him; whether he is confident to live the life which God grants to him. The question is a very serious one. For by the same judgment of God he is a sinner and yet a justified sinner, lost and yet saved, a victim to death and yet raised again from death to life. God's sentence on him pronounces all this as an indivisible whole. God's sentence sets him irresistibly in the movement from that past to this future. But if he is not able to grasp this promise and enter this way, how does it stand with the genuineness of his knowledge of sin and confession of sin, of his accusation of himself and bewailing of his estate? What is the basis of it, however deep and powerful it may be, however violent and fierce, perhaps far surpassing in its vehemence that of the Psalmists and Paul? It is quite possible to have a very human defeatism and pessimism whose agitations and convulsions, accusations and bewailings, have nothing whatever to do with the sentence of God and submission to it. It is quite possible that—in this way—man is only trying to escape the sentence of God. It is quite possible that

---

[EN149] creation out of its opposite
[EN150] creation
[EN151] justification of the godless
[EN152] justification

§ 61. *The Justification of Man*

all his expressions of despair are only the symptoms of the old unbroken pride in which he now withdraws to the last and perhaps the surest citadel, that of a violent self-abnegation. Has this man really given God the right against himself, has he really accepted His sentence, if he has to accept the fact—and he declares that he has to accept it—that he knows himself to be negated and rejected by God, but cannot make anything of the Yes of God, and does not see anything of the future which is opened up to him, of the right to live which is granted to him? If anyone tries to resist this, if he can and must resist it, then he simply shows that it is not the No of God which he maintains that he accepts and to which he maintains that he submits. His vanity still peeps out through the very rents in his garment. The No of God is never without the Yes which follows it. It is not an autonomous Word. It is only an indispensable foreword. It is the repudiation, the meaning and goal of which is the promise. The man who can hold aloof from the promise has not heard the repudiation. His knowledge and confession of sin cannot therefore be genuine, no matter how serious they may be.

[594]

> In the modern novel there are not lacking portrayals which give us the impression that the author originally had in mind something like God's pardon of sinful man. But in fact they do not go beyond what is often a strikingly honest depiction of his vileness. Such portrayals cannot be totally sincere any more than those of earlier periods, the vileness of which consisted in the fact that they would not accept the vileness of man, but ascribed to him qualities which in the circumstances could not be real qualities but only an illusion of real qualities.

The knowledge and confession of sin are serious only where in and with them there is the only true penitence in which man gives up all his proud boasting, even the humbly proud boasting of his corruption and lost estate, and grants that God is wholly in the right, accepting His Yes no less than His No, and in fact more so, because in it we have to do with His positive will. True penitence will show itself as such in the fact that man will not rest in what he was and still is and has to accept and confess, but will resolutely turn to what he will be and already is. In true penitence man makes in simple obedience the turning for which he is pronounced free in the justifying sentence of God, which is therefore both legitimate and possible. He bows to the one total and indivisible disposing of God. He does not leave out the first step. But in and with the first he makes the second; in and with the confession of sin he lays hold of God's promise of grace. God's pardon demands this total obedience. And where it is accepted by man, he finds it. The man who will not recognise that he is a justified sinner is just as disobedient, and more so, than the man who tries to deny that only as a sinner is he justified.

The justification of man begins in his past and it is completed in his future. But as his past as a sinner is still his present, so his future as a righteous man is already his present. The fact that although he is still a sinner he is already righteous, that in the same present in which he comes out of his past as a sinner he goes forward to the future as a righteous man—this fact is the promise addressed to him in the judgment and sentence of God. There is no doubt

3. *The Pardon of Man*

that it speaks of his future. This other man, the righteous, the one he was not and still is not, is the man he will be. This future is promised to him as the past is repudiated. But the promise that he will be this man is addressed to him here and now, to-day, in the midst of the present. It is not an uncertain promise like the hopes which he might create for himself or which might be created for him by circumstances and relationships and even other men. It is the promise the power of which is the irrevocable decision of God in which he is already this other man, the righteous. It is not a general promise like the great ideas of humanity, to hear of which may be a very different thing from relating them to oneself, but the promise of his God, which applies to him with a supreme immediacy and directness. It is not an empty promise like the fine expectations which may gladden and comfort but of which we cannot for the moment make anything in practice, but the promise of the eternal God, which as it is given and received can be used at once as such, to which we can hold and with which we can at once begin to live. The future which it promises to man is not just any future. It is the *futurum exactum*[EN153] of God. As man accepts it, as he reaches out for it, as he apprehends it as the promise of God, its fulfilment is no longer distant only, but already near even in its distance. He does not live and think and act any longer simply as the man he was and still is, but in the leap which he can now make forward, in anticipation of the man he will be, as already that other man, the righteous, which he was not and which in the light of the past he is not yet. In the receiving and presence of the promise and his relationship to it he is already the man he will be. That is the completion of man's justification.

[595]

Naturally there can be no question of a simple equality or identity between future and present, between the fulfilment as such and the promise, between what man will be and what he is. Even on this side the being of the justified sinner is a differentiated being, and as such it is stretched like a bow. But, again, there cannot be any question of a mutual exclusion, of a future which is distant and not near, and therefore of a present which is apart from the future, of a fulfilment which has still to come, and therefore of an empty promise, of the righteous man who will be as now absent, and therefore of the exclusive presence of the one who was not and still is not righteous.

And the distinction which we have to consider is one which cannot properly be described in quantitative terms, as though that which is ascribed to the justified man with the promise and therefore in the present is only a little thing, whereas that which we expect in the future is a greater, as though the one is only a part and the other the whole. When an inheritance reverts to a man, and it is quite certain, it is not smaller because he has not yet entered into it (except in the form of a first instalment or a pledge). The moment it

---

[EN153] determined future

§ 61. *The Justification of Man*

becomes his it becomes his altogether. The wrong which according to the divine sentence is behind man is all his wrong. The death from which he comes is his whole death. So, too, the right and life which are before him according to the same sentence are his whole right and life. In his past, as it reaches into the present, he is wholly in the wrong and dead. So, too, in his future as with the promise it reaches into the present he is wholly in the right and alive. The only thing is that as long as he lives in time and considers his own person, he is both together: *simul peccator et iustus*^{EN154}, yet not half *peccator*^{EN155} and half *iustus*^{EN156}, but both altogether. And the pardon of man, declared in the promise concerning him, the reality of his future already in the present, is no less than this: *totus iustus*^{EN157}. That this is the case will be clear if we try briefly to unfold the content of the promise in the receiving of which the justification of man is completed.

We can gather together the whole of the promise, as the Creed does, (1) under the term, the forgiveness of sins. From the point of view of every human present this is undoubtedly something which is altogether future—the completed justification to which the justified man looks and moves. There is no moment in his life in which he does not have to look for and await and with outstretched hands request both forgiveness and therefore freedom from his sins. No one can evade the fifth petition of the Lord's Prayer. Its force can never grow less in the Christian life. A second test of the genuineness of a man's justification as his being in transition is whether the actuality of this petition forces itself increasingly upon him or whether that actuality is lost, whether in this case it has ever been actual, whether, therefore, he does live in this transition which is his justification. If he does live in this transition, he can understand the forgiveness of sins only as the work in which God comes to him as he has absolute need of forgiveness in the light of his past and his present, not as the state in which he for his part goes forward to God. He can have forgiveness of sins only as he receives it from God, as God gives it to him. There can be no question of any other receiving, or having, or possessing of forgiveness, of any other certainty concerning it. This is all true as the act of God takes place for him, as the gift of God is recognised and taken by him. The content of the promise is that God wills to do and will do this act for him, that he can recognise and take this gift. To receive the forgiveness of sins means, therefore, to receive the promise of the forgiveness of sins. To have the forgiveness of sins means to hold to the promise, to look forward with confidence in it, to go forward obediently to its direction. To be certain of the forgiveness of sins means finally not to doubt the promise of it as such for its own sake. If he looks behind him, or into the depth of his present as determined by his past, man

---

^{EN154} sinner and righteous at the same time
^{EN155} sinner
^{EN156} righteous
^{EN157} wholly righteous

3. *The Pardon of Man*

can never receive or enjoy the comfort of the forgiveness of sins; he cannot have it. He has it only as it comes to him in the promise, not otherwise.

But what does the forgiveness of sins mean? It is only in appearance that its reference is merely to the past. It has this reference. But only in the sense that it denotes the line which is put under his past, making it the past and marking it off as such. But at what point in my past do I see this line clearly put under it? Even if I thought I knew some such place, what about all that has become the past since? And with what justification and certainty can I affirm that it is put under it as I come from my past? When do we not have to look continually for it to be put under it? It is only in this way that this cancellation can be the content of the promise addressed to man. We ask: What is meant by this cancellation? Forgiveness obviously does not mean to make what has happened not to have happened. Nothing that has happened can ever not have happened. The man in whose life what had happened came not to have happened would not be the same man. He is this man in the totality of his history. He stands before God and is known to Him as this man. The man who receives forgiveness does not cease to be the man whose past (and his present as it derives from his past) bears the stain of his sins. The act of the divine forgiveness is that God sees and knows this stain infinitely better than the man himself, and abhors it infinitely more than he does even in his deepest penitence—yet He does not take it into consideration. He overlooks it, He covers it, He passes it by. He puts it behind Him, He does not charge it to man, He does not "impute" it (2 Cor. 5^{19}), He does not sustain the accusation to which man has exposed himself, He does not press the debt with which he has burdened himself, He does not allow to take place the destruction to which he has inevitably fallen victim. That God forgives means that He pardons. But the divine pardoning is not a weak remission. As pardoning it is the great—we might almost say the wrathful—act of divine power and defiance. God proves His superiority to all the contradiction and opposition arrayed against Him. He proves His unshakable lordship over man. He does so by despising the sin of man, by ignoring it although it has happened, by not allowing His relationship to man to be determined by it. Again, the divine pardoning is not an unlawful remission. As pardoning, it is the exercise of His supreme right, and at the same time the restoration of a state of right between Himself and man, the effective assertion of His glory in relation to man. Again, it is not merely a verbal remission. As pardoning, it is the effectual and righteous alteration of the human situation from its very foundation. If God's sentence concerning man is that He will know nothing of this stain, then the stain is washed away and removed, and although man still bears it, in spite of it he is without stain, in spite of his wrong he is in the right. The divine pardoning is not a remission "as if" man were not a sinner. As pardoning, it is the creative work of God, in the power of which man, even as the old man that he was and still is, is no longer that man, but is already another man, the man he will be, the new man. That is the forgiveness of sins as the final stroke under man's past.

[597]

§ 61. *The Justification of Man*

[598] But obviously we cannot understand it as such without seeing that not only has an old page been closed but a new one opened. And it is by this that it is truly characterised as the future to which man is continually summoned to look and move. If it is God's powerful and righteous and effective and indeed creative covering and overlooking and despising and disparaging of his pride, then obviously it does not merely create a *tabula rasa*^{EN158}, a clear field into which any new thing may come. By the divine pardon man is placed in a very definite new situation from which to start. For one thing it is only in this way, but in this way seriously, that he definitely becomes one who knows the grace and therefore the love and therefore the kingly freedom of God and of His right and will. Again, it is in this way, and radically in this way, that he becomes one who knows himself as the creature to whom God in pardoning him can only be gracious, about whom He can only be concerned. And finally, however great and powerful his sin may be, however accusingly and temptingly it may stand before him, he can think of it now only as the stain which is covered and overlooked and despised and disparaged by God and not worthy of further consideration. These are the three moments of the new freedom of the man whose sin God has forgiven: He can hold to the grace and will and right of God; he can learn humility; and he can confidently and definitively turn his back on his sin. His ability to do this is the new page which is opened with the forgiveness of sins. But where and when did we ever find this new situation in our own past, so that we have only to recall it to live in the power of this recollection? Where and when do we find it as an assured state in our present? If we ever could or can find it, then it is surely only as the promise which is given us by God and which we had and have to recognise and take as such. It is only as the future to which we could go forward and have in fact gone forward with more or less certain steps, only to be instructed again and again that it would be newly disclosed to us as our future, that it will be disclosed to us as such even in our present.

But we do not forget that the promise is the promise of God, and that forgiveness as its content is the total forgiveness of God. As pardoning, as that concluding stroke, as freedom for a new being, it is His complete forgiveness of all our sins. The fact that it is for us something future, that enclosed in the promise of God it can only be hoped and awaited and prayed for, does not in any way limit it or lessen its power. It does not mean that as man lays hold of the promise he cannot receive it here and now with unconditional certainty and unlimited fulness. No, he can and should receive it and have it in the same present in which he knows that he is always utterly in need of it. Where and when the promise is given to him, it is true and reliable; it cannot fail in anything of its content. As eschatology it is "realised eschatology." In and with it,

[599] its whole content enters the present of man. Where and when man trusts the promise, where and when he dares to treat it as directed to himself, to apply it

---

^{EN158} blank state

3. *The Pardon of Man*

to himself, to accept it as true of himself, there the forgiveness of sins takes place, that line is drawn, the new situation from which he can set out is created. There absolution is not simply pronounced to him. It takes place. There he receives forgiveness, the divine pardon, and the freedom of a new and the only true capacity. There he already has it, and he can and should dare to live as one who is forgiven.

The phrase "the forgiveness of sins" is well adapted to sum up all that has to be said in this connexion. But it is better not to try to sum it all up in this phrase. The content of the promise in the receiving of which the justification of man is completed is (2) his institution into a specific right which replaces the wrong which he has committed and which God has ignored. His justification is completed in this positive work of God, in virtue of which he becomes one who can lift up his head and hold it high because he can stand before Him, because he is pleasing to Him, because he is God's righteous man. He will be this righteous man. How can we ever put this in any but the future tense? The man who in the light of his past sets himself before the God who encounters him can never do anything but spread out before Him his wrong, with the petition: *quod vixi, tege*[EN159]. But there is a right which even as the one who is in the wrong with God he can receive, with which God wills to and will clothe him even though he is stripped of every right in His presence—and in such a way that he can boldly claim and assert it as his right, boasting of it, being confident of his case under its protection. It is not merely the restored right of the creature and the covenant-partner; according to the New Testament witness, it is the right of the child of God. In spite of his sin man is justified by God and before God not merely in the sense that God confirms and maintains him as His creature and covenant-partner, but in the sense that He receives him into His house, that He accepts and addresses and treats him as essentially His. Beyond the very real and intimate co-existence of God and man, as the final goal of their reconciliation, as the final meaning of the peace re-established between them, the term "child of God" signifies the unprecedented fact of a kinship of being which God has promised and guaranteed to man. It therefore signifies something which is more than reconciliation and peace, which rather seals the reconciliation and peace of man with God, which makes it so sure that it cannot be abrogated or lost, an ontological relationship in which the event of reconciliation, the restoration of peace between man and God, is crowned, and its result is anchored. It does not signify merely that man is bound to God, but also and primarily that God is bound to man. For if God calls man His child, if therefore man *is* His child, then God acknowledges that He is his Father, and therefore He *is* his Father. God has bound Himself to man and therefore He is bound to man in the same way that He has bound man to Himself and man is therefore bound to Him. The divine sonship of man is not his divinity. It is only ascribed to him, imparted to him, given to

[600]

[EN159] cover up the way I have lived

§ 61. *The Justification of Man*

him. He is only received and adopted by God as His child. He is only instituted as such. But in it he belongs to God by a kinship of being. He does so on the basis and in the power of the fact that God declares that He Himself belongs to him, and makes it so. If God is his Father, and he is the child of this Father, God is as little God without him as he is man without God, and he has the right of a son in relation to God as God has the right of a Father in relation to him—the right to a being with Him, the right to immediate access to Him, the right to call upon Him, the right to rely upon Him, the right to expect and to ask of Him everything that he needs. This right of sonship is the essence of every right of man. And the promise of this right is the completion of the justification of sinful man. It is with the promise of this right that God encounters and defies and withstands sin and wrong, the chaos which has invaded His creation. The existence of such children of God is the Yes with which He overcomes the No of man. It is also the meaning of His own No in face of the fall of man. It is what God wills with man, and what He wills victoriously in justifying him as a sinner. With it—with the fact that He calls man His child, and causes him to be His child—He definitively draws that line under his past and places him in the new situation from which to start, a situation behind which he cannot go. With it He gives him a future, a future which with a final and supreme clarity and certainty is new and different.

Do we need to emphasise particularly that the right of divine sonship ascribed to him is really his future, the given promise, to the fulfilment of which he can only look and move in every present? Who amongst us looking backward to his past has ever found that he is a child of God and therefore in a kinship of being with Him, just as indispensable to God as God is to him, in possession of this whole and truly princely right in relation to Him? We know this, if at all, only as that which God promises and ascribes, and as we trust and receive and accept God's promise. We are "begotten again unto a lively hope" (1 Pet. 1³) in this being. But in this connexion we must also emphasise that in and with the promise of God, included in it, and only to be apprehended in and with it, in this "lively hope," the divine sonship of man comes right into his present, so that it has not only to be considered and admired and awaited and longed for as a distant goal, but lived out already here and now. "We are the children of God" (Rom. 8¹⁶, 1 Jn. 3²). It may be covered over and concealed by that which overshadows and burdens and harasses us from our past, and basically so, so that there can be no question of any perception. "It doth not appear what we shall be" (1 Jn. 3²). But this cannot alter the fact. This cannot either remove it or diminish even a fraction of its relevance. What we are according to God's promise, those to whom God has bound Himself, calling them His children, what we have, the right to hold to this and to appeal to it, the right to cry "Abba, Father" (Gal. 4⁶, Rom. 8¹⁵), is the immutable thing which, although it may now be concealed from us, cannot be even touched, let alone shaken or overthrown, by any questioning of circumstances and relationships, of the judgment of other man, or of our own uncertainties and doubts, however

3. *The Pardon of Man*

superficial or profound. It is the irrevocable right of man. In the light of the promise which comes to us from God, we stand here on the rock of our justification which never moves and which will always bear us. Even in the most powerful assaults from behind, even in the severest conflict with all that we are "still" or "not yet," we are not merely permitted but commanded without fear or awe, without what would here be a false shame and reserve, to boast of the fact and continually to proclaim: "We are the children of God." In so doing we do not usurp anything that is not ours. Rather we would again be encroaching on the honour of God if we were not willing to boast of it and continually to return to it—so long as it is the bold and humble boasting of and returning to His promise and therefore to our justification by His gracious and miraculous act.

But the totality of completed justification must be considered from a further standpoint which is related to the one just mentioned and yet different from it. It is (3) man's placing in a state of hope. We can, of course, describe hope simply as the supreme form of the right of the children of God. We can also describe the whole state of the justified sinner as his state in hope, in so far as in the forgiveness of sins proclaimed to him, in the divine sonship ascribed to him, he has to do with the promise of God and therefore with that which he has to hope and expect from God.

But, again, it is not at all self-evident that man should live in this hope and expectation, that he should not refrain but should actually dare to look and to move forward to the goal which is set before him, that he should be aware of and accept the fact that the promise reaches into his present, that he should rouse himself and continue to hold to it and to find true and radical comfort in it, that he should not grow tired of doing this. Who amongst us has ever found in his past this inflexible hope corresponding to the inflexibility of the promise? where and when in his past? and how far even now in his present? The fact that he hopes, and therefore that he lives in and with the promise, the fact that here and now he allows himself to be told the future thing: "Thy sins be forgiven thee," the fact that here and now he confidently repeats what he is told in the promise: "We are the children of God," the fact that he is the man who not only represents himself as doing this but actually does it: this is obviously a thing apart, and yet again it is the content of the promise in which his justification is completed. In this context it tells us: Thou mayest hope and thou canst hope; indeed, thou art the man who actually will hope; thou art the man on whose heart this lively hope is already written; as the man who has this lively hope thou art already on the other side of that line, born again as the child which thou art as addressed by God. This address or promise obviously has to be apprehended, for the very reason that in it it is a matter of its apprehension as such, of confidence in it, of hazarding it and keeping to it. Just as we can and must pray for the ability to pray and for actual prayer, so with all seriousness we can and must hope for the ability to hope and for actual hope, for

[602]

§ 61. *The Justification of Man*

this is itself the content of the promise to whose fulfilment we continually look and move.

But there is more to it than that. In the hope in which man's justification is fulfilled it is not merely a matter of the looking and reaching out for the promised forgiveness of sins and divine sonship which has to be new every day and every hour. It is a matter of that. But it is clear that hoping for it as such implies a looking and reaching out for a goal at which the state of the justified man as indicated by the forgiveness of sins and divine sonship, although not different, will be revealed and shown and will work itself out in a different way from anything that can or will ever take place on his pilgrimage from an ever new past through an ever new present to an ever new future, in his movement, his history, in time. His justification takes place in the temporal course of this history, and everything that he is and does as justified by God is only in this transition. It is genuine and complete, but contradictory, concealed under this contradiction. It is only in the being together of that which is antithetical, in the form of a riddle, in the mystery of the *simul peccator et iustus*[EN160]. The justified man exists—this is the completion of his justification—as he hopes from day to day and hour to hour, in the hope—which we now have to write with big letters—for a final goal of his hope, for the solution of the riddle, the removal of the contradiction, the revelation of the mystery of his history in all those transitions which he continually has to make. He does not grope in the dark. He knows the way on which he finds himself—not only its direction but its goal. He knows that he is not caught up in a futile vacillation or movement in a circle. He lives in the constant differentiation of his future from his past, his right from his wrong, his life from his death. He lives by the constant projection of his future, the constant prevailing of the promised forgiveness of sins and divine sonship against the accusation and menace from which he comes, by the superiority, the forward-pointing thrust of the divine sentence: *totus iustus*[EN161], in face of the backward-pointing *totus peccator*[EN162]. But it is still the case that in every present the past is still present, that the forgiveness of sins and the divine sonship enclosed in the promise has to be sought and apprehended afresh every moment out of the deepest need, that he cannot hear the *totus iustus*[EN163] without being willing continually to hear the *totus peccator*[EN164]. It is still the case that he can hold to that which is promised, to the unshakable and indestructible thing which cannot be lost, because it cannot be revoked, only in the assured but continually renewed striding, only in the joyful and confident but hazardous and laborious movement which is described by Paul in Phil. 3^{12}: "Not as though I had already attained, either were already made perfect: but I follow after, if that I may apprehend that for

---

[EN160] sinner and righteous at the same time
[EN161] wholly righteous
[EN162] wholly sinful
[EN163] wholly righteous
[EN164] wholly sinful

3. *The Pardon of Man*

which also I am apprehended ... " This is neither vacillation nor movement in a circle. But neither is it a *progressus in infinitum*^{EN165}. In it all he obviously looks to a decision in which the relativity and contradiction and provisional nature of the decisions in consequence of which he now exists are taken away, in which the movement in which he now goes through these decisions, from the one to the other, comes to rest because it has attained its goal, in which the forgiveness of sins and the divine sonship, the fulfilment of the promise given to him, do not need to be sought and apprehended any more, in which the *totus iustus*^{EN166} will be the final word, the only, uncontradicted word. On the way itself he knows about this goal, about the end of this form of his righteousness before God, about the beginning of its new and definitive form. And as he treads the way he moves forward to this goal. Essentially the goal is not different but just the same as that towards which he now moves every day and every hour—his right before God, his life under the protection of this right—but it will be the goal beyond which there is no need of any further movement. According to the strong expression of 2 Cor. 5^{21}, he will have become the righteousness of God. He will no longer be merely expecting and seeking his right to be with God beyond that concluding stroke, his right to an existence in the glory of the service of God, his right to eternal salvation. He will no longer have to pray that he may have it. He will simply have it and exercise it. He will simply be in the possession and under the protection of this right, because he will live in the immediate fellowship of his being with the being of God who is the source and essence of all right and life, of all being and salvation. He will be unconditionally free to serve Him. He will be at the point to which he is now on the way. And this arriving will simply be the revelation of his journeying, of his history in time. His eternal life will consist in the disclosing of the justification of his life in this world. It will be this temporal life itself in the newness which is already ascribed to it in the judgment and sentence of God, in the righteous form which is already given to it by the divine pardon, when the old and sinful form has finally been left behind and cannot again reach into the present. It will be pure present, a present which is wholly and exclusively determined and filled by the future ascribed in the divine promise, without any togetherness with the past, a present in which nothing at all can be said of him but *totus iustus*^{EN167}, in which he can know himself only as such. But in this way it will be the full present of life and service and salvation and glory [604] which is now the hidden thing in every present, which now in this temporal present he has to traverse step by step, which he can traverse confidently and joyfully just because that which is hidden in it is this future thing, the pure present of eternal life.

---

^{EN165} advance into the infinite
^{EN166} wholly righteous
^{EN167} wholly righteous

§ 61. *The Justification of Man*

"And if children, then heirs" is what we are told in Rom. 8^{17}, and again in 1 Pet. 1^3: "Begotten again to a lively hope." "Inheritance" is the decision, the hidden thing in all the decisions in which here and now the justified man can have the full forgiveness of all his sins and be a full child of God. "Inheritance" is the being which is the hidden thing in the righteous being which here and now is promised to him without reserve in the divine promise. "Inheritance" is the present of eternal life which is the hidden thing in every temporal present in which he finds himself in this transition. The entry into and taking possession of the inheritance will be the revelation of this hidden thing, the drawing aside of the veil by which it is now concealed, the removing of the contradiction, the solving of the riddle, the dispersing of the mystery of his temporal being. To have the forgiveness of sins and to be a child of God means to be one who awaits this inheritance and moves towards it. To be justified (Col. 1^{12}) is to be "made meet to partake of the inheritance of the saints in light." This making meet to partake of the inheritance is the completion of man's justification. The righteous man is the one who is waiting in this way, the one who is made a partaker, the one who irrevocably and with all that it implies is appointed an heir, the one who already lives as this heir, who moves towards the revelation of justification and in it eternal life. He will live in and by this great hope as it is given to him as such. As such he will never lose sight of the promise, he will never be hesitant to lay hold of it, nor will he ever fail or fall away in obedience to its direction. He will know the hidden thing in every time as the eternal thing, the depth of every present in which he moves already to the future of the pure present. He will wait patiently for the revelation of it, and in so doing he will constantly rise up with wings like an eagle—a pilgrim who is hard pressed but not pressed down, often weary but not exhausted, often distressed but not in despair, often astray but not lost, seeking but also finding, asking but also receiving, and in the last analysis—in the light of his ultimate goal—merry and joyful. The pardon of man, the completion of his justification, is his appointment as this pilgrim, his institution into the state of the great hope. His sins are forgiven him in order that he may be this pilgrim. In this consists his supreme right as a son. It is clear that the promise, too, is a future which he has continually to seize and apprehend, that it stands continually before him and wills to be continually lived. But it is clear again that in this form too, as a concrete possibility, the promise reaches into every present of the justified man. It is to-day, to-day, that it stands before him as the future. Therefore it is to-day, to-day, that it can and should be affirmed and seized and apprehended and put into effect as such. It is to-day, to-day that its content, the great hope, can and should be lived—the power of the world to come as the power of this world. The righteous sentence of God opens wide to sinful man even in this world the gate of the world to come. If he subjects himself to this sentence, if he abandons the self-sufficiency of his pusillanimity, if he gives God the right against himself—the God who in this way enters the lists so powerfully on his behalf—what else is there for him to do but to go through this gate, to be the

3. The Pardon of Man

one who hopes with a great hope, which he is permitted and indeed commanded to be by God, which he is already by the divine sentence?

To close our discussion we will consider something of the witness of the Old Testament Psalter. Paul undoubtedly had the Psalter in mind when in Rom. 7 he spoke of the beginning of justification in the midst of the sin and lost estate of man, and then in Gal. 2 or Rom. 8 or Phil. 3 of its completion in the pardon of man. And with the words of the Psalter the first community responded to the evangelical record of the obedience, the humility, the humiliation and the crucifixion of the Lord, to the history of the beginning and completion of their—and not only their—justification proclaimed in and with this record. It is also worthy of note that it was by studying and meditating on the Book of the Psalms that Luther was impelled to his remarkable rediscovery of justification: his movement was from the Psalms to Romans, Galatians and Hebrews, not *vice versa*[EN168]. Nor must we overlook the fact that as the self-attestation of the Old Testament people of God which lives by the promise and therefore the pardoning of sinful man by the gracious God the Psalter both as a whole and in detail has the irreversible direction of that history, that its emphasis and controlling note are therefore on the revealing of what the Israelite knows as his future and therefore as his present when God is the righteous Judge and is at work as such. For all its variety the Psalter is, as it were, a single voice: the attestation of that to which the individual Israelite believes he holds and does in fact hold, both as a member of his people and for his own person, in reliance on the divine sentence and promise; the attestation of his right as not only maintained and confirmed but triumphantly renewed by God in spite of his sin and the loss which it involved; the attestation of his hope, in which he dares to live already in the present, to find comfort and even to rejoice in his holy and angry God in the midst of all his trials. It is no accident that whether its statements are directly addressed to God or speak of God in the third person, the Psalter is always a prayer-book. The background from which the man who speaks in it comes is not forgotten. For the most part the Psalmists bring it out explicitly. Where they do not do so, it has to be read in in order to understand them: the oppression and need and lost estate of this people and its individual members in the world around them which are the result of their sin; the past of their unfaithfulness and therefore of their perdition which reaches into their present and completely obscures it. It is from this darkness, and completely enveloped in this darkness, that the Psalmists come before God in prayer. And in this we see the transition, justification as history. (Has the Psalter ever been consistently examined and appraised as a reflection of the history of Israel?) Side by side with Psalms 78 and 106, in which the guilt and punishment of Israel are in great measure recalled, we have to set a Psalm like 136, where this same past which elsewhere is judged so negatively is already set unconditionally against the eternally enduring goodness of God. And in Psalms 32 and 51, with their painful and shocking recollection of the origin of the individual Israelite, we have already seen the tendency which makes it difficult for the reader to understand them altogether as Penitential Psalms and not rather as a peculiar type of Psalms of thanksgiving and praise. The Psalter as a whole ends on this note—it must have been a tremendous Nevertheless in the time of its redaction—not looking backward but forward. But we will allow some of the individual witnesses to speak for themselves.

And first of all, corresponding to the great hope of the justified man of which we have just been speaking, the hope which already fills and determines the present, Ps. 116$^{5f.}$: "Gracious is the Lord, and righteous; yea, our God is merciful .... Return unto thy rest, O my soul; for the Lord hath dealt bountifully with thee. For thou hast delivered my soul from death, mine eyes from tears, and my feet from falling. I will walk before the Lord in the land of the living.

[606]

[EN168] the other way around

§ 61. *The Justification of Man*

I believed, therefore have I spoken: I was greatly afflicted .... What shall I render unto the Lord, for all his benefits toward me? I will take the cup of salvation, and call upon the name of the Lord .... Precious in the sight of the Lord is the death of his saints. O Lord, truly I am thy servant; I am thy servant, and the son of thine handmaid: thou hast loosed my bonds. I will offer to thee the sacrifice of thanksgiving, and will call upon the name of the Lord ... in the courts of the Lord's house, in the midst of thee, O Jerusalem. Praise ye the Lord." And then Ps. 118$^{14f.}$: "The Lord is my strength and song, and is become my salvation. The voice of rejoicing and salvation is in the tabernacles of the righteous: the right hand of the Lord doeth valiantly. The right hand of the Lord is exalted: the right hand of the Lord doeth valiantly. I shall not die, but live, and declare the works of the Lord. The Lord hath chastened me sore: but he hath not given me over unto death. Open to me the gates of righteousness: I will go into them, and I will praise the Lord. This is the gate of the Lord, into which the righteous shall enter. I will praise thee; for thou hast heard me, and art become my salvation. The stone which the builders refused is become the head stone of the corner. This is the Lord's doing; it is marvellous in our eyes. This is the day which the Lord hath made; we will rejoice and be glad in it." And on the same level Ps. 16$^{5f.}$: "The Lord is the portion of mine inheritance and of my cup: thou maintainest my lot. The lines are fallen unto me in pleasant places; yea, I have a goodly heritage .... Therefore my heart is glad, and my glory rejoiceth: my flesh also shall rest in hope. For thou wilt not leave my soul in hell; neither wilt thou suffer thine holy one to see corruption. Thou wilt shew me the path of life: in thy presence is fulness of joy; at thy right hand there are pleasures for evermore." These are, of course, statements on the very highest level, like the song of praise in Is. 26$^{2f.}$: "Open ye the gates, that the righteous nation which keepeth truth may enter in. Thou wilt keep him in perfect peace, whose mind is stayed on thee: because he trusteth in thee. Trust ye in the Lord for ever: for the Lord Jehovah is the rock of ages."

To assess these statements we must first take a few steps backward, entering into the shadow of the present in which man can only grasp the promise as such, but enlightened and strengthened by it can already look to the height, the future, whose light can, on the other hand, make his present so bright. It is at this distance that Ps. 130 speaks (in the familiar Prayer Book version): "Out of the deep have I called unto thee, O Lord: Lord, hear my voice. O let thine ears consider well: the voice of my complaint. If thou, Lord, wilt be extreme to mark what is done amiss: O Lord, who may abide it? For there is mercy with thee: therefore shalt thou be feared. I look for the Lord; my soul doth wait for him: in his word is my trust. My soul fleeth unto the Lord: before the morning watch, I say, before the morning watch. O Israel, trust in the Lord, for with the Lord there is mercy: and with him is plenteous redemption. And he shall redeem Israel: from all his sins." There is to some extent a backward reference in Ps. 25$^{10f.}$, but not at the price of its forward direction: "All the paths of the Lord are mercy and truth unto such as keep his covenant and his testimonies. For thy name's sake, O Lord, pardon mine iniquity: for it is great. What man is he that feareth the Lord? him shall he teach in the way that he shall choose .... The secret of the Lord is with them that fear him; and he will shew them his covenant. Mine eyes are ever toward the Lord; for he shall pluck my feet out of the net. Turn thee unto me, and have mercy upon me; for I am desolate and afflicted. The troubles of my heart are enlarged: O bring thou me out of my distresses. Look upon mine affliction and my pain; and forgive all my sins .... O keep my soul, and deliver me: let me not be ashamed; for I put my trust in thee .... Redeem Israel, O God, out of all his troubles." Ps. 143$^{1f.}$ goes further back, but always with the same direction: "Hear my prayer, O Lord, give ear to my supplications: in thy faithfulness answer me, and in thy righteousness. And enter not into judgment with thy servant, O Lord: for in thy sight shall no man living be justified." And v. 5 f.: "I remember the days of old; I meditate on all thy works; I muse on the work of thy hands. I stretch forth my hands unto thee: my soul thirsteth after

3. *The Pardon of Man*

thee, as a thirsty land. Hear me speedily, O Lord: my spirit faileth; hide not thy face from me, lest I be like them that go down into the pit. Cause me to hear thy loving-kindness in the morning; for in thee do I trust; cause me to know the way wherein I should walk; for I lift up my soul unto thee." And v. 10 f.: "Teach me to do thy will; for thou art my God: thy spirit is good; lead me into the land of uprightness. Quicken me, O Lord, for thy name's sake: for thy righteousness' sake bring my soul out of trouble."

But then, and from that very point, we have the new advance of those whose back is to the wall and yet who do not fear, the new hold and leap into the future (Ps. 142^5): "I cried unto thee, O Lord: I said, Thou art my refuge and my portion in the land of the living." And (in v. 7): "Bring my soul out of prison, that I may praise thy name: the righteous shall compass me about; for thou shalt deal bountifully with me." Ps. 18$^{1f.}$ puts it even more dramatically: "I will love thee, O Lord, my strength. The Lord is my rock, and my fortress, and my deliverer: my God, my strength, in whom I will trust; my buckler, and the horn of my salvation, and my high tower." Then in v. 6: "In my distress I called upon the Lord, and cried unto my God: he heard my voice out of his temple, and my cry came before him, even into his ears." But then everything becomes different and the one who was anxious and oppressed seems to rise up with an almost superabundant vitality in v. 28 f.: "For thou wilt light my candle: the Lord my God will enlighten my darkness. For by thee I have run through a troop; and by my God have I leaped over a wall. As for God, his way is perfect: the word of the Lord is tried: he is a buckler to all those that trust in him. For who is God save the Lord? or who is a rock save our God? It is God that girdeth me with strength, and maketh my way perfect. He maketh my feet like hinds' feet, and setteth me upon my high places. He teacheth my hands to war, so that a bow of steel is broken by mine arms. Thou hast also given me the shield of thy salvation: and thy right hand hath holden me up, and thy gentleness hath made me great. Thou hast enlarged my steps under me, that my feet did not slip." We find the same movement in Ps. 17$^{6f.}$: "I have called upon thee, for thou wilt hear me, O God: incline thine ear unto me, and hear my speech. Shew thy marvellous loving-kindness, O thou that savest by thy right hand them which put their trust in thee from those that rise up against them. Keep me as the apple of the eye, hide me under the shadow of thy wings." And then the voice of the redeemed in v. 15: "As for me, I will behold thy face in righteousness: I shall be satisfied, when I awake, with thy likeness." Similarly in Ps. 73$^{21f.}$: "Thus my heart was grieved, and I was pricked in my reins. So foolish was I, and ignorant: I was as a beast before thee. Nevertheless I am continually with thee; thou hast holden me by my right hand. Thou shalt guide me with thy counsel, and afterward receive me to glory. Whom have I in heaven but thee? and there [608] is none upon earth that I desire beside thee. My flesh and my heart faileth: but God is the strength of my heart, and my portion for ever. For, lo, they that are far from thee shall perish: thou hast destroyed all them that go a whoring from thee. But it is good for me to draw near to God: I have put my trust in the Lord God, that I may declare all thy works."

And then Ps. 103 plainly looks back from the goal upon the whole way and its starting-point in the unforgettable praise of the Lord to which the Psalmist calls his soul, his very self, because he finds himself called to it: the Lord (v. 3 f.) "who forgiveth all thine iniquities; who healeth all thy diseases; who redeemeth thy life from destruction; who crowneth thee with loving-kindness and tender mercies; who satisfieth thy mouth with good things; so that thy youth is renewed like the eagle's." For (v. 8) "the Lord is merciful and gracious, slow to anger, and plenteous in mercy. He hath not dealt with us after our sins; nor rewarded us according to our iniquities. For as the heaven is high above the earth, so great is his mercy toward them that fear him. As far as the east is from the west, so far hath he removed our transgressions from us. Like as a father pitieth his children, so the Lord pitieth them that fear him." With this we may compare Ps. 85, which is bold to say the same expressly of the people of Israel as such: "Lord, thou hast been favourable unto thy land: thou hast brought

§ 61. *The Justification of Man*

back the captivity of Jacob. Thou hast forgiven the iniquity of thy people, thou hast covered all their sin. Thou hast turned away all thy wrath: thou hast turned thyself from the fierceness of thine anger" (v. 1 f.). "Surely his salvation is nigh them that fear him; that glory may dwell in our land. Mercy and truth are met together; righteousness and peace have kissed each other. Truth shall spring out of the earth; and righteousness shall look down from heaven" (v. 9 f.). Finally, we must follow word for word the best-known and most inexhaustible of all the Psalms, Ps. 23: the confession of the man whose shepherd is the Lord, who therefore will lack nothing, who will be led on the right path, who need fear no evil but is comforted as he goes through the valley of the shadow, for whom a table is prepared and fully provided in the presence of his enemies, whose head is anointed with oil, who expects to be followed by goodness and mercy all the days of his life, and to dwell in the house of the Lord for ever—that, and so far only that. Every sentence speaks of the completion of the justification of the sinful man, of his pardon. Therefore every sentence is in the strict sense "eschatological," looking into the furthest and final future, and from there back again into the present. Every sentence is like the call of those who wait for the morning in Ps. 130$^{6f.}$ but for that reason every sentence is the word of thanksgiving and praise of a man who to-day, to-day, can rejoice in the coming morning. Ps. 23 is a summary of the whole Psalter, and therefore the explanation of the clear songs of triumph with which the book closes from Ps. 145 onwards. It is the self-documentation *in nuce*$^{\text{EN169}}$ of the existence of the sinner justified by the gracious God.

4. JUSTIFICATION BY FAITH ALONE

When we speak of the man who is pardoned in this judgment of God and therefore justified, the man of this history, of this transition, who moves from wrong to right, from death to life, whom do we really mean? Who is he? What man is this?

[609]

The man of some century, perhaps the 16th or the 1st of our era, which was particularly affected by religious revolution and renewal? Or the man of the European Middle Ages who was so near to the earth and the sea and the forest and the beast of prey, who was preoccupied with the struggle for existence, who was still so familiar with death, who still continued to live cheerfully in the paganism of his fathers, who was therefore self-evidently open to every kind of mysticism and magic and mythology? Or the painfully civilised man in the framework of the firm traditions which were refashioned in the 17th century and since then have determined the 19th century and the beginning of our own—the conservative Liberal for whom Christianity, like the political and social order, was a much discussed but obviously effective factor, who if he was not a libertine or an extreme rationalist did not want to live altogether apart from the Church ("From time to time I view the old with favour, and take care not to break with it"), for whom missions and evangelisation and life in community, and also the reform of manners and jurisprudence, pacifism, the emancipation of women, the race-question, the social question, even socialism—and right into the 19th century the emancipation of slaves—were still novelties in which he had to be interested only by special prophets and "movements," and in which he was interested only unwillingly and in the teeth of every kind of reaction? Or the modern spiritual man, who not only was not prevented but was actually impelled by his exposure to rapid scientific and technical progress to form for

---

$^{\text{EN169}}$ in miniature

4. Justification by Faith Alone

himself, as an idealist or a romantic (with or without Christian influences, and perhaps applying the newly discovered ancient Asiatic wisdom), a more or less solid counterpoise to it, or an "island of the blessed" in the form of aesthetic culture or a corresponding stoical or enthusiastic *ethos*? Or the deeply discontented man of the Nihilists at the beginning of our century, who had learned from Schopenhauer and Nietzsche, Ibsen, Björnson and Strindberg (the remarkable Northern disciples of Kierkegaard), Tolstoy and Dostoievski, that more or less everything worth while had perished, that it was better—if only we knew where to go—to contract out of the world as out of a club whose achievements we could no longer view with favour, and who sometimes turned to the New Testament at any rate for confirmation of this frame of mind? Or, finally, ourselves, the fathers and sons of the generation of threatened over-population and the working out of the soil by obvious exploitation, of the awakening of Asia and Africa—the man of the first and second and the dreaded third world war? The man who after all the individualism, criticism and scepticism from which he has come can find nothing more sensible than life in the avowed friend–foe relationship of nations and classes and races and economic claims and interests? The man who has no better way of correcting this unhappy relationship than by the ideology and establishment of totalitarian states, and who seems to have learned from the recent collapse of a first form of this totalitarianism nothing more than what we see before us in the rise and development of two new totalitarianisms which are rivals and very dissimilar, but which at heart belong very closely together? The man who momentarily believes and imagines that he sees himself in existentialism, although it is open to dispute whether what he sees is supposed to be his vileness or his divinity, or finally his wise and benignant humanity after the pattern of a reviving classical humanism? Or the man who tries to keep himself healthy, or to stave off destruction, or at a pinch to arrest himself on the very verge of madness, with the help of a refined psychology and pedagogy? Or simply the man who is uprooted both inwardly and outwardly, the displaced man, the man who has been led into every kind of error, the man who is our fellow-man to-day in so many known and so many more unknown forms? in which we must not overlook the remarkable but undeniable fact that this modern man is confronted by the phenomenon—if not of the Gospel, at least of the Church which ostensibly or actually proclaims the Gospel, of its factual power (however it may be interpreted), and that in disillusionment, agitation, protest or repudiation he has to reckon with it in a way which certainly could not have been foreseen even forty years ago. In all the phases and developments of the past there did exist, and at the present day there still exists with a greater or lesser definiteness and authenticity, the consciously and actively Christian man, it may be in the great Churches, it may be in all kinds of separate societies, it may be as an individual in the most diverse positive and negative relationships to the spirit and tendency of the age. Of this man we shall have to speak particularly in the two final sections, of the community existing in the world, and of the individual Christian as such living within it.

[610]

Our question here concerns the man justified by God, the man to whom there refers, and of whom there has to be said, everything that we have heard concerning the judgment of God passed upon him and the pardon of God applying to him and valid for him. Is there such a man? Does he even exist? Has he ever existed? Will he ever exist? The Christian does not really need to look at the heathen and unbelieving and indifferent to be forced to ask this question. Is he himself, the Christian, the man justified by God? Does he know himself as a man who is really on the way from Rom. 7 to Rom. 8, who can take Ps. 23 sincerely on his heart and therefore legitimately on his lips in this movement and as the subject of this history?

§ 61. *The Justification of Man*

Nor is there any sense in thinking that the question: Where and who is this man? is one which has become a burning question only in relation to our own environment, to the man and the men of our own age—we probably take ourselves much too seriously as such. We would seek this man with just the same uncertainty and difficulty if we could transport ourselves into 16th century Wittenberg or Geneva, or into the streets and cathedrals and cloisters of the German Middle Ages, or into the Italy of Francis of Assisi, or into the empire of Constantine which had so suddenly found itself Christian, or into the gatherings of the earliest Christian communities, or even into the catacombs—not to speak of the world outside, in which the light of Christianity has shone for so long, and still shines.

The history of theoretical atheism in the West, which Fritz Mauthner (1920 f.) was at pains to write in four big volumes, shows us at any rate (together with H. Reuter's older work, *Geschichte der religiösen Aufklärung im Mittelalter*, 1875) that what has been propagated as theoretical godlessness in our own age (and much less energetically to-day than half a century ago) was only an irruption of the same thinking which had lived on strongly enough in a more hidden stratum of the European spirit through all the preceding and ostensibly Christian centuries—and very deeply indeed in the full flower of what was supposed to be a Christian mysticism. What would be revealed if ever a history of practical atheism were written, e.g., concerning the real relationship between the general hostility to religion of the present-day East and the Christianity of the modern West on both sides of the Atlantic? It is with particular reference to practical atheism both old and new that the question: Where and who is the man justified by God? forces itself to our notice.

[611] What is he then, measured by the actuality not only of modern man, but of humanity as a whole as we have so far seen it, of which we can hardly expect that it will be essentially different in the future from what it has been in the past and still is to-day? Is it that all the time we have simply been speaking of an idea, constructing an ideal picture, recounting a fairy-story, a myth: the myth of a turning and pilgrimage which can at least be thought and conceived by man. of the history whose subject he would like to imagine himself; a myth which lacks nothing in meaning and beauty, but only in reality, as something "which never was on land or sea;" a myth which may like any other illusion alternately interest or bore us, give us pleasure or annoy us. We ourselves do not accept the view that the man justified by God is an idea, an ideal construction, a myth, an illusion. We believe that we have to recognise and confess his reality. But if this is not to be a mere opinion, as against which we might equally well be of a different opinion, we must consider closely the grounds on which we have to adopt it.

The difficulty in relation to the existence or non-existence of the man justified by God is by no means small. Indeed, if it is not noted, it will at once gain in strength and be fatal. In its more harmless form, which is always well to the forefront, it consists in the universal and very serious questioning of the existence of this man throughout the whole range of history both secular and ecclesiastical. Whether we look at the past or at the present there is unfortunately not a little but very much to be said for the nagging suspicion that when we maintain it we have to do perhaps only with an ideal or mythical construction and therefore with an illusion.

If we try to dispute this, we must be careful that our argumentation does not

4. *Justification by Faith Alone*

unconsciously and all the more weightily serve to confirm it. This is necessarily the case if we set the existence of this man in some kind of transcendent sphere, proclaiming and describing him only as a kind of guiding intellectual concept, and thus secretly giving up all attempt to maintain and prove his actual being. What can this mean except that the questioning is affirmed and indeed that it is laid down as self-evident that the only possible answer is a simple negation of that which is questioned? And what else does this involve than that the whole doctrine of justification—the whole answer, remember, to the question concerning the God who is gracious to man—is made the theme of a hypothesis airily constructed with the aid of religion and thought and poetry? We must be clear that if in the doctrine of justification we are not dealing with a hypothesis of this kind, but with a well-founded answer to this question, then we cannot accept the calling in question of this man. It is necessarily destroyed and swept right away, and with it both that simple negation and that nagging suspicion.

But the real difficulty, the great difficulty, does not arise from the questioning. It results rather from the nature of the self-demonstration of the man justified by God, by which the questioning is in fact destroyed and the suspicion swept away. It is in fact a matter of his self-demonstration. He has actually the power to do it, and he exercises it. But this means that the one who accepts it, who rests upon it, who in face of all history both secular and ecclesiastical, including the present and his own life's history, counts on the existence of this man and dares calmly and publicly to count on it in the presence of others, has from the very first and radically to give up all attempts to be sure of himself, to prove himself to himself, to proclaim and represent himself as the man who destroys this questioning and sweeps away this suspicion. He must be clear and he must accept the fact that it is not he who controls the reality and existence and the revelation of this man, that he is not in a position to introduce him or to point to him even with his little finger, that he is not in a position to come forward as an advocate to argue and fight for him. He must know that he will betray and corrupt the matter, which is the whole doctrine of justification, just as much and perhaps even worse than the one who puts the existence of this man in some transcendent sphere, if he sets out even in the slightest degree to declare and conduct himself as owner, lord and master. He must abandon every claim to be able to do anything himself in this matter. He cannot expect any effect or success of himself. Why not? Not because the historical question, the problem of experience with which he is confronted, is so terribly difficult, the calling in question of justified man by everything else that we know of man so serious, the nagging suspicion that it is all a myth or something of that kind so hard to dispel. These are all child's play compared with the fact that the thing or person that we here have to recognise and confess will and can be recognised and confessed of himself and as such, according to his sovereign nature, only in the response to and on the basis of his self-demonstration, of the fact that he does not accept any advocate, that he strikes

[612]

§ 61. *The Justification of Man*

all arguments out of the hands of those who come forward as such. This is the great inherent difficulty of the matter which we have to face because we are definitely caught in it if we do not see and recognise it, although there is the risk that we will not be able to escape it even if we do. It consists in this. The existence of the justified man proves and maintains and establishes itself as real to itself with sovereign power. It is more real than all human conceptions of history both secular and ecclesiastical. But while this is true, we can never master it, we can never control it, we can never avail ourselves of it, we can never use it, we can never make anything of it. All that we can do (a riddle and a miracle even to ourselves) is simply to know about it, without any claim and in the most profound thankfulness. All that we can do, again without any claim and in the most profound thankfulness, is to be its witness, and again without any attempt to advocate it. Of course, when we do that it will be with an absolutely unconditional and joyful certainty. But then and only then. Not otherwise. If we are not ready to conceal—submerge—ourselves, if it is too small a thing for us to be those who humbly know and witness, if we are of the opinion that there must be some better way which by-passes the simple self-demonstration of what has to be demonstrated, if we will not cease to look for such a way, then we will merely show that we ourselves have not yet caught sight of what has to be demonstrated, that we are not qualified to speak on this matter. More than that, we will compromise the only possible and effective demonstration—the self-demonstration of the man justified by God—because we will regard it as incredible and ineffective in our own person. But who is ready to accept this? to agree that this is our situation in the question concerning this man? not to try in some way to evade and escape this situation? It is such a temptation to regard it as impossible and to act accordingly. The great difficulty is that the recognition and confession of justified man is not possible except at this price, on the surrender of every claim to our own human assertion of it, or is possible only in the form of an empty and hollow and ineffective substitute. But the payment of this price is not self-evident. Why not? Because it is not self-evident that anyone has the price to pay, that anyone can conceal himself as he should in order to be qualified to speak in this matter, as a witness of the man justified by God. No one is by nature. No one is on the basis of a religious disposition. No one is because he lives in and by a definite cultural or ecclesiastical tradition and the stimuli and forces of that tradition. No one is because he receives the sacraments, or is a genius, or a brave man, or baptised—even as a believer—or converted, or a passably good Christian. No one. And naturally the great temptation in this great difficulty is to agree that we are unable, and thus to fold our hands, to refrain from doing what we have to do—as though it were not possible for all of us every moment to do what has to be done. For the ability required is a genuinely and concretely human ability, but the possession of it can be shown only by the use made of it, and when a man does make use of it it is shown not to be an ability which he himself has contributed and exchanged as a presupposition, in the form of a capacity of

4. *Justification by Faith Alone*

his own. He is just the man who does actually do this and can do it. He stands at a new beginning which he has not made himself but which is made with him. And if he ever does this again, and therefore can do it, it will be without any presupposition; it will again be a new beginning. And the essence of every such new beginning will be the demonstration in which the man justified by God shows himself to be real and existent to himself. The man who knows about him in this way, and is made his witness in this way, will of himself find himself placed where he belongs as such: summoned to, and made able and ready for, the action of humility which corresponds to this recognition and confession. No one can create for himself or take to himself or maintain as his own possession this direction into humility and therefore the adaptation for this action. Again, no one who follows after it, in the self-revelation and demonstration of the justified man, the holding fast to his reality and existence, will not at once have it and put it into effect, in the discovery and the gift of this encounter, in the readiness of the thanks to which he will definitely find himself summoned in this encounter. [614]

We are speaking of what takes place in the genuinely and concretely human situation of faith. It is faith which can do what has to be done and what cannot be done by anyone naturally. It is in faith that a man surmounts the great difficulty which consists in the fact that he is not adapted of himself to do justice to the sovereign self-demonstration of the justified man—not to speak of the lesser difficulty caused by the historical questioning of this man, the anxiety whether he is not after all a myth or an illusion. Having passed through the first door which was closed, he will not be halted for a single moment by this second door. In faith he has the price of humility which has to be paid, and he pays it. Faith is itself the absolutely humble but absolutely positive answer to the question of the reality and existence of the man justified by God, to the question who and where this man is. The one who can and does believe knows this man well. He will confess him, and therefore he will confess the judgment and pardon of God, the reality of that history, of that transition of man from his Yesterday to his To-day. In his own person? Yes, but in his own person in its solidarity with all other men, and therefore virtually and prospectively in their persons too. Because he recognises and confesses him in his own person, he also recognises and confesses him in the riddle of the man of every age and clime; he recognises and confesses his infinitely greater reality as compared with every opposing human picture. He will regard his own being in contrast to his reality, and therefore the riddle of his own person, as not less but much more dubious than all the dubieties which he might encounter in past and present history both secular and ecclesiastical. If his faith is the taking away of that which separates himself from the man justified by God, how can it hold back in relation to others, how can it not be virtually and prospectively a faith for others?—however much he may see the reality and existence of the man justified by God called in question by them, however tempted he may be to

§ 61. *The Justification of Man*

that nagging suspicion in relation to them. Faith breaks through the calling in question, the suspicion, radically and therefore all along the line.

We have now reached the point where we can and must consider the great catchword, the concept which became so well-known in theology, but which so far we have prudently avoided and kept in the background: that the justification of sinful man is his justification by faith alone.

The combination of the words δικαιοσύνη^{EN170} and πίστις^{EN171} is obviously a special element in the theology of Paul. He spoke of δικαιοσύνη πίστεως^{EN172} (Rom. 4^{13}), or τῆς πίστεως^{EN173} (Rom. 4^{11}), of δικ. ἐκ πίστεως^{EN174} (Rom. 9^{30}, 10^{6}), and in Phil. 3^{9} of δικ. διὰ πίστεως^{EN175} and ἐπὶ τῇ πίστει^{EN176}. In Paul all these combinations indicate the place where and the manner in which man's relationship to the redemptive activity accomplished in the judgment and sentence of God, His δικαιοῦν^{EN177}, the δικαιοσύνη θεοῦ^{EN178} in its actuality, is known and accepted and apprehended, is in fact "realised" on the part of man. There is no instance of the combination δικ. διὰ τὴν πίστιν.^{EN179} This means that from the standpoint of biblical theology the root is cut of all the later conceptions which tried to attribute to the faith of man a merit for the attainment of justification or co-operation in its fulfilment, or to identify faith, its rise and continuance and inward and outward work with justification. The pardon of sinful man in the judgment is God's work. His δικαιοῦν^{EN180}, His δικαιοσύνη.^{EN181} Paul has not marked this off so sharply from any supposed or ostensible δικ. ἐκ νόμου^{EN182} or ἐν νόμῳ^{EN183} or ἐξ ἔργων^{EN184}, from any ἰδία δικ.^{EN185} (Rom. 10^{3}) or ἐμὴ δικ.^{EN186} (Phil. 3^{9}), from any justification of man by his own attitude and action, merely in order to accept this other human attitude and action, the work of faith, as the true means to create the right of man. As a human attitude and action faith stands over against the divine attitude and action described as δικαιοῦν^{EN187}, without competing with it, or preparing it, or anticipating it, or co-operating with it, let alone being identical with it. As far as I can see—the passage in 1 Cor. 12^{9} where πίστις^{EN188} is called one of the gifts of the Holy Spirit is not relevant—Paul nowhere says explicitly that there can be faith only on the basis of a divine work and gift. But if this is so, it is merely because it was for him the most self-evident presupposition. Yet even as grounded in the work and gift of God the work of faith is still a human work. And its part in the justification of man is that it alone is the human work—we can say this quite definitely in the sense of Paul—which is adapted, which corresponds on

---

EN170 righteousness
EN171 faith
EN172 righteousness of faith
EN173 of (the) faith
EN174 righteousness from faith
EN175 through faith
EN176 by faith
EN177 justifying
EN178 righteousness of God
EN179 righteousness by virtue of faith
EN180 justification
EN181 righteousness
EN182 righteousness by the law
EN183 in the law
EN184 by works
EN185 own righteousness
EN186 righteousness of mine
EN187 justification
EN188 faith

4. Justification by Faith Alone

the human side, to his divine justification. Not because of its intrinsic value. Not because of its particular virtue, or any particular power of its own. But because God accepts it as the human work which corresponds to His work. Because, according to the phrase adapted from Gen. 15^6 (Gal. 3^6, Rom. 4$^{3f.}$) it is "reckoned" ($\dot{\epsilon}\lambda o\gamma i\sigma\theta\eta$) to man by God as $\delta\iota\kappa\alpha\iota o\sigma \acute{\upsilon}\nu\eta$ [EN189], as a righteous human work, i.e., a work which corresponds to His righteousness. God recognises, not that by this action man fulfils a condition or attains something which makes him worthy of the divine pardon, but that in this action of man, and this action alone, His pardon actually comes fully into its own. God recognises that in this way, and only in this way, but in this way seriously and fully. His work and Word will be accepted, "realised" by man, that in this action of man to which He awakens and calls him, His own action has its counterpart and analogy—in Rom. 3^3 the one word $\pi i\sigma\tau\iota s$ [EN190] can denote both the action of God and the analogous human action. God recognises that in the man who is caught up in this action He meets the man who makes a faithful and authentic and adequate response to His own faithfulness; that He finds the man who does this, who believes, adapted to be the hearer and witness of His pardon. It is the good-pleasure of God which singles out from all others this particular human action. But by that good-pleasure it is, of course, radically singled out from all others. The election and calling of Abraham are manifested in the fact that he believes, and that his faith is imputed to him for righteousness. Thus far Paul.

As the doctrine of "justification by faith" (alone) this conception of Paul was rediscovered in the century of the Reformation, and as such it was both attacked and defended. It was understood and misunderstood on both sides and in the centre in the most diverse ways. And it finally became one of the most important (the most important of all in Lutheranism) of the basic doctrines of Evangelical Christendom. In our discussions up to this point we have concentrated all our attention upon the "objective" content of the doctrine of justification. The time has now come when we must turn to what has become this very important "subjective" side.

"Justification by faith" cannot mean that instead of his customary evil works and in place of all kinds of supposed good works man chooses and accomplishes the work of faith, in this way pardoning and therefore justifying himself. As his action, the action of sinful man, faith cannot do this. Nor does it make any odds whether a man means by faith a mere knowledge and intellectual understanding of the divine work and judgment and revelation and pardon (*notitia*[EN191]), or an assent of the mind and will to it, the acceptance as true of that which is proclaimed as the truth of this work of God (*assensus*[EN192]), or finally a heart's trust in the significance of this work for him (*fiducia*[EN193]). It is not in and with all this that a man justifies himself, that he pardons himself, that he sets himself in that transition from wrong to right, from death to life, that he makes himself the subject of that history, the history of redemption. There is always something wrong and misleading when the faith of a man is referred to as his way of salvation in contrast to his way in wicked works, or his true way of salvation in contrast to his way in the supposed good works of false faith and superstition. Faith is not an alternative to these

[616]

[EN189] righteousness
[EN190] faith
[EN191] knowledge
[EN192] assent
[EN193] trust

§ 61. *The Justification of Man*

other ways. It is not the way which—another Hercules at the crossroads—man can equally well choose and enter, which he can choose and enter by the same capacity by which he might go any other way. Even in the action of faith he is the sinful man who as such is not in a position to justify himself, who with every attempt to justify himself can only become the more deeply entangled in his sin. He is awakened and called to will and achieve this by the work of God (otherwise he certainly will not do it). But in so far as it is his own—as it must be—even in his faith he confirms and repeats himself. Even as a believer he can represent himself to God only as the one he is in virtue of his past, only with the request: "God be merciful to me, a sinner." If his faith is his justification, his pardon, if in faith he can recognise the man justified by God in his own person, if, because in his own person, he can see in the man justified by God the divine mystery of grace of the existence of all his fellow-men, he does not owe this in the very least to what he is and feels and thinks and says and does as a believing man. He is as little justified in faith as in his other good or evil works. He needs justification just as much in faith as anywhere else, as in the totality of his being. In relation to it, considering himself as a believer, he cannot see himself as justified, he cannot be certain of his own justification or of the justification of man in general and as such. In faith he will be no less aware of his transgression and need and shame than in his other states and achievements. The image of himself as a believer—in so far as he has time and the desire to concern himself with it—can only incite and impel him to that other request: "Lord, I believe; help thou mine unbelief" (Mk. 9^{24}). There is as little praise of man on the basis of his faith as on that of his works. For there is as little justification of man "by"—that is to say, by means of—the faith produced by him, by his treading the way of faith, by his achievement of the emotions and thoughts and acts of faith, by his whole consciousness of faith and

[617] life of faith, as there is a justification "by" any other works. Faith is not at all the supreme and true and finally successful form of self-justification. If it tried to be this, if man tried to believe with this purpose and intention and claim, then even if his faith was not a "dead" faith, even if it was a most "hearty" faith, even if it was a fiduciary faith most active in love, it would be the supreme and most proper form of his sin as the sin of pride. To play off a faith in which man thinks that he can and should pardon and justify himself against other attempts at self-justification in the form of fidelity to the Law and good works is not merely nonsensical. It is the enterprise and conduct of a Pharisaism which is the most evil Pharisaism of all: the Pharisaism of the publican. It may well happen that the most audacious man of works, the Christian or secular pietist or activist, will go back to his house justified rather than this man: not by his little works but because—who can tell?—there is perhaps behind his works in some hidden form a real faith which is completely lacking in the one who simply justifies himself in all his righteousness of faith. If it is in his real righteousness of faith that a Christian can and should boast, then he above all men must know better than this; he must not on any account regard it as his own; he

4. Justification by Faith Alone

must not on any account tread the way of self-righteousness as one who is justified by faith, but only the way of the real publican.

Of the Reformers Calvin made this distinction with particular sharpness. Faith as such cannot contribute anything to our justification: *nihil afferens nostrum ad conciliandum Dei gratiam*[EN194] (*Inst.* III, 13, 5). It is not a *habitus*[EN195]. It is not a quality of grace which is infused into man (on *Gal.* 3⁶; *C.R.* 50, 205). *La foi ne justifie pas entant que c'est une oeuvre que nous faisons*[EN196]. If we believe, we come to God quite empty (*vuides*), *non pas en apportant aucune dignité ni mérite à Dieu*[EN197]. God has to close His eyes to the feebleness of our faith, as indeed He does. He does not justify us *pour quelque excellence qu'elle ait en soy*[EN198], but *tellement que d'autant qu'elle défaut*[EN199]; only in virtue of what it lacks as a human work does He justify man (*Serm. on Gen.* 15; *C.R.* 23, 722 f.). For that reason there is no point in inquiring as to the completeness of our faith. Exegetes who understand the ἐλογίσθη[EN200] of Gen. 15⁶ as follows: *Abram a esté reputé preud'homme et que c'a esté une vertu à luy de croire à Dieu*[EN201] are condemned by Calvin quite freely and frankly: *ces chiens-là nous doivent bien estre abominables. Car voilà les blasphèmes les plus énormes que Satan puisse dégorger*[EN202] (*ib.* 688). As if there were nothing worse than this confusion! And, indeed, according to the fresh Reformation understanding of the Pauline justification by faith there could not be anything worse than this confusion. It is clear that if faith was to be a virtue, a power and an achievement of man, and if as such it was to be called a way of salvation, then the way was opened up for the antinomian and libertarian misunderstanding, the belief that a dispensation from all other works was both permitted and commanded. And the objection of Roman critics was only too easy, that in the Reformation *sola fide*[EN203] this one human virtue, power and achievement was wildly over-estimated at the expense of all others. Even at the present day there is still cause most definitely to repudiate this misinterpretation, for which the Pauline text is not in any sense responsible.

But what is faith? What is the meaning of it as the human action which makes a faithful and authentic and adequate response to the faithfulness of God, which does justice to the reality and existence of the justified man created by God's pardon, which meets with the divine approval in its suitability to this object, which is recognised and judged and accepted by Him as right, in which therefore the knowledge of justification is a genuinely and concretely human event? Let us say at once that there is more to be said of faith than that in it and by it man comes to his justification, to justification in general and as such, i.e., that he is aware and certain of it and of the happening of it as the work of God, of its application to his person, *pro me*[EN204], but to his person in

[618]

[EN194] bringing nothing of our own to procure the grace of God
[EN195] disposition
[EN196] Faith does not justify by virtue of being a work which we do
[EN197] not bringing to God any dignity or merit
[EN198] on account of some excellence with it has in itself
[EN199] on the basis that it lacks
[EN200] 'reckoned'
[EN201] Abraham has been reckoned righteous, and that belief in God was a virtue which he possessed
[EN202] those dogs must be an absolute abomination to us, for these are the most enormous blasphemies which Satan could vomit forth
[EN203] by faith alone
[EN204] for me

§ 61. *The Justification of Man*

solidarity with all men, and therefore for all men, *pro nobis*[EN205]. On this specific aspect faith is indeed the life of the Christian community and individual Christian life within the world and the human race in its totality. But the justification of sinful man, the restoration of his peace with God, is only one of the problems of the Christian life. And so faith has other dimensions than that of its relation to man's justification. It has other forms than that in which it is the knowledge, the apprehension, the realisation of the right addressed to man in the judgment and sentence of God. This is its centre. This is faith in the truest sense. But the centre has a circumference. We will return to this in the final section of this first part of the doctrine of reconciliation. For the moment our inquiry concerns its relation to the justification of man, or, to put it briefly and in a rather misleading way, justifying faith.

Now if we are going to answer this question we cannot avoid taking a few further steps along the way of criticism which we intimated at the very outset. If demythologising is anywhere necessary and demanded, it is at this point. Our very first task was to set aside *a limine*[EN206] a basic misunderstanding, to reject the idea that, in virtue of an inner quality of what the believing man does, faith is the real means which man can use to justify himself and himself to declare the divine pardon. In order to grasp the essential nature of the faith in which man comes to justification we must at once develop the principle underlying this rejection.

Faith, we have said, is wholly and utterly humility. To put it negatively, it takes place in faith that man's affirmation and approval of his pride, his satisfaction with it, is completely destroyed. Not that he will finally amend himself in faith. It is the sinful man, the proud man, who believes. But in believing he has nothing more to do with his pride, with himself as the proud man he is. He has no further use for himself as such. And therefore he has no use—primarily and finally—for any kind of pride of faith. Faith is the abdication of vain-glorious man from his vain-glory. We do not say, his liberation from it, its defeat and destruction. It would be the supreme triumph of vain-glorious man if he could just control his vain-glory, exercising it one minute and then suddenly or gradually shaking it off like the snow on his hat. That would be the new pride in which man would only show that he has not yet begun to believe. No, even in the believer we have to do with very vain-glorious man. The only thing is that—although he still exercises vain-glory—he has acquired a distaste, a radical and total distaste for it. The only thing is that he cannot find any more pleasure in what he does as vain-glorious man, that he despairs of himself as this man. He no longer expects anything of what he does as such. He sees the corruption of his utterly proud action. He sees that he will not attain what he continually hopes from it. He sees into what trouble it is bringing him, that at the end of all his vain-glorious ways—the vain-glorious ways of all men—

[EN205] for us
[EN206] from the outset

4. *Justification by Faith Alone*

disillusionment awaits him, ridicule, defeat, meaninglessness, indeed nonsense and contradiction, destruction, nothingness and death. He is under no misapprehension as to the fact that he still goes these ways, with their ever new and concealed turnings. The only thing is that now he cannot affirm and approve them, he cannot affirm and approve himself as he goes them. The fact that he believes means for him—this is how we must put it—that he has become a bankrupt sinner, a proud man humbled, a proud man who with a terrible certainty has become aware of the limitations of his pride, and therefore of the limitations of all his being and activity, his own limitations, who is forced to say No to his pride, and therefore to all his being and activity, and therefore to himself. It is a No which he cannot and will not fulfil, i.e., put into effect, of himself—otherwise he would not be despairing of self, but would again be regarding himself as unlimited. Yet it is a No which he cannot avoid saying, with which he simply has to live in self-negation as the man he is within these limits. This is a general and rather formal description of the critical work of faith. It is obvious that the man who does it cannot be uncritical of himself in relation to this work too, and therefore that as a believer—in face of his pride—he can only think humbly of this work of his in itself and as such.

Faith is not a self-chosen humility, like the Colossian error (Col. 2^{23}). It is not the humility of pessimism, scepticism, defeatism, misanthropy, a weariness with the world and oneself and life. These are possibilities which a man can choose for himself, and in fact often does choose. They cannot be substituted for the humility of faith. They differ from the humility of faith in this, that we need not surrender to them, that we can take courage and be persuaded against them, that with or without the help of clever psychology we can liberate ourselves from them or let them take their course. They differ from the humility of faith in the fact that there is nothing at all of humility in the man who lays hold of them, that they are simply particular forms of the same pride in which he might equally well choose the very opposite possibilities. As against that, choosing the humility of faith is not something which a man can either do or not do. And when he does choose it, it is not a form of his pride, but he admits that he is proud, and is ashamed of the fact.

But faith is not an enforced humility, an acquiescence, a withdrawal, a surrender which is imposed upon him by fate and circumstances. Such compulsion is not in any sense a guarantee that that to which man is compelled is true humility and not a pride which is for the time being somewhat intimidated and suppressed. And such compulsion has only the character of a negation, a deprivation and limitation which comes upon man, so that the apparent humility to which it gives rise is a passive and unwilling and therefore a joyless humility. The humility of faith, on the other hand, while it is a necessity for man, and not something which he can control, is still a matter of his free and, at bottom, joyful decision, even though it does consist in the fact that a man is dissatisfied with his own action, deeply mistrustful of his vain-glory and openly discontented with all his ways. But faith does not mean unhappiness—on the

[620]

§ 61. *The Justification of Man*

contrary. Humility has nothing to do with discouragement—on the contrary. And if others pity a man because he is humbled, they only show that they have completely misunderstood him. Their pity ought to be for themselves if they for their part know nothing of this humbling. The humility of faith is a genuine but a comforted despair. And it is better to despair in the comfort of this humility than to be comforted without its despair.

Faith is the humility of obedience. It is no accident that at this point we have to turn to the thought which is decisive for the christological view which we have followed throughout: the humble obedience of the Lord who for our sake became a servant. But for the moment we will keep this connexion in reserve. Let us conclude our provisional description. Faith differs from any mere thinking and believing and knowing, or indeed from any other trusting, in the fact that it is an obeying. For that reason its humility is neither a matter of our own choice nor of an outward compulsion. It is a free decision, but made with the genuine necessity of obedience. To put it the other way round, it is a necessary decision, but made with the necessity of a genuine and therefore a free obedience. For that reason the despair without which faith would not be faith is a comforted despair. On the one hand it is the believer's own self-affirmed self-despair: he cannot and does not want to be rid of it. He declines every suggestion for ridding himself of it. He refuses every mitigation of it. He believes in his own freedom when he accepts it, when he dares to live in and with it. But, on the other hand, it is not his own choice and invention. It is laid upon him. He is not responsible for it. He cannot on account of it justify himself either to himself or others. It is not his guilt. It does not belong to it. It is despair at his guilt, a despair in which he is lifted above his guilt—not by his own effort and contriving, but as it is laid upon him. He cannot let it be talked or taken away from him. He gives himself to it and he persists in it in obedience—and neither he himself nor anyone else can absolve him from this obedience. From both these sides—the humility of faith is the humility of obedience—it is not a wild and desperate despair but a comforted despair, *desperatio fiducialis*[EN207] (Luther).

We must bear all this in mind if we are to understand the great negation in the Pauline and Reformation doctrine of justification by faith, and especially Luther's *sola fide*[EN208]: the opposition of faith to all and every work; the two statements (1) that no human work as such either is or includes man's justification (not even the work of faith as such), but (2) that the believer is actually the man justified by God. This second and positive statement obviously needs to be worked out and established, and we must now address ourselves to this task. But clearly it can be meaningful only when the way is cleared for it by the first and negative statement, i.e., when the faith of the man justified by God is opposed to all his works (even the work which he does when he believes), and

---

[EN207] confident desperation
[EN208] 'by faith alone'

4. *Justification by Faith Alone*

opposed in such a way that there can be no returning to the view that his works might either be or include his justification. The one who is righteous by faith can only live in an atmosphere which is purified completely from the noxious fumes of the dream of other justifications. That is what Paul and the Reformers said in their negative statement.

The works to which they referred in this context are the thoughts and words and achievements of sinful man, including the works which he is able and willing and ready to do and produce as such in relation to the revelation of God and in obedience to His Law. The negative statement of Paul and the Reformers is that no human works, not even those which are demanded by the Law, which can be seriously expected of man and regarded as good, either are or include his justification. As works to advance his justification they are not expected of him and they are not good.

In this context Paul obviously meant by ἔργα[EN209] the works which the Old Testament demanded of the members of God's chosen people Israel to mark their distinction from other peoples or positively to attest the fact that they belonged to the covenant which He had made with them. He did not reject or under-estimate these works of the Law as such. According to accounts in the Acts of the Apostles, which it is better not to reject, he did himself, as a Christian and an apostle, occasionally perform such works. But—as he saw it, not in contradiction to, but in agreement with this Law, as a legitimate interpretation of it— he unconditionally rejected the idea that the doing of any of the works demanded by the Law either is or includes the justification of any sinner. And if, as the Galatian errorists taught, the fulfilment of the works of the Law is placed side by side with faith, as something which will justify a man, if it is commanded as a necessary completion of the work of faith, if it is to be laid and enforced upon Gentile believers as necessary, then this is judged to be an apostasy from faith and its radical denial. Faith is relentlessly opposed to the works of this Law, and Gentile believers are in practice forbidden to allow themselves to be won over to the doing of this Law, the introduction of circumcision, the keeping of the Sabbath, purifications, etc. This was an antithesis which could not come easily to a man who was not a stranger to the world of these works but quite at home in it if not bound by it. It is a complete misunderstanding to think that in Galatians and Romans and Philippians, and Colossians [622] too, he is involved in a wilful movement of emancipation and liberation, as do the Jews who hate him for it and the Liberals of all times who cannot sufficiently praise him. But, as contained in these Epistles, the message of this conservative and not at all revolutionary Jew of the dispersion was bound to have that ring once faith as the place at which man comes to justification was exposed to the rivalry of works, the works of that Law which to him was still and indeed only now genuinely holy. As he saw it, the Law was not at all given for this purpose. The justification of man cannot be accomplished or revealed by the fulfilment of its works. When this question arose, Paul could see only an Either-Or between faith and the works of the Law. And faced with this alternative he could see only one outcome—the rejection of all its works in favour of faith, and for Gentile Christians only faith and the works of faith, which cannot as such be considered as justifying works. The *sola fide*[EN210] does not actually occur in the Pauline texts. Yet it was not an importation into the texts, but a genuine

---

[EN209] works
[EN210] by faith alone

§ 61. *The Justification of Man*

interpretation of what Paul himself said without using the word *sola*^{EN211}, when Luther translated Rom. 3²⁸: "Therefore we conclude that a man is justified by faith alone without the deeds of the law." Say what we will about the possibility and the freedom and the right and the compulsion and the practical necessity of the doing of works—the works of the Law or the works of faith—according to Paul a man is not justified by the fact that he does these works, and therefore to that extent he is justified χωρὶς ἔργων νόμου^{EN212}, without them. And the faith by which a man is justified stands alone against this "without," even though it is not without works, even though it is a faith which "worketh by love" (Gal. 5⁶). But if he is not justified by the works of the holy Law of God, but by faith, then obviously he is justified only by faith, by faith alone, *sola fide*^{EN213}. The Reformers dared to see the situation in their own time in the light of the situation of Galatians, and therefore indirectly (and often very directly) to equate the Law of Israel with the cultic and general order of the late mediaeval Roman Church, the doing of its works with the achievements of the ostensible or actual piety of their contemporaries in correspondence with that order, the Galatian errorists with the exponents of the ecclesiastical doctrine of justification current in their day, and finally the apostle as the preacher of the faith which alone justifies—with themselves. We have only to read Luther's exposition of the Romans in 1516, and especially his commentary on Galatians in the definitive form of 1535, to see to what extent exposition and application—this exposition—intermingle with one another almost from the very first verses of the New Testament text to the very last. And fundamentally the same is true of the commentaries of Calvin, who was a much more careful exegete, and who occasionally at least did bring out the difference between the two ages. The risk involved in this kind of *explicatio*^{EN214} and *applicatio*^{EN215} was a very big one. The strength of Reformation theology is the directness with which it tried to place itself under Scripture and listen to it and allow it to speak, the power with which it dug out its buried centre, allowing it to illuminate the tangle of corruptions and new beginnings, the dissolution of old and the development of new ties in its own day, the courage in that light to decide with God and to call for decisions in the name of God. But this very strength was perhaps its weakness—a too hasty identification of the biblical situation with its own, and therefore as a result of its own impetuous understanding of the present a failure to see many of the nuances, and the other aspects and parts of the biblical texts, or conversely, because of its impetuous exposition of the texts, a lack of many, of the necessary nuances and differentiations in its judgment of the present. Only those who have tried to understand and expound the Bible, and especially Paul as a man of his own day, only those who have happily escaped the dangers which threaten us on these two sides (exposition and application), are entitled to cast the first stone. Certainly in Galatians (not to speak of other parts of Paul's writings and of Scripture generally) there were and are many more things to be discovered than what Luther discovered then. Certainly there was and is much more to be said of the Roman Church and Roman theology both then and since than what the Reformers said then within the *schema* of Galatians. We do not need to consider ourselves bound either in the one respect or in the other by their attitude.

But in the relationship between the original and Reformation Paulinism there is one very important thing which is unaffected by any doubts we may have about Reformation exegesis. For it cannot well be denied that it was only at the time of the 16th century Reformation that, if not the whole of the New Testament or the whole of Paul, at least Paul in his conflict

---

^{EN211} alone
^{EN212} apart from the works of the law
^{EN213} by faith alone
^{EN214} exposition
^{EN215} application

4. *Justification by Faith Alone*

with Judaism in the Church, was again understood at all adequately and sympathetically. From its very beginnings in the 2nd century the Catholic Church did not understand this Paul (with the exception of Marcion who misunderstood him). At a later date even Augustine, the only name we can consider, did not understand him as the Reformers did. He did not understand the principle underlying the Pauline distinction of faith and works. He did not understand the passion of the antithesis, of the mutual exclusiveness with which he viewed the two. He did not understand the bearing of the antithesis on the exposition either of faith or works or especially of justification itself. How could Augustine—and in his wake all Catholic exegesis and dogmatics—possibly have understood justification as a process which is fulfilled in the human subject, allowing it simply to begin with faith and to be completed with the infused grace of love, if he had had before him the contrast of Galatians as it revealed itself afresh to Luther? The most primitive post-apostolic Church had moved too far away from the world of the Old Testament, and conversely it had too quickly become a doublet of the community and order of the Old Testament, to be able to adopt the Pauline view of the Law as the order of life which is revealed and holy but of no value at all for the justification of man. A detour was necessary to rediscover what the Law did and did not mean for Paul. The Reformers—and in the first instance Luther—had to be confronted by the problem of another order of life, the order of life and the redemptive system of the Roman Church, which was there and was administered and imposed on mediaeval man with a claim to justifying power, which introduced man to the outworking of that process. These are exegetical points—I am mentioning only the most important in our narrower context—the illumination of which by Reformation theology we cannot very well deny, no matter how arbitrary that theology may have been in matters of detail.

Even in its application of the Pauline insights to the contemporary scene, we have to note that it cost Luther in particular no less than it did Paul to win through to his understanding of the "Law" as we find it in his writings—to the most radical departure from the view that man can and must attain his justification as a sinner by the fulfilment of the works prescribed by the Law. The Law was for him primarily and concretely the demand of the monkish regulations which had become obligatory by reason of his oath. He had expected his justification by the observance of these regulations no less seriously than Paul had once expected his by the observance of the Law of Moses. And by Law in its wider sense he meant the whole structure of duties with which the Church had surrounded the way to the sacraments and their reception and therefore access to the grace of God, the life which is well pleasing to God within the framework of the *corpus christianum*[EN216]. With Luther, too, it was not a repudiation of this Law as such, nor was it a demand for freedom in opposition to it, which led him to his doctrine of justification by faith alone. By nature Luther was even more conservative than Paul. And the situation was even more complicated for him than it was for Paul to the extent that what the Law meant for him was normative as the Law of the Church of Christ and therefore as the Law of faith, e.g., the monkish oaths were an exposition of the evangelical sayings, the system of indulgences, which brought about an open breach was an exposition of the evangelical summons to repentance, and the ecclesiastical and especially the papal authority which guaranteed the whole was the authority of the Lord and His apostles which it was never his intention to repudiate. It is common knowledge with what hesitancy he won through to the perception that all this was not the Law of Christ and the Gospel, that it was not the holy and just and good Law of God as Paul had seen it in the Law of Israel. It is common knowledge with what reluctance he first stood out against this supposed Law of God except in so far as it was a matter of remedying palpable abuses, and with what anxious and, to those near and rather more distant from him, almost painful reserve he

[624]

[EN216] Christian society

§ 61. *The Justification of Man*

time and again confessed that he had no interest in, indeed that he was opposed to, the contesting of this Law as such. To the Law and its works he did not really oppose freedom but (even in his proclamation of the *libertas Christiana*[EN217]) faith. It is wrong to censure him, and a grotesque misunderstanding to applaud him, as a Liberal. And in this respect Zwingli and Calvin, too, were fundamentally in agreement. They did not come as he did from the cloister, but from a pious humanism. By nature they were much less conservatively inclined. They were never so attached as Luther to the whole idea of the *corpus christianum*[EN218]. But in attitude, doctrine and action they were the very reverse of arbitrary innovators. It was not by a boldly snatched inspiration, or a sudden insight, or, as it were, a flick of the wrist that any of the Reformers—Melanchthon seems to come relatively the nearest—made the step from the exposition of Paul to the contemporary application, thus adopting his position and making his doctrine the lever for their own reforming enterprise.

And above all, in relation to this aspect of the matter, we can only maintain that the reaction of the Roman Church and theology to the doctrine of justification as presented by the Reformers in succession to Paul did allow that the Reformers were in the right at least to this extent, that in the opposition to them there is no sign of any understanding of the Paul of Galatians and Romans, or of the antithesis and exclusiveness of faith and works which he there develops in the question of justification.

Among the more notable Romanist theologians of the 16th century there were a few of whom it can be said that they did at least hear and understand the thesis of the Reformers and tried to treat it seriously. I will cite as an example Cardinal Caspar Contarini, who at the time of the colloquy of Ratisbon around 1541 wrote a treatise, *De iustificatione*, in which he tried to consider and present the matter, as it were, on two different levels: a first, on which to the great offence of his own party he described it in propositions which Luther himself might almost have written; and a second on which his expositions moved along the usual lines of contemporary Romanist theology. As he saw it, the righteousness of the justified man is at one and the same time one which is imputed to him, the righteousness of Christ which can be apprehended only in faith, and an inherent righteousness which has to be put into effect in works of charity. His intention was that precedence should be expressly given to the first aspect over the second. It is not surprising that both parties accused him of temporising. And although he ought to be mentioned here, he did not found any school, and it was only perhaps his early death which saved him from ecclesiastical censure. The Church was not willing to learn anything in this matter but only to continue unaltered, and that is what it did.

The Roman Church adopted an official attitude to the Reformation teaching in the decree of the Council of Trent on justification (*Sess.* VI, 1547). And, unfortunately, we have to admit that in this decree it laid down its attitude for all time. The decree itself is theologically a clever and in many respects a not unsympathetic document which has caused superficial Protestant readers to ask whether there might not be something to say for it. But if we study it more closely it is impossible to conceal the fact that not even the remotest impression seems to have been made upon its exponents by what agitated the Reformers or, for that matter, Paul himself in this whole question of faith and works. Even more depressing is the reason for this lack of understanding: that what was not only to the Reformers but to Paul the climax of justification in its character as a divine work for man was to them a completely unknown quantity. Otherwise how could they possibly have described the death of Christ as the mere *causa meritoria*[EN219] of justification (*c.* 7), transferring justification itself into the

---

[EN217] Christian liberty
[EN218] body of Christ
[EN219] meritorious cause

4. Justification by Faith Alone

sphere of the Church which controls sacramental grace on the one hand, and of the believer who makes use of the Church's means of grace on the other? How could they possibly have described it as a process in the man who enjoys the blessings of the Church's redemptive system and fulfils its demands? What was this but the very idea which Paul had contested so vehemently, that there is a justification which can be attained in the sphere of the institution of the Law by the accomplishment of its provisions? Does it sufficiently mark off the happening envisaged in the Tridentinum from that to which Paul so sharply opposed justification by faith that in the former it is set under the sign of the *meritum Christi*[EN220] and the stipulation of infused grace? Where in Paul—not only the Paul of Galatians but Paul generally—do we find anything like the *gratia praeveniens*[EN221] in virtue of which even before a man believes and is baptised he is set in motion *ad convertendum se ad suam iustificationem*[EN222], that is, to the "disposing " (*c.* 5 and *can.* 4–5) of himself for grace as his own *liberum arbitrium*[EN223], which has only been weakened (*c.* 1), assenting to it and co-operating with it (*assentiendo et cooperando*[EN224])? Does Paul know anything of a natural man who, by reason of this *gratia praeveniens*[EN225], is in a position to accept the revelations and promises of God, out of fear of Him to turn to His mercy, to trust in the goodness addressed to him *propter Christum*[EN226], to begin to love Him, to hate and despise his sins and to repent, and finally to ask for baptism and a new life and obedience (*c.* 6)? And could Paul possibly have described baptism as the *causa instrumentalis*[EN227] of what he called δικαιοσύνη[EN228], as the Council of Trent does (*c.* 7)? Is there in Paul anything like a sacramentally infused and therefore inherent righteousness (*c.* 16)? Could he have described true Christian faith as a mere *initium salutis*[EN229] (*c.* 8) and therefore as something which needs to be filled out in relation to justification? Could he have forbidden it to a Christian as a *vana et omni pietati remota fiducia*[EN230], the very words of the Tridentinum (*c.* 9), to cling in faith and to find comfort in the fact that his sins are forgiven? Could he have regarded it as a "heretical and schismatic" opinion that Christian faith has an unconditional and not a conditional assurance of this, and that so far as it does not have this unconditional assurance it is not the true Christian faith which justifies a man? Where did he ever say, and how could he possibly have said, that (*c.* 9) although the Christian ought not to doubt the mercy of God, the merits of Christ and the power of the sacraments, yet in view of his own *infirmitas*[EN231] and *indispositio*[EN232] even in faith there can be no absolute assurance *de sua gratia*[EN233], in the question whether there is grace for him? Above all, where did he ever bring the sanctification of a Christian and his justification into the relationship which forms the substance of the positive teaching of the Tridentinum: that justification is only completed in sanctification, in the doing of the good and meritorious works provoked and made possible and accomplished by the grace of justification (*c.* 16)—a grace which only begins with the forgiveness of sins (*c.* 7)? Where did he ever say, and how could he possibly say, that faith justifies a man in so far as it works by love? How could he

---

[EN220] merit of Christ
[EN221] prevenient grace
[EN222] to turning himself to his own justification
[EN223] free will
[EN224] in assenting and co-operating
[EN225] prevenient grace
[EN226] on account of Christ
[EN227] instrumental cause
[EN228] righteousness
[EN229] beginning of salvation
[EN230] trust, apart from every vain piety
[EN231] weakness
[EN232] indisposition
[EN233] of grace for himself

§ 61. The Justification of Man

possibly speak of an *incrementum*^{EN234} or *augmentum*^{EN235} of the grace of justification by the practice of love, by the accomplishment of certain works, which carries with it an augmentation of the glory to be expected in eternity (*c.* 10 and *can.* 24 and 32)? Or finally of a repetition of justification—the actual phrase is *rursus iustificari*^{EN236}—in view of the situation of a fall from grace which constantly arises in practice in the life of every Christian, a repetition which has to take place in the sacrament of penance by means of priestly absolution and the annexed satisfactions on the part of the one who is restored to grace (*c.* 14)? Is not all this in effect a very exact parallel to the whole institution and enterprise in face of which, in the matter of man's justification, Paul gave to faith that isolated and exclusive position? Does it not mean that in spite of Gal. 2^{16} there is "flesh" which is justified by "the works of the law"? The decisive polemical sentence of the Tridentinum is as follows: *Anathema sit*^{EN237}, whoever maintains, *fidem iustificantem nihil aliud esse quam fiduciam divinae misericordiae peccata remittentis propter Christum, vel eam fidem solam esse, qua iustificamur*^{EN238} (*can.* 12). Now Paul certainly spoke of love and hope as well as faith, and if our thinking is to be Pauline we must follow him in this. But in the matter of man's justification he spoke only of faith. And if faith undoubtedly has for him other dimensions than that in which in relation to man's justification it is *fiducia divinae misericordiae peccata remittentis propter Christum*^{EN239}, yet there can also be no doubt that in the contexts in which he connects δικαιοσύνη ^{EN240} and πίστις ^{EN241} faith is just this and nothing but this: the confidence of sinful man in the demonstration of the undeserved faithfulness of God as given in Jesus Christ, a demonstration in which he finds that his sins are forgiven. If there is any corresponding faithfulness of sinful man to the faithful God, it consists only in this confidence. As he gives God this confidence, he finds himself justified, but not otherwise. That was what the Reformers maintained.

They did not have the unequivocal backing of Paul for all their statements. But they undoubtedly had it for this statement. If the Roman Church of the time had been circumspect but open, it could have pointed to certain undeniable gaps in the Reformers' understanding of Paul and the Bible generally; but for its own part it would have been ready to learn from this statement of Reformation theology, thus taking the initiative in the comprehensive reformation of the whole Church (and its better unification). But by placing this statement under anathema it placed itself under the ἀνάθεμα ἔστω ^{EN242} with which Paul was ready to defend himself in Gal. 1$^{8f.}$ even against an angel from heaven, if he chanced to preach any other gospel than that which he himself championed against the Galatian errorists in this letter. It is difficult to see in the Tridentine doctrine of justification anything better than what Paul meant by another gospel. It has no light from above. It is admirably adapted to serve as a touchstone to show where we all stand in the matter. There are Protestant doctrines of justification—we will not enter into them now—which do not pass this test because they themselves are far too Tridentine. The aim of that Council was to be a reforming Council, and in many of its practical decisions this is what it actually was. But with its doctrine of justification the Roman Church closed the door to self-reformation and

---

^{EN234} increase
^{EN235} augment
^{EN236} 'justified again'
^{EN237} Let him be anathema
^{EN238} that justifying faith is nothing other than trust in the divine mercy which forgives sins on account of Christ, or that it is that faith alone by which we are justified
^{EN239} trust in the divine mercy which forgives sins on account of Christ
^{EN240} righteousness
^{EN241} faith
^{EN242} let him be anathema

4. Justification by Faith Alone

deprived itself of all possibility of seizing the initiative in uniting the divided Church. It was impossible for the Evangelical Churches to return to fellowship with Rome when the decisive point of dispute was handled in this way. They could not surrender truth to unity. This reaction of the Roman Church was convincing proof that the Reformation application of the Pauline (and not only the Pauline) texts to the contemporary situation was both meaningful and necessary here at the very heart of the tragic controversy, and that it will remain so—seeing that the Roman Church cannot very well go back on that decree. A Church which maintains that its official decisions are infallible can commit errors which are irreformable. It has more than once done so.

We have said that justifying faith, the faith which recognises and apprehends man's justification, is the obedience of humility. We have also said that in relation to man's justification it excludes all works. When it is a matter of the recognising and apprehending of justification, it denies the competence, the relevance, the power and the value of all human action. The two propositions mutually condition and determine each other. We can and must interpret them in the light of each other. [627]

Because faith is obedient humility, abnegation, it will and must exclude any co-operation of human action in the matter of man's justification. It will and must be alone in this matter. It will and must be only faith. If it hesitated to be this, if in the recognising and apprehending of justification it tried to base itself on any human action which takes place either before faith or in faith or as a result of faith, it would cease to be obedience; it would cease to be the humility of obedience. It would be trying to be something more and better than man's comforted despair, comforted because as the decision of obedience it is both free and necessary. There would be no real renunciation and No to pride, no real distaste for it, seeing that in addition to the fact that he believes man would still be leaning and relying on himself. If all works are not excluded and do not continue to be excluded in this matter, he cannot and will not attain to the recognising and apprehending of his justification in his faith.

But, again, this proud isolation of faith, the *sola fide*[EN243] and therefore the exclusion of all competing works can have meaning and truth only in the fact that it is based upon the humility of faith. There can be no question of any arbitrary defiance, of any titanic self-assertion of man even in this form. And therefore human works as such cannot be regarded with contempt or indifference, and rejected. They are the (in itself) inevitable and good actualisation of the (in itself) good creaturely nature of man. They can and must be done. And faith itself would not be faith if it did not work by love, if it were not as Luther put it "a living, active, busy thing." The resignation, distaste, negation and despair of humility do not relate to man's activity as such but to the pride which is at work in all his activity. We recall that the humility of faith can have nothing

---

[EN243] by faith alone

§ 61. *The Justification of Man*

to do with pessimism, scepticism, defeatism and the like. Nor can the exclusion of works on the basis of this humility have anything to do with indifferentism, quietism or libertinism. We have to see to it that we are not led astray by suspicions and objections at this point, so that we fall back again into the error of works. As Rom. 6 shows, such suspicions and objections were raised already against Paul's own preaching of faith and justification. We also have to see to it, of course, that we do not think and speak and live in ways which give substance to these objections and suspicions. Where there is justification, there is also sanctification. Where there is faith, there are also love and works. The man who, justified by faith, has peace with God has also peace with his neighbour and himself. That he lives as one who is righteous by faith to the exclusion of all works is something that he will establish and attest in his works—the particular doctrine of justification that we find in the Epistle of James. If in relation to justification no work is important and every work indifferent, in relation to this confirmation every work is important and none indifferent. It cannot be otherwise if it is really in the humility of faith (not in something arbitrary) that he has the certainty and joy of faith, and in faith of justification.

But we must now go deeper. We have described faith as the humility which involves necessarily the exclusion of works. In so doing we have obviously described it in its negative form. We must now face up to the question of its positive form. But this is a question which we cannot answer until we see why it must first of all and above all have this negative form.

How is it that many writers could describe it, and had to describe it, as an empty outstretched hand? How is it that Calvin described it as an empty vessel, as man's *exinanitio*[EN244] before God (*Inst.* III, 11, 7), as a *res mere passiva, nihil afferens nostrum*[EN245] (*ibid.* 13, 5)? How is it that we find such trenchant statements as: *Dieu besogne en telle sorte qu'il n'y a rien de nostre costé*[EN246] (*C.R.* 23, 706)? Or: over against the *misericordia*[EN247] of God to which man must cling in faith there stands nothing but the *miseria*[EN248] of man, who can meet God only as *prorsus nudus et vacuus*[EN249] (*Inst.* III, 11, 16)? Luther put it in much the same way: "I must go out naked from all service, works and merit" (*Pred. üb.* Ex. 19[14f.], *W.A.* 16, 420, 12). We may also recall a verse which Zinzendorf wrote as the prolegomenon to his famous song, "Go forth ... " It runs as follows:

> "Rise up, rise up, O Zion, rise in thy misery
> And poverty and dust, and thine will be the day.
> Have nothing, but believe,
> That the Lord, the soul's true husband, can be thy stay."

Was it really such a new and strange and shocking thing when in my exposition of the

---

[EN244] emptying
[EN245] things purely passive, bringing nothing of our own
[EN246] God requires it such that there is nothing on our side
[EN247] mercy
[EN248] misery
[EN249] utterly naked and empty

4. Justification by Faith Alone

Epistle to the Romans in 1921 I described faith as a "vacuum"? Do we not have to describe it in this way too? Yet why do we have to describe it in this way—negatively?

One thing is certain, that as an abstract admission of human weakness and nothingness such statements cannot have any meaning as a self-confession of the faith which according to 1 Jn. 5^4 is the victory which overcometh the world. That we are good for nothing is true, but it is not so relevant that the confession of this truth has independent significance. Nor can the negative form of faith, faith as a vacuum, be asserted as a singular magnifying of the glory of God, as though that glory were the greater the less man is before it, and greatest of all when man is absolutely nothing. It is significant even for the negative form of faith that it is faith in God. Before God man is not nothing but something, someone. God is far from finding pleasure in the nothingness of man as such. Above all, we do not have here a directive to mystical self-emptying, to entrance into the night of quiescence, of silence, of an artificial anticipation of death: not even (and more especially not) when such experiments appeal expressly to the example of the death and passion of Christ and are portrayed as the mystic's imitation of this event. Certainly there is an imitation of this event in faith. But it is a return to the conception of a faith which justifies man [629] *per se*^{EN250} if the imitation of the work of Christ is described as a work which man can do to attain his own justification, as a task which is laid upon him in this sense; if therefore the basis of the humility of faith, and of its exclusiveness in face of every work, is sought in the necessity of this self-emptying, in a theology of the *imitatio Christi*^{EN251} which understands itself in this way. There is nothing, nothing at all, to justify the belief that God has created us for the practice of this self-emptying, or that it has to be recognised and adopted as the way to reconciliation with God. When a man ventures to make this experiment, where does he find himself but in the enclosed circle of his proud being and activity? If faith in its negative form is indeed an emptying, then it is certainly an emptying of all the results of such practices of self-emptying. It begins at the point where all the works of man are at an end, including his quiescence and silence and anticipatory dying. Christian faith is the day whose dawning means the end of the mystical night.

Christian faith has this negative form of renunciation because positively it is the appropriate response to what at the beginning of this section we described as the self-demonstration of the man justified by God. It is this self-demonstration of his justification which in faith a man recognises and accepts as true and certain, to which in faith he clings as he has to cling to it, as he can alone cling to it. The appropriate response to this self-demonstration of his righteousness can only be the humility which regards it as adequate and indeed perfect and therefore exclusively adequate, in which all the weapons and instruments and keys with which he might try to demonstrate to himself

---

^{EN250} of itself
^{EN251} imitation of Christ

§ 61. *The Justification of Man*

his justification fall away of themselves, in which all the gadgets and engines which he might have invented and constructed for this purpose come to a halt of themselves, in which he of himself renounces the invention and construction of any further devices of this nature, in which he is ready to let this self-demonstration of his righteousness speak for itself, and simply to be the hearer of it and obedient to it. And because it is a matter of the triumphing of this self-demonstration over him, faith has to have this negative form; it has to be humble obedience to the exclusion of all his own works.

But the self-demonstration of the justified man to which faith clings is the crucified and risen Jesus Christ who lives as the author and recipient and revealer of the justification of all men. It is in Him that the judgment of God is fulfilled and the pardon of God pronounced on all men. In the second and third sections of this part, and therefore in our whole description of the term justification, we have been speaking of Him and therefore of justified man, of His history and therefore of our own, of His transition from the past to the future, from sin to right, from death to life, and therefore of ours, of His present and therefore of ours. It happened that in the humble obedience of the Son He took our place, He took to Himself our sins and death in order to make an end of them in His death, and that in so doing He did the right, He became the new and righteous man. It also happened that in His resurrection from the dead He was confirmed and recognised and revealed by God the Father as the One who has done and been that for us and all men. As the One who has done that, in whom God Himself has done that, who lives as the doer of that deed, He is our man, we are in Him, our present is His, the history of man is His history, He is the concrete event of the existence and reality of justified man in whom every man can recognise himself and every other man—recognise himself as truly justified. There is not one for whose sin and death He did not die, whose sin and death He did not remove and obliterate on the cross, for whom He did not positively do the right, whose right He has not established. There is not one to whom this was not addressed as his justification in His resurrection from the dead. There is not one whose man He is not, who is not justified in Him. There is not one who is justified in any other way than in Him—because it is in Him and only in Him that an end, a bonfire, is made of man's sin and death, because it is in Him and only in Him that man's sin and death are the old thing which has passed away, because it is in Him and only in Him that the right has been done which is demanded of man, that the right has been established to which man can move forward. Again, there is not one who is not adequately and perfectly and finally justified in Him. There is not one whose sin is not forgiven sin in Him, whose death is not a death which has been put to death in Him. There is not one whose right has not been established and confirmed validly and once and for all in Him. There is not one, therefore, who has first to win and appropriate this right for himself. There is not one who has first to go or still to go in his own virtue and strength this way from there to here, from yesterday to to-morrow, from dark-

4. *Justification by Faith Alone*

ness to light, who has first to accomplish or still to accomplish his own justification, repeating it when it has already taken place in Him. There is not one whose past and future and therefore whose present He does not undertake and guarantee, having long since accepted full responsibility and liability for it, bearing it every hour and into eternity. There is not one whose peace with God has not been made and does not continue in Him. There is not one of whom it is demanded that he should make and maintain this peace for himself, or who is permitted to act as though he himself were the author of it, having to make it himself and to maintain it in his own strength. There is not one for whom He has not done everything in His death and received everything in His resurrection from the dead.

Not one. That is what faith believes. And in believing that it is justifying faith, i.e., a faith which knows and grasps and realises the justification of man as the decision and act and word of God. It is faith in Jesus Christ, who was crucified and raised again for us—faith in Him as the One in whom our judgment has taken place, our pardon has been pronounced. Faith comes about where Jesus Christ prevails on man, and in Jesus Christ the self-demonstration of the justified man. Faith knows Him and apprehends Him. It lets itself be told and accepts the fact and trusts in it that Jesus Christ is man's justification. It affirms and receives the fact that He is for us, that our redemptive history—that of all men and every man—has taken place in Him. The believer looks to Him and in Him to himself and his fellow-man of every age and clime, both near and distant, to find in Him their righteousness before God, their yesterday and to-morrow, their end, their beginning, their pardon, their peace with God, the whole reality which is the subject of the 23rd Psalm, and therefore man's justification. [631]

It is this positive aspect which makes the negative form of faith so necessary. For because it is faith in Jesus Christ, it can be true and living faith only as the humility of obedience; it has to be an empty hand, an empty vessel, a vacuum. It can be said of the believer at all times and in all circumstances: "What hast thou that thou didst not receive?" (1 Cor. 4^7), and: "By the grace of God I am what I am" (1 Cor. 15^{10}). What is he in relation to Jesus Christ, to his own justification as it is an event in Him, except the recipient of it living by the grace of God? He believes that Jesus Christ, and in Him God, is for him. But if Jesus Christ, and in Him God, is for him, of what importance are all the thoughts and words and attitudes and enterprises and achievements in which he tries to be for himself? He cannot expect anything from them, from his works, as far as the attainment of his justification is concerned. If he looks to Jesus Christ, to the event of his own redemptive history as it has taken place in Him, how can he also look to himself and his works? what interest can he have in them? how can he expect and claim that in them and therefore in himself there is, as it were, a little redemptive history, the completion, the continuation, the real fulfilment of the great history which has taken place in Jesus Christ? If he believes in Him, he knows and grasps his own righteousness as

§ 61. *The Justification of Man*

one which is alien to him, as the righteousness of this other, who is justified man in his place, for him. He will miss his own righteousness, he will fall from it, if he thinks he can and should know and grasp and realise it in his own acts and achievements, or in his faith and the result of it. He will be jeopardising, indeed he will already have lost, the forgiveness of his sins, his life as a child of God, his hope of eternal life, if he ever thinks he can and should seek and find these things anywhere but at the place where as the act and work of God they are real as the forgiveness of his sins, as his divine sonship, as his hope, anywhere but in the one Jesus Christ. To the extent that he tries to rely on himself and man and the will and achievement of man, he will be forced to despair of himself and man. For he himself, the man on whom he can rely, is not here but there, in that One. He lives in His history. He must be sought and found in Him. Faith ceases to be faith, it becomes its opposite, unbelief, hating and despising God, rejection, the crucifying afresh of the One in whom He gave Himself for us, if it looks anywhere but to Him, if the believer tries to look at himself and to rely and trust on his own activity and accomplishment. We have already eliminated the false bases of the *sola fide*[EN252], the exclusiveness of faith. We will not return to this. But the true basis is the exclusiveness of the One in whom faith believes. What is the *sola fide*[EN253] but a faint yet necessary echo of the *solus Christus?*[EN254] He alone is the One in whom man is justified and revealed to be justified. He alone has fulfilled the penitence in which the conversion of man to God is actually and definitively accomplished. He alone has prayed in Gethsemane: "Thy will be done." He alone has judged the world by letting Himself be judged by it and for it. He alone has shown Himself the One who in our place has destroyed the old and brought in the new. He alone was the One who was able to do this, who was sent into the world to do it, who was ordained to do it from all eternity as the Son of the Father. He alone as such is raised again from the dead and lives and rules as the man who exists for all others and justifies them all in His own person, at every moment of time, and then to all eternity. He alone: no creature either in heaven or on earth beside Him; no man who is justified in and of himself or otherwise than in Him; no man in whom the justified man can give that self-demonstration of his existence and reality. He gives it, but He alone. And because faith is faith in Him, for that reason it is justifying faith only in that isolation. For that reason it spurns and rejects the rivalry and co-operation of any attempts of man to bring about his own conversion to God, to try to accomplish of himself the destruction of the old and the introduction of the new, of right and life, the evening of the past and the dawning of the future. This is forbidden and prevented by the object of faith, by that to which it looks, and clings, by which it lives, in which it rejoices, by which it is continually renewed, in which it has its basis as faith. In

---

[EN252] by faith alone
[EN253] by faith alone
[EN254] Christ alone

4. Justification by Faith Alone

His own isolation Jesus Christ directs faith in Him into the same isolation; He gives to it the defiance in which it wills to be alone as the reception of the divine pardon, as the assurance of the forgiveness of sins, the divine sonship and the hope of eternal life, in which it wills to be nothing but pure trust in the effective and manifest mercy and gracious act of God, and therefore trust in the good right of man. It is impossible to see how the *solus Christus*[EN255], the *sola iustitia Christi*[EN256] can have any other correlative than the *fides Christi*[EN257] as the *sola fides*[EN258], which absolutely excludes any other helpers or helps, the faith which will constantly renew itself in this exclusion, the faith which will always have the character of humble obedience and which in this humble obedience will defy all competition. If we have even the remotest idea of what is meant by positive faith, we cannot try to have or state it otherwise. We will always think of faith and works as strict alternatives in this particular context.

[633]

In this light, what else is there to say concerning the positive form of justifying faith? It has this positive form. Or, rather, its form as humble obedience, in which it is renunciation, openness to its object and therefore faith in Jesus Christ, is in the last resort negative only in appearance. As openness to this object, as the knowing and grasping of the alien righteousness of Jesus Christ, it can be only a maintaining of that humble obedience, a comforted despair, in so far as it is a human form of being, a human act and experience. But what does "only" mean when the object with which the believer has to do, the object which encounters him and is encountered by him, is Jesus Christ and his own justification in Him? when it is from this point that he is plunged into this comforted despair? Certainly all vain-glory is excluded in this encounter. But a quite different glory is promised. This encounter obviously means the end of all reliance on man, of all dependence on his own resources, of all anxiety concerning himself, of all worry about making the decision which means his conversion to God, of all responsibility for this decision. Faith means that man can be, in virtue of the object of faith and therefore of Jesus Christ, because he really is in Him, because his true history has taken place in Him. Faith means that at every moment and in every situation man can rely on the fact that the movement between God and man which has taken place in Jesus Christ has taken place in supreme reality for him and therefore is his movement. Faith means that man can have confidence in relation to this alien righteousness fulfilled there in Jesus Christ with a twofold reference, to yesterday and to-morrow. It is his righteousness fulfilled with this same twofold reference. The Now of Jesus Christ is his Now. Everything depends on the fact that faith is not empty in so far as it does not look into the void, in so far as it is not directed at the formless mystery of something supernatural, but has this concrete object. Everything depends on the fact that it is being in encounter with the

---

[EN255] Christ alone
[EN256] justification alone of Christ
[EN257] faith in Christ
[EN258] faith alone

§ 61. *The Justification of Man*

living Jesus Christ, a being from and to this object. That is what is meant by Christian faith. That is the meaning of the form of being, the act and experience in which man can believe in response to the Christian message. He knows and affirms and understands himself in Christian faith, not in the abstraction of his being for himself—he is not for himself but Jesus Christ is for him—but from and to what he is in Jesus Christ. He is what he is in so far as this One is for him. He knows and affirms and understands himself in the light and power of the promise which is given thereby. He accepts this promise, and in such a way that he refers it to himself and therefore to all his fellows. He looks away from everyone and everything else to this promise. He bows to the judgment accomplished in virtue of it. He accepts the pardon pronounced in it on himself and all men. He dares to live as one on whom this judgment has passed, to whom this pardon applies. He dares to consider all other men in the light of the fact that this judgment has been passed on them, this pardon applies to them. He makes a legitimate use of this pardon which is plain to understand as it applies to himself and all men, as it is heard by himself and all men. He knows that he is free *realiter*[EN259]: free from the old which has passed, free for the new which is coming. Faith is the liberation which comes to man in encounter with Jesus Christ in whom God is for him. The man who believes knows that he has not come to God but God has come to him, that he has done nothing for God but God has done for him not only that which is necessary but far more, that He has come to his side and indeed taken his place as a brother, that He has set him right, that He has drawn him irrevocably to Himself. Faith is life in the freedom which is given thereby, on the basis of the right order which is created thereby. Faith can never be anything else but a venture. Faith can never be lived except in a Notwithstanding: notwithstanding all that man finds himself and his fellow-men to be, notwithstanding all that he and his fellow-men may try to do. But it is lived in the Notwithstanding which has its basis in the divine Therefore of its object, in the existence and reality of the justified man in the one Jesus Christ. It is simply the venture of obedience and therefore of the deepest humility, which is the only thing possible in face of the self-demonstration of justified man. But ventured in this relationship, and therefore in this humility, it is the being of sinful man in which he finds that he is really and truly justified, that his sins are forgiven, that he is a child of God, and an heir of the hope of eternal life, but in which there also opens up a view of his fellow-men, for whom all this is true and actual in Jesus Christ however it may be with their individual faith.

And now as our final word along the christological line to which we finally had to submit in explanation of justification by faith alone, we have to say expressly that in faith in its character as justifying faith we do have to do with an *imitatio Christi*[EN260]. We have more than once touched on the fact that as a

---

[EN259] in reality
[EN260] imitation of Christ

4. *Justification by Faith Alone*

human attitude, as emerges from the twofold use of the word πίστις^EN261, it does represent an imitation of God, an analogy to His attitude and action. It is the confidence of man which gives a corresponding and appropriate answer to the faithfulness of God as effective and revealed in His judgment and sentence. But in particular and concretely, it is an imitation of Jesus Christ, an analogy to His attitude and action.

> It is expressly demanded of Christians in Eph. 5¹ that they should be "imitators of God." In this connexion may I recall what I wrote in *C.D.* I. 1, 272 f. concerning the "divine conformity" of faith. And in relation to the imitation of Christ in particular, the important idea of discipleship is obviously relevant, although we can only refer to it here without developing it. The term πίστις^EN262 is brought into direct combination with ἀναλογία in Rom. 12⁶: the ἀναλογία τῆς πίστεως^EN263 is the norm which true prophecy must observe and which distinguishes between the true and the false. To whom faith and prophecy are analogous—not identical, but corresponding, similar in all their dissimilarity—there can, of course, be no question as far as Paul himself is concerned. The μορφή^EN264 which is to be shown in Christians—and in Galatians this definitely means in the justifying faith of Christians as opposed to all righteousness of works—is the μορφή Χριστοῦ^EN265 (Gal. 4¹⁹). Phil. 2⁵ speaks of a definite φρονεῖν^EN266, which primarily, originally and properly is in Jesus Christ, is His own φρονεῖν^EN267, but which is to be repeated in those who are "in Christ Jesus," in those who know and apprehend themselves as being in Him. And, according to Phil. 2³ᶠ·, this Christ-like φρονεῖν^EN268 of Christians is the ταπεινοφροσύνη^EN269 in which each esteems others better than himself. In so far as Jesus Christ has practised and demonstrated it, it must necessarily be reflected *ceteribus imparibus*^EN270 in those who belong to Him—that is, in those who believe in Him.

[635]

We return for the last time to the form of faith as the obedience of humility. In the first instance we called this the negative form of faith, and we understood it in its character as pure receptivity in relation to its object. But in view of the fact that faith is receptivity in relation to this object, we then had to amend as follows: that it is negative only in appearance, in its human and external aspect, and that it is the fulness of faith, its object, which gives to it this character. Now we must advance a further step and say that when we call faith humility, the obedience of humility, we say the most positive possible thing that we can say of it as a human form of being, a human act and experience. For in this way it imitates Jesus Christ in whom it believes, it corresponds to Him, it has a similarity with the One who "for your sakes became poor, that ye through his poverty might be rich" (2 Cor. 8⁹). Similarity with Him in the high mystery of the condescension in which as the Lord He became a servant, in which as a

---

EN261 faith
EN262 faith
EN263 analogy of faith
EN264 shape
EN265 shape of Christ
EN266 attitude
EN267 attitude
EN268 attitude
EN269 humble attitude
EN270 all other things being unequal

§ 61. *The Justification of Man*

child He lay in a crib in the stall at Bethlehem, in which in Jordan He entered the way of penitence, in which He was hungry and thirsty and had nowhere to lay His head, in which He washed the feet of His disciples, in which He prayed alone in Gethsemane, in which He was rejected by Israel and judged and condemned by the Gentiles, in which He hung in opprobrium on the cross of Golgotha. Faith is a weak and distant but definite echo or reflection of all this. It cannot be otherwise. For it is the mystery of the true Godhead of Jesus Christ that He was able and willing to do what He did do in obedience according to Phil. 2^{7-8}: that He emptied Himself, humbled Himself. And a man finds his justification as he believes in this One who became poor. Faith itself, therefore, becomes a poverty, a repetition of this divine downward movement, a human reflection of the existence of the One who, according to Is. 53^2, was like "a root out of a dry ground," who had "no form nor comeliness; and when we shall see him, there is no beauty that we should desire him," a human imitation of what God has done for man in this One. Not that faith for its part either wills or does anything for him. Not that it justifies him because there is in it this repetition, reflection and imitation, because it is so poor, because it is an analogy to Jesus Christ in the form of that humility, in its form as an empty hand, an empty vessel, and therefore a comforted despair. As a human form of being, a human act and experience, it will always be a profoundly imperfect correspondence, it will always be similar only in the greatest dissimilarity, it will not therefore give to man any glory or merit. It is not faith if it does not renounce all such glory and merit and even the brightness of its poverty, if it looks even momentarily to itself as the copy instead of to the original, if it places any of its confidence in the former and not all its confidence in the latter. For if it does this, even if it is a supremely perfect analogy of humble obedience, seeing it can never be more than an analogy, it can have as little substance as a shadow on the wall in relation to the figure which it reflects. Yet it cannot be denied that justifying faith is in fact a concrete correspondence to the One in whom it believes, and that if it is not, it is not justifying faith. It is not a mere figure of speech to say that in faith man finds that the history of Jesus Christ is his history, that his sin is judged in Him, that his right is established in Him, that his death is put to death and his life is born in Him, that he can regard himself as justified in His righteousness because it is his own righteousness, because his faith is a real apprehension of his real being in Christ. It is, therefore, quite unavoidable that there should be a correspondence to his being in Christ in the sphere of his own being as differentiated from it, his being in the flesh and therefore his walking in faith. The great humility of the Son of God must and will make its impress on the lesser humility of the man who believes in Him. The faith of that man will be characterised by it. If he believes in Him, if he trusts and relies on Him as the One who has taken his place and lives for him, then that means that that One has prevailed over him and that he has become obedient to Him. To believe and to realise that He lives for us means (without any claim but quite unquestioningly) to live with Him. If we have not become obedient to

4. Justification by Faith Alone

Him, how can we trust and rely on Him, how can we believe in Him? But if we have become obedient to Him, it is inevitable that the divine humility in which Jesus Christ is the righteous man should be the pattern which we who believe in Him should follow.

This will be the starting-point for at least one section of theological ethics as presented from the particular standpoint of the atonement. But it has brought us already to a consideration of the second sphere of the doctrine of reconciliation itself, in which we have to set the doctrine of sanctification over against that of justification. We will not therefore pursue it in the present context. But in so far as in Christology we have reached the climax of the doctrine of justification, what we can say is that, even in its emptiness and passivity, justifying faith has this character of supreme fulness and activity, and that without it it would not be justifying faith: the character which is proper to it because Jesus Christ who is the object of it is, in the words of Heb. 12^2, its author and finisher, and therefore the One who forms it.

[637]

Christology in the sense of a reference to Jesus Christ as the object and content and therefore the formative norm of justifying faith may very well be described as the climax of the doctrine of justification. In their inter-relatedness and correspondence the terms "justification" and "faith" are like the two sides of the foundation of a Gothic building, from which the two pillars or arches rise up, first parallel and then converging until they finally come to rest in a vertex and keystone, thus acquiring meaning as the bearers of the vault which, in a perfect structure of this kind, seems rather to float above them than to be borne up by them. The comparison is quite a good one for the doctrine of justification by faith, which, like all doctrines, necessarily has something of the character of a building. And in it we cannot overemphasise as *tertium comparationis*^{EN271} the floating of the vault (i.e., the ultimate truth of God) above the pillars and the keystone. As regards the thing represented in this construction, we must be clear that in this matter Jesus Christ is not the last word but the first, not the climax but the foundation (in 1 Cor. 3^{11} the θεμέλιον) of the whole. Everything that has to be regarded as the reality and truth of justification and faith and their mutual relationship begins in Him and derives from Him. In Him on the one hand there takes place the demonstration of the justified man, and He Himself on the other hand is the One who prevails on man in faith as the knowing and apprehending of justification. At one and the same time he is both the ontic and the noetic principle, the reality and also the truth of both justification and faith.

This is the witness of the writing which has a particular importance in this connexion as a source and a criterion, the Epistle to the Galatians. The didactic and polemical strength of this Epistle, its whole secret, lies in the strictness with which Paul thought and spoke of justification and faith not only with reference to Jesus Christ but in the light of Jesus Christ. We will bring to a close our presentation not only of the relationship of the two concepts but of the whole doctrine of justification with some references to the central substance of this Epistle. It is our belief that any doctrine of the inexhaustible truth and reality of justification—if it is to present the only Gospel and not another—will not only close with a reference to this centre but will have to be continually renewed from it.

First of all some answers to the question: Who is Paul himself, that he dares to represent himself and obviously has to represent himself as the preacher of the only Gospel beside

---

EN271 basis of comparison

§ 61. *The Justification of Man*

which there is no other? At the very outset (1^1) we are confronted by the abrupt contrast: He is an apostle, the human doer of this human work, the human preacher of this human word—not of man or by man, not of himself, but "by Jesus Christ, and God the Father, who raised him from the dead." If he had been called and commissioned and authorised by men he might have preached, he would have had to preach, another Gospel. Because Jesus Christ lives, because he is sent by Him, he can only preach the justification which has taken place in Him and therefore justification by faith alone. For who is Jesus Christ? He is (1^4) the One "who gave himself for our sins, that he might deliver us from this present evil world, according to the will of God and our Father." Paul is committed to Him, to this One who was delivered up for the sins of all, for the taking away of those sins, and therefore for the redemption of all. He is instructed by His revelation and by that alone (1^{12}). For the event of his calling, in which he recognises his eternal election, from which he can therefore as little separate himself as he can cease to be himself, is ($1^{15f.}$) that it pleased God to reveal His Son in him, and to make him a witness of this living One in whose self-sacrifice men are liberated from their sins and therefore redeemed, awakening him to faith, to faith in this living One, to the πίστις Χριστοῦ Ἰησοῦ[EN272] and therefore to the knowledge of the true and actual justification of man, and therefore to a knowledge of the impossibility of a justification ἐξ ἔργων νόμου[EN273] (2^{16}). By His Law, the Law of this living One, he has died to the "Law"— the error of a justification of man by the fulfilment of another law than this—in order that he may now live for God. In His crucifixion he himself is crucified and therefore destroyed and done away, the man who willed to justify himself in this impossible way. It has become impossible for him to try to go further along this impossible way (2^{19}). But this means that the life of Jesus Christ has become his true and actual life, that his life in itself and as such his ζῆν ἐν σαρκί[EN274] has become only his sphere and opportunity for faith, that it can be lived only as his life in the faith in Him, "the Son of God, who loved me and gave himself for me" (2^{20}). The bridge behind him has been broken. The boats on which he might have set out on the way back have been burned. He has no ground or air or light for any other life. Any such life, any further seeking of a justification by the Law, would only mean that he rejects the grace of God, that he thinks Christ might have died in vain, that he transgresses the true and actual Law under which he stands. He cannot do this. He is prevented by this living One, by His revelation, by the identity of His present with his own. He cannot escape His law. Therefore it only remains to live in faith in Him. That is why he does not know anything else in which to glory (6^{14}) but "the cross of our Lord Jesus Christ, by whom the world is crucified unto me, and I unto the world." This means that in and with the crucifixion of Christ a humanity which is directed to self-justification and which undertakes such self-justification has become non-existent for him, and he for it. What he has given up, what it has cost him to leave this world behind—that it needed a crucifixion, the crucifixion of Jesus Christ, to cause him to pay this price, or rather to pay it for him—we can infer from the passage 1^{13-14}, in which he recalls the past in all its splendour: his conversation amongst the Jews, his persecuting and wasting the Church of God, the distinction which he won by it above many of his own contemporaries and fellow-countrymen, his existence as one who was particularly zealous (ζηλωτής) for the traditions of the fathers. He was at home in this world. It was his own. Any other than Jesus Christ—the One he persecuted—could not have uprooted him from it. But He brought about what is described in $1^{15f.}$. And even the moment of *imitatio Christi*[EN275] is not concealed: "I bear in my body the marks (στίγματα) of Jesus" (6^{17}). He is marked off

---

[EN272] faith in Jesus Christ
[EN273] by works of the law
[EN274] life in the flesh
[EN275] imitation of Christ

4. *Justification by Faith Alone*

for Him. He cannot seek to please men. If he did he would not be the servant of Christ (1^{10}). This is Paul according to his own picture of himself. This is the necessity in which as an apostle he has to say what he does say in this Epistle. He does not say it because it suits him, or because the logic of his theology demands it, but because he finds himself in the power of Jesus Christ.

He is confronted by the Galatian Churches. The seriousness of the situation is revealed by the fact that in 1^2 he refrains from addressing them directly as the Churches of God or of Christ. The continuation of the letter shows indisputably that he did not dream of denying them this character. God has called them "by the grace of Jesus Christ" (1^6) no less than himself. Jesus Christ the Crucified has been "evidently set forth" before them (3^1) so that everything Paul says about His power over himself has to be recognised by them as His power over them. He tells them quite without reservation in 3^{26}: "For ye are all the children of God by faith in Jesus Christ." They have been baptised into Him. They have put Him on (3^{27}). They belong to Him (3^{29}, 5^{24}). Paul is the witness of all this. They had once received him not only as an angel of God—Paul has no great good to say of angels in this letter, as we see from 1^5 and 3^{19}—but as Jesus Christ Himself (4^{14}): an expression which, as he uses it, can hardly indicate simply a supreme degree of human warmth and respect, but beyond that the seriousness with which they received him in accordance with his mission, in accordance with the "I live, yet not I, but Christ liveth in me." "Ye did run well," he can testify elsewhere (5^7). [639] He does not think of this as something which has not happened. He does not wipe it out. He does not treat the Galatians as renegades. In face of the situation which has arisen in Galatia he certainly believes that something like a regeneration is necessary. He compares himself to a woman (4^{19}) who must travail again for a child which has already been born. But it is only that Christ may again win a form ($\mu o \rho \phi \acute{\eta}$) among them and in them; that their faith may again acquire the form in which alone it can be faith in Jesus Christ and therefore justifying faith. The danger in which he sees them is a terrible one. In the light of Christ all these positive things can be said of them, yet he sees that they have fallen under a spell (3^1) by which not merely some things but all things are compromised. He is afraid that he has bestowed his labour upon them in vain (4^{11}). Yet there is no passage in the whole letter from which it may be deduced that he has given them up, that he has ceased to see and address them in the light of Christ. There is no passage in which his faith in the divine act which justifies man does not enter in in relation to them. He holds them fast in this faith: "I have confidence in you through the Lord, that ye will be none otherwise minded" (5^{10}) In this we have to see a consequence of his institution as an apostle, which was not of man but of Jesus Christ, of his firm foundation in his election and calling. If his office were in his own power, he would think and speak like the member or leader of a party, and he could simply abandon and anathematise the Galatian Churches. He cannot do this because they are not "his" Churches, in which he can rejoice or be mistaken, which he can recognise or reject as such, but in spite of everything they are the Churches of Jesus Christ. For that reason it is not they but their seducers that he places under the anathema of 1^{8-9}. He calls them "foolish" Galatians, but he does not cease to call them $\dot{\alpha}\delta\epsilon\lambda\phi o\acute{\iota}$^{EN276} ($3^{15}$, $4^{12\ 31}$, 5^{13}, 6^1). We may well ask whether this faithfulness of the apostle, in which he follows the faithfulness of God, does not speak just as eloquently for the cause he represents in this Epistle as anything that he says expressly in its favour.

But the faith in which and on which he addresses them—this is said no less than three times in the one verse, 2^{16}—is the $\pi \acute{\iota} \sigma \tau \iota \varsigma$ $X \rho \iota \sigma \tau o \hat{\upsilon}$^{EN277}, and as such—we have this combination three times in the same verse—it is the faith in which man knows and apprehends his

---

EN276 brothers
EN277 faith in Christ

§ 61. *The Justification of Man*

justification, the justification which can be known and apprehended and realised only in this work—this again is maintained three times in 2^{16}—and not in doing the works of the Law. Why not? Not because faith as such is better than these works. In all Galatians there is not a single word of praise for faith as such, nor is there a single word in which works as such are disparaged. Of the three factors—justification, faith and Christ—the basic and controlling one is obviously the last. The next verse (2^{17}) goes on at once to speak of ζητοῦν δικαιωθῆναι ἐν Χριστῷ[EN278]. In Jesus Christ the blessing of Abraham has come on the Gentiles (3^{14}). As those who belong to him, they are the direct seed of Abraham and heirs according to the promise (given to him) (3^{29}). God has sent His Son in the fulness of time, born of a woman, subject to the Law, in order to redeem them that were under the Law, that they might receive the υἱοθεσία[EN279] ($4^{4f.}$). It is He who has done this, redeeming us from the curse of the Law by Himself being made a curse, as it is written: "Cursed is every one that hangeth on a tree" (3^{13}). And by doing it He has made us free for liberty (5^1). We are called unto liberty (5^{13}). We have our liberty already (2^4). Because He has made it for us, because He has called us to it, because it is our freedom in Him, the general proposition is true: "By the works of the law shall no flesh be justified" (2^{16}); not because of the weakness of the flesh which cannot do these works, but because of the perfection with which Christ has done them. For the same reason the great imperative of Galatians is: "Stand fast in the liberty wherewith Christ hath made us free, and be not entangled again with the yoke of bondage" (5^1); not because freedom is a fine and a good thing in itself and as such (in itself and as such it can also be the freedom of the flesh, 5^{13}), but because it is a freedom which has been won for us by Him. And in what can it actually consist but in freedom to believe in Him, in the renunciation of all efforts aimed at self-justification, in the one decision of trust in Him, and therefore in the blessing of Abraham, in life in the divine sonship, in entry into the status of heirs, and therefore in participation in the divine justification? It is the freedom of those in whose hearts there dwells the Spirit of His Son, who for that reason are no longer slaves but sons, and can call God their Father ($4^{6f.}$). There is one way out from the conclusion that all men are under sin, but only one: the promise of the πίστις Ἰησοῦ Χριστοῦ[EN280] (3^{22}). As one who has received this promise and therefore who simply believes, Paul speaks to the Galatians as those who have also received it and who ought also simply to believe. "And as many as walk according to this rule (τῷ κάνονι τούτῳ), peace be on them, and mercy, and upon the Israel of God" (6^{16}).

To turn aside from this rule, to give up this freedom which has been won by Christ and is found in Him, to give up justifying faith, is the temptation into which the Galatians have been led by the false teachers who have entered in and won some success amongst them. As appears from the letter, and as Paul expressly says, it is only a question of a "little leaven" (5^9), of a slight modification of the Christian position and teaching, which might easily be represented as a mere externality, but which in fact—"a little leaven leaveneth the whole lump"—is bound to put everything on a different basis, to give a different meaning and direction to the existence of these communities and the whole faith of the Galatian Christians. Concretely we learn two things: Circumcision ($5^{3\ 6\ 11}$, $6^{13\ 15}$) and the observance of the Jewish feasts (4^{10}) are to be made obligatory. In other words, they are to be made to give to their Christian faith and life the form of a variation of the Jewish religion of Law. It is by the doing of these works that they are to stand on the foundation of the divine covenant and therefore in the sphere of the divine justification of man. Their faith in Jesus Christ is to become a particular form within the redemptive system appointed by the Old Testament

---

[EN278] 'seeking to be justified in Christ'
[EN279] adoption
[EN280] faith in Jesus Christ

4. Justification by Faith Alone

Law. It can be developed only within this system, on the presupposition of the fulfilment of its demands. There is no question of setting aside faith or the Gospel, but rather of domesticating it, of integrating it into the well-known and natural view of man that his relationship with God is something in which he can and must help himself, that the grace of God is something which he can and must create and assure to himself by definite observances. The point at issue is the attachment of the Christian community to the great continuity of religious history, in which not without reason Judaism was conscious of having the last word in face of all kinds of local and historical peculiarities of a different origin by virtue of its appeal to the revelation entrusted to it by God. And from the point of view of faith in the Gospel, the point at issue was its necessary completion, consolidation and founding off—which need not be taken too tragically as a matter of external form—by a *conditio sine qua non*[EN281] within which it was still possible to speak about grace quite comfortably and seriously and profoundly. This proposal was most illuminating to the Galatian communities. They did not notice—this is why Paul calls them "foolish" in 3^{1f}—the basic difference between the reformation to which they gave themselves and their foundation as Christian communities, the apostolic preaching which they had received. They believed that this change of position was both necessary and possible. They probably thought (like the Israelites when Aaron made for them the golden calf) that in making it they would set themselves on the way to healthy ecclesiastical development; that it was the natural transition from the heavenly revelation to its earthly development, from the event to the institution, from the Spirit to its tenable and necessary form in the world.

The remarkable surprise which Paul had for them in his letter was the uncovering of the basic contradiction in which they had entangled themselves; not only their contradiction to him, but to themselves, to their foundation and existence as Christian communities, above all to Jesus Christ, whom they did not wish to deny but in their own way to confess, although, in fact, they did not confess but deny Him. They have been led astray (5^{10}), they have been hindered so that they do not obey the truth (5^7), he tells them. What they have begun in the Spirit they are trying to complete in the flesh (3^3). Not, therefore, as they imagined, to complete in the necessary and salutary giving of form to the Spirit, but in alienation from the Spirit, in a relapse into non-spiritual humanity. Not in an appropriate and demanded development of the heavenly, but in its transmutation into something earthly. Not (as though this were necessary) in the insertion of the Gospel into the context of the covenant which God made with Abraham, but—this was the hardest thing of all that Paul said to them, $4^{3f.}$—in apostasy from this covenant, in a relapse into heathenism, into bondage to natural forces, the στοιχεῖα τοῦ κόσμου[EN282], from the service of which they had been snatched by the preaching of the Gospel when they believed, in betrayal of the καινὴ κτίσις[EN283] which had been promised to Abraham, which had been offered to them as his children, which had already dawned for them, and in the light of which there could be no question of circumcision or uncircumcision or any other ordinances (6^{15}). They want to make themselves the Israel of God by the way on which they have entered, but if they go that way they deny themselves as the Israel of God. So much for your ecclesiastical progress, is the message which they have to hear from Paul.

[641]

But what is he contending against and what is he contending for with his complaint, with his earnest appeal, with his unconditional demand that they should return at once and completely renounce this way? Against a worse and in favour of a better order of salvation and life and religion and theology and Church government? This is how the matter appears

---

[EN281] necessary requirement
[EN282] elements of the cosmos
[EN283] new creation

§ 61. The Justification of Man

on the outside, and we shall obviously have to consider and estimate it from this standpoint. But, in fact, what Paul does is simply this. Speaking both on behalf of and in opposition to the Galatian communities, he sets against the supposed reformation in Galatia Jesus Christ Himself, Jesus Christ, the One who has called both him and them, Jesus Christ as his and their true and only righteousness, to which we can do justice and in which we can participate only in faith in Him, and not in any circumstances or in any sense in a form of faith discovered and stylised and systematised by man as obedience to the Law of God. The only thing which counts is the "new creation." But the new creation is real in Christ and nowhere else. Therefore the only thing which counts can be known and apprehended and realised by man only in faith in Him and not in any other way: not because faith as such is better than circumcision and the other works of the Law; but because Jesus Christ and therefore the true justification of man can be known and apprehended and realised by man only in faith. Therefore the decisive argument of Paul against the Church-reformation in Galatia is this—that the persuasion ($\pi\epsilon\iota\sigma\mu o\nu\acute{\eta}$) to which the Galatians have fallen victim does not come from the One who has called them (5^8). If they obeyed His voice, they could not go this way. "In Christ Jesus neither circumcision availeth ($\mathit{i}\sigma\chi\acute{u}\epsilon\iota$) anything, nor uncircumcision, neither Judaism nor heathenism—nor any other '-ism'—but faith which worketh by love" (5^6). Strong in faith and therefore believing in Christ, they could not even enter into this discussion of an improvement of the Gospel and of faith. They could only break it off. They could only retrace at once any steps they had gone in this direction. Such steps could and can only lead them out of the freedom won for them by Jesus Christ and into bondage, making their life in righteousness of no effect. If they were right, then Jesus Christ had died in vain (2^{21}). More than that, they ought logically to accuse and condemn as a servant of sin the One who in His death won that freedom for them (2^{17}), taking their place at the side of those who crucified Him. If they persist in that way, it will not help them (5^2). They can tread it only in separation from Him, only as they destroy their being in Him and His being in them (5^4). Note that the moment of $\mathit{imitatio}^{\text{EN284}}$ can be seen on this side, too: those who go this way will be spared the offence of the cross, the threat of persecution under which those who believe in the Crucified continually stand (5^{11}, 6^{12}). For at bottom (and it can easily be seen in practice) this way is simply a fresh accommodation to the world, the evil world from which they are delivered by Jesus Christ (1^4). A Christianity which has been fitted into the system of human self-justification, which has become a religion, which has been domesticated, has never brought down persecution upon itself. Paul knows and counts on it that all these things are far from the mind and intention of the Galatian communities. But for that very reason he shows them that no less is at stake. It is not a matter merely of the Gospel or the Law, faith or works, himself or the false teachers, but Christ or no Christ—or, as Luther boldly but not unjustly put it—Christ or Belial. And this being the case, everything is at stake—the Gospel and faith and righteousness. As a righteousness which is hid with Christ in God, it is only in faith that it can be the hope of the Christian and that it can be awaited as such (5^5).

The strength of the Reformation exposition of righteousness by faith alone consisted in a word in this, that it saw and made plain that the living Jesus Christ—and His righteousness as man's righteousness—is the scarlet thread which runs through Galatians and therefore through the rest of Holy Scripture. This is something that we cannot say of so many expositions of this matter both old and new. That is why in the substance of our understanding of this matter we definitely have to take our stand with them.

We will conclude by quoting without comment a section of the *Heidelberg Catechism*, of

---

EN284 imitation

4. Justification by Faith Alone

which it may well be said that it represents the insight and confession of all the Reformation Churches of the 16th century.

Question 60: How art thou righteous before God?

Answer. Only by true faith on Jesus Christ. In such a way therefore that although my conscience accuses me that I have grievously sinned against the commandments of God, and have failed to keep them, and am always inclined to every form of evil, yet without any merit of my own God of His mere mercy gives me the perfect satisfaction and holiness of Christ, and accounts that I have never committed or had any sin, but have myself fulfilled the obedience which Christ has achieved for me, if only I receive this benefit with a believing heart.

Question 61: Why dost thou say that thou art righteous only by faith?

Answer. Not because I please God by reason of the worthiness of my faith, but because only the satisfaction, righteousness and holiness of Christ is my righteousness before God, and I cannot receive and appropriate it in any way except only by faith.

Question 64: But doth not this doctrine make wild and careless folk?

Answer. No, for it is impossible that those who are implanted into Christ by true faith should not bring forth the fruit of thanksgiving.

[643]

§ 62

THE HOLY SPIRIT AND THE GATHERING OF THE CHRISTIAN COMMUNITY

The Holy Spirit is the awakening power in which Jesus Christ has formed and continually renews His body, i.e., His own earthly-historical form of existence, the one holy catholic and apostolic Church. This is Christendom, i.e., the gathering of the community of those whom already before all others He has made willing and ready for life under the divine verdict executed in His death and revealed in His resurrection from the dead. It is therefore the provisional representation of the whole world of humanity justified in Him.

1. THE WORK OF THE HOLY SPIRIT

A simple picture will help to make clear the previous course of our presentation of the doctrine of reconciliation and the meaning of the final turn in which we must now give to its development (within the framework of this first part). The Christology is like a vertical line meeting a horizontal. The doctrine of the sin of man is the horizontal line as such. The doctrine of justification is the intersection of the horizontal line by the vertical. The remaining doctrine, that of the Church and of faith, is again the horizontal line, but this time seen as intersected by the vertical. The vertical line is the atoning work of God in Jesus Christ. The horizontal is the object of that work; man and humanity. We now come to the final aspect (within the event of reconciliation) of this whole encounter. The particular problem involved might be described as the subjective realisation of the atonement. The one reality of the atonement has both an objective and a subjective side in so far as—we cannot separate but we must not confuse the two—it is both a divine act and offer and also an active human participation in it: the unique history of Jesus Christ; but enclosed and exemplified in this the history of many other men of many other ages. We could develop the Christology only with a constant recollection of this other side. The doctrine of sin has shown us who and what the man is whose active participation in the act of God is in question. In the doctrine of justification we made the transition from the one to the other. It only remains to show what is involved in this other as determined by it, in this active participation of man in

[644] the divine act of reconciliation. We will describe it in this section in terms of the Christian community and then in a final section in terms of Christian faith. The adding of the adjective "Christian" to a human action—the action of the

1. The Work of the Holy Spirit

Christian community and the Christian individual—indicates that we are now dealing with man as he stands in a particular relationship to Jesus Christ, and to that extent with the subjective realisation of the atonement. (In this context we can only mention these presuppositions, but for a more explicit treatment, cf. *CD* I, 1, §§ 6 and 12; I, 2, §§ 16–18, and II, 2, § 25.)

There is no μετάβασις εἰς ἄλλο γένος [EN1]. There is no abandonment of the sphere of the greed. It is significant that at this point, the transition from the second to the third article, the word *credo* [EN2] is specifically mentioned. It tells us that we can know the man who belongs to Jesus Christ only in faith. Nor is there any abandonment of the christological subject-matter of the doctrine of reconciliation. The history which we consider when we speak of the Christian community and Christian faith is enclosed and exemplified in the history of Jesus Christ. In a way which is still hidden, the history of Jesus Christ is the history of the reconciliation of the world with God. It is not exhausted in the history of the Christian community and Christian faith. But in this history—as the proclamation of the meaning of world history which has yet to be revealed—we do have to do with the history of Jesus Christ. And it is not as though now, from the standpoint of human history, existence and activity which is now maintained, we are really coming to grips—as so much mythology would say—with the real heart, the "existential" relevance, the substance of the Christian message, to which the Christology and the doctrine of justification are related as the husk to the kernel. Here, too, of course, we do have to do with the substance of it, but not separated from the substance which we had to present in the Christology and the doctrine of justification. We are not now in a different sphere; we are simply looking at it from a different angle. The Christian community and Christian faith belong to the substance of the one confession which has its centre in Jesus Christ. In the Christian Church we have to do with man, his history, existence and activity in this peculiar but provisional form. If the Christology and the doctrine of justification are a myth, so, too, is what we now have to say of man, for it is no less strange, no less amazing, no less inaccessible from the point of view of man's self-knowledge, no less a mystery. And if it is a mystery but not a myth, so, too, it is with the Christology and the doctrine of justification, in which we have to do with the basis and object of everything that we must now see and say concerning man. The fact that according to the third article there is a man who actively participates in the divine act and offer in the form of the Christian community and Christian faith, the fact that this part belongs as such to the greed, is not at all self-evident. Indeed, to be precise, it is far less self-evident than creation, or than the incarnation of the Son of God. It is far less self-evident because in it the mystery of creation and of the incarnation is now in a sense brought home to us, because in the Christian community and its faith man is directly strange

[645]

[EN1] change of category
[EN2] 'I believe'

§ 62. The Holy Spirit and the Gathering of the Christian Community

and amazing and inaccessible to himself. All this takes place only in his concrete adherence to Jesus Christ, only on the basis of the reality of the justification as it has taken place in Him, only in virtue of the truth of the divine verdict as it has been pronounced in Him. The fact that there is the Christian community and Christian faith and therefore this man is, of course—we are reminded of the remarkable pause indicated in the New Testament between the ascension and Pentecost—a new thing, another dimension of the one mystery, a further step in the way and progress of the one God in His address to man, and yet not a new thing in the way and progress of the one God in the context of His own work, but only its provisional end as it had been in view from the very first. It is not identical with creation and the incarnation. Conceptually it has to be kept apart. Yet it had been in view, it had been envisaged in the incarnation and even in creation. It is actual and comprehensible only as it derives from and is related to them. It cannot, therefore, be separated from them.

In this concluding phase of our presentation, the concept and reality of the Holy Spirit must be the centre of our attention. He is the controlling theme of everything that Christianity believes and must confess in the third article: *credo in Spiritum Sanctum*[EN3]. We speak of human experience and action when we speak of the community and faith, and therefore of the subjective realisation of the atonement. Yet it is that human experience and action which is not of man's "own reason and power" or in virtue of his own capacity, resolve or effort, but (Luther) "the Holy Spirit has called me by the Gospel, enlightened me with His gifts, sanctified and maintained me in a right faith, as He calls and gathers and enlightens the whole of Christendom, keeping it to Jesus Christ in the true and only faith." The Holy Spirit is the "*doctor veritatis*[EN4]" (Tertullian), the *digitus Dei*[EN5] (Augustine), by whom this takes place. Man is sinful, proud and fallen man who has neither arm, nor hand, nor even a finger to do it for himself, who as such is neither willing nor able to participate actively in the divine act of reconciliation. If this is to take place in the Christian community and Christian faith, if man is to will what of himself he cannot will and do what of himself he cannot do, then it must be on the basis of a particular address and gift, in virtue of a particular awakening power of God, by which he is born again to this will and ability, to the freedom of this action, and under the lordship and impulse of which he is another man, in defiance of his being and status as a sinner. God in this particular address and gift, God in this awakening power, God as the Creator of this other man, is the Holy Spirit. It is still God Himself in this work, in the strict sense in which the same must be said of the work of creation and the objective realisation of the work of atonement in Jesus Christ. Man, however, is not of himself open or ready or willing for a

---

[EN3] I believe in the Holy Spirit
[EN4] teacher of truth
[EN5] finger of God

1. *The Work of the Holy Spirit*

profitable, a living knowledge of this objective realisation and therefore for its subjective realisation. He can only be amazed at himself when he finds himself caught up in it, when he can count on the fact that the verdict pronounced in Jesus Christ applies to himself with everyone else, that the justification of sinful man accomplished in Him is his justification and that of all men. He can never understand this in any way but that God has opened his eyes to this knowledge, that God has made him free and ready for it, that a miracle has taken place in him. He will not claim it as his own conversion, but maintain it only as God's own converting of him to Himself. In all the experiences in which it takes place, in all the insights which he gains by it, in all the decisions which he makes and executes in it. He will give God the glory. They are undoubtedly his experiences and insights and decisions and actions, but in relation to all of them he will simply be thankful. In any other attitude he would merely betray the fact that he does not know what he is doing when he confesses the Christian community and Christian faith, no matter how sincerely and earnestly he may do it. The Holy Spirit, for whose work the community, and in and with the community the believing Christian, is thankful, is not the spirit of the world, nor is He the spirit of the community, nor is He the spirit of any individual Christian, but He is the Spirit of God, God Himself, as He eternally proceeds from the Father and the Son, as He unites the Father and the Son in eternal love, as He must be worshipped and glorified together with the Father and the Son, because He is of one substance with them. He is not man's own spirit and He never will be. He is God, attesting Himself to the spirit of man as his God, as the God who acts for him and to him. He is God, coming to man, and coming to him in such a way that He is revealed to him as the God who reconciles the world and man to Himself, in such a way therefore that what He is and does for him as such becomes the Word which man can hear and actually does hear, in such a way, therefore, that man allows himself to be reconciled with Him (2 Cor. 5^{20}). God's self-attestation makes what He does the Word which is spoken to this man and received and accepted by him. The Holy Spirit is God in this His self-attestation—God in the power which quickens man to this profitable and living knowledge of His action. He is God intervening and acting for man, addressing Himself to him, in such a way that He says Yes to Himself and this makes possible and necessary man's human Yes to Him.

From all this it is self-evident that neither the Christian community nor the individual Christian can subjugate or possess or control Him, directing and over-ruling His work. He makes man free, but He Himself remains free in relation to him: the Spirit of the Lord. He awakens man to faith, but it is still necessary to believe in Him, *in Spiritum Sanctum*[EN6], in the very same fellowship with Him and the very same distance from Him with which we believe *in*

[647]

[EN6] in the Holy Spirit

§ 62. The Holy Spirit and the Gathering of the Christian Community

unum Deum Patrem^{EN7} and *in Jesum Christum, Filium eius unicum*^{EN8}. The relationship of the Christian community and the individual Christian to Him is not created by them but by Him—with a supreme reality and certainty. But this means that it can only be one of obedience and of prayer for His new coming and witness and quickening: *Veni creator Spiritus*^{EN9}. In everything that we have to say concerning the Christian community and Christian faith we can move only within the circle that they are founded by the Holy Spirit and therefore that they must be continually refounded by Him, but that the necessary refounding by the Holy Spirit can consist only in a renewal of the founding which He has already accomplished. To put it in another way, the receiving of the Holy Spirit which makes the community a Christian community and a man a Christian will work itself out and show itself in the fact that only now will they really expect Him, only now will they want to receive Him; and where He is really expected, where there is a desire to receive Him, that is the work which He has already begun, the infallible sign of His presence.

But the Spirit and therefore the awakening power which is the presupposition of the community and faith is the Holy Spirit. The word "holy" does not merely repeat and emphasise the fact that He is divine, that He is Himself God. According to 1 Cor. 8^5 there are many gods, and to attest them there are many spirits. The real operation of these spirits is not, of course, a secret, but they can be understood as the many forms of the spirit of the world and man as they correspond to the nature of those gods. Man can possess the spirits no less than they possess him. At bottom he has as much control over them as they have over him. But the Holy Spirit is clearly marked off from these spirits by the fact that He is the Spirit of the God who acts in Jesus Christ, reconciling the world to Himself and revealing Himself in the world as the doer of this work. He does not attest to man something quasi-divine (not even if it claims to be transcendence itself). He does not mediate to him the knowledge of a supposed higher wisdom. He does not subject him to the yoke of a supposed power. He attests to him the Son, who in obedience to the will of the Father took up and trod to the very end the way into the far country—his Judge who gave Himself to be judged in his place. He attests his transition from wrong to right, from death to life, as it was fulfilled in this judgment. He attests that which was accomplished thereby as his justification. He attests the verdict of the Father on the world and himself as spoken in His death and revealed in His resurrection. He attests the grace of God as the righteousness of God and the righteousness of God as the grace of God. And all this, not as the impartation of an abstract historical truth, not as abstract doctrine, but in attestation of the living Jesus Christ Himself: nothing, therefore, but what is His history, nothing but what is true and actual in Him, nothing but what is Himself. He actually

---
^{EN7} in one God, the Father
^{EN8} in Jesus Christ, his only Son
^{EN9} Come, Spirit creator!

1. *The Work of the Holy Spirit*

spends Himself in His attestation in so far as He is the Spirit of the Father and of the Son who accomplishes and reveals the will of the Father. He is the Spirit of Jesus Christ, His power awakening man to a knowledge of the God acting in Him. In this way He is the Spirit of God. In this way He is holy, and He makes man holy.

And this involves the final point, that He is sent by Jesus Christ and comes to man. According to Jn. 20^{22}, He blows as His breath in the freedom described in Jn. 3^8. He is the form of His action, in which His action is not excluded and does not cease because it has taken place, in which it cannot become the object of historical impartation or abstract doctrine. It is the form of His action in which this action continues, in which it is made present to the man to whom He gives Himself and who receives Him as the action which in its singularity takes place to-day, in which as he is free to know and grasp it in faith, as he participates in it, it makes him its contemporary. It is the form of His action in which this action hastens from His resurrection as its first revelation to a few to its final and general revelation to all. It is the expression and confirmation of His life as the theme of that action.

It is strange but true that fundamentally and in general practice we cannot say more of the Holy Spirit and His work than that He is the power in which Jesus Christ attests Himself, attests Himself effectively, creating in man response and obedience. We describe Him as His awakening power. Later we will have to describe Him as His quickening and enlightening power. To that extent we have not yet said of Him everything that there is to say. But fundamentally and generally there is no more to say of Him than that He is the power of Jesus Christ in which it takes place that there are men who can and must find and see that He is theirs and they are His, that their history is genuinely enclosed in His and His history is equally genuinely enclosed in theirs. Anything beyond this description of fact is either a report of His history as such: His way, His act and experience, His life as the subject of the action in which God reconciled the world to Himself, or it is an account of its significance and relevance and effect in the life of the community which recognises and confesses Him as the Lord, in the life of the faith and—as we shall see later—of the love and hope of the Christian. The confession: *credo in Spiritum Sanctum*^{EN10}, in which we are concerned with the relationship, the fellowship, indeed the unity between Him and the community, between Him and the individual Christian, occupies in the creed a strangely isolated position—almost, we might say, as though it were naked and empty. But if the decision is made in Him, it is in Him that the whole is both questioned and answered.

How gladly we would hear and know and say something more, something more precise, something more palpable concerning the way in which the work of the Holy Spirit is done! How does it really happen that the history of Jesus Christ, in which the history of all men is virtually enclosed and accomplished,

[649]

---

^{EN10} I believe in the Holy Spirit

§ 62. *The Holy Spirit and the Gathering of the Christian Community*

is actualised, in the first instance only in the history of a few, of a small minority within the many of whom this cannot so far be said, but even in the history of the few typically for the history of the many? How can it really be—the question of the Virgin in Lk. 1³⁴—that there is an actualising of this history in other human histories? By what ways does God bring it about that in the perverted hearts, in the darkened knowledge and understanding, in the rebellious desires and strivings of sinful men—for that is what even the few are—there takes place this awakening, in which they can know Jesus Christ as theirs and themselves as His? How is there really born in them the new man who knows and recognises and confesses Jesus Christ? How can there be in history such a thing as Christianity, and men who seriously want to be Christians?

The confession *credo in Spiritum Sanctum*^{EN11} does not tell us anything concerning this How. It merely indicates the fact that all this does take place, did take place and will continually take place again. It merely tells us that the God who created man on the earth and under heaven, who has reconciled him to Himself in His Son, has done and does and will do this as well, the opening of blind eyes and deaf ears, the raising up of lame feet, the training of useless hands, the awakening of dead hearts to the hearing and obedience of His Word. Even the New Testament, although time and again it places the Holy Spirit between the event of Christ on the one hand and the Christian community and Christian faith on the other, does not really tell us anything about the How, the mode of His working.

And the saying about the wind which blows and is heard, but we do not know whence it comes or whither it goes (Jn. 3⁸), seems to repel any question as to the explanation of the fact that it does blow and is heard. All that is said of it is an attestation and confirmation of the fact that the Holy Spirit is the Spirit of Jesus Christ, that His power is on certain men, that He comes to them as such, that He is "poured out" on them, that He "sits" on them and "fills" them (Ac. 2¹ᶠ·), that He is effective and manifest in the rise of the community and the existence of Christian men to the extent that they receive Him or begin to receive Him. Beyond the description and assertion of this fact there did not emerge any doctrine of the Holy Spirit and His work even in the secondary and later theology of the Church. All that could be done was to refer forward to this special work of God from Christology and the doctrine of justification (or sanctification or calling), and to refer backward to it from the doctrine of the Church and of faith (or love or hope).

[650] It is obviously futile to try to go beyond this twofold reference. God Himself—concretely, the work and Word of the living Jesus Christ—stands between the two, His free gift and creation, so that here, if anywhere, apart from this twofold reference, we can only say: "Let everything in us keep silence." This is what makes the preaching of Pentecost so difficult and so easy. This is what is expressed in the preaching of Pentecost with such crystal clarity and yet with

---

^{EN11} I believe in the Holy Spirit

2. *The Being of the Community*

such mystery—*N.B.* not only or primarily in the preaching of Whitsunday, but as the clarity and mystery of all preaching, all proclamation of the relationship, the fellowship, the unity which exists, which has to be continued and renewed, which has constantly to be founded anew, between Jesus Christ on the one hand and the Christian community, the Christian and man in general on the other.

The "demonstration of the Spirit and (therefore) of power" to which Paul referred in 1 Cor. 2⁴ is shown unmistakably by the context not to be a demonstration which Paul thought he had given or could give in Corinth, but the demonstration which God had given and would continue to give there in Jesus Christ. Not without the apostolic preaching of Him, or the apostolic direction and instruction and guidance for the building up and maintaining of the community, but as the apostle pointed forward from the one and backward from the other to this centre as the point where his teaching reached its limit and therefore could only be silent, because there, and from there, the decision was reached whether his teaching of Jesus Christ and of justification as it took place in Him was the proclamation of a myth or God's own Word, whether his teaching of the Church and of faith was again the proclamation of a myth or God's own Word. Paul simply attested the ἀπόδειξις πνεύματος καὶ δυνάμεως.^{EN12}

For this reason (in view of what we have said earlier) this introductory section can be very brief. It will be enough if we simply write below all that we have said so far and above all that we have still to say the confession which is the confession of this sovereign goal and presupposition of all Christian teaching: *credo in Spiritum Sanctum*^{EN13}.

2. THE BEING OF THE COMMUNITY

As the work of the Holy Spirit the Christian community, Christendom, the Church is a work which takes place among men in the form of a human activity. Therefore it not only has a history, but—like man (*CD* III, 2 § 44)—it exists only as a definite history takes place, that is to say, only as it is gathered and lets itself be gathered and gathers itself by the living Jesus Christ through the Holy Spirit. To describe its being we must abandon the usual distinctions between being and act, status and dynamic, essence and existence. Its act is its being, its status its dynamic, its essence its existence. The Church *is* when it takes place that God lets certain men live as His servants, His friends, His children, the witnesses of the reconciliation of the world with Himself as it has taken place in Jesus Christ, the preachers of the victory which has been won in Him over sin and suffering and death, the heralds of His future revelation in which the glory of the Creator will be declared to all creation as that of His love and

[651]

---

^{EN12} demonstration of the Spirit and of power
^{EN13} I believe in the Holy Spirit

§ 62. *The Holy Spirit and the Gathering of the Christian Community*

faithfulness and mercy. The Church *is* when it happens to these men in common that they may receive the verdict on the whole world of men which has been pronounced in the resurrection of Jesus Christ from the dead. By the pronunciation of this verdict, which they can receive and have received by the awakening power of the Holy Spirit, they are gathered and they allow themselves to be gathered, they gather themselves, as they have received it and do receive it. The Church *is* when these men subject themselves to the law of the Gospel, "the law of the Spirit of life" (Rom. 8^2), when they become obedient to it, when they keep to the fact, as to an imperative which is true of all of them in common, that God was and is and will be faithful to man in His great wrath against man's unfaithfulness to Him, that He has given Himself up for him in His Son, that in this One He has re-established His own damaged right and the lost right of man, that in Him He has maintained and fulfilled His covenant and concluded eternal peace. The Church *is* when these men as the first-fruits of all creation can know and have to acknowledge the Lord of the world in His faithfulness as the Lord of the covenant which He has maintained and fulfilled, and therefore as their Lord. The Church *is* in the particular relationship of these men, when this is possible and actual under the sovereignty of Jesus Christ in their common hearing and obeying, when they can make a common response with their existence to the work of Jesus Christ received by them as Word.

In all this we are simply paraphrasing the basic meaning of the word ἐκκλησία[EN14]. The Latin rendering in *Cat. Rom.* (I, 10, 2) is correct: *Significat ecclesia evocationem*[EN15]. The Church is a community which hastens towards and comes together in a public convocation. In the same text, and also in *C.A.* VII and VIII, it is a *congregatio*: a *coetus*[EN16], to use a favourite (if rather static and institutional) phrase of the days of orthodoxy; or even further removed from the original sense, a *societas*[EN17], a *corpus*[EN18].

The English equivalent "church" or "kirk," and the German "Kirche," is usually explained to be a mutilated rendering of the adjective κυριακή[EN19]. But it may go back to the same root to which the Latin words *circare, circa, circum, circulus*[EN20], etc., belong, indicating the circumscribed sphere in which this gathering, this hastening and coming together of the community, takes place, or even more concretely the half-circular apse with the altar and the bishop's throne on which the assembled congregation was focused in its worship in churches built after the older Roman style. A third guess is that the word "church" comes from the term κηρυγεία[EN21]. (the office of a herald). None of these explanations is completely satisfying. What is certain is that Luther preferred not to use the word at all, but to speak of the "community," the "congregation," the "company" or "little company," or even "Christendom." There is no doubt that we do have to fill it out and interpret it in this sense in accord-

---

[EN14] church
[EN15] 'Church' means 'calling out'
[EN16] congregation: an assembly
[EN17] partnership
[EN18] legal body
[EN19] 'of the Lord'
[EN20] to go around, around, about, circle
[EN21] heralding

2. *The Being of the Community*

ance with its New Testament use and the Old Testament original *qahal*. The Church as ἐκκλησία[EN22], as *evocatio*[EN23] or *congregatio*[EN24], is a description of an event. The same is true of the explanatory formula added to the description of the *ecclesia*[EN25] in the creed, the *communio sanctorum*[EN26], no matter whether by the word *sanctorum*[EN27] we mean the *sancti*[EN28] (the *fideles, vocati*[EN29]), those who enter into fellowship with one another in the Church, or the *sancta*[EN30], the redemptive occurrence attested in the Church's *kerygma*, in which its members have their specific and conscious part. It is unquestionable that the *communio*[EN31], too, is not the being of a state or institution, but the being of an event, in which the assembled and self-assembling community is actively at work: the living community of the living Lord Jesus Christ in the fulfilment of its existence. [652]

The Church *is* when it takes place, and it takes place in the form of a sequence and nexus of definite human activities. In these human activities as such it can be studied from the very beginning of our era by all those who have the opportunity and give to it the necessary attention. It is a phenomenon of world history which can be grasped in historical and psychological and sociological terms like any other. There is, there takes place, a gathering and separation of certain men to this fellowship. This involves—in varying degrees of strictness or looseness—an ecclesiastical organisation and constitution and order. In this gathering and separation there takes place its cultus, teaching, preaching, instruction, theology, confession, and all in definite relationships to the political and economic and social conditions and movements, to the scholarship and art and morality, of the surrounding world. It all develops in and with this world, but according to its own laws, with a tradition which is in many ways related and in many ways differentiated, with its distinctive purpose and stamp, but with obvious connexions and similarities and reciprocal actions in relation to other human phenomena and their history. It is a specific and yet also an integrated, a distinctive and yet not a unique element in the whole of human culture, its achievements and its destinies. In all this—to use the term which has become classical—the Church is visible, *ecclesia visibilis*[EN32]. It is one historical factor with others, asserting itself and immediately noticeable as such. Nor is it, as it were, accidental or *per nefas*[EN33] that it is visible in this way. It is essential to it to be so; just as essential as that in another sense it should be invisible: *ecclesia invisibilis*[EN34]. The work of the Holy Spirit to

---

[EN22] Church
[EN23] 'calling out'
[EN24] congregation
[EN25] church
[EN26] communion of saints
[EN27] saints
[EN28] saints
[EN29] believers, those called
[EN30] 'holy events'
[EN31] communion
[EN32] a visible church
[EN33] wrongly
[EN34] an invisible church

§ 62. *The Holy Spirit and the Gathering of the Christian Community*

which it owes its existence is something which is produced concretely and historically in this world. It is the awakening power of the Word made flesh, of the Son of God, who Himself entered the lowliness of a historical existence in this world, who as very God became and is very man. Like begets like. The Christian faith awakened by Him is a definite human activity and therefore a definite human phenomenon. For all the peculiarity of his activity the Christian is an ordinary man with other men. Similarly the Christendom in which there are Christians is a human work and as such a human phenomenon which can be generally observed. Where there is this awakening, where the Church is born of the Word of God (Zwingli), itself "the mother which conceives and bears every Christian by the Word of God which it reveals and produces, enlightening and kindling the hearts so that they grasp and receive and cling and hold fast to it" (Luther), there there arises in some form a historical quantity which can be observed, which is at work and which can be calculated in historical terms.

[653]

> According to the Gospels, the Church came into being quite visibly with the calling of the twelve apostles who were all named and who correspond in number to the twelve tribes of Israel. It developed visibly with the addition of the thousands on the day of Pentecost, and among the Gentiles in the form of the ἐκκλησίαι^{EN35} of Asia Minor, Greece and Rome, and later the whole Mediterranean littoral, and then the far North and East and South—a very visible counterpart to the visible temporal Empire. In the world of Constantine the Great and of Charlemagne and later of the Houses of Saxony and Hohenstauffen, it assumed visible forms which can only be described as terrifying. It again took historical form in consequence of the denial of Evangelical renewal in the 16th century, and the necessity to re-establish itself in relation to this renewal. And the Reformers guarded themselves very carefully against the idea that by the Church they meant only a *civitas platonica*^{EN36}, the pure idea of a Christian community and therefore only an invisible Church. They at once gave themselves to the task of building on the ruins of the past a new and visible Church based on the newly perceived Word of God and in new obedience to that Word. And they succeeded well enough in a form which is also to some extent terrifying. And since then, whenever it has been thought that such reconstruction is necessary and possible, it has always been—and no sect, however spiritual, can completely escape it—with a certain visibility, with a separation which every eye can see, with the establishment of certain cultic and intellectual and legal and social and aesthetic forms which mark it off more or less distinctively from other temporal or religious societies or from other forms of the Christian community. The Church never has been and never is absolutely invisible.

There is an ecclesiastical Docetism which will not accept this, which paradoxically tries to overlook the visibility of the Church, explaining away its earthly and historical form as something indifferent, or angrily negating it, or treating it only as a necessary evil, in order to magnify an invisible fellowship of the Spirit and of spirits. This view is just as impossible as christological Docetism, not only in point of history, but also in point of substance. For the work of the Holy Spirit as the awakening power of Jesus Christ would not take place at

---

^{EN35} churches
^{EN36} ideal republic

2. *The Being of the Community*

all if the invisible did not become visible, if the Christian community did not take on and have an earthly-historical form. The individual Christian can exist only in time and space as a doer of the Word (Jas. 1²²) and therefore in a concrete human form and basically visible to everyone. Similarly the Christian community as such cannot exist as an ideal commune or universum, but—also in time and space—only in the relationship of its individual members as they are fused together by the common action of the Word which they have heard into a definite human fellowship; in concrete form, therefore, and visible to everyone. If we say with the creed *credo ecclesiam*^{EN37}, we do not proudly overlook its concrete form; just as when we confess *credo resurrectionem carnis*^{EN38} we cannot overlook the real and whole man who is a soul and yet also a body, we cannot overlook his hope as though the resurrection was not also promised to him. Nor do we look penetratingly through this form, as though it was only something transparent and the real Church had to be sought behind it; just as we cannot overlook or look through the pleasing or less pleasing face of the neighbour whom we are commanded to love. We look at the visible aspect of the Church—this is the state of it. And as we look at what is seen—not beside it or behind but in it—we see what is not seen. Hence we cannot rid ourselves in this way of the generally visible side of the Church. We cannot take refuge from it in a kind of wonderland. The *credo ecclesiam*^{EN39} can and necessarily will involve much distinguishing and questioning, much concern and shame. It can and necessarily will be a very critical *credo*^{EN40}. In relation to the side of the Church which is generally visible it can and necessarily will express what does not amount to much more than a hope and a yearning. But it does take the Church quite seriously in its common visibility—which is its earthly and historical existence. It confesses faith in the invisible aspect which is the secret of the visible. Believing in the *ecclesia invisibilis*^{EN41} we will enter the sphere of labour and conflict of the *ecclesia visibilis*^{EN42}. Without doing this, without a discriminate but serious participation in the historical life of the community, its activity, its upbuilding, its mission, in a kind of purely theoretical and abstract churchliness, no one has ever seriously repeated the *credo ecclesiam*^{EN43}. Those who try to repeat it in a way which looks above the Church, only dreaming of its existence in time and space, must see to it that they are not secretly pandering to a christological Docetism as well, or, at any rate, that they are really taking seriously the true humanity of Jesus Christ. Faith in His community has this in common with faith in Him, that it, too, relates to a reality in time and space, and therefore to something which is at bottom generally visible. If,

[654]

---

^{EN37} I believe in the church
^{EN38} I believe in the resurrection of the dead
^{EN39} I believe in the church
^{EN40} I believe
^{EN41} invisible church
^{EN42} visible church
^{EN43} I believe in the church

§ 62. The Holy Spirit and the Gathering of the Christian Community

then, we believe in Him, we cannot refuse—however hesitantly or anxiously or contentiously—to believe in His community in its spatio-temporal existence, and therefore to be a member of it and personally a Christian. We will return to the implications of this in the second part of the doctrine of reconciliation under the title of the true humanity of Jesus Christ. For the moment it is enough to point to it by way of demarcation.

When we have done this, the emphasis in the present context must be upon the fact that the community called into being by the Holy Spirit, although it does not exist and must not be sought abstractly in the invisible, also does not exist and must not be sought abstractly in the visible. It does exist openly in a very concrete form, a historical phenomenon like any other. But what it is, the character, the truth of its existence in time and space, is not a matter of a general but a very special visibility. Without this it is invisible. What is visible to all is the event of the *congregatio*[EN44] and *communio*[EN45] of certain men, its characteristic activities and achievements, its peculiarities by which it is distinguished from other historical structures, its deficiencies which it has with them in common, its relative advantages. But what actually takes place, what this is in truth, is not visible to all; it is visible to Christians only in this particular way or not at all. Without this special visibility all that can be seen is the men united in it and their common activity, and this will be explained in terms of the categories which are regarded as the most appropriate for the understanding and appraisal of common human activities, with an attempt to subordinate it to some picture of the world and of history. On this view it can be understood as a religious society within human society generally and side by side with other organisations. The attention paid to it will be with reference to its past and present in this connexion and on this level. Its structure and message and claims and activity as this particular society within or side by side with others, its greater or lesser, welcome or unwelcome significance and co-operation and power in the spheres of culture and the state, will be registered and either lauded or tolerated, supported or contested, with varying degrees of attention. It will be taken seriously, but within the limits of the two-dimensional view in which it can be generally known, as one earthly-historical factor with others. And when we say that we are already saying too much, because on this view there cannot be any other but earthly-historical factors.

> In this connexion we may recall the level on which and the manner in which the Church is usually spoken of by the average statesman or politician, by the journalist who pontificates concerning the Church and the Churches and things ecclesiastical and by the pure historicist, psychologist and sociologist. All these very obviously and obstinately keep to the external picture which is visible to them, and with a mixture of ignorance, irony and nervousness they steer clear of anything wider.

It is plain that fundamentally the Church is forced to acknowledge the pic-

---

[EN44] congregation
[EN45] communion

2. *The Being of the Community*

ture which it offers on this view. Indeed it is essential to it to be external, to exist in the dimensions of this level, and therefore to offer this external picture. It is equally plain that for its own part it cannot agree to be seen and understood for what it is in this external picture as such. It has to know the third dimension of its existence. Yet it also has to know that it is defenceless against the interpretations to which it is subject on this two-dimensional view. For where there is not this special visibility, where there cannot be an insight into its earthly and historical form, even what it can confess and ever so impressively explain concerning its true being as visible in this external picture will, of course, have its greater or lesser interest as its particular ideology and may even be noted with a nod of the head, but it will at once be translated onto the historical and psychological and sociological level and irresistibly absorbed into the external picture as such. No matter what attitude it takes up, what it is will still be invisible, and for the first time genuinely invisible. And then it will always be tempted to give way, to see and understand itself only in this external picture, to acquiesce in it, to be a kind of religious society, to build itself up and to develop as such, to be active, setting itself aims and achieving results as such, to live peaceably with the rest of society on this basis and in this sphere, even to assert itself—perhaps with a certain measure of triumph but certainly with assurance, because, like everything else on this level, religion can always present itself as a necessary human need, and because it is unquestionably in a position to meet that need. But this is a temptation which comes to the Church from without, from its own humanity. From within it will never find itself tempted to try to exist only in two dimensions and therefore in an abstract visibility. From within, in the light of its awakening by the Holy Spirit, it will always have to see and understand and confess itself in three dimensions, whether this is understood from without or not. [656]

If in the great Schleiermacher's *Glaubenslehre* we have, as it were, a fall of Christianity, or the canonisation of it, this is to be found in the wonderfully logical introduction in which on the basis of ethics (what Schleiermacher calls the general philosophy of history) it is defined and described as a "pious society"—naturally of a particular kind—that is to say, "a monotheistic form of faith related to the teleological direction of piety," and essentially distinguished from all others by the fact "that everything in it is connected with the redemption accomplished by Jesus of Nazareth" (§ 11). In this definition everything has been more or less correctly perceived. The only thing is that the third dimension, in which the Church is what it is, is completely absent.

To be sure, the confession *credo ecclesiam*[EN46] does refer necessarily to a human society which exists concretely in history and which may at a pinch be defined as a pious society or something similar. But its true reference is to what this society *is* in its concrete historical form, and therefore to a character which is proper to it not in its general but its particular visibility, a character in which it is invisible without this particular visibility. In this character, notwithstanding

---

[EN46] I believe in the church

§ 62. *The Holy Spirit and the Gathering of the Christian Community*

its concrete historical form, indeed in this form as in everything declared by the Christian confession, the Church has to be believed. No one really needs to believe the Christianity defined and described by Schleiermacher: in its own way it is a historical phenomenon like all others, and as such it can at bottom be perceived generally. What Christianity really is, the being of the community as "the living community of the living Lord Jesus Christ," calls for the perception of faith, and is accessible only to this perception and not to any other. It has this character in virtue of the reconciling and self-revealing grace of God, in virtue of the mission and work of the Holy Spirit, and therefore in the power of Jesus Christ Himself. Only in this power is it recognisable in this character. The glory of Jesus Christ was hidden when He humbled Himself, when He took our flesh, when in our flesh He was obedient to God, when He destroyed our wrong, when He established our right. So, too, the glory of the humanity justified in Him is concealed. And this means that the glory of the community gathered together by Him within humanity is only a glory which is hidden from the eyes of the world until His final revelation, so that it can be only an object of faith. What it is, its mystery, its spiritual character, is not without manifestations and analogies in its generally visible form. But it is not unequivocally represented in any such generally visible manifestations and analogies. The men united in it and their action are in every respect generally visible. They are so as the elect and called of God, and their works as good works. But the being of the community in its temporal character is hidden under considerable and very powerful appearances to the contrary. There is no direct identity between what the community is and any confession, theology or cultus; any party, trend, group or movement in the being of the community as it may be generally perceived; anything within it which can be demonstrated or delimited or counted or formulated in a purely human way; or, of course, any of the individuals assembled and active within it. There is nothing within it which does not prompt, which may not itself be, the question whether and how far it has a part in what the community is. There is nothing within it which does not continually have to receive again this part, which does not have to be believed in its participation. The gathering and maintaining and completing of the community, as the mystery of what its visible form is on this level, is in the hand of God, and as His own work, a spiritual reality, its third dimension, it is invisible, it cannot be perceived but only believed. For in what its generally visible history is on that level it does not belong only to the creaturely world but actually to the world of flesh, of fallen man. It is always sinful history—just as the individual believer is not only a creature but a sinful man. Woe to it if what it is is directly identical with what it is as generally visible, or if it accepts as its being its concrete historical form, equating itself with it and trying to exist in it abstractly! For we should then have to say of it that it is not Israel but Edom or Moab, that it is not the Church of Jesus Christ but the synagogue of Antichrist. This is the sword which always and everywhere hangs

2. The Being of the Community

over the *ecclesia visibilis*[EN47]. According to the will and in the power of the act of God, even in its visibility it can and should attest its invisible glory, i.e., the glory of the Lord justifying man and of man justified by the Lord. But it loses the ability to do this, it becomes unserviceable to the will and act of God, to the extent that in its visible being it wants to be something more and better than the witness of its invisible being, if it is content or indeed insists on representing and maintaining and asserting and communicating itself as a historical factor, taking itself and its doctrine and sacraments and sacramental observances and ordinances and spiritual authority and power in the more usual sense of the word to be the meaning of its existence, its greatness, its true and final word, in place of the underlying and over-ruling power of Jesus Christ and His Spirit. The question whether it does this has to be directed not only to the Papal Church and the other great world Churches, but no less seriously to even the smallest of Church groups, the modesty of whose external existence often seems to stand in strange relationship to the notorious arrogance of their claims. It is always and everywhere a living question, wherever the Church is and is therefore visible, in face of every cultus or law or confession or theology. Where the Holy Ghost is at work the step to visibility is unavoidable, but it is always and everywhere surrounded by this temptation. The third dimension from which this step is made must remain open. It can be made legitimately only when we remember that the men gathered into the community and acting as such still stand in need of the grace of God, i.e., of their invisible Lord and His invisible Spirit; that it is He who controls the Church without in any sense being controlled by it. [658]

Where and when does it not hang by a knife's edge whether or not there is this remembrance in the community? If there is not, the Church not only becomes like the world, but denying its true secret it becomes especially worldly. Luther knew what he was talking about when he dared to say (*Pred. üb. Matth.* 28 ^{1}, 1531, W.A. 34^1, 276, 7): *Non est tam magna peccatrix ut Christiana ecclesia*[EN48]. It is the Church which prays, "Forgive us our trespasses," which therefore knows and confesses that it needs the forgiveness of sins. It is always God's redemption of a sinful Church when it is aware of that denial of its secret and therefore of its extreme worldliness. We have to do with this redemption, or rather with this Redeemer, who alone can guarantee its hidden character, when we confess: *credo ecclesiam*[EN49].

No concrete form of the community can in itself and as such be the object of faith. Even the man Jesus as such, the *caro Christi*[EN50], cannot be this, just as the individual Christian cannot believe in his faith as a work. The community can believe in itself only when it believes in its Lord and therefore in what it is, in what it really is in its concrete form. The work magnifies the master. The visible attests the invisible. The glory of the community consists in the fact that it can give God the glory, and does not cease to do so. Its glory can appear only

---

[EN47] visible church
[EN48] There is no sinner so great as the Christian church
[EN49] I believe in the Church
[EN50] flesh of Christ

§ 62. *The Holy Spirit and the Gathering of the Christian Community*

where there appears the glory of Jesus Christ and the sinner justified by Him. But as long as time endures, until the final manifestation of God and man in the future of Jesus Christ, the place where this takes place is hidden in its concrete form, with which it is only indirectly and not directly identical. For that reason this occurrence must be believed in the concrete form of the history which is visible to all.

It is worth noting that even in the *Cat. Rom.* (I, 10, 17–18) we find this expressly recognised: *Cum igitur hic articulus (sc. de ecclesia) intelligentiae nostrae facultatem et vires superet, iure optimo confitemur, nos ecclesiae ortum, munera et dignitatem non humana ratione cognoscere, sed fidei oculis cernere* .... *Neque enim homines huius ecclesiae auctores fuerunt, sed Deus ipse immortalis* .... *Nec potestas, quant accedit, humana est, sed divino munere tributa. Quare, quemadmodum naturae viribus comparari non potest, ita etiam fide solum intelligimus, in ecclesia claves caelorum esse eique potestatem peccata remittendi, excommunicandi verumque Christi corpus consecrandi traditam*[EN51]. For the moment we may leave it open whether excommunication is one of the most important functions of the Church, or whether the consecration of the true body of Christ is one of its functions at all. What matters is that *in thesi*[EN52] it is maintained: *fide solum intelligimus*[EN53].

If only there were something corresponding to this in the encyclical of Pius XII, "*Mystici Corporis*" (1943), which is normative for the modern Romanist view! But instead of that it does not even speak of the necessity of faith in the Church, and in the decisive explanation of the term *Mysticum corpus*[EN54] (Herder edit., 1947, 60 f.), although we do not find a conceptual equation, we have what amounts to the same thing, an unconditional identification of the mystery of the Church as created and maintained and ruled by Christ through the Holy Spirit with its historical action and judicial organisation. It is the Holy Spirit who exalts the Christian above all other communities and every natural order. Its external structure is a very secondary matter (*aliquid inferioris omnino ordinis*[EN55]) (p. 64). But since it derives directly from Jesus Christ, even the visible and organised Church is a *societas perfecta*[EN56] (p. 66). Between it and the invisible Church of the Spirit and love there is no antithesis worth mentioning: *nulla veri nominis oppositio vel repugnantia*[EN57]. What is visible in the Church as human weakness is not the fault of its constitution but of the deplorable evil disposition of individuals (the *lamentabilis singulorum ad malum proclivitas*[EN58])—a weakness which its divine author knows how to handle for the best and with supreme wisdom even though it may be found in higher placed members of the body. Of the Church as such it can be finally confessed with triumph: "Without any fault at all (*utique absque ulla labe*) the pious mother shines forth in the sacraments by which her children are borne and nourished, in the faith which

---

[EN51] Since therefore this article (sc. on the church) exceeds the faculty and powers of our intelligence, we confess with the best right that we understand the origin, the offices and the dignity of the church not by human reason, but that we see it with the eyes of faith ... For men were not the authors of the Church, but the immortal God himself ... The power which it has received is not human power but is attributed to the work of God. So, just as it is not able to be compared with the powers of nature, so we can understand only by faith, that the keys of heaven are in the church, and that the power to forgive sins, to excommunicate, and to consecrate the true body of Christ have been handed to her

[EN52] in principle
[EN53] we can understand only by faith
[EN54] mystical body
[EN55] something altogether of a lower order
[EN56] perfect society
[EN57] no opposition or conflict in a real sense
[EN58] the woeful tendency of individuals to wickedness

2. *The Being of the Community*

she has always kept inviolate, in the most holy laws to which she engages all, and in the evangelical counsels which she gives, finally in the heavenly gifts and graces by which she produces with inexhaustible fertility whole hosts of martyrs, virgins and confessors. We cannot make it a matter of reproach to her if some of her members are sick or wounded. In their name she makes her daily prayer to God: 'Forgive us our trespasses,' and with the strong heart of a mother she makes their spiritual nurture her unceasing concern" (p. 68 f.).

Note that it is in the name of individual offenders among its members that it makes the petition mentioned by Luther. When it does this there is no question of praying in its own name and therefore of acknowledging itself *ecclesia peccatrix*^{EN59}. It itself is always right in everything. What the Church is is not hidden. It does not need to be believed. It can be directly deduced from what the Church is and does as the visible Church, from the excellence of its existence as it may be seen by all. But why call it "mystical" if it can be perceived directly without any difficulty? We must not overlook the fact that within modern Roman Catholicism there are those who think and speak of the Church in a way which is very different and which seems to give fresh life to the *fide solum intelligimus*^{EN60}, cf. the stimulating writings of H. U. v. Balthasar (*Geschleifte Bastionen*) and F. Heer (*Das Experiment Europa*). But for the moment it is hard to see how there can be any further discussion with the official Roman Catholic doctrine of the Church when it so obviously continues to harden in this way.

Looking forward once more to the second part of the doctrine of reconciliation, we emphasise the fact that if the *credo ecclesiam*^{EN61} contains within it a critical caveat in face of its whole earthly and historical form, if it sets it in question, it does not negate it so that there can be no question of an escape into invisibility. On the contrary, if this reservation is taken seriously as such, [660] then we are both challenged and permitted not to burk but resolutely to take the unavoidable step into visibility. *Credo ecclesiam*^{EN62} then means that the Church can take itself seriously in the world of the earthly and visible, with all humility but also with all comfort, at once directed and established by its third dimension. According to its best knowledge and conscience, it can and should create the forms which are indispensable to it as the human society which it essentially is, the forms which are best adapted to its edification and the discharge of its mission. It can and should think and discuss and decide with the necessary prudence and boldness concerning such things as canon, dogma, constitution, order and cultus. In its great hours it has always rightly done this and will continue to do so. It must do it in faith and obedience. It has to remember that it is not itself God but is responsible to God, that it does not have the last word. But with this reservation in relation to itself, with a consciousness of the relativity of its decisions, their provisional nature, their need of constant reform, standing under and not over the Word it can go to work with quiet determination, accepting the risk, but with the courage and authority of faith and obedience, and therefore without the false affectation which in order not to do anything questionable will never do anything at all, which in

---

^{EN59} sinning church
^{EN60} we can understand only by faith
^{EN61} I believe in the church
^{EN62} I believe in the church

§ 62. *The Holy Spirit and the Gathering of the Christian Community*

every conditional assertion scents an attempt at the unconditional, which out of a simple fear of hardening, orthodoxy, authoritarianism and hierarchy can never get past the stage of questioning and protesting (as though in the last resort formlessness and therefore chaos is the condition which is best pleasing to God). If the Church has a good conscience in its relation to the "Jerusalem which is above, which is the mother of us all" (Gal. 4^{26}), and therefore to its basis in God, and therefore to itself, it will find it all the more humble and appropriate to give itself to the task of earthly and historical ordering in every form, instead of trying to imitate the unconditioned nature of God by refusing the conditions which are indispensable to its community and its service in earth. If it lives also and primarily in its third dimension, it can and should act confidently on the level of its phenomenal being. If the Church continues in the humility of its Lord and therefore in respect for His and its own secret, then the sword of rejection which hangs over all Church life is the protective sword of its election and calling. It lives by the awakening power of the Holy Spirit. In the world it can never be anything other than an *église du désert*[EN63], anything better than a "moving tent" like the biblical tabernacle. But it does live by the awakening power of the Holy Spirit. It is called to tarry for Him and to obey Him. The Church which does this seriously will in the long run prove to be the best Church even in the visibility of history.

[661] But what is this being of the community, this spiritual character, this secret, which is hidden in its earthly and historical form and therefore invisible, or visible only to the special perception of faith? The answer—which does indeed point to a third dimension—can only be this: The community is the earthly-historical form of existence of Jesus Christ Himself. The time has now come to adopt the New Testament term used to describe this matter. The Church is His body, created and continually renewed by the awakening power of the Holy Spirit. Jesus Christ also lives as the Crucified and Risen in a heavenly-historical form of existence; at the right hand of the Father, before whom He is the advocate and intercessor for all men as the Judge who was judged in their place, the One who was obedient for them all, their justification. But He does not live only and exclusively in this form, enclosed within it. He does not live only above human history on earth, addressing Himself to it only from above and from afar and from without. He Himself lives in a special element of this history created and controlled by Him. He therefore lives in an earthly-historical form of existence within it. This particular element of human history, this earthly-historical form of existence of Jesus Christ, is the Christian community. He is the Head of this body, the community. And it is the body which has its Head in Him. It belongs to Him, and He belongs to it. We can put it even more strongly: Because He is, it is; it is, because He is. That is its secret, its being in the third dimension, which is visible only to faith.

But because He is its Head, the Christian community which is His body is the

---

[EN63] wilderness church

2. *The Being of the Community*

gathering of those men whom already before all others He has made willing and ready for life under the divine verdict executed in His death and revealed in His resurrection from the dead. This is the creation of the body by its Head, of the body with which He co-exists as the Head and which co-exists with Him as its Head, which as the body is the earthly-historical form of existence of the Head. What distinguishes the men united in the community and therefore the community itself is that they acknowledge what has been done from God by Him, the Lord who became a servant, not only for them but for all men; that they recognise as such the One who is not only their Lord but the Lord of the whole world; and that they confess Him with their life. The verdict of God pronounced in Him not only on them but on the whole world is accepted by them and in force. It has found in them open ears and a ready heart. Ultimately the community will not be alone in this. Rather, "at the name of Jesus every knee shall bow, of things in heaven and things in earth, and things under the earth; and that every tongue should confess that Jesus Christ is Lord, to the glory of God the Father" (Phil. $2^{10f.}$). But this will not take place in the continuity of earthly history, but in its breaking off, in the end and goal of all time as brought about by God the Father (again in the—general—revelation of Jesus Christ). That will be the irruption of the other side of all human history. What distinguishes the community is that there is already revealed to it in faith that which as it concerns all will then be revealed to all. It realises, it sees and acknowledges and confesses "already before all others" what has been done for all in Jesus Christ, and what, as it has been done for all, will be seen and acknowledged and confessed by all when He appears as the Judge of the quick and the dead. It exists already before all others in the light of Easter Day as the dawning of the Last Day—already, i.e., within the as yet unbroken continuity of earthly history. It exists eschatologically, i.e., in correspondence with the "already" of Easter Day, which was the dawning of the Last Day within earthly history. In this existence which looks back to Easter Day and forward to the Last Day the community belongs together with the living Lord Jesus Christ Himself because He belongs together with it, because this its existence is the earthly-historical form of His existence. As it subjects itself to the divine sentence pronounced in Him, it lives with Him as His people, His fellowship, His community, in this choice and decision and work. The only thing is that of all other human choices and decisions and works this particular choice and decision and work does not arise spontaneously from the spirit of the men united in it, but from their awakening by the Holy Spirit. Its basis and truth and continuance are therefore in the choice and decision, the work and the living Word of Jesus Christ Himself. Thus in the particular activity which distinguishes it as His community in the world it does not belong to itself, but to Him; it does not live of itself, but can only follow the movement of His life; it has not to present and maintain and carry through to success its own cause, but (notwithstanding all the humanity, all the corruption and lostness which characterise the men united in it) can reflect and illustrate and in that way attest in its own activity

[662]

§ 62. *The Holy Spirit and the Gathering of the Christian Community*

His activity. The people which has not assumed and cannot assume or continue, but to which it is given and of which it is and will be demanded, to do this, is the Christian community. It believes that it is this people when it confesses: *credo ecclesiam*[EN64]. And that it undeniably is and will be and continually becomes this in its concrete form—for its faith is not empty, but faith in Jesus Christ—is the secret of Church history, which cannot be destroyed by the "medley of error and force" which it may also appear to be, but which shines out in world history only by its own power, and can therefore be perceived only by the faith which sees it shine in this power and is itself awakened by it.

We must now explain briefly the remarkable New Testament expression σῶμα Χριστοῦ[EN65]. And first it will be as well to try to survey together the different meanings within which the word σῶμα[EN66] oscillates. To understand the New Testament usage we must not forget that in the first instance it means a dead body, a corpse. But in relation to the human body it also means the living body, either as contrasted with the soul, or with its individual parts, the members, or even with the blood in which it has its life (as in the texts relating to the Lord's Supper). From this we may conclude that σῶμα[EN67] is the seat of the earthly-historical life, so that being in it can indicate the time of man's being on earth, and the σῶμα[EN68] in which he lives the limitation of that time. But σῶμα[EN69] is also the medium of man's experience and suffering, the organ or instrument of his activity. We must also not forget that (in Rev. 18¹³) it can indicate the bodily possession, or slave, and (in Col. 2¹⁷) the body which throws a shadow in distinction from the shadow. In the sequence Χριστός-σῶμα-ἐκκλησία[EN70] the word σῶμα[EN71] can have all these different meanings with greater or lesser pregnancy.

We will start with the main passage, 1 Cor. 12¹². Here primarily we have to note that in the first instance it is not the community which is called a body, or compared to it, but Christ Himself. He is a body. By nature He is not simply one (for a body is the unity of many members), but one in many. It is not that σῶμα[EN72] is a good image for the community as such, but that Jesus Christ is by nature σῶμα[EN73]. Hence the force of Paul's argument in 1 Cor. 12⁴⁻³¹ for the necessity of the unity and plurality of gifts in the community (which, although they differ from another, are all gifts of the one Spirit). It is in the "bodily nature," in the simplicity and plurality of Jesus Christ Himself, that the Corinthians are able to recognise the necessary order, the relatedness and the freedom of their life as His community. From Him they are one as ἐκκλησία[EN74], that is to say, they are His body, and members of this body in the reception of the different gifts of the one Spirit granted to them: ὑμεῖς δέ ἐστε σῶμα Χριστοῦ καὶ μέλη ἐκ μέρους[EN75] (1 Cor. 12²⁷). The community is not σῶμα[EN76] because it is a social grouping which as such has something of the nature of an

---

[EN64] I believe in the church
[EN65] body of Christ
[EN66] body
[EN67] body
[EN68] body
[EN69] body
[EN70] Christ-body-Church
[EN71] body
[EN72] body
[EN73] body
[EN74] church
[EN75] you are one body of Christ, and members individually
[EN76] body

2. *The Being of the Community*

organism, which reminds us of an organism, which, *ceteris imparibus*[EN77], can therefore quite suitably be compared with it, which can be called a σῶμα[EN78] It is σῶμα[EN79] because it actually derives from Jesus Christ, because of Him it exists as His body. The relationship to Him, or rather from Him, is everywhere evident: οἱ πολλοὶ ἕν σῶμά ἐσμεν ἐν Χριστῷ[EN80] (Rom. 12⁵). He is the "Head" of this body, the centre which constitutes its unity, organises its plurality, and guarantees both (Col. 1¹⁸, Eph. 5²³). "From Him (ἐξ οὗ) all the body by joints and bands supported, and knit together, increaseth with the increase of God" (αὔξει τὴν αὔξησιν τοῦ θεοῦ, Col. 2¹⁹, Eph. 4¹⁶). The work of the ministry of the saints is for the edification of His body (Eph. 4¹²). "We are members of his body" (Eph. 5³⁰), and He is its Saviour (Eph. 5²³). Apart from Jesus Christ there is no other principle or *telos*[EN81] to constitute and organise and guarantee this body. Even the *kerygma*, baptism, the Lord's Supper, the faith and love and hope of Christians, the work and word of the apostle, cannot have this function. It is the function of Jesus Christ alone. As the Head He is Himself and primarily the body, and He constitutes and organises and guarantees the community as His body.

He does this as the One who was crucified on Golgotha. Of course as the One crucified there He was raised again on the third day and is therefore able to act. All the same, to understand who it is that acts, we must first think of the meaning of σῶμα[EN82] as a dead body or corpse, as in Rom. 7⁴: "Ye also are become dead to the law by the body of Christ," or, again, Col. 3¹⁵: "Ye are called to peace in one body" (His), or Col. 1²²: "He hath reconciled us in the body of his flesh through death," "by the cross" (Eph. 2¹⁶), or 1 Pet. 2²⁴: "He bare our sins in his own body on the tree," or Heb. 10¹⁰: "We are sanctified through the offering of the body of Jesus Christ once for all." He lives and acts as the One who was put to death in the body, who offered up His earthly-historical existence, who was deprived of it, who in His body delivered up to death, bore and bore away "the body of sin" (Rom. 6⁶), the "body of the flesh" (Col. 2¹¹), the "body of this death" (Rom. 7²⁴). In Him it was all humanity in its corruption and lostness, its earthly-historical existence under the determination of the fall, which was judged and executed and destroyed, and in that way liberated for a new determination, for its being as a new humanity. It was the body of everyman which became a corpse in Him and was buried as a corpse with Him. All men, "Jew and Greek, bond and free, male and female," as they are now representatively gathered in the community, were one in God's election (Eph. 1⁴), were and are one in the fulfilment of it on Golgotha, are one in the power of His resurrection, one in Jesus Christ (εἷς, Gal. 3²⁸), His body together in their unity and totality.

[664]

This is revealed in His resurrection from the dead, in the light of which it can and must be said to the community: "Ye are the body of Christ" (1 Cor. 12²⁷). In His risen body the sinful, fleshly humanity which had fallen a prey to death and had been destroyed in Him is awakened to being in a new right and life. "The body without the spirit is dead" (Jas. 2²⁶). Without the Holy Spirit the body of Jesus Christ and in it all humanity can only be dead. But the body of Jesus Christ was not a body abandoned by the Holy Spirit. The Holy Spirit has shown Himself to it as the life-giving Spirit. The body of this One who was slain has become a body which is alive by the Spirit: σῶμα πνευματικόν[EN83], 1 Cor. 15⁴⁴). During the forty days He appeared to His disciples in this body. He, the one man Jesus of Nazareth, who had been raised from the dead—that is the concrete history of the forty days. But not He alone,

---

[EN77] other things not being equal
[EN78] body
[EN79] body
[EN80] we many are one body in Christ
[EN81] goal
[EN82] body
[EN83] spiritual body

§ 62. The Holy Spirit and the Gathering of the Christian Community

abstractly as this one man, just as He had not died alone, abstractly as this one man. But the one man who as their Representative and the Representative of all men, the bearer of their sin and flesh and death, had delivered all this up to the past in His death, dying on the cross—this one man now appeared to His disciples (in their own person first and then of all humanity) as the bearer of their new right and life, and as such the Revealer of their future, Himself in His person, in His body, the promised πνεῦμα ζωοποιοῦν[EN84], which is His remarkable title as the "last Adam" (1 Cor. 15⁴⁵). The content of Easter Day and the Easter season consisted in this, not in an "attesting miracle," not merely in a parthenogenesis of the Christian faith, but in the appearance of the body of Jesus Christ, which embraced their death in its death, their life in its life, their past and their future in itself, thus including them all in itself. As He encountered them in this corporeity, the disciples heard addressed to themselves as such, to the ἐκκλησία[EN85] which arose in virtue of it, the call which is the disclosure of the secret of His earthly-historical existence: "Ye are the body of Christ."

Therefore the mystery of the community is not in the first instance its own. In the first instance it is His mystery: the mystery of His death in which He was this Victor; the mystery of His resurrection in which He was this Revealer. In His body He is elected, called and instituted from all eternity as this Victor and Revealer. It is His body which includes them all to their salvation and the salvation of the world. Because it includes them, it is their body and they are His body. In Him they themselves have turned away from sin and flesh and death as their past and have turned to the right and life as their future. His mystery is theirs. Having been given life by the Spirit, and Himself a life-giving Spirit, He has made it known to them—His election and birth and calling and institution as their Head and the Head of all men, His earthly-historical existence as that of their Representative and Substitute and Advocate, and therefore as the truth of their own earthly-historical existence. He is always the Head of this body. He is the giver and they are the recipients. He is the Master and they are the brethren (Mt. 23⁸). He is the vine and they are the branches (Jn. 15⁵). "Without me ye can do nothing"—you cannot be my body, you cannot be a body at all. For only He, Jesus Christ, the "last Adam," is the unity in plurality of humanity which the first Adam could only prefigure. He alone can be the Head of a body which includes them all—so that if they are to be a body, they can only be His body.

The mystery of the community is not in the first instance its own mystery in the further sense that its Head Jesus Christ was elected the Head of all humanity (as the last and true Adam, 1 Cor. 15⁴⁵ᶠ·), that He was made the one Mediator between God and all men (1 Tim. 2⁵), that He died for the sins of the whole world (1 Jn. 2²), and that He rose again as the Revealer of the right and life of all men (1 Cor. 15²¹ᶠ·). The New Testament never expressly uses the term body of humanity as a whole, of the totality of Jews and Greeks, slaves and free men, males and females. It uses it only of the Christian community. For only in this community is there a dispensing and eating of the bread which is broken in common. Only in it is there the visible fellowship (κοινωνία) of this body, the perceiving and attesting of His real presence, the recognisable and recognised union of a concrete human fellowship with Him (1 Cor. 10¹⁶). ὅτι εἷς ἄρτος: "Because it is the one bread which the many break and eat (together)"—ἓν σῶμα οἱ πολλοί ἐσμεν[EN86]: "we, the many, are one body"—οἱ γὰρ πάντες ἐκ τοῦ ἑνὸς ἄρτου μετέχομεν: "for we are all partakers of the one bread" (1 Cor. 10¹⁷). Their communion with one another, their common action in remembrance of Him, their common proclamation of the death of the Lord until He comes (1 Cor. 11²⁶), as it takes place in this action, does not create and put into effect their union with Jesus Christ Him-

---

[EN84] life-giving Spirit
[EN85] church
[EN86] body of Christ

2. *The Being of the Community*

self—which is unnecessary; it reveals and publishes and documents that union, it is that union *in concreto*[EN87], as the earthly-historical activity and experience of these particular men. Where there is not this communion, we cannot speak with the New Testament of a union of men with Jesus Christ and therefore of a real presence of His body. To that extent the expression σῶμα Χριστοῦ[EN88] is in the New Testament an esoteric expression. The reality indicated by it is to be seen only in the concrete life of the community. A saying like 1 Cor. 12^{27} ("Ye are the body of Christ, and members in particular") is obviously not a part of missionary preaching. It is clearly a kind of repetition of the call which in the forty days was not directly addressed to humanity as a whole but to the few whom the risen One encountered. But it is open to question whether the same can be true of the saying in 1 Cor. 12^{12} in which Jesus Christ Himself is called a body. For how can we proclaim His death and resurrection to Jews and Gentiles as their own death and the promise of their right and life without proclaiming Him as the Head and Representative and Mediator of all men, the "last Adam"? And how can we do that without approximating very closely to the concept of the body of Christ including and uniting all men? That logic drives us in this direction is something we have to remember for an understanding of the being and mission of the community. As σῶμα Χριστοῦ[EN89] it is not an end in itself. In the first instance and originally Jesus Christ as the Head is the one body visible in the bread, and the community only because He is this one body and calls it to be and makes it a unity. Similarly, the community itself, participating in the bread, is only the arrow which points to that unity of the many which is grounded and—although hidden—actual in the fact that He is the Mediator and Substitute and Representative of all men. How can it be the body of this Head if it tries to be a house with closed doors and windows, if it tries to exist like a ghetto, if as the body of Christ it wants to be defined by its own limits? If it has a right understanding of itself in its common breaking and eating of the one bread and therefore in its concrete life as a community, then as the body of Christ it has to understand itself as a promise of the emergence of the unity in which not only Christians but all men are already comprehended in Jesus Christ. The great truth of Eph. 1^{23} can never be forgotten but must always shine out in it. As His body it is "the fulness of him that filleth all in all." And the same is true of Eph. 1$^{9f.}$: God has "made known unto us the mystery of his will, according to his free resolve purposed in himself and to be accomplished in the fulness of times ἀνακεφαλαιώσασθαι τὰ πάντα[EN90]: to give to all things their head in Christ—to all things, both which are in heaven, and which are on earth, in him, in whom also we have obtained an inheritance, being predestinated according to the purpose of him who worketh all things after the counsel of his own will, that we should be to the praise of his glory, who already have our hope in him" (προηλπικότες, lit. those who have hoped before in Him).

This is the Magna Carta of the being of the community in Him. We do not decrease but bring out its true glory if we understand the exclusiveness in which it is called and is His body in the world as an exclusiveness which is relative, provisional and teleological. Sayings like Col. 1$^{18\ 24}$: "The church is his body," or, conversely, Eph. 1^{23}: "His body is the church," or Rom. 12^5, in which the many are one body in Him, or the direct statement in Eph. 5^{30} that "we are members of his body," speak of the glory of the being of the community in so far as they speak properly of the glory of Jesus Christ Himself and therefore of the σωτὴρ τοῦ κόσμου[EN91] (Jn. 4^{42}; 1 Jn. 4^{14}), of His being and work for the whole of humanity which is

[666]

[EN87] in concreto
[EN88] body of Christ
[EN89] body of Christ
[EN90] uniting everything under one head
[EN91] saviour of the world

§ 62. *The Holy Spirit and the Gathering of the Christian Community*

both one and many. In the first instance they are christological and therefore teleological statements, and only as such ecclesiological.

For that reason they do not provide any basis for the idea of a Church which exists *ipsa quasi altera Christi persona*[EN92], as fully proclaimed in the encyclical "*Mystici corporis*" (p. 54). There are not two or possibly three bodies of Christ: the historical, in which He died and rose again; the mystical which is His community; and that in which He is really present in the Lord's Supper. For there are not three Christs. There is only one Christ, and therefore there is only one body of Christ.

For the same reason there is no need to take the statements symbolically or metaphorically. As His earthly-historical form of existence, the community is His body. His body is the community. Why, and to what extent? Because the community and those who belong to it have received the "manifestation of the Spirit" (1 Cor. 12^7) in the unity and diversity of His gifts (Rom. 12^6), because they have "drunk" with Him (1 Cor. 12^{13}) and therefore are free to confess Jesus as *Kyrios*[EN93] (1 Cor. 12^3). To put the same thing in another way, because the Gospel once and still proclaimed to them has shown itself powerful and effective and fruitful to and in and among them, as described in the thanksgivings with which Paul opens a whole series of his letters. The equating of the body of Christ and the community is valid only with reference to this divine action, but it is unconditionally and actually valid with this reference. With this reference these sayings can be uttered with no less definiteness than the great christological statements concerning the death of Jesus Christ implying our death as it has already taken place in Him, and the resurrection of Jesus Christ implying our future resurrection. Here we have the invisible being of the community, the being which is visible only to faith. This is what permits and enjoins us to celebrate "thanksgiving" ($\epsilon\dot{\upsilon}\chi\alpha\rho\iota\sigma\tau\acute{\iota}\alpha$) within it, to give thanks as Paul does for its existence. For in the community the truth of these christological statements, the justification of man as it has taken place in Jesus Christ, is known, in as much as Jesus Christ has shown His power and revealed and asserted Himself within it. For in Him "ye heard the word of truth, the gospel of your salvation; in whom also after that ye believed, ye were sealed with that holy Spirit of promise, which is the earnest of our inheritance, until the redemption of the purchased possession, unto the praise of his glory" (Eph. $1^{13f.}$). With the foundation and preservation of the community this event actually takes place in the space and time of these men, in the sphere of their experience and activity, although it is an event which, according to 1 Cor. $2^{9\ 14}$, cannot be brought about by any human experience or activity. In the light of this event, as the Spirit who raised up Jesus from the dead dwells within them (Rom. 8^{11}), the community can be referred to as the body of Christ, and its members as members of this body. In the light of this event its earthly-historical existence can be known as the earthly historical existence of Jesus Christ Himself (who, as its Head, is in heaven at the right hand of the Father), so that He can concretely ask the persecutor of the community (Ac. 9^4): "Saul, Saul, why persecutest thou me?", and He can say no less definitely of that which is done (or not done) to the least of His brethren (Mt. $25^{40\ 45}$): "Ye have done it (or not done it) unto me." With reference to this event the equation of the body of Christ and the community has itself to be described as a very secondary christological statement, but one which is of decisive practical importance for the time of the community in the world.

We must be clear that the community is not made the body of Christ or its members members of this body by this event, by the Spirit of Pentecost, by the fulness of His gifts, by the faith awakened by Him, by the visible, audible and tangible results of the preaching and receiving of the Gospel, let alone by baptism and the Lord's Supper (as so-called "sacra-

---

[EN92] as if as another very person of Christ
[EN93] Lord

2. *The Being of the Community*

ments"). It is the body, and its members are members of this body, in Jesus Christ, in His election from all eternity (Rom. 8^{29}, Eph. 1^4). And it became His body, they became its members, in the fulfilment of their eternal election in His death on the cross of Golgotha, proclaimed in His resurrection from the dead. In this respect, the insight of patristic tradition cited in "*Mystici Corporis*" (and combining Jn. 19^{40} and Gen. 3^{20}) is not only ingenious but substantially correct: *in cruce ecclesiam e latere salvatoris esse natam instar novae Evae matris omnium viventium*[EN94] (p. 28). The only thing is that we at once have the usual encroachment when this "new" Eve is equated with the infallible teaching and ruling ecclesiastical institution (p. 32) which is focused on the papacy as the visible head of this Church in place of the invisible Christ (p. 40). There can be no doubt that the work of the Holy Spirit is merely to "realise subjectively" the election of Jesus Christ and His work as done and proclaimed in time, to reveal and bring it to men and women. By the work of the Holy Spirit the body of Christ, as it is by God's decree from all eternity and as it has become in virtue of His act in time, acquires in all its hiddenness historical dimensions. The Holy Spirit awakens the "poor praise on earth" appropriate to that eternal-temporal occurrence, the answer to the Easter message in the hearts and on the lips of individual men, faith and the one and varied recognition of obedience to the Son of God as the Head of all men. "Thou worthy Light, shine here below / Teach us our Saviour Christ to know / That we in Him alone may stand / Who brought us to our fatherland. *Kyrie eleis*[EN95]." It is the work of the Holy Spirit that the Lord does do this in His mercy, that He shines on men to give them this knowledge of Jesus Christ and themselves. And in this knowledge, in and with Jesus Christ, His body is known as His community, His community as His body. It is known because this union has already been created in that eternal and temporal happening. It is known in such a way that its being precedes the knowledge of it, and the knowledge of it can only follow its being.

Where the knowledge of it does follow its being, there the men who share this knowledge are necessarily called to it and claimed by it. The mystery of Jesus Christ is then in fact the mystery of their own existence. The Corinthians are necessarily summoned (1 Cor. 12^{4-31}) not only to the preservation of their unity but also to the freedom of varied movements in the sphere of the one and manifold Spirit and His gift and gifts given to them: "God hath tempered the body together" (v. 24); "But now hath God set members every one of them in the body, as it hath pleased him" (v. 18); "But it is the same God which worketh all in all." If they confess Jesus Christ as Lord, which can only be by the Holy Spirit (v. 3), they confess themselves as His body, and therefore the necessity not to deny either the unity of the community or the diversity of its membership, not to suppress either but to maintain both. How they would misunderstand themselves as the community and its members, how they would misunderstand the one Spirit and His many gifts, if they were ever in danger of doing this, if they were ever tempted to do it, if it became to them a source of self-will and arrogance and division! God does not tempt anyone (Jas. 1^{13}) and neither does His Holy Spirit. Such dangers cannot derive from their being as the community of Jesus Christ. When they are awakened by the Holy Spirit, when they know Jesus Christ and in this knowledge are really in Him as He is in them, "in the midst" (Mt. 18^{20}), then they are in the one bread which they break and eat together and in that way represent and attest both Him and themselves—His body as it was crucified on Good Friday and raised on Easter Day; then they are representatives and precursors of all the Jews and Greeks, the slaves and the free men, the males and the females who are many in Him and who are also one in Him. Their unity cannot jeopardise their plurality, nor their plurality their unity.

[668]

[EN94] that on the cross the church was born from the side of the Saviour, in the likeness of a new Eve as a mother of all the living
[EN95] Lord, have mercy

§ 62. The Holy Spirit and the Gathering of the Christian Community

We are again reminded of the temporary, provisional and teleological character of this special being of the community as the body of Christ when we think of Jas. 1^{18}: "Of his own will begat he us with the word of truth, that we should be a kind of first-fruits ($\dot{a}\pi a\rho\chi\acute{\eta}\ \tau\iota s$) of his creatures;" or of 1 Pet. 2^9: "Ye are a chosen generation, a royal priesthood, an holy nation, a people of possession; that ye should proclaim the manifestations of power ($\dot{a}\rho\epsilon\tau a\acute{\iota}$) of him who hath called you out of darkness into his marvellous light;" or finally of Mt. 5^{14}: "Ye are the light of the world," which stands in a similar relationship of apparent contradiction and real agreement to Jn. 8^{12}: "I am the light of the world," as does Paul's reference to the body which is the body of Christ and as such His community.

The concept the body of Christ necessarily comprehends the perception of the being of the community as visible in faith. It will now be our task to expound this perception in the form of an analysis of the four predicates given to the *ecclesia*[EN96] in the Nic.-Const. creed (381): *Una, sancta, catholica, apostolica*[EN97].

Credo unam ecclesiam[EN98]. The Christian believes—and there is—only one Church. This means that it belongs to the being of the community to be a unity in the plurality of its members, i.e., of the individual believers assembled in it, and to be a simple unity, not having a second or third unity of the same kind side by side with it. The statement follows necessarily from all that we have seen concerning it. In all the riches of His divine being the God who reconciled the world with Himself in Jesus Christ is One. Jesus Christ, elected the Head of all men and as such their Representative who includes them all in Himself in His risen and crucified body is One. The Holy Spirit in the fulness and diversity of His gifts is One. In the same way His community as the gathering of the men who know and confess Him can only be one.

At this point we must quote word for word the passage in Eph. 4^{1-7}, because it says *in nuce* all that has to be said: "I therefore, the prisoner of the Lord, beseech you that ye walk worthy of the vocation wherewith ye are called, with all lowliness and meekness, with longsuffering, forbearing one another in love; endeavouring to keep the unity of the Spirit in the bond of peace. There is one body, and one Spirit, even as ye are called in one hope of your calling; one Lord, one faith, one baptism, one God and Father of all, who is above all, and through all, and in you all. But unto every one of us is given grace according to the measure of the gift of Christ." The limit within which there can be a real plurality among those who are addressed in this way is plain. It is the plurality of these individuals within the community, corresponding to the plurality in which they are elected and reconciled in Jesus Christ and called and endowed by His Spirit. In the event their calling and endowment follows their gathering to the equally real unity of His body. They are therefore included in it once and for all—with the absolute uniqueness of the Lord whom they all know and confess. That is how the matter is stated in 1 Cor. 12^{4-31} and Rom. 12^{3-8}. In the New Testament there can be no question of a plurality of unities. The unity is a single unity. Otherwise it is not what the New Testament knows as the $\dot{\epsilon}\kappa\kappa\lambda\eta\sigma\acute{\iota}a$[EN99].

For this reason (1) the visible and the invisible Church are not two Chur-

---

[EN96] church
[EN97] one, holy, catholic, apostolic
[EN98] I believe one church
[EN99] church

2. *The Being of the Community*

ches—an earthly-historical fellowship and above and behind this a supernaturally spiritual fellowship. As we have already seen, the one is the form and the other the mystery of one and the self-same Church. The mystery is hidden in the form, but represented and to be sought out in it. The visible lives wholly by the invisible. The invisible is only represented and to be sought out in the visible. But neither can be separated from the other. Both in their unity are the body, the earthly-historical form of existence of the one living Lord Jesus Christ.

For the same reason (2) the *ecclesia militans*[EN100] and the *ecclesia triumphans*[EN101] are not two Churches but one Church. In the one case, it is still gathered, and builds up itself and lives by its mission, both as a whole and in its members, to-day. In the other, it did so in past days or centuries, so that it already belongs to-day to the sphere of completion. But the dead no less than the living have a part in the "communion of saints." It is not only the living who speak and act. but their predecessors, their words and works, their history, which does not end on their departure, but on their departure often only enters its decisive stage among their successors, standing in an indissoluble relationship with the history of the present. Always and everywhere the Church exists in these two dimensions. We to-day, therefore, exist only as confronted not only with the persons and problems of to-day, but (whether we are aware of it or not) with the persons and problems of all Church history. The *ecclesia triumphans*[EN102] is "with Christ" (Phil. 1^{23}). With Him, the Head of the body, it takes part in the glory which is still hidden from the *ecclesia militans*[EN103]. But for this very reason it can never be far from it. Christ Himself is not far from it. As the heavenly Head of His whole body on earth He is in the midst of it. And with Him the *ecclesia triumphans*[EN104] is also with it and in the midst of it. Actively and not merely passively engaged with it, it waits for the completion of the whole as the presupposition of every present. It impels it towards its completion. Conversely, in the *ecclesia triumphans*[EN105] the *ecclesia militans*[EN106] has, as it were, its spearhead in the sphere of completion, in which it already exists eschatologically. Therefore the Church which was and the Church which is are very concretely one Church. And the Church which will be will still be the one Church. "All live unto him" (Lk. 20^{38}): not only on that side, but on this; not only on this side, but on that. And because they live to Him, they are one community.

For the same reason (3) the people of Israel in its whole history *ante et post Christum*[EN107] and the Christian Church as it came into being on the day of

---

[EN100] Church militant
[EN101] Church triumphant
[EN102] Church triumphant
[EN103] Church militant
[EN104] Church triumphant
[EN105] Church triumphant
[EN106] Church militant
[EN107] before and after Christ

§ 62. The Holy Spirit and the Gathering of the Christian Community

Pentecost are two forms and aspects (*CD* II, 2, § 34, 1) of the one inseparable community in which Jesus Christ has His earthly-historical form of existence, by which He is attested to the whole world, by which the whole world is summoned to faith in Him. For what the Christian Church is, Israel was and is before it—His possession (Jn. 1^{11}), His body. He Himself in the one person is the crucified Messiah of Israel who as such is the secret Lord of the Church, the risen Lord of the Church who as such is the manifested Messiah of Israel. In its Old Testament form the community attests Him as the man elected and called by God who as such was invested with the sins of the whole world, and bore the judgment of God, and in this form of a servant was truly the Lord. In its New Testament form the community attests Him as the God electing and calling man, who has not given Himself in vain, but to have mercy on His own, to set him right, for him. In its form as Israel it attests the justification which begins strangely and terribly in the midst of a world of sin and death, its *terminus a quo*^{EN108}. In its form as the Church it attests its *terminus ad quem*^{EN109}, its strange and glorious consummation in a new world of right and life. On the one hand there is the promise, on the other its fulfilment. On the one hand there is the man who hears, on the other the man who believes. On the one hand there is the perishing form, on the other the form which comes. In its form as Israel the community is still identical with a nation. In the Church its mission as a community for the world is actualised in the fact that it gathers into itself not only Jews awakened to faith in their Messiah but Gentiles, i.e., men from all nations who believe in Him as the Saviour of the world. But how can we distinguish or separate except *a parte potiori*?^{EN110} The man who suffers the judgment of God, the secret of the Old Testament history, is revealed as the faithful servant of God in the New. The God attested by the New Testament witnesses, the God who in His mercy creates right and life, is the God who was not concealed from the Old Testament witnesses. Does the Church no longer know the beginning of justification? Did Israel not know of its consummation? Was the promise empty for Israel because it was not fulfilled? Now that it has been fulfilled, does the Church not need to hold with Abraham to the promise as such? Has Israel heard without in any sense believing? Is not the faith of the Church based on simple hearing? As this chosen people, was not Israel potentially the Church for the world? Is not the Christian world of Jews and Gentiles a little Israel within the nations which border it? There are differences which we cannot overlook. We are dealing with two forms, two aspects, two "economies" of grace. But it is the one history, beginning there, having its centre in Jesus Christ, and here hastening to its culmination. It is the bow of the one covenant which stretches over the whole. It was therefore essential to the Church from the very beginning, and it always will be, to represent this unity in

---

^{EN108} starting point
^{EN109} end point
^{EN110} with respect to emphasis

2. *The Being of the Community*

itself and to exist in it. That is why it has always read the Old Testament with the New, and the Old before the New, as the attestation of the one work and the one revelation of the one God. That is why, from the very first, it has thought of itself as the Church of Jews and Gentiles, and to that extent as the "Israel of God" (Gal. 6^{16}), as "all Israel" (Rom. 11^{26}). To try to deny this unity would be to deny Jesus Christ Himself.

[671]

Where the Church has taken Rom. 9–11 seriously, it has not been able to escape or explain away the fact that its unity in this sense is compromised by the existence of a Judaism which does not believe in Jesus Christ. More than anything else, this makes its own existence problematical. For it belongs to its nature and situation as the community in the world to be separated from all kinds of religions and religious communities. Its very aim as a missionary community is to call men out of these, to call them from false gods to the true God. But this being the case, the existence of the Synagogue side by side with the Church is an ontological impossibility, a wound, a gaping hole in the body of Christ, something which is quite intolerable. For what does the Church have which the Synagogue does not also have, and long before it (Rom. 9$^{4-5}$)— especially Jesus Christ Himself, who is of the Jews, who is the Jewish Messiah, and only as such the Lord of the Church? The decisive question is not what the Jewish Synagogue can be without Him, but what the Church is as long as it confronts an alien and hostile Israel? "Jewish Missions" is not the right word for the call to remove this breach, a call which must go out unceasingly from the Church to these brethren who do not yet know their unity with it—a unity which does not have to be established but is already there ontologically, who will not accept what they already are, and what they were long before us poor Gentiles. And what a dreadful thing when the Church itself has so little understood its own nature that it has not only withheld this knowledge from its brethren but made it difficult if not impossible for them! *Credo unam ecclesiam?*^{EN111} This confession gives rise to other and very difficult questions. But here in the so-called Jewish question we face the deepest obscurity which surrounds it. The Jewish question? If Paul is right, then in the light and context of that confession it is really the Christian question.

Because the community is a single unity we have to say finally (4) that we can legitimately speak of historically existent Christian "Churches" in the plural only with reference to the geographically separated and therefore different congregations. We must not forget that it is in the concrete event of its gathering that the community has its invisible and also its visible being, that it is the earthly-historical *communio sanctorum*^{EN112}, that the Lord Himself is in the midst of it by His Spirit, that it is His own earthly-historical form of existence, that it lives as the body of which He is the Head. If this gathering takes place there as well as here, if in essential accordance with its commission it has to

---

^{EN111} I believe one church
^{EN112} communion of saints

§ 62. *The Holy Spirit and the Gathering of the Christian Community*

take place in many localities, it is also essential to it that in its unity it should exist in this geographical separation and difference: a difference which corresponds to its environment and history and language and customs and ways of life and thought as conditioned by the different localities, and also to its personal composition. In this respect the same thing does not suit every Church or every place and time. This has never been taken seriously enough in our missionary thinking. But it can, of course, be taken too seriously, as has often happened. The local presuppositions and conditions of a Christian community cannot have the significance and function of factors which underlie and therefore actually separate the Churches, nor should they be thought of in this way. The local community, with its local characteristics, cannot be basically and essentially another community in relation to others. Each in its own place can only be the one community beside which there are no others. Each in and for itself and with its local characteristics can only be the whole, as others are in their own locality.

> The New Testament plural ἐκκλησίαι[EN113] does not speak of a plurality of Churches genuinely and radically different from each other. It is one and the same community, separated only by geographical distance and what it involves. This one community is grounded in the same Gospel, and awakened and maintained and ruled by the same Spirit, although as the community of the same Lord it exists at one and the same time in Thessalonica, Galatia, Corinth and Rome. Whatever we may understand by the seven Churches of Asia Minor with their seven angels (Rev. 2–3), none of them has its own Lord or Spirit or Gospel. Each of these individual communities in relation to the concrete event of its gathering is called and trusted and expected by the One who is over them all to be the community of the Lord in its own locality, immediately and directly in the fulness of the gifts and the corresponding responsibility given to it. It was on this presupposition that Paul addressed the communities founded or otherwise commissioned by him. It was in this sense—and only in this sense—that the Reformers could occasionally speak of the "Churches" (as in the first words of the *Confession of Augsburg*: *ecclesiae magno consensu apud nos docent*[EN114]).

Each community has its own locality, its own environment, tradition, language, etc. But in that locality, as established and appointed by the Lord of all the communities, it should be the one complete community. It should take itself seriously as such, and know that it is responsible as such. When this is the case; then geographical distance and difference cannot give rise to any genuine or essential difference or distance, but the community in one place can and must and will recognise itself in the community of another, and *vice versa*[EN115]. The unity of the community will then be mutually attested and affirmed in spite of the differences. Everywhere the edification and ministry and mission and confession will be unanimous. But this unity, and mutual recognition in this unity, the *magnus consensus*[EN116] of the *ecclesiae*[EN117], can be

---

EN113 churches
EN114 the churches among us with great agreement teach …
EN115 the other way around
EN116 great agreement
EN117 churches

2. *The Being of the Community*

basically and necessarily and infallibly and unconditionally guaranteed only by the fact that each community is individually founded by the one Lord of all the communities, and that, founded in Him in obedience to His Spirit, it is continually ruled by Him. All human mediation of this unity, all the mutual understanding and agreement and co-ordination between the individual members, can only be a free human service. It cannot supply, let alone create, the guarantee of unity, the mutual recognition of the individual communities. This does not mean that the existence of a particular organ of mediation, an institution which demands and maintains the oneness of the locally separated communities, is completely impossible. What it does mean is that such an organ or institution is not an integral constituent of the essence of the Church. The one Church does not exist either in an ideal or in an organised or organising totality to which the individual communities stand in the relationship of participating Churches (like the digits in a figure or the notes in a chord). The one Church exists in its totality in each of the individual communities. [673]

It is evident that even in New Testament days there were some helpful and serious human links between the Churches. The mutual ἀσπάζεσθαι[EN118] which there was according to the letters of Paul was hardly a mere formality. Individuals seem often to have been on the way between them. Above all, of course, we have to think of the ministry of the apostles which had precedence over them all and was more or less respected by them all. What we do not find in the New Testament is the existence of what might truly be called a Church government which is superior to the individual communities and the external guarantee of their unity as the community of Jesus Christ.

The discussion in Ac. 15 between Paul and Barnabas as the delegates of the community in Syrian Antioch and the "apostles and elders" in Jerusalem has often been described as an Apostolic Council. Was this, then, the beginning of the synodal direction of the Church? But the result of it was not a decree or dogma conjointly accepted by this assembly, but the consolation which, according to v. 31, was sent by the believers of Jerusalem to their brethren at Antioch. And the incident as a whole did not involve the appearance of an institution, but the *ad hoc* introduction and execution of an act, the practical result of which was accorded only a partial and occasional respect. What can be gathered from this passage (as from 2 Cor. 8–9) is that in relation to the other and later communities that at Jerusalem occupied a position of peculiar dignity at any rate up to A.D. 70. But there can be no question of the others being ruled through it or by it.

As far as the apostolate of Paul is concerned, it is plain from his Epistles that his relationship to the communities was definitely not that of a universal bishop. If he had adopted towards them an attitude veering in this direction, this would have appeared, e.g., in 1 Cor. 1 and 3 in his reaction to the parties at Corinth. He would not have put his own group on the same level as that of Apollos and the others, but singled out their views as normal because those of the whole Church. And from the fact that he had "planted" in Corinth, whereas Apollos had only "watered" (1 Cor. 3⁶), he would have deduced the clear precedence of his own work over that of the other teacher. But in vv. 7–8 he calmly says: "So then neither is he that planteth anything, neither he that watereth; but God that giveth the increase. Now he that planteth and he that watereth are one: and every man shall receive his own reward

---

[EN118] receiving

§ 62. *The Holy Spirit and the Gathering of the Christian Community*

according to his own labour. For we are labourers together with God: ye are God's husbandry, ye are God's building." None of this smacks of the hierarchical guaranteeing of the unity of the Church. Naturally Paul came to the communities with a higher authority—but with that of the servant and, as a called apostle, of the unique and not the institutional servant of Jesus Christ. With this unique apostolic authority he speaks like the other first and direct witnesses to the Church of every age. But as, according to Gal. 1^1, he had received it "not of men, neither by man, but by Jesus Christ," so he exercises it simply in the fact that he makes the authority of Jesus Christ visible and audible in the Churches. He teaches and warns and beseeches "in Christ's stead" (2 Cor. 5^{20}). He does not rule in His place. He is not His vicar. His place is in the διακονία τῆς καταλλαγῆς[EN119] (2 Cor. 5^{18}). We are again reminded of the way in which the unity of the Church is proclaimed in the great passage in Eph. $4^{1f.}$. If this is the word of a Deutero-Paul, he has understood the apostle in a remarkable way. And the saying in 2 Cor. 1^{24} is unquestionably Pauline: "Nor for that we have dominion over your faith, but are helpers of your joy"—and this to the community at Corinth, which—we might think—had such bitter need of an earthly lord over their faith to represent the heavenly Lord and the whole Church. Neither here nor anywhere else does Paul place himself over his community. Even where he speaks most definitely he places himself alongside it, questioning, arguing, beseeching, even pleading and imploring. Or rather, he places himself within it. We never find him playing the role of a superior even in relation to the heads of the individual communities, who in any case are not very often mentioned (cf. Rom. 12^8, Phil. 1^1).

Strangely enough, it is even more difficult to show that Peter (cf. O. Cullmann, *Petrus*, 1952, 251 f.) exercised any total rule over the individual communities. From the very first he assumed a position of leadership among the disciples. He had had a special part in the resurrection appearances. In the first days he was the leader of the Church in Jerusalem. But then he gave up this position to James, the Lord's brother, at the time (why?) when Jerusalem ceased to be the only Christian community. In subordination to James he then seems to have headed the mission to the Jews. On the basis of later sources it seems tenable that he finally came to Rome (why?) and that he died there as a martyr. But if we are not to put too much credence in later reports, it cannot be proved that he was ever the Bishop of Rome, and even if he was, it cannot be proved that as such he had a function in relation to the whole Church.

It certainly cannot be maintained that the existence of a synodal or episcopal organ to guarantee the unity of the communities is essential to the New Testament idea of the Church, even if the texts do not record all the actual and perhaps very strong connexions which did exist in New Testament days. If these connexions did exist in any form, and if their organs (if there were any) were of great practical value for mutual correlation and co-ordination, it is still obviously the case that no one thought of them as basically indispensable for founding and maintaining the unity of the communities, that no one, therefore, thought of them as necessary to salvation, that no one ascribed to them either infallible authority or unconditional efficacy. Rather, those who proclaimed the authority of Jesus Christ pointed to Him and His Spirit as the creator and guarantee of their unity (even of their unity one with another)—confident that fundamentally He was a sufficient guarantee in the matter, and presupposing that there could not be any other beside Him. Our own decision will have to be the same in relation to it.

As far as the correlation and co-ordination of individual communities is concerned, love and prudence may prove many things to be necessary by way of

---

[EN119] ministry of reconciliation

2. *The Being of the Community*

service in this matter of unity. But that is another matter, as is also the question what possible forms of Church government must be considered and which is relatively the best. We will return to these items in the second and third parts of the doctrine of reconciliation, when we have to consider the building up and the mission of the community. But our present question is the gathering of the community by the Holy Spirit, the one single being of the one single community. And we can name only one authority which is fundamentally indispensable, necessary to salvation, infallible and unconditionally effective to guarantee its existence as such in the geographically separate communities: the Lord who attests Himself in the prophetic and apostolic word, who is active by His Spirit, who as the Spirit has promised to be in the midst of every community gathered by Him and in His name. He rules the Church and therefore the Churches. He is the basis and guarantee of their unity. [675]

We cannot name any other legitimate plurality of Churches, one which does not destroy but affirms their unity, other than those which we have mentioned already, the visible and the invisible, the militant and the triumphant Church, Israel and the Christian community, and the local congregations. Any other plurality means the co-existence of Churches which are genuinely divided. That is, in the event of their gathering, and therefore by their basis and invisible being, in their faith, although they all regard it as the Christian faith, they are so different from one another and confront one another as such strangers that they cannot recognise and acknowledge one another, at any rate seriously, as the community of Jesus Christ. At best they will be able kindly to tolerate one another as believing differently, and at worst they will fight against one another, mutually excluding each other with some definiteness and force. The existence of this kind of plurality of "Churches" is in conflict with both Eph. 4 and the *credo unam ecclesiam*[EN120]. Under no head and in no sense can it be regarded as legitimate. Certainly it is possible to understand and explain historically the separation and opposition of such Churches. Certainly in the sphere of state and society their co-existence and opposition can be made tolerable for participants and non-participants alike with the assistance or under the supremacy of the doctrine of toleration. Certainly it can be stabilised and canalised in terms of practical law. Certainly among the more enlightened on both sides, or perhaps with some depth even among a majority of those who believe differently, there may arise a tacit or to some extent perhaps even an explicit agreement as to the relative and temporary nature of the opposition, with more or less radical glimpses of a unity which is already present in some point of convergence. It may also be that for good reasons or bad the consciousness of existing differences becomes blunted in whole groups of Churches, so that they become an external factor without internal necessity. There is no justification theological, spiritual or biblical for the existence of a plurality of Churches genuinely separated in this way and mutually excluding one another

---

[EN120] I believe one church

§ 62. The Holy Spirit and the Gathering of the Christian Community

internally and therefore externally. A plurality of Churches in this sense means a plurality of lords, a plurality of spirits, a plurality of gods. There is no doubt that to the extent that Christendom does consist of actually different and opposing Churches, to that extent it denies practically what it confesses theoretically—the unity and the singularity of God, of Jesus Christ, of the Holy Spirit. There may be good grounds for the rise of these divisions. There may be serious obstacles to their removal. There may be many things, which can be said by way of interpretation and mitigation. But this does not alter the fact that every division as such is a deep riddle, a scandal. And in face of this scandal the whole of Christendom should be united in being able to think of it only with penitence, not with the penitence which each expects of the other, but with the penitence in which—whatever may be the cost—each is willing to precede the other. If a man can acquiesce in divisions, if he can even take pleasure in them, if he can be complacent in relation to the obvious faults and errors of others and therefore his own responsibility for them, then that man may be a good and loyal confessor in the sense of his own particular denomination, he may be a good Roman Catholic or Reformed or Orthodox or Baptist, but he must not imagine that he is a good Christian. He has not honestly and seriously believed and known and confessed the *una ecclesia*[EN121]. For the *una ecclesia*[EN122] cannot exist if there is a second or third side by side with or opposed to it. It cannot exist in opposition to another Church. It cannot be one among many.

> It is an impossible situation that whole groups of Christian communities should exhibit a certain external and internal unity among themselves and yet stand in relation to other groups of equally Christian communities in an attitude more or less of exclusion. It is an impossible situation that such groups should confront each other in such a way that their confession and preaching and theology are mutually contradictory, that what is revelation here is called error there, that what is heresy here is taught and reverenced as dogma there, that the order and cultus and perhaps the ethics of the one should be found and called strange and alien and unacceptable and perhaps even reprehensible by the other, that the adherents of the one should be able to work together with those of the other in every possible secular cause, but not to pray together, not to preach and hear the Word of God together, not to keep the Lord's Supper together. It is an impossible situation that either tacitly or expressly, with an open severity or a gentler friendliness, the one should say to the other, or, in fact, give it to be understood, or at any rate think of the other: You have another Spirit; You are not within but without; You are not what you presumptuously call yourselves, the community of Jesus Christ.
>
> We have to recall the effects of this disunity on the mission fields of Asia and Africa, in the face of Islam and Buddhism. But we have also to recall its effects on the so-called home fields of the Christian Church which were evangelised a thousand years ago and more, where with the dispelling of the mediaeval illusion of a Christian West the Church is mercilessly confronted—in all its disunity—with the tremendous alienation of the baptised masses from the Gospel. We have to think of the Church's difficulty in being impressively and credibly and

---

[EN121] one church
[EN122] one church

2. *The Being of the Community*

convincingly, even to its own more or less living members, "the church of the living God, the pillar and ground of the truth" (1 Tim. 3^{15}), when it is constituted in this way; when it exists as the Church only in co-existence with separate Churches, of which each one involves for every other criticism, competition, disruption and hostility. Where it ought to be a matter of true faith, does not the constant possibility of a comparison between faith and faith constitute a threat to the very question of the true faith and the answering of that question? What is the Church if it can only express itself as a repetition of the plurality and contradictions of the world of heathen religions and the conflicts of secular totalitarianism? What is the objective truth of its message if it has to contradict itself so evidently in its subjective realisations? Is there not a good deal to be said for the thesis of E. Hirsch, who rather disconcertingly begins his *Geschichte der neueren evangelischen Theologie*, 1949 f., with the Peace of Westphalia of 1648, because then the general consciousness of Europe learned to acquiesce in the fact that Europe was divided religiously into two and even three great confessions, and it began to wonder at these conflicting absolutes, these bearers of revelation, each of which claimed for itself alone the truth and God? "Lutheran, Papist, Calvinist, All three faiths are present, But where, we ask, is Christianity?" Other powerful factors may have contributed at the same time or later, but the Peace of Westphalia was, as it were, the original manifestation of the historical forces which conceived and bore and produced modern Evangelical theology, the historicist, psychologist and relativist theology of Neo-Protestantism. Is there not something in this? In the great process of the modern alienation between the Church and countless numbers of its members—which as a process of disillusionment in relation to the mediaeval idea may not be altogether bad—the co-existence and opposition of the Churches in place of the one Church has, at any rate, been a very potent factor for evil, constituting a serious difficulty even for serious Christians, although not one which is inherent in the nature of the matter itself. [677]

For the disunity of the Church is not grounded in the nature of the matter—in the existence of the Church, for example, in the temporary and imperfect conditions of the time between the ascension and the coming again of Jesus Christ. It was not created or sent out into this time in this plurality when the risen Jesus Christ breathed on His disciples. Exegetically it was not perhaps so strained as appears at first sight when the early Church found an exhortation to unity in the seamless robe of Christ which was woven of a piece and which the soldiers did not wish to rend at the cross, but for which they cast lots (Jn. 19^{23}). Certainly there is no trace of this plurality in the New Testament, and in view of the being of the community as the body of Christ it is—ontologically, we can say—quite impossible; it is possible only as sin is possible.

We must not try to explain and justify it as a development of the riches of the grace given to man in Jesus Christ, a development which derives from the Holy Spirit and which is therefore normal and acceptable. We must not try to explain and justify it by the image of the different elements and forces and functions in the one organism, or of the different branches and twigs of the one tree, or of the different families of a human clan. We must not deduce this plurality of Churches from some principle, as though the contradictions were necessities of the *una ecclesia*^{EN123}, as though this Church had to be divided into the Churches of the East and the West, as though the Church of the West had to be divided into the Romanist and Evangelical, as though the Evangelical Church had to be divided into the Lutheran and Reformed and Anglican, as though the wider divisions all proceeded necessarily from the nature of the case, as though in all this there was no trouble, no disorder, only the outworking of a law immanent in the Christian community. All this is simply the arbitrary view of a philosophy of history. It is not in accordance with the law of the matter itself. It is

---

EN123 one church

§ 62. The Holy Spirit and the Gathering of the Christian Community

not permitted even by the thought of God's providence which certainly does over-rule in all this and traces of which can clearly be seen. For the matter itself (we should read Jn. 17^{21-23} word by word) demands always, and in all circumstances, *unam ecclesiam*[EN124]. And if history contradicts this, then it speaks only of the actuality and not the truth. Even under the fatherly and effective providence of God which can cause it to work for good, a scandal is still a scandal. The disunity of the Church is a scandal. And there are some cases where the scandal is not even serious, but has only the character of a foolish embroilment.

The question is: What is the meaning of the confession: *credo unam ecclesiam*[EN125], in face of this scandal? We shall have to return to this in detail when we speak of the upbuilding of the community. For the moment we will simply give the main outline.

[678] One thing is certain—this *credo*[EN126] cannot consist in a movement of escape up or on from the visibility of the divided Church to the unity of an invisible Church. It is such a movement when the individual believer withdraws in disgust or superiority from his own and therefore from all other Churches, when he shuts himself off with his God and Christ and Holy Spirit in some hermit's retreat or ivory tower, enjoying his own private faith, being happy after his own fashion, and possibly with the contemplation of the *una sancta*[EN127] which for the moment has its only representative in his own person. This is to abandon not only the distress but the hope of the community and indeed oneself. For there are no retreats and towers of this kind. We are either in the *communio sanctorum*[EN128] or we are not *sancti*[EN129]. A private monadic faith is not the Christian faith. Again, it is a movement of flight when one of the divided Churches or a number of them try to bring unity nearer by ceasing to take themselves seriously, by letting slip the special responsibility which they have, by denying and renouncing their special character for the sake of internal or external peace, by trying to exist in a kind of nondescript Christianity. The way to a self-chosen supra-confessionalism is not by a long chalk the way to the unity of the Church, but the way to a new separation, the particular feature of which will be its featurelessness as a Church. Where the Church is divided in the way which now concerns us, the division reaches right down to its invisible being, its relationship to God and Jesus Christ and the Holy Spirit, and it develops from this, the external division being the result of an internal disruption, so that neither individuals nor the whole Church can overcome it by a flight to the invisible, but only by a healing of both its visible and its invisible hurt.

For the same reason we cannot try to realise the *credo unam ecclesiam*[EN130]

[EN124] one church
[EN125] I believe one church
[EN126] I believe
[EN127] 'one holy'
[EN128] communion of saints
[EN129] holy
[EN130] I believe one church

2. The Being of the Community

externally *in abstracto*[EN131]. Self-evidently this cannot be done by a *cogite intrare*[EN132], by any political or social pressure exercised by one Church or group of Churches on another. But again, it cannot be done by any form of understanding or agreement concerning the relative and reconcilable nature of the differences, or by any form of unconditional mutual recognition or practical co-operation which leaves open the questions which have to be mutually posed, or by any form of artificial suppression of the mutual difficulties which are the basis of disunity. What is demanded is the unity of the Church of Jesus Christ, not the externally satisfying co-existence and co-operation of different religious societies. To establish the latter is not too difficult on the basis and under the dominion of the idea of toleration, provided there is sufficient good will. Alliances and pacts and unions are often possible on this basis and have been attempted often enough and even seem to have been successful. Supposing, however, that on both sides the necessity and freedom of faith are not considered, but faith has to suffer shipwreck in favour of the attainment of political and social and moral and practical tactical ends to which it is subordinated, and before which it is reduced to silence, together with the confession of it? Supposing that at bottom this, too, is a movement of escape? Supposing that a conscious or unconscious spirit of indifference is the father of the thought and the corresponding acts and enterprises? To believe in the unity of the Church of Jesus Christ in its disunity can never be the work of a feeble or uncertain or uncritical faith, or of a Church which takes itself less seriously, but only of a Church which takes itself more seriously, and of a faith which is strong and certain and genuinely critical. [679]

From this we can go on to say that the distress and scandal consists in the fact that in its visible and also in its invisible being, in its form and also in its essence, the one community of Jesus Christ is not one, and that neither the community itself in its divided and opposing communions nor the individual Christians united in them can simply evade this disunity or overcome it by any kind of passivity or activity, notwithstanding the fact that to overcome it is undoubtedly envisaged and demanded by the *credo unam ecclesiam*[EN133]. The individual communions and all of us in and with them find ourselves at some point and with some distinctness in this disunity of the one Church, and therefore on the one side or the other—not in the Eastern Church, shall we say? but the Western, not Roman Catholics but Evangelicals, and Evangelicals, it may be with conviction or with reservations, but preponderately in the form of Lutherans or Reformed or Anglicans or Baptists or Mennonites. Why not? Each of these Churches is still the Church even in the disunity. In each communion it confesses: *credo unam ecclesiam*[EN134]. And every Christian stands more or less resolutely on the ground of his own communion, it may be by

---

[EN131] in the abstract
[EN132] 'compelling them to come in'
[EN133] I believe one church
[EN134] I believe one church

§ 62. The Holy Spirit and the Gathering of the Christian Community

baptism, environment and upbringing, it may be by his own choice and decision. The division is a shame and a scandal, but this does not alter the fact that concretely the gathering to the community means for each of us the gathering to one of these divided communions. And it is not an acceptance of the scandal or an acquiescence in the shame if we say that we are not only permitted but commanded to start from this fact in our confession of the *una ecclesia*[EN135]. All Churches and all the Christians united in them are called upon primarily to take themselves seriously even in their distinctness and therefore in their separate existence and confession—not necessarily to remain in them, and certainly not to harden in them, but to reach out from them to the one Church. If they do not do this here, they will not do it at all. If they jettison and abandon what they are as the Church in the disunity of the Church, how can they know its unity or be zealous and active in relation to it? Just as the knowledge of justification cannot begin anywhere else or in any other way than with the recognition of the sin of the man justified by God, so the knowledge of the one community of Jesus Christ can begin only with its recognition in one of the forms of its unfortunate disunity, and not without a humble loyalty to one, to this specific confession which is, without doubt, highly contestable in its separation and isolation. The one depends on the other. The man who knows the justification of himself and all men in Jesus Christ, and who therefore acknowledges himself a sinner with all men and as such looks and moves forward to his right and life, will look and move forward to the one Church only from the place where he is ecclesiastically a Roman Catholic or Lutheran or Methodist or some other, a place which in its isolation and exclusiveness is a sinful place. And it is here, too, in its very doubtful particular existence that each Christian community or group of communities has to come to grips with its summons to the one Church. But what does it mean, to begin here, to go on from here, and therefore, and above all, to be loyal here in humility?

It will certainly mean attentively to pursue the intentions of this particular Church to their origins and actual meaning, to try to follow them out, to work out and to put into effect the various possibilities within this sphere, to pay attention and to give a voice to this particular witness. The promise of the Lord that where two or three are gathered together in His name He is there in the midst (Mt. 18[20]) will be true of this Church in spite of the doubtful nature of its separate existence. At some time, in some antithesis, when its fathers came forward with its particular confession and order, it was born of a choice and decision of faith, having its relative necessity and right as the complement to some omission or error on the other side. But a relative necessity and right may still give at least a relative justification for its continuance. It may be, therefore, that it and the Christians who belong to it have, for the time being, no cause to renounce their particular existence and doctrine and form of life,

---

[EN135] one church

2. *The Being of the Community*

but, on the contrary, they find that they are called upon to cherish and renew and develop it.

But that is a possibility which naturally all Churches are only too ready to regard as applicable to their own case. Therefore we have to be more precise. A Church can appeal with a good conscience to this possibility of its own relative justification only when and to the extent that it is honestly and seriously committed to it for the sake of Jesus Christ; only when and to the extent that it not merely thinks but believes it can serve Him in accordance with the intentions which distinguish it from others; only when and to the extent that its particular existence and teaching and form as distinct from others are necessary to its faith and salvation; only when and to the extent that it has to recognise and confess that it is bound, not by its own confession, but by the Word of God. If this is the case, then it not only can, but ought to, maintain its cause. It ought not to be confused in it by any appeals for love and peace. Where the question of truth is sacrificed to that of love and peace, we are not on the way to the one Church. But it is no light thing when an individual Church maintains that for the sake of the truth and faith and eternal salvation and Jesus Christ it can do no other, it can only persist in its individual existence. Is it really sure? Can it be sure? There are other grounds for this persistence, just as there were other grounds for the emergence of the separation in question: national peculiarities, particular historical and social groupings, the existence of leading personalities, with whose spirits the Holy Spirit seems at the time to have been strangely united; and to-day, the understandable attachment of the sons to the fathers, the natural weight of all and especially religious traditions, perhaps laid down in the most respected texts and established by written law and even property and endowment, the usage and custom of the land, the instinct of self-preservation, the requirements of prestige natural to every human society and especially to one which looks back to so great an antiquity. Is the difference and opposition of this or that Church something which really cannot be surrendered in relation to others? Do we really believe, or do we only think, that we have to cling to it? Can we really do no other, in response to the question of truth, or does it only seem that we can do no other, in consideration of certain actualities? Must we really accept the continuance of the bastions which separate us or can they be in part or totally broken? Have we perhaps overlooked the fact that they have been broken long since, or exist only as an external factor and in the interpretative historical phantasy of a relative minority? These are questions which no individual Church—however large or small—should basically exclude or allow to rest, let alone deliberately suppress.

[681]

Why not? Because each individual Church lives by the certainty and the claim, not only that it is the Church as well as others, but that it especially is the Church, that it is the Church in a peculiar way, that in a sense it alone among the Churches is the Church, the authentic, true, living and faithful Church of

§ 62. *The Holy Spirit and the Gathering of the Christian Community*

Jesus Christ. It may be in relation to its particularly ancient and assured tradition, if possible reaching right back to the apostles by the succession of its ministers. It may be in relation to its particularly zealous reformation in accordance with Holy Scripture, or the particular zeal and conscientiousness with which it exercises itself to follow Jesus in practice. Now there is good reason why every Christian fellowship—even to the many more or less influential liberal and unitarian movements, and often these most seriously—should in some way claim Jesus Christ especially for itself. Each individual Church should let itself be burdened with this certainty and claim. For it is in this that the unity of the Church is proclaimed in all its perverse plurality. If only we would pay attention to it as proclaimed in this way! If only we would everywhere allow Jesus Christ genuinely to speak and to rule, genuinely and continuously subjecting ourselves to His guidance and instruction and direction, genuinely allowing Him to be the Lord of the Church! Naturally not in the theory, the historical or speculative philosophy, the dogma, the particular Christology, in which He has been imprisoned and, as it were, encysted, but Himself, the living Lord, speaking by the Holy Spirit to the Church to-day in the witness of the prophets and apostles. He is appealed to as such on every hand. The older and also the more recent traditions all remember Him as such. His real presence as such is held to become an event in the world in the Roman mass, the Lutheran Lord's Supper, the Reformed exposition of Holy Scripture, the Methodist preaching of conversion, the eloquent or silent testimony of fraternal spiritual fellowship, or practical turning to one's fellows in accordance with His will. What would be the result if His real presence as the living and speaking Lord was genuinely accepted, if it was not merely maintained but allowed to become an event in the form in which it is earnestly believed? What would take place in and with it in every Church—great or small, old or new—would definitely be the question directed to it, not from without, not by those who believe otherwise, but from its own heart, by the Lord whom it believes and knows and confesses, the question of truth which is put to it from above: whether and to what extent in its particular tradition and teaching and form it really serves Him, it really proclaims Him, it is really faithful to Him, and therefore—since it honestly and sincerely believes that it is His Church—to itself?

And where would He not have to ask this question, where would He not actually ask it, if there were an unconditional openness to His work and an unconditional committal to His Spirit? If His real presence were really allowed to become event instead of simply being cherished, then everywhere there would be a crisis in ecclesiastical self-consciousness, rather like the proving by fire described in 1 Cor. $3^{12f.}$, in which every man's work is made manifest, that which he has so far built on the one foundation beside which there is no other: gold, silver, precious stones or wood, hay, stubble. The problem of the individual existence of Churches, which had been regarded as settled and set aside, would then be reopened, and radically reopened, in such a way as it had never

2. *The Being of the Community*

been opened by external protests on the part of more or less friendly or hostile "sister-Churches," in such a way that the reopening of it could not be resisted with a good conscience or with any basic reservation. All would then find themselves drawn up in their own place, and doubt, scepticism, indifference and the like would be everywhere impossible. From their own place all would orientate themselves to the centre which in loyalty to their own cause they regard as their own peculiar centre. But from that place—presupposing that they are really willing to be controlled from it—they would themselves be orientated. The unity of the Church—which is not under the power of any man because the living Lord Jesus Christ in His own power is Himself this unity—would then begin not only to be a reality but to be realised as such in the many Churches. In face of the scandal of the divided Church *credo unam ecclesiam*^{EN136} would obviously mean in the first instance not merely the ascription, but—in the very place where every man is, in his own separate Church —the actual granting to Jesus Christ of the power to open this problem of the one Church and therefore the calling in question of the contrary plurality. In and with Him, the One, the unity of His body and therefore of the Church cannot for very long remain completely hidden from the faith which will ascribe and actually grant to Him the power to do this. [683]

If appearances are not deceptive, it was the prophetic intention of Count Zinzendorf in the founding of his remarkable "brotherhoods", not to split the confessional Churches, not to replace them by a super-Church, but as they came together freely as loyal members of the particular Churches to confront them typically with the unity which they had not lost and actually could not lose in Jesus Christ Himself, who remarkably enough was elected their common Elder Brother. It is no accident that the very man who in his preaching and poetry and dogmatics (so far as he had any) was perhaps the only genuine Christocentric of the modern age (fools would say: Christomonist), must also perhaps be called the first genuine ecumenicist, i.e., the first really to speak and think wholly in terms of the matter itself.

We cannot begin by contesting or waiving aside the confessions and orders of the separated Churches, by an over-hasty and arbitrary and self-confident breaking of the bastions, by a dissolution of the law. It is a matter of its fulfilment. It is a question of everywhere taking seriously faith in the real presence of Jesus Christ, or rather the real presence as it is believed, in obedience to His Word and Spirit. In spite of every current error and misunderstanding, He will have kept His promise to be in the midst even in the disunited Church. If we really grant Him His Word and the exercise of His power, He will not say from the very outset a general and exclusive No to the various particular traditions and doctrines and forms. Even in the proving by fire in 1 Cor. 3 it is not everything which is burned up. And when it is a matter of the unity of the divided Churches from and in Jesus Christ, the burning up of that which is individual is not the first and most important consequence. Certainly when He is allowed to speak and rule the inevitable crisis of the individual, the radical reopening

---

^{EN136} I believe one church

§ 62. The Holy Spirit and the Gathering of the Christian Community

of the problem of the existence of particular Churches, will ineluctably involve the fact that—in his own place—every man will be committed to what is on the human level, the level of Church history, a humble loyalty to his own cause, which means, of course, that he will be open to the particular traditions and doctrines and forms of other Churches, very practically and concretely open to the question whether and to what extent they, too, might not stand under a particular Yes of the living Lord Jesus Christ which has not yet been heard or is no longer heard on this side; whether and to what extent there ought not to be on this side a willingness to learn from them instead of simply opposing them. Who knows: Is it really possible to be glad and confident in our own faith so long as we regard ourselves as sheltered and secure in that faith against the faith of those who believe otherwise, so long as we think that we can simply shutter up ourselves against it?

[684] It is at this point that what we said earlier about penitence really enters in. No one, none of the separated Churches, can expect the others to hold or even to consider its case against them. They stand and fall to their own Lord. If we are seriously to hear Jesus Christ, then we must hear them even if they for their part give no sign that they are willing and able to hear us. They are perhaps harder of hearing than we are. But all the same, it may be that they can say something to us which we have to hear for our own sake. And perhaps the only way to call them out of their isolation, to cause them to hear us, is first of all to hear them. But this is not the place for tactical considerations. A prudent guest at the Lord's table (Lk. 14^{10}) will seat himself with the other guests whatever proud looks he may have to face.

In the realisation of faith in the one Church in face of its disunity, the decisive step is that the divided Churches should honestly and seriously try to hear and perhaps hear the voice of the Lord by them and for them, and then try to hear, and perhaps actually hear, the voice of the others. Where a Church does this, in its own place, and without leaving it, it is on the way to the one Church. It is clear that in so doing it has already abandoned its claim to be identical with the one Church in contrast to the others, and in this sense to be the only Church. The claim has been dashed out of its hand by the One who is the unity of the Church. If it will not accept this, it cannot be on the way to the one Church, and with its exclusive *credo unam ecclesiam*^{EN137} it can only confirm the disunity of the one Church. But if it really hears the Lord afresh, it has already abandoned its claim and this *credo*^{EN138}. And if it lets Him open the question of its individual existence, then it will automatically be open to the other Churches in the sense that it will be willing and ready to let them say something to it, thus renouncing, in fact, its isolation as the only Church, its exclusion of all other Churches.

But then there seriously arises the practical question what is to become of its

---

^{EN137} I believe one church
^{EN138} I believe

2. The Being of the Community

individual existence, its particular confessions and ordinances? It is quite clear that this question does confront it. It may be that it will be necessary to scrap, or at least to revise or modify, its particular constitution. It may be that at many points it will need to be liberated or renewed in its separate existence. Note that it is not true to itself if at bottom it tries to resist this. Or it may be that much that is proper to it will now prove for the first time to be right, that it will be committed to the cherishing and continuance of it with a genuine joy and stringency. No Church will emerge from this fiery trial unscathed, unaltered, unrenewed, authorised merely to persist: something of wood, hay and stubble will necessarily have to be sacrificed. But—with constant reference to the promise of the Lord—it is not merely probable but certain that everywhere there will be preserved and established something of gold, silver and precious stones. And even if the form is not exactly one and the same, will not that which remains in the one place be so near and similar to that which remains in the other that on both sides we will actually find that we are positively on the way to unity and we must and will mutually perceive that we find ourselves on this way? But we must not close our eyes to this. And, above all, we must not cease to move further along this way—which means, that we must not be afraid to enter the way of the *credo unam ecclesiam*[EN139] at its very beginning, at the acknowledged centre of every Christian community, and therefore at the lordship of the One to whom the Church belongs, whose body it is, who is Himself its true unity. As we look from Him, the actual unity of the Church will certainly be visible at a greater or lesser distance.

[685]

Credo sanctam ecclesiam[EN140]. Holy means set apart, marked off, and therefore differentiated, singled out, taken (and set) on one side as a being which has its own origin and nature and meaning and direction—and all this with a final definitiveness, decisively, inviolably and unalterably, because it is God who does it. The term indicates the contradistinction of the Christian community to the surrounding world, and in particular to the other gatherings and societies which exist in the world. It is not a natural society after the manner of the nations, nor is it based on social contracts, or agreements, or temporary or permanent understandings and arrangements. It is not a society of necessity and compulsion like the state, nor is it a free society for a particular purpose like an order or a club or an economic or cultural union. It has its own basis and its own goal. It cannot, therefore, understand itself in the light of the basis of other societies or follow their goals. In what it does it goes its own way and makes use of its own method, which it cannot exchange for those used by other societies, but which, again, it cannot try to force on those societies. In assessing the greatness or the littleness, the value or the shame, the success or the lack of success of what it does, it has its own standard, so that it cannot

---

[EN139] I believe one church
[EN140] I believe the holy church

§ 62. The Holy Spirit and the Gathering of the Christian Community

judge itself by the standards which apply to other societies. It has quite different conditions even in the question of its membership; or, strictly speaking, it has only one, and from its own point of view, a very definite condition, although one which in the last resort is incomprehensible to every other human society, the condition of faith. It cannot possibly waive this condition, just as it necessarily has to waive all those which may apply elsewhere. In short, it has its own law, and in its life it is pledged to that law and that law alone.

But it is still undoubtedly a human society in and like others, with its own sphere of power and interests and influence. Its members are still men like others, and they may also belong to some, or even many, human societies. It is still in a sense the neighbour of these societies. For all its distinctiveness, what it does is not beyond comparison with what they do. It can be compared with it at many points. In many respects it runs parallel with it. It is bound to it in practice by all kinds of relationships. We obviously have to underline the *credo ecclesiam*[EN141] in this respect too. That is to say, the invisible being of the Church in its visibility is in this respect too the matter of a special knowledge which is not accessible and cannot be attributed to every man, which is not amenable to the control of man at all. As long as the community lives in the world its holiness, like its unity, is covered by its actual likeness and relationships to other societies, by the twofold citizenship of its members, of Christians, in itself, but also in more than one of these other *civitates*[EN142]. If the confession is true, *credo sanctam ecclesiam*[EN143], then it is a matter of revelation and of the knowledge of revelation. The confession does not describe a matter which is open to all, but a discovery which no one can make without the Holy Spirit and to which no one can hold without a continuance of His revealing work. But on this presupposition, which cannot be omitted or forgotten, this means that the community is (in the sense which we have sketched) holy, and holy with a final and categorical definitiveness, inviolably and unalterably.

To understand this matter it is very much to the point to remember that the Creed says: *credo ecclesiam*[EN144], not *credo in ecclesiam*[EN145]. We cannot believe in the Church—the holy Church—as we believe in God the Father, Son and Holy Spirit. According to the third article we can believe only in God the Holy Spirit, and as we know and confess His work we can also believe the existence of the holy Church, just as later we can believe the forgiveness of sins as He declares it to man, or in the first article the heaven and earth as created by God the Father. If it is seriously true and can be known in faith, the holiness of the Church is not that of the Holy Spirit but that which is created by Him and ascribed to the Church. It is He who marks it off and separates it. It is He who differentiates it and singles it out. It is He who gives it its peculiar being and

---

[EN141] I believe the church
[EN142] states
[EN143] I believe the holy church
[EN144] I believe the existence of the church
[EN145] I believe in the church

2. *The Being of the Community*

law of life. It is holy as it receives it from Him to be holy. But though it is holy it is still a part of the creaturely world in which there can be no question of believing as we believe in God.

Calvin laid great stress on this: *Idea enim credere in Deum nos testamur, quod et in ipsum ut veracem animus noster se reclinat et fiducia nostra in ipso acquiescit; quod in ecclesiam non ita conveniret*[EN146] (*Instit.* IV, 1, 2). But the *Cat. Rom.* also explains (I, 10, 19) that in relation to the Church we must be content with the *credo*[EN147] without the *in, ut hac etiam diversa loquendi ratione Deus omnium effector in creatis rebus distinguatur, praeclaraque omnia quae in ecclesiam collata sunt, beneficia divinae bonitati accepta referamus*[EN148].

What else can the holiness of the Church be but the reflection of the holiness of Jesus Christ as its heavenly Head, falling upon it as He enters into and remains in fellowship with it by His Holy Spirit? He is the One who is originally differentiated and singled out as the eternal Son of God appointed the Reconciler of the world with God, and then as the executor of the divine counsel in His incarnation and the work of obedience on the cross, and as the recipient of the divine verdict in His resurrection. In the existence of the community we have to do with the earthly-historical form of His existence. As it is gathered and built up and commissioned by the Holy Spirit it becomes and is this particular part of the creaturely world, acquiring a part in His holiness, although of and in itself it is not holy, it is nothing out of the ordinary, indeed as His community within Adamic humanity it is just as unholy as that humanity, sharing its sin and guilt and standing absolutely in need of its justification. "And for their sakes I sanctify myself, that they also might be sanctified through the truth" (Jn. 17^{19}).

[687]

Hence Calvin says (*Serm. on Mt.* 2^{23}, *C.R.* 46, 455 f.) that there is no *plénitude de saincteté sinon au Chef*[EN149]. Just as Joseph among his brethren and Samson among his people were both set apart (Nazirites) for their sake and as their liberators, so in fulfilment of these Old Testament types the "Nazarene" Jesus was *separé d'avec tous les autres fidéles*[EN150] in order to make common cause with them. *Pourquoi donc ceste discrétion a elle este mise? C'est afin qu'il ait luy seul toute preeminence, afin que chacun s'addresse a luy, que nous puisions de ceste fontaine, qui ne tarit jamais: et que cependant nous ne laissions pas toutefois d'estre conjoints a luy*[EN151]. And again in astonishing agreement with Calvin the *Cat. Rom.* (I, 10, 12): the Church is holy *inter tot peccatores ... quod veluti corpus cum sancto capite, Christo Domino, coniungitur*[EN152]. There is a fine voice from modern Evangelical theology to the same effect, that of M. Kähler (*Wiss. d. chr. Lehre*, 1893, p. 389): As the assurance of the justified rests on the holiness of the self-

---

[EN146] Therefore we confess that we believe in God, and that our minds lean on him as faithful, and our trust rests in himself. It is not appropriate, therefore, to trust in this way in the church
[EN147] I believe
[EN148] in, so that God, the author of all things, might be distinguished from all that he has created, by this different manner of speaking, and so that we might describe all the wonderful things which are conferred upon the church as blessings received from God's goodness
[EN149] fullness of holiness except in the head
[EN150] set apart from all other faithful
[EN151] Why then has this distinction been made? So that He might have all the pre-eminence for himself, so that each one might point to Him, so that we might draw from this fountain which never runs dry. And, that we might nevertheless not fail to be joined to Him
[EN152] amidst so many sinners ... just as the body is joined with the holy head, Christ the Lord

§ 62. *The Holy Spirit and the Gathering of the Christian Community*

sufficient God and His electing grace, so, too, does the holiness of the Church. "In its claim to this quality which it cannot lose there lies the confession of the power of the Reconciler which overcomes the world." The measure of agreement seems to be particularly great in this important insight.

But the insight has far-reaching consequences of a positive as well as a critical nature. We will begin with two positive affirmations.

The community as the body of Jesus Christ is holy because and in the fact that He, the Head, is holy: in its connexion with Him, in its unity with Him, in the light which falls necessarily upon it from Him when it belongs to Him in the work of the Holy Spirit. But if this is true then obviously the converse is true, (1) that all the corresponding holiness of individual members on the basis of His relationship with them and theirs with Him, all the differentiation and separation of individual men by the gift of the Holy Spirit, by their awakening to faith and the knowledge of Him, is equivalent to the fact that they are members of His body and therefore that they are in the community. Where and when He calls these men—and not others, addressing and setting aside this man or that woman as His own, it does not mean, as the matter has often been put, and is still put, in a very doubtful way, that there arises between Him and them a private relationship. The fact that these individuals can as such partake of His grace and live with Him and for Him has no autonomous or ultimate significance. It has significance only as in so doing they become members of His body, or, rather, are revealed to be such to themselves and others. To be awakened to faith and to be added to the community are one and the same thing. Therefore there are not two separations or differentiations: an individual one for its own sake, and therefore the creation of certain *homines sancti*[EN153] whose existence can be an end in itself, satisfying both the One who calls them to it and those who are called; and then a collective one which is necessary and meaningful in some quite different way, the gathering and separation of these individual Christians into a community. There is only one separation, that of the *communio sanctorum*[EN154]: the awakening of the faith of individuals, the purpose of which is their gathering into the community—the gathering of the community in the form of the awakening of the faith of individuals.

In the Old Testament the partner of *Yahweh* was the people Israel as it existed, of course, in the totality of those who belonged to it. In and with Israel the individual Israelite was also the partner of *Yahweh*, but only as the representative of his people. So, too, the partner of Jesus Christ attested in the New Testament is the community which, of course, exists and is seen in the faith of its individual members, the ἡμεῖς [EN155] of the Lord's Prayer, the ὑμεῖς [EN156] of the Epistles; not a Christian individual who is not as such, or is merely subsequently and incidentally and not primarily and essentially, within the community. It is not a matter of the higher

---

[EN153] holy men
[EN154] communion of saints
[EN155] we
[EN156] you

2. *The Being of the Community*

value of the collective as compared with the individual, but if we like of a definite order and sequence. We can put it this way: the collective is the purpose and the individual the form of the subjective admission of reconciliation by the work of the Holy Spirit. The two terms can be used only when we relate them to a single point. If we take them to indicate two competing realities then they can only prevent us from understanding the point at issue. The community lives in Christians, Christians live in the community, and in this way Jesus Christ lives in the world. In this way they are holy in Him and with Him.

Note that in the first proposition we have said something which is very like but not exactly the same as the well-known dictum: *extra ecclesiam nulla salus*[EN157]. We find the substance, if not the actual words, of this dictum in many of the fathers (*C.D.* I, 2, 212). In the strict sense it claims that without participation as a member in the being and life of the Church there can be no participation in the reconciling act of divine redemption. But this is what we must be careful not to say. In this sense it would be true to say: *extra Christum nulla salus*[EN158]. But the Church as His body is only the form of existence in which He encounters the world historically, the community of those who know and confess their salvation and that of the world in Him. It serves Him in the world reconciled by Him. It proclaims the redemptive act of God as it took place in Him. Yet it is not outside adherence to the Church, but outside the adherence of all men to Him as known and confessed and proclaimed by the Church, that there is no salvation. We must also be careful not to maintain that participation in the salvation of the world grounded in Jesus Christ is bound absolutely to the mediation of the Church and therefore to its proclamation. We have to reckon with the hidden ways of God in which He may put into effect the power of the atonement made in Jesus Christ (Jn. 10^{16}) even *extra ecclesiam*[EN159], i.e., other than through its ministry in the world. He may have provided and may still provide in some other way for those who are never reached, let alone called to Him, by the Church. It does not detract from the glory of the community or weaken its commission if we keep at least an open mind in this respect. What we can say of the community is only this, though we can say it in all seriousness: *extra ecclesiam nulla revelatio, nulla fides, nulla cognitio salutis*[EN160]—and in so far as the knowledge and revelation of Jesus Christ and faith in Him and the ministry of the proclamation of His name constitutes the holiness of the Church: *extra ecclesiam nulla sanctitas*[EN161]. What is true is that the typical and ministerial separation of an individual, in virtue of which he is distinguished and marked off from other men as one who believes and knows, is as such his separation to life and ministry in and with the community. If he does not have it as such, he does not have it at all. And if he withdraws from the fellowship of the Church, in so doing he denies himself as *sanctus*[EN162], as one who believes and knows. What is true is that there is no legitimate private Christianity. The question which in this light we have to address not only to all forms of mysticism and pietism but also to Kierkegaard is plain to see. As Calvin puts it (*Instit.* IV, 1, 10), to try to be a Christian in and for oneself is to be a *transfuga et desertor religionis*[EN163] and therefore not a Christian. *Discessio ab ecclesia*[EN164] is a *Dei et Christi abnegatio*[EN165] and therefore worse than the position of the one who, never having come to faith and knowledge, is *extra ecclesiam*[EN166],

[689]

[EN157] no salvation outside the church
[EN158] no salvation outside of christ
[EN159] outside the church
[EN160] no revelation, no faith, no knowledge of salvation outside the church
[EN161] no holiness outside the church
[EN162] holy
[EN163] fugitive and a deserter of religion
[EN164] Departure from the church
[EN165] denial of God and of Christ
[EN166] outside the church

§ 62. *The Holy Spirit and the Gathering of the Christian Community*

has no part in its differentiation and separation, is not a *sanctus*^{EN167} and perhaps never will be. Such a *transfuga et desertor religionis*^{EN168} may even risk and forfeit his salvation, i.e., his participation in the reconciliation of the world with God. It may be something akin to the sin against the Holy Ghost of which he is guilty. For the Holy Ghost leads him directly into the community and not into a private relationship with Christ. *Nec ullum atrocius fingi crimen potest, quam sacrilega perfidia: violare coniugium, quod nobiscum (nobiscum*^{EN169} not *mecum) unigenitus Dei Filius contrahere dignatus est*^{EN170} (Calvin *l.c.*).

The community is holy because and as Jesus Christ is holy. But if this is true, then we can say of it (2) that, as what it is as differentiated in essence from the world and all its *civitates*^{EN171}, it is indestructible. In this respect the older dogmatics called it infallible. What was meant by this expression in Evangelical dogmatics was that the separation in which it exists cannot be reversed, that it cannot lose its distinctness and separateness within the world. Because it is from Jesus Christ, because it is His body, it cannot cease to be this, it cannot become something else, it cannot be subjected to another law than that which is laid upon it. It has not taken it upon itself to be holy, and it cannot set aside its calling. It has it from God and no man can take it from it—just as Israel never could or can in any crisis of its history in the covenant of God with it cease to be the people elected and called and commissioned by God. The Church exists in unity with this people of the old covenant. The perennial nature of Israel as the people of Jesus Christ is that of the Church.

The community may sometimes be pushed to the wall, persecuted, suppressed and outwardly destroyed, as has actually happened to Israel in many of its historical forms both past and present. What is worse, it may, like Israel, be guilty of failure and error. It may deny its Lord and fall from Him. It may degenerate. Indeed it has never existed anywhere except as a Church which has degenerated to a greater or lesser, a more serious or a less serious degree: not even in the New Testament period and certainly not according to the records of Church history, and, worst of all, where it has been most conscious and boasted most loudly of its purity—just as, according to the Old Testament, Israel does not seem at any time to have been—and, least of all, in the times of supreme self-consciousness—what it was ordained to be in faithfulness to its faithful God. The Church stands in the fire of the criticism of its Lord. It is also exposed to the criticism of the world and this criticism has never been altogether false and unjust. It has always needed, and it always will need, self-examination and self-correction. It cannot exist except as *ecclesia semper reformanda*^{EN172}—if only it had always understood itself in this light and acted accordingly! Its acts and achievements, its confessions and orders, its theology

---

^{EN167} holy/saint
^{EN168} fugitive and deserter of religion
^{EN169} There can be no more terrible crime that the sacrilege of treachery: to violate the marriage, which the only Son of God has condescended to contract with us (with us)
^{EN170} with me
^{EN171} states
^{EN172} church always to be reformed

2. *The Being of the Community*

and the ethics advocated by it and lived out by its members, never were and never are infallible at any point; and, again, they are most fallible where there is the arbitrary attempt to deck them out with infallibility—not least the ethics lived out by Christians. When has Christian ethics not wavered between a pharisaical legalism and an antinomian libertinism, between a "spiritual" sectarianism and a complacent respectability, between a weary pietism and a feverish activism, between the attractions of conservatism and those of revolution (or perhaps only of Bohemianism)? When has it been the case that men could simply see the good works of Christians and had to glorify their Father which is in heaven (Mt. 5^{16})? Taking it all in all, the community of Jesus Christ in the world may at times be clothed with every kind of pomp and glory; but what a frail vessel it is, exposed to every kind of assault, and actually assaulted both outwardly and above all inwardly!

> It was most apposite and ought not to have been discontinued that in 17th and 18th century Basel (after the daily sermon) the prayer was used in all Churches: "Have mercy, O Lord, upon the most pitiful and parlous state of thy dear Church in Germany, France, Piedmont, England, Hungary, etc., and most of all in an honourable Confederacy and surrounding territories." Yes, indeed, to this very day: *Kyrie eleison*$^{\text{EN173}}$. And as Luther used to emphasise: "Forgive us our trespasses"—to be prayed not merely in the name of individuals but by the Church as such in its own name.

But in face of all that has come and still comes upon the Church, in face of all that can be said concerning it and against it, *credo sanctam ecclesiam*$^{\text{EN174}}$. The *credo*$^{\text{EN175}}$ is obviously indispensable. We cannot say this except as a confession of faith. But it belongs to the confession of faith to say it.

> What Jesus said in Mt. 16^{18} is still true: "The gates of hell shall not prevail against it." And what He said in Lk. 22$^{31\text{f.}}$ to Peter (who three times denied Him): "Simon, Simon, behold, Satan hath desired to have you, that he may sift you as wheat; But I have prayed for thee, that thy faith fail not." And again in Jn. 17^{15}: "I pray not that thou shouldest take them out of the world, but that thou shouldest keep them from the evil." The perennial nature of the community rests only on this promise and prayer. But it does rest on it. To deny the perennial nature of the community is to deny the power of this prayer and promise. *Item docent, quod una sancta ecclesia perpetuo mansura sit*$^{\text{EN176}}$ (*Confession of Augsburg* VII).

The body of Jesus Christ may well be sick or wounded. When has it not been? But as the body of this Head it cannot die. The faith of the community may waver, its love may grow cold, its hope may become dreadfully tenuous, but the foundations of its faith and love and hope, and with it itself, are unaffected. The reflection of what the Holy Spirit was in eternity and will be in eternity does not cease to fall on it. It finds itself on a way which is not of its own seeking. It has not set itself on this way, and it cannot leave it. No one can

[691]

EN173 Lord, have mercy
EN174 I believe the holy church
EN175 I believe
EN176 Similarly, they teach that one holy church will remain in perpetuity

§ 62. The Holy Spirit and the Gathering of the Christian Community

arrest it on this way, nor can it halt of itself. It may limp on it and stumble and fall. It may lie on it apparently dead, like the man who fell among thieves on the way from Jerusalem to Jericho. But death is behind it. "Being born again, not of corruptible seed, but of incorruptible, by the word of God, which liveth and abideth for ever" (1 Pet. 1^{23}), it cannot again fall victim to it. It has always risen again, and it always will rise again, beaten down justly by God or justly or unjustly by man, but not cut off from the world, perishing in the one form to begin again with new power in another, almost or altogether extinguished in one place to build itself up the more joyfully as a young Church in another. Its authority and effects and influence and successes may be small, very small. They may threaten to disappear almost or altogether. But the authority and power of God are behind it and it will never fail. It may become a beggar, it may act like a shopkeeper, it may make itself a harlot, as has happened and still does happen, yet it is always the bride of Jesus Christ. Its existence may be a travesty of His, but as His earthly-historical form of existence it can never perish. It can as little lose its being as He can lose His. What saves it and makes it indestructible is not that it does not basically forsake Him—who can say how deeply and basically it has often enough forsaken Him and still does?—nor is it this or that good that it may be or do, but the fact that He does not forsake it, any more than *Yahweh* would forsake His people Israel in all His judgments.

From this it is clear that it is always a responsible and dangerous matter to criticise the Church. Again and again there may be the possibility of doing this with justice, and therefore the necessity to do it. But when we feel impelled to do it we must see to it that it really is necessary, that is to say, that it is demanded. A tacit criticism of the Church may be more relevant and effective than a violent one. But the danger is always that not only the Christians who direct and represent the cause of the Church, but in these weak brethren and their action Jesus Christ Himself will be criticised, attacked, condemned and perhaps rejected. To the fact that the Church can serve Him only according to His attestation in Holy Scripture, and can therefore speak and act only with a relative and provisional and therefore at bottom contestable authority, there corresponds the further fact that any criticism can only be relative and itself limited by the attestation of Jesus Christ in Holy Scripture. Spiritual things must be spiritually discerned, on the basis of a serious hearing, in the form of a conscientious distinguishing between that in which in any given case the Church does err, giving place to alien voices and powers and denying its Lord, and that in which in all its weakness and corruption it does perhaps contend for the truth. attesting the voice and power of the good Shepherd, being faithful to Him in all its unfaithfulness. If we can never hear the Church without some scruple, if we always have some cause to object to its word and attitude, in the strict sense we can confront it only with more or less searching questions, not with apodictic repudiations and condemnations and rejections; and whether the utterance of them be loud or quiet, it must proceed always from the recognition: I myself am in the *ecclesia semper reformanda*^{EN177}, and responsible for it. The first question must therefore be addressed to myself: What is the basis of my scruple and objection? to what extent am I really authorised to make it? The legitimate, prophetic, reformation attack upon the Church and its doctrine and order and life and attitudes can be conducted only on its own ground, in the

---

^{EN177} church always to be reformed

2. *The Being of the Community*

name of Jesus Christ, and with the intention of re-establishing it more firmly on this ground which it is perhaps on the point of denying, and with a new and better awareness of this ground. Do I myself stand on this ground when I criticise the Church? Am I concerned to serve its cause? Have I the ability to hold out something new and better? Legitimate scruples and objections can have nothing to do with the cheap anti-clerical clamour of the gutter. They can derive only from the solidarity in which we subject ourselves first—and then the Church—to the criticism to which it is subjected by its living Lord. For that reason, even though they may go very deep and have to be expressed sharply, they can never be made legitimately and therefore effectively except with a final brotherly mildness, restraint and consideration, except with a final respect for the Church's holiness. How much justifiable and necessary criticism of the Church has at bottom failed simply because it has not derived from this solidarity and has not, therefore, been made with this mildness and respect!

All this is relevant to the mutual relationship of the Churches as distinct from one another in spite of the unity of the Church, to their unavoidable criticism of one another within this relationship. Their division rests on the doubtful light in which they appear to one another, on the scruples and objections which they have to raise against each other. But, however doubtful may be the light in which one Church appears to the other, this other must not forget that it, too, is holy only from its living Lord, and that the other may also be holy from the one living Lord. Therefore no matter how well grounded and necessary and sharp may be the criticism which it brings against it, it can never harden into an absolute condemnation and rejection. Ultimately it can have only the character of a penetrating question addressed to it. As the rejection and condemnation of another Church it might well be directed against Jesus Christ Himself. It can succeed only in the humility in which we on this side—perhaps better than the other—know that the holiness of the community on both sides is His work, the gift of His Holy Spirit, so that it cannot either be claimed as a possession on the one side or called in question as the work and gift of the Lord on the other: as though our own Church were the mistress of the Lord and the other were not under His lordship. In the last resort it was Luther himself who in answer to the question (*W.A.* 40¹, 69 f.) how Paul, in spite of everything, could still address the Galatian communities as ἐκκλησίαι[EN178] stated quite plainly: *Sic et nos hodie vocamus Ecclesiam Romanam Sanctam et omnes episcopatus sanctos, etiamsi sint subverstet ministri eorum impii. Deus enim regnat in medio inimicorum,* (item) *Antichristus sedet in templo Dei et Satan adest in media filiorum Dei. Idea ecclesia etiamsi sit in medio nationis pravae et perversae ... luporum et latronum, hoc est tyrranorum spiritualium, nihilominus Ecclesia est*[EN179]. Even in the city of Rome (although it is worse than Sodom and Gomorrha) baptism and the Lord's Supper and the voice and word of the Gospel and Holy Scripture and the ministry and the name of Christ and the name of God still remain. Where these are found in a people, that people is holy. *Ideo Romana Ecclesia est sancta.* Luther could expressly say the same (71, 19) of the communities of the *phanatici*[EN180], but only on the same basis, and it was on this basis alone that he claimed the character of holiness for his own Church in Wittenberg (69, 29). *Ego, tu, sancti sumus: ecclesia, civitas, populus sanctus est non sua sed aliena, non activa sed passiva sanctitate*[EN181] (70, 19). It is another matter whether and to what extent

[693]

[EN178] churches

[EN179] So we today also call the Roman Church holy, and all the sees holy, even if they be corrupted, and wicked servants of themselves. For God reigns amidst his enemies, the Antichrist is seated in the Temple of God, and Satan is present in the midst of the sons of God. Therefore even if the Church be in the midst of a wicked and perverse nation ... of wolves and robbers – that is, of spiritual tyrants – it is nevertheless still the Church

[EN180] radicals

[EN181] We are holy, you and I; the Church, a state, a people holy not by its own holiness, but by that of another, not with an active, but a passive holiness

§ 62. The Holy Spirit and the Gathering of the Christian Community

Luther did justice to this insight in his polemics against Rome and the *phanatici*^{EN182}. It is certainly no light or simple task actually to do it justice in a given case. What is certain is that even in the most extreme cases the mutual judgment in the relationship between the divided Churches cannot go further than the affirmation that in its character as a community of Jesus Christ the one is more or less and perhaps completely hidden from the other so that it can neither see it nor understand it. It cannot therefore go beyond a very serious question concerning this quality of holiness. But is it hidden from itself as a community of Jesus Christ? Does it not have to believe that it is such without seeing it? On this basis its judgment cannot become a judgment which rejects the other Church altogether as a Church of Jesus Christ. For only Jesus Christ Himself can pronounce this judgment on it. Pronounced by another Church which itself lives by His holiness, it is not merely presumptuous but worse, for it means that the rejecting Church runs the most serious danger, and has perhaps already fallen victim to it, of rejecting in the rejected Church Jesus Christ Himself and the holiness in which He allows it to participate, thus making itself definitely unholy and ceasing to be His community.

We turn from the positive to some critical conclusions from the fact that the holiness of the community has to be understood wholly as the reflection of the holiness of Jesus Christ and therefore only as the gift of His Holy Spirit.

If this is the case then (1) we have to consider that its separation in the world does not, as it were, automatically, necessarily and consistently coincide with the peculiarity of its common being and activity in which it often distinguishes and marks itself off from the activity of the world and that of other neighbouring human societies. To quote Luther again: *christiana sanctitas non est activa, sed passiva sanctitas*^{EN183}. We have seen that the Church does exist in activity, and indeed in a specific and special activity, the human activity directed in accordance with its own law. But it is not the Church which makes its special activity holy. It is not itself which by its special activity in the world marks itself off from that of other societies. But this means that it does not lie in its power or under its control to give to its own activity the predicate "Christian." It would do well always to apply this adjective to its own activities only with the greatest reserve and therefore relatively seldom. In all seriousness there are what we may call "Christian" activities, which are as such different from all others and as such holy, a holy activity of the community within the world. There is in fact a coincidence of its divine separation and its own separations in and with its activity (in its preaching, in its worship, in its constitution, in its ordinances, in its theology, in its attitude in questions and decisions which affect the world). There are human acts and attitudes which are holy as such, i.e., which have the character of real witness to the One whose earthly historical existence the Church is allowed to be. But that they have this character is always dependent upon the answering witness of the One whom they aim and profess to attest. It is a matter of His special care, of His free grace which He has promised to address to His community without committing it into the hands of His community. In respect of its holiness the community is bound to

---
^{EN182} radicals
^{EN183} Christian holiness is not active, but passive holiness

2. *The Being of the Community*

Him—and He to it—only to the extent that He constantly wills to bind Himself and does in fact bind Himself to it. He is always the Subject, the Lord, the Giver of the holiness of its action. Its action as such can only be a seeking, an asking after holiness, a prayer for it. And not the community but He Himself decides the rightness of its seeking, asking and prayer, and therefore whether and to what extent He will hear it, confirming and blessing its action as a true witness to Him. Neither in great things nor in small can it be holy of itself and therefore without His Holy Spirit. And in great things and in small the presence and gift of His Holy Spirit are directly His own work. It can be in the right in its activity, therefore, only to the extent that it acquires this right from Him. If He does not give it, then even its ostensibly most holy work is profane: its preaching is simply a kind of explanation and instruction, or enthusiastic protestation; its baptism and Lord's Supper are religious rites like others; its theology is a kind of philosophy, its mission a species of propaganda, etc. They may all have their interest and importance and practical value from other standpoints—intellectual, moral, psychological, sociological—but they cannot be holy without the work of the living Lord of the community. No institutions within which its activity is done, no good will on the part of the men who act, no old or new technique which is used, can make them holy or prevent them from again becoming secular. The community is wholly in the hands of its Lord, and that means that it is thrown back on His having mercy upon it and making its unholy activity holy and acknowledging it as such.

This does not contradict its indestructibility. Its indestructibility consists in this open relationship to Him, in the fact that it is entirely in His hand and thrown back on hope in Him, in the sovereignty in which He turns to it and the acknowledgment in which it, for its part, turns to Him. It cannot attain it in any other way. It is holy and indestructible in the fact that it *abdicata omni sua sapientia a Spiritu Sancto doceri se per verbum Dei patitur*[EN184] (Calvin, *Instit.* IV, 8, 3).

If it is the case that the holiness of the community is the reflection of the holiness of the Lord and therefore the free gift of His Holy Spirit, then (2) we have also to consider critically that its separation and holiness will not automatically, necessarily and consistently take place in the mere fact that certain men unite together in it, or enter its existing unity, thus becoming and being members of it. This does, of course, take place as well wherever the community arises or is present. It belongs to the aspect which is visible to everyone that such and such men come to it with their profession of faith and desire to receive baptism and are received by it and actually become members and, as such, are Christians, or, at any rate, appear to be. But to be Christians, and therefore holy members of the holy community means—for "if any man hath not the Spirit of Christ, he is none of his" (Rom. 8⁹)—that they have actually been awakened to faith in Him. that they have found themselves members of

[695]

[EN184] renounces all of its own wisdom, and allows itself to be taught by the Holy Spirit through the Word of God

§ 62. *The Holy Spirit and the Gathering of the Christian Community*

the community in this fact, that in fulfilment of their faith and election and calling they have asked for baptism and received it as a confirmation, that with a lively faith they are Christians and therefore in the community. Is this really true of all those of whom the community is composed as visible to every man? Of how many of them is it true? Of which of them? This was the question which, in the 16th century, deeply disturbed not only the Anabaptist communities and other so-called sectarians but the great Churches of the Reformation. They all wrestled with this question in their confessional writings or in other ways. It is a question which is deeply disturbing even to-day. The Church which is not deeply disturbed by it is not a Christian Church. It is the question which runs parallel to that of the holiness of its common action and is indissolubly connected with it—the question of the holiness of its members. If it is in its members, if its common action is their action, then the holiness of its action and its own holiness obviously stands or falls with that of the Christians assembled in it. But which are the holy members? Who are the true Christians?

Est autem ecclesia congregatio sanctorum[EN185] (*Confession of Augsburg* VII). What is meant emerges unmistakably from the German text: "the congregation of all believers." And it is affirmed by Art. VIII even in the Latin that the Church is *proprie* (properly) the *congregatio sanctorum et vere credentium*[EN186]. But is there a community which is holy only *improprie*[EN187]? The continuation of Art. VII is well known: *in qua evangelium pure docetur et sacramenta recta administrantur*[EN188]. This is correct—although not exhaustive—as an answer to the question of the holiness of its activity. But can we separate this question from that of the holiness of its members who are the subjects of its activity? Is there no relationship at all between that *pure*[EN189] and *recta*[EN190] and the *vere credere*[EN191] of those who are gathered into the community and are active as such? Can we simply ignore this second question, as Art. VIII seems to come near to doing, merely so as not to provide an opening to the Donatist heresy? Can we be content simply to make the true enough statement that the truth of the Gospel is not tied to the worthiness or unworthiness of the Church's ministers? Is not the question inescapable if the Church is not only a sphere *in qua*[EN192] this action takes place but, as the obvious subject of this action, the "congregation of all believers"? It could not actually lie dormant even in the great Churches of the Reformation but always demanded some kind of answer.

But when it is posed, there were and are attempts to answer it which are far too facile. On the surface they are opposed to each other, but in fact they are complementary. They are both illegitimate and, for that reason, they can both be set aside at a stroke.

The first points to baptism as the factor by which a man is placed in the *communio sanctorum*[EN193] and on the basis of which he is a true member of it. It is in and by the fact that he is baptised that he receives the Holy Spirit and comes to a true faith, thus becoming a member of the body of Christ and a holy member of His holy community. The number of

---

[EN185] The church is the congregation of the saints
[EN186] the congregation of the saints and of those who believe truly
[EN187] improperly
[EN188] in which the Gospel is purely taught and the sacraments rightly administered
[EN189] purely
[EN190] rightly
[EN191] believe truly
[EN192] in which
[EN193] communion of saints

2. *The Being of the Community*

true Christians is therefore the number of the baptised. How can it be otherwise when baptism has this power *ex opere operato*[EN194]? We are not concerned for the moment whether this is good baptismal teaching. Nor are we considering the absurd result that in this way (*via* infant baptism) whole populations of whole countries have automatically been made and can automatically be made the holy community. Even if we did not have to face this practice, the decisive objection to this view is that in it the question of the gathering of the community by the Lord Himself is mischievously evaded, the spiritual mystery of the community being replaced and crowded out by an arrogantly invented sacramental mystery. What kind of a conception of the Holy Spirit is it, of His presence and operation, of the awakening to faith, and of membership of the body of Christ, when all this can be imparted to a man simply by the correct fulfilment of an action initiated by men? What kind of a conception of the community is it when the community has the power to constitute and augment itself as a holy community simply by this action?

[696]

But it was no better when the attempt was made to recognise the holiness of Christians (and therefore the holiness of the community) by certain attitudes and actions which distinguish Christians from other men: perhaps by their regular attendance at service and Holy Communion, or more seriously by their conversion to the faith under certain conditions, or by what they do or do not do, by a certain style or habit of Christian life, by ways of life which are usual or even unusual, and all presupposing the existence of some law or standard by which the presence of these distinguishing marks of Christianity can be established. But where is the law which can serve as a measure to distinguish who has or has not the Holy Spirit, who believes or does not believe, who belongs to the community of the saints or does not belong? What decides and distinguishes in this case is not a sacramental *opus operatum*[EN195] but a religious and moral *opus operantis*[EN196]—as though the Lord, the Holy Spirit and His gift could be enclosed in the sphere of certain human works thought out by men. Again it is obvious that the question of the Holy Spirit and His gathering of the community has been—we can only say mischievously—evaded. Again the real mystery of the community has been replaced and crowded out by one which has been arrogantly invented (this time a religious and moral). What kind of a conception of the holiness of its members and therefore of its own holiness is this? What kind of a conception of the Holy Spirit?

There can only be vacillation in face of these two attempts to answer our question. There can never be either a valid and clear-cut decision or any kind of compromise between them. As a rule, the result will be either the reaction of a powerful moralism against the recognised danger of sacramentalism, or that of a powerful sacramentalism against the recognised danger of moralism. It is to be hoped that on neither side the reaction will be too powerful because the *aporia*[EN197] into which we are betrayed when we try to choose either one or the other is quite hopeless. But if we try to combine the two, will not the combination simply aggravate the evil which attaches to both? In both cases the answering of the question is made too facile. In both cases we have to do with imitations, substitutes. Both rest on illusions. Both miss the one point on which everything turns. Therefore both have to be abandoned.

We will try to answer the question from our presupposition, and we will begin by stating that at all times and in all situations holy members of the holy Church, and therefore true Christians, were and are the men assembled in it

---

[EN194] automatically
[EN195] work worked
[EN196] work of the one working
[EN197] impasse

§ 62. The Holy Spirit and the Gathering of the Christian Community

who are thereto elected by the Lord, called by His Word, and constituted by His Spirit: just so many, no more and no less, these men and no others. It is He who knew them and willed them and created them as such. It is He who knows and preserves them as His saints.

But are there "others" in His community, who have not come to it by Him, who have not been baptised and are not members on the basis of His affirmation, who take their confession on their lips and in some way participate in the life of the community—but only in appearance, who are not therefore saints, true Christians? It would be an obvious exaggeration to try to maintain that this is not possible. There is no doubt—and this is what the eyes of the world see—that the Church is also a human *civitas*[EN198] or *societas*[EN199], a union of men. Hidden in this it lives as the body of Jesus Christ. But it does exist and recruit as this union on the basis of human insights and judgments and decisions. We cannot expect that these human insights and judgments and decisions (conditioned and limited as such) will be plainly and automatically and directly identical with those of its Lord, or that they can prejudice or even anticipate His, His knowledge of men and resolve concerning them, His activity by which He makes them members of His body. It may well be that they are blessed and ratified by Him, and to that extent are made in His name, not merely in claim but in truth. But the community constitutes and recruits itself knowing the fact, and knowing it as its limit, that in this, too, it is in His hand and is thrown back on the hope of His ratification and blessing, on the free grace of His Holy Spirit. It can constitute and recruit itself only in faith in Him. In this respect, too, it must acknowledge His sovereignty. But this involves an acknowledgment that it may make mistakes, that even amongst those who belong to it in the eyes of men there may be some who are not members of His body, who are not at all elected and called by Him, who are not awakened by His Holy Spirit to faith in Him.

> As we see from the parable in Mt. 13$^{24f.}$, there may be tares among the wheat, or from that in Mt. 13^{47f} there may be bad fish amongst those which come into the net. Who knows how many tares? Who knows how many bad fish? There was a Judas even among the twelve apostles. And so *C.A.* VIII reckons with the fact that "in this life there remain many false Christians and hypocrites and even notorious sinners among the faithful." It may well be, therefore, that the fellowship of the Church as such can only be called a *societas mixta*[EN200], and in that case only *improprie*, improperly, the body of Jesus Christ.

We have to take this possibility into account, not on the obvious but very doubtful ground that when we look at supposed fellow-Christians we have every reason to think of the tares rather than the wheat, but because the final and authoritative decision whether such and such baptised and professing

---

[EN198] state
[EN199] society
[EN200] mixed society

2. *The Being of the Community*

members of the community whom we regard as genuine believers are really such is not our affair but His, while we can only go by what we see.

But in the strict sense it would also be an exaggeration if we thought we knew and tried to maintain that it is not only possible but actually the case that in the community there are, in fact, both believing Christians and unbelieving, both true Christians and false, so that we can regard what we see as the Church only improperly as the community of Jesus Christ, treating it as such only with a limited seriousness. For how can we know this if it is really the Lord who decides the emergence and development of His body and therefore who is or is not a true member of it and therefore a true member of His community? Why should it not be His pleasure actually to think much better and make much more of all those who as baptised and professing Christians are visibly members of His community like ourselves than we can ever imagine in our general or particular mistrust of supposed fellow-Christians? And how can we possibly know how many and which He has placed on His right hand as His own people, and how many and which He has placed on His left hand as those who are not called or as Judases? According to the standard of human knowledge and judgment the community can and must decide whom it must and will accept and recognise as visible adherents, or whom it must and will refuse to recognise or expel. There are serious grounds for both, and in this connexion we shall have to consider at a later stage the problem of Church discipline. But there is no Church discipline—and it is a misunderstanding and misapplication of the saying about the keys of the kingdom of heaven in Mt. 16^{19} to expound it in this way—in which it is given to men to decide what men are or are not members of the body of Christ and therefore true Christians and therefore saints. As we can only believe the Christian community as such in its identity with the holy community of Jesus Christ, so we can only believe ourselves and others as its holy members.

[698]

We are obviously thrown back entirely on faith even if in a supposed awareness of the mixed character of the Church union we try to seek out an "inner circle" of true believers or to make common cause with certain others as *sancta ecclesiola in ecclesia*^{EN201}. It is evident that Luther did occasionally toy with this idea. But fortunately he neither developed it systematically nor attempted to apply it in practice. For who is to decide and who is able to decide who belongs or does not belong to this *ecclesiola*^{EN202}?

But if it is a matter of the perception of faith, then we all do well to begin with the question how it is with ourselves. According to *Qu.* 54 of the *Heidelberg Catechism*, when I look at the community elected to eternal life from the whole of the human race by the Son of God, gathered and protected and preserved by His Spirit and Word in the unity of the true faith from the beginning of the world to its end, I may and can and should believe with supreme confidence and joy "that I am and will eternally remain a living member of the same." I am

---

^{EN201} holy church-within-the-Church
^{EN202} church-within-the-Church

§ 62. *The Holy Spirit and the Gathering of the Christian Community*

[699] not asked or allowed, indeed I am forbidden, to doubt this. But—since I cannot see myself as this living member—I can cease to doubt it only in faith. And faith means that I look to Jesus Christ, that I subject myself to His verdict and cling to it, that in Him and in virtue of His verdict, in spite of everything which is against me, I am not condemned but justified, not rejected but accepted, not outside but inside, although I cannot know anything for myself but the consciousness of my faith ("Lord, I believe; help thou mine unbelief"), my baptism and my profession. If I believe this for myself, it obviously means that I give myself into His hand with all that is against me and with all that I think I know positively of myself trusting, but genuinely into His hand. When I do this I do not need to doubt my election and calling, my true Christianity, my holiness; indeed I cannot and must not do so. But if this is the case with me, why should it be otherwise with my supposed fellow-Christians? In relation to them I can obviously only believe that they are not merely supposed Christians, Christians in appearance only, or even Judases. In relation to them I am obviously not summoned to doubt but to believe, and to this end, in relation to them, too, to look to Jesus Christ to whose verdict they are ready to subject themselves in virtue of their baptism and their profession: notwithstanding all that speaks against them and as I see it seems to speak against them. In relation to myself and to them, and therefore to them as well as myself, what can I do but commend both myself and them, them and myself, to His hand and His decision? To them as to me, to me as to them, it is the hidden decision of His free grace which I cannot forestall either positively or negatively. But I can—and obviously should—accept it in advance as right, both for them and for me, for me and for them. He is the Holy One, and as such the Lord and the Head, the Creator and Preserver of His holy community and its holy members. Can I really show my holiness in any other way than by trusting Him as Paul did in the salutations of his Epistles (as in 1 Cor. 1^2), trusting that my fellow-Christians are not Christians only in appearance or Judases, but on the basis of His decision and act living members of His body and holy, although their holiness can be just as little perceived and established as my own? Am I not myself acting as a Christian only in appearance, and as a Judas, if I refuse to do this, if I will not allow to be in their favour that which is in my favour? Certainly we do not have any knowledge of that which is invisible in this respect, and we ought to maintain that we do not have it. But when we believe in Jesus Christ, presupposing that we are in the community which is before us and that we live with it, we are required to accept as a working hypothesis that other members as well as ourselves can be holy and not unholy; not on the basis of their own thought and will and action, but in spite of the doubtful nature of all human thought and will and action, as those who are separated by the Lord of the community and therefore genuinely, as real Christians. It is only on this presupposition that the admittedly serious problem of Church discipline can be meaningfully faced. It can never be exercised seriously except among those who are mutually ready to accept each other as Christians.

2. *The Being of the Community*

From the knowledge of the origin of the holiness of the community in that of Jesus Christ there follows (3) the critical question of its obedience. We cannot develop this in the present context. The second part of the doctrine of reconciliation will be the right place to do this. For the moment, in order to prevent a threatened misunderstanding, we have simply to remember that the question is posed, and posed acutely. The statement of Luther that the Church's holiness is not active but passive must not be taken to mean that the Church, with its activity and members, is only as it were covered by a holiness which Jesus Christ places over it from without, so that although its human and visible existence is certainly protected by its invisible holiness it is also blurred by it as by a shade, so that it is not affected or disturbed by it, but is left to go its own way in independence of it. It does not mean that on this great presupposition, for good or evil, according to the best conscience of the men united in it, the community can and must develop and shape and order and control itself and its movements, and always with the comfortable assurance that though this may be more for evil than for good, it cannot itself create and maintain its holiness, but can live only by the holiness of its Lord. It does not mean that its holiness has only—in the deepest sense of the word—a theoretical and not a practical and concrete significance for its human and visible existence. If our previous understanding of the holiness of the community is right, that it is the working in it and to it of the free act of grace of Jesus Christ and the gift of His Holy Spirit, then a deduction of this kind is quite impossible. It is true enough that in this holiness it remains invisible to the world and even to itself apart from faith. It is imparted to it only in so far as there is this working in it and to it. It cannot and will not be visible to every man. It cannot and will not become a predicate of its historical existence which can be maintained in neutrality. It will never be visible even to itself except with reference to its Lord, with the prayer for His Holy Spirit, and for His working within it. It will be visible only in faith. It is not a hypostasis which hovers statically over it and in the knowledge and confession of which it can rejoice in a this-sidedness which for its part both rests and moves in itself. Jesus Christ is not the Holy One for Himself, but for the world and in the first instance for His community in the world. He is not the Holy One in some height or distance above its earthly and historical existence but in it and to it (as His own earthly-historical form of existence). It is not for nothing, therefore, that it is in His hand and even in its this-sidedness, but in its very this-sidedness, in its human doing and non-doing, in its common action and the life of all its members it is continually confronted with His presence as the Holy One, it is continually exposed to His activity, it is continually jolted by Him, it is continually asked whether and to what extent it corresponds in its visible existence to the fact that it is His body, His earthly-historical form of existence. How can it believe and know and confess itself as His holy community, how can its adherents believe and know and confess themselves as its holy members, without looking to Him? But how can they look to Him without being continually asked how they are really conducting themselves in

[700]

[701]

§ 62. The Holy Spirit and the Gathering of the Christian Community

their relation to Him in their existence here? And how can they find themselves questioned in this way without hearing His instruction, without being called to obedience to Him, without being asked concerning their obedience? It would be a singular faith which refused to be asked concerning its character as obedience—as love to the One in whom it is reposed. No, it cannot create and assure its own holiness. It can only trust His holiness and therefore its own. But there is another No, which is this: No, it cannot legitimately trust His holiness and therefore its own without recognising and confessing and respecting it as the imperative and standard of its own human activity, without finding that indolence and self-will are both forbidden and distasteful, without being very definitely stirred into action by His holiness, the holiness of the living Lord, without being summoned to a very definite expectation and movement. His holiness is not given to it as a kind of umbrella under which it can rest or walk up and down at will, but as a pillar of cloud and fire like that which determined the way of the Israelites in the wilderness, as the mystery by which it has to direct itself in its human Church work—although it always remains a mystery. Whether it does this or not, whether it does it in part or altogether, is the question of obedience which is put to it. It cannot answer this question of its holiness by any answer of its own. It can never make itself holy by its human Church work—not even when it has nothing with which to reproach itself in the doing of it. For when it has done all that it has to do, because it is commanded, it will have good reason to know and confess with Lk. 17^{10} that we are unprofitable servants. The question of its holiness—and that of its activity and members—can be answered only with reference to the holiness of its Head. The basis of its holiness is its living Head, present to it as His body and acting in it and to it. This being the case, it is the *conditio sine qua non*[EN203] of the only possible answer to this question of its holiness that it accepts the question of obedience which is raised by it, and takes it into account in every aspect of its human Church work.

Credo catholicam ecclesiam[EN204]. The adjective "catholic" means general, comprehensive. It speaks of an identity, a continuity, a universality, which is maintained in all the differences. Applied to the Church it means that it has a character in virtue of which it is always and everywhere the same and always and everywhere recognisable in this sameness, to the preservation of which it is committed. In the character of this sameness it exists and shows itself to be the true Church, the Church of Jesus Christ. Where it does not exist and is not recognisable in this sameness, where it is not concerned to preserve it, where it is not "catholic," it is not the true Church, the Church of Jesus Christ. The term "catholic" speaks explicitly of the true Church activating and confirming its identical being in all its forms. Implicitly it speaks of the contrast between the true Church and the false. It is the false Church in every form in which it

---

[EN203] necessary condition
[EN204] I believe the catholic Church

2. The Being of the Community

does not activate or confirm its identical being but has and reveals and maintains an alien being. It is then a "heretical" Church, i.e., a Church which chooses for itself such an alien being. At the very worst it may even become an "apostate" Church, i.e. one which falls away, which turns its back on the being of the true Church and denies it. Either way it is *eo ipso*[EN205] a schismatic Church, i.e., one which breaks away from the fellowship of the true Church, a sect which has cut itself off from it. The word "catholic" signifies, therefore, that element in the concept Church which both unites and divides, which is both irenical and polemical. It speaks of what rivets the Church together as a Church. But by this riveting it means something definite, something which cannot be exchanged for anything else. To that extent it speaks of what separates the Church from that which is only ostensibly or supposedly the Church, but which is not the Church.

> The Reformation and the Evangelical theology of the 17th century did not allow their claim to the catholicity of their cause to be spoiled by the fact that it was so violently disputed by the Romanist Church under this very name. And in England the refusal to give up this word has persisted not merely in Anglicanism but right up to our own days in Congregationalism. The surrender is, in fact, quite impossible. A Church is catholic or it is not the Church. It was a sign of the greatest thoughtlessness and weakness on our part when in common usage we allowed the word to be taken from us, so that as a title it is now for the most part abandoned to the Romanists and we ourselves are—wherever possible with great emphasis and pleasure—described as a-catholics, heretics, schismatics and sectarians, and it is to us a most derogatory matter if we think we can establish or even report of someone that he is guilty of "catholicising" or "catholic" tendencies. As though a genuine Church and theology could have any other tendency at all than one which is not merely "catholicising" but seriously "catholic!"

Credo catholicam ecclesiam[EN206] simply means that—although I do not have faith in it but in the Holy Spirit and through Him in the Father and the Son—I believe in the existence of a community which in the essence which makes it a Christian community is unalterable in spite of all its changes of form, which in this essence never has altered and never can or will alter. And negatively, I do not believe that a community which is different in essence is the Christian community. To bring the two together, I believe in the existence of a true Church and not in that of a false Church.

The plurality or variety which is embraced by the Church in virtue of its unalterable essence or against which it maintains and is pledged to maintain its unalterable essence was at first understood primarily in a geographical sense. The Church is the same in all countries and in all parts of the earth, and in essence it has to present itself as the same in all of them. "Catholic" had, therefore, and in the first instance still has, the narrower sense of "ecumenical", i.e. identical in the whole inhabited world, in all parts of the globe where men live and where it can exist as the Church.

[703]

[EN205] by definition
[EN206] I believe the catholic Church

§ 62. The Holy Spirit and the Gathering of the Christian Community

"Because" ecumenical "only brings out one dimension of the term" catholic "we may deplore the fact that it has been chosen to describe the modern attempts at reunion and unity. Some part of the responsibility must be attributed to the meaningless but passionate opposing of the terms" Catholic "and " Protestant."But there are signs that as progress is made in these attempts the wider term" catholic "will fill out or burst through the narrower term " ecumenical."

From the geographical meaning of the word there has derived and still derives the wider sense in which the reference is to the relationship of the Christian community to the other natural and historical human societies. In essence the Church is the same in all races, languages, cultures and classes, in all forms of state and society. If it is to remain the true Church, it cannot be essentially determined by any of these societies. It cannot allow its conception of itself to be dictated by them. It cannot adjust itself to them. In all the apparently unavoidable accommodations of a practical and technical kind, it must see to it that it does not become guilty of deviation from the way which can only be the same in all spheres, or of disloyalty to the commission which it has to discharge in them all. With greater ease or difficulty it can enter into symbiosis with all societies, but it cannot accept any kind of essential dependence on them. Christians will always be Christians first, and only then members of a specific culture or state or class or the like. Similarly in all these different spheres the Church must always be the Church first, and only then, in the first instance in the advocacy of its own cause, and to that extent always with a certain alienation, can it enter into positive relationships with these other spheres.

Christianity exists in Germany and Switzerland and Africa, but there is no such thing as a German or Swiss or African Christianity. There is a Church in England, but in the strict sense there is no Church of England. It was quite intolerable when some twenty years ago the rise of Hitler was seriously claimed as a kind of divine revelation, or when to satisfy the racial laws of National Socialism it was proposed to found special congregations of Jewish Christians. How much longer will it be possible in the United States and South Africa to ratify the social distinctions between whites and blacks by a corresponding division in the Church, instead of calling it in question in the social sphere by the contrary practice of the Church? And in the tension of this present age will it be given not merely to the Churches of the Eastern bloc but above all to those of the supposedly free West to escape in time, and effectively, the influence of the world around them upon their message and function? Every Church in every age has good reason to ask concerning its catholicity in this sense. Does it exist only as a kind of respectable local, regional or national tradition valued and cherished by certain circles and sections? Or as one of the instruments of the power of society or the ruling class in society? Or—as happens again and again—as a union which is cleverly tolerated or even encouraged by statesmanship to satisfy certain religious needs or to buttress the morality and outlook which is desired for the well-being of the state? By its very antithesis (e.g., the combating of a materialistic philosophy) may it not be guilty of self-betrayal as a secularised Church? Does it exist of its essence and in faithfulness to its essence? We must never think that we can arrive at a position where we will not be disturbed by this question.

But the term catholic then has an even wider temporal dimension. It tells us that the Church has maintained itself and has to maintain itself in the identity

2. The Being of the Community

of its essence even in the historical sequence of its forms. It exists in history. It is history. It makes history. But this being the case, it is clear that in this respect it exists only in change. It is on a way which is surrounded by a continually changing landscape and in which it is itself continually subject to change—but in which it can never become anything other than itself, in which it is obliged and summoned always to be the same and continually to maintain itself as the same in forms which are always new.

At this point we must resist with equal firmness two imminent errors.

The "catholic" and therefore the true Church is not the oldest Church as such. It is not, therefore, that Church which at a later time and even to-day can appeal with the greatest certainty to the continuity and conformity of its structure with that of the most primitive Church. In this respect the *Scots Confession* of 1560 remarked dryly but correctly (Art. 18) that in point of age and the dignity which it confers Cain ultimately has precedence over both Abel and Seth. It is not because it was the oldest community, but because it was that of the direct witnesses to Jesus Christ that the community of the New Testament is for every age the typical, "catholic" community. Even in the form which immediately followed the Church was at once questioned concerning its catholicity, so that in an answering of the question of the catholicity of the Church in its later forms this form is not without interest and importance but cannot claim to be in any basic sense normative. All honour to the apostolic fathers and the rest of the 2nd century. All honour, too, to the churchmanship and theology of the early days of the Reformation and their confessional statements. But the question of the true Church cannot possibly resolve itself simply into that of conformity with any forms which are earlier in point of time. Reaction in the form of a return to any fathers is ecclesiastical romanticism; it has never been the way to maintain or restore the catholicity of the Church. For the same reason the character of the Church as a true Church can never be deduced from or established by the proof of a legal succession (we will return to this question) of its ministry linking it with the ancient or most ancient Church. The Church of any age, ancient or modern, most ancient or most modern, is the true and therefore the catholic, the general and comprehensive Church, only to the extent that in its own age it participates in the essence of the one Church, being faithful to it and knowing how to do it justice in its visible expression.

Conversely, it is not the newness, the modernity, the up-to-dateness of a Church which as such proves and commends it as the true and catholic Church. There was a proud *theologia moderna*[EN207] even in the 15th century. At the time of Protestant orthodoxy the introduction of Aristotelianism was the last word in modernity about 1600, as was that of Cartesianism a little later. After 1700 the modern theology was one which knew how to be orthodox, pietistic and enlightened at one and the same time. Naturally all the different forms of theological and ecclesiastical Liberalism boasted of their modernity as a sign of truth. According to Troeltsch and his contemporaries in age and controversy, "Neo-Protestantism" was definitely the most important of all the keys to the kingdom of heaven. And we must not forget that at that time there was in the Church and in theology a trend and school of "modern positivism." But modernity, up-to-dateness, has nothing whatever to do with the question of the truth of the Church. For that reason the idea of progress is a highly doubtful one as applied to the Church. What counts in the Church is not progress but reformation—its existence as *ecclesia semper reformanda*[EN208]. *Semper reformari*[EN209], however, does not mean always to go

[705]

[EN207] modern theology
[EN208] the Church always to be reformed
[EN209] always to be reformed

§ 62. The Holy Spirit and the Gathering of the Christian Community

with the time, to let the current spirit of the age be the judge of what is true and false, but in every age, and in controversy with the spirit of the age, to ask concerning the form and doctrine and order and ministry which is in accordance with the unalterable essence of the Church. It means to carry out to-day better than yesterday the Christian community's one task which needs no revision, and in this way to "sing unto the Lord a new song." It means never to grow tired of returning not to the origin in time but to the origin in substance of the community. The Church is catholic when it is engaged in this *semper reformari*[EN210], so that Catholicism has nothing to do with conservatism either, but very much to do with the sound common sense of the prayer of the robust Nicholas Selnecker (which is still to be found even in the new Swiss hymnbook): "Against proud spirits stand and, fight, / Who lift themselves in lofty might, / And always bring in something new, / To falsify thy teaching true." Therefore neither flirtation with the old nor flirtation with the new makes the Church the true Church, but a calm consideration of that which as its abiding possession is superior to every yesterday and to-day and is therefore the criterion of its catholicity.

But the Church is also the catholic, the general and comprehensive and therefore true community of Jesus Christ in its relationship to its individual members, to Christians. The Christian is first a member of the Christian community and only then, and as such, this individual Christian in his particular Christian being and nature and presence. And this means that the Christian faith is first the faith of the Christian community and only then and as such, affirmed and shared by them, the faith of the men united in it. It does not have in them, as it were, its original and normative form. It is not the sum, as it were, of the different individual acts of Christian faith, which would necessarily mean the cross-cut, agreement and compromise between them. In and with their individual faith Christians participate in and with the faith of the community. In this their faith has its basis, norm and limit. It derives from it and is built up on it. And the same is true of all the personal knowledge and confession of faith. It is, as such, basically co-ordinated with and subordinated to the knowledge and confession of the community. It is true in so far as it is "catholic" and therefore has a part in the knowledge and confession of the community. As personal knowledge and confession it has its own place and right and freedom within the knowledge and confession of the community, not outside it, not elsewhere, not *in abstracto*[EN211]. It is true that the community for its own part has no external power to prevent its members going beyond and therefore leaving the place and right and freedom of their own within the comprehensive unity of the common faith, knowledge and confession. But it is responsible for their not being able to do this without a serious attestation of that which makes them the community or its members. And above all it is responsible for their maintaining in a pure and living form their being as the Christian community in face of all the caprices of individuals and whatever may be the individual ways of its members. As the body of Jesus Christ conjoined with its Head it has priority over its members and it has to maintain this

---

[EN210] always to be reformed
[EN211] in abstraction

2. The Being of the Community

priority not only for the sake of the Head but also for that of the members. That is what "catholic" means in this dimension.

It hardly needs to be said that we are dealing here with a point of view which has been most flagrantly neglected in modern Protestantism since the 18th century. From the visible standpoint our Protestant national Churches are little more than great unions, or communities of interest, of individuals who are Christian or are called Christian, individualists, each of whom—like the people of Israel in the time of the Judges—does that which is right in his own eyes, so that although some may act together in particular *ecclesiolae*[EN212] called movements, we cannot inquire too closely what it really is that unites them. Even less can we inquire what these Churches are as a whole, a question which would yield the most gratuitous and to a large extent unconvincing answers. If we will and can and must maintain the form revealed in them, then we can only sigh: *Kyrie eleison*[EN213]. Destroying as they do the relationship between the community and its members, they are hopelessly a-catholic Churches, hardly distinguishable, if at all, from heretical sects, or sects which verge on heresy, in the matter which now concerns us.

The most obvious example is the 1911 *Constitution of the Evangelical Reformed Church of the City of Basel*. It begins with a kind of hymnal introit to which a conscientious exegete could hardly give any but an Arian sense: "In the name and to the glory of God our Creator and Father, who has given us Jesus Christ as our Saviour and Redeemer and through Him called us out of darkness into His marvellous light. Amen." Then it is explained that the Church of Basel is a "member of the universal Christian Church," the heir and successor in law of the Church which in 1529 "was renewed by the decree of the people and congregations on the basis of Holy Scripture", and one of the Churches "which resulted from the Reformation." The remarkable interpretation of this "resulted from" is that the basis of its teaching is "Jesus Christ and His Gospel, which it has sought out from the Bible under the guidance (not of the Holy Spirit but) of Christian conscience, experience and scholarship, and which it proclaims and endeavours to put into practice" Further: "In loyalty to the basic principles of Protestantism it expects its members to come to a personal conviction in the great Evangelical truths on the basis of reflection and experience." But who are these members? "All Protestants residing in the canton of the city of Basel," or (according to the official commentary) "all Christians of Evangelical profession who have not expressly declared their withdrawal." In spite of this, or by this means, it is their aim "to contribute to the furtherance of the kingdom of God on earth by the Gospel as the unfailing source of eternal life and personal and social progress."

The faith which dares to maintain the *credo unam sanctam ecclesiam*[EN214] in face of a Church which expresses and manifests itself in this way will have to be strong enough to remove a few by no means negligible mountains. We may certainly ask whether—if this is the state of affairs, as it is not merely in Basel and Switzerland—it is not, after all, better that it should be stated in the solemn and shameless way which is customary in Switzerland. But, however that may be, it makes no odds: *rebus sic stantibus*[EN215] the community of Jesus Christ obviously has to be and wills to be believed even as expressed and manifested in this or some similar form. Just as a zealous Roman Catholic will not hesitate to confess the *Una Sancta*[EN216] even when he thinks of Alexander VI and its representation in him, so we will not be ashamed to do the

[707]

[EN212] churches
[EN213] Lord, have mercy
[EN214] I believe one holy Church
[EN215] as things stand
[EN216] One Holy

§ 62. *The Holy Spirit and the Gathering of the Christian Community*

same even in relation to the constitution of the Church of Basel and similar depressing phenomena.

But as long as the voice of theology is not entirely stilled even in the sphere of Churches of this kind, we cannot refrain from addressing to them the following question: What is really at the back of their minds? On the one hand they expressly call themselves a member of the universal (catholic) Church, resulting from the Reformation and referred back to Jesus Christ and His Gospel. On the other, they deduce this reformation on the basis of Holy Scripture historico-politically from a decision of the people and congregations made in the year 1529; they hand over the exposition and proclamation of the Gospel unreservedly to the Christian conscience, experience and not very closely defined scholarship of its members—those who have not expressly declared their withdrawal; and apparently they do not expect from these members anything more necessary than that they should "come to a personal conviction" in the Christian "truths on the basis of reflection and experience." And all this as a contribution to the furtherance of the kingdom of God on earth. Fortunately this only stands on paper, or is accepted only in the hearts and minds of unruly "Protestants," while all the time *Dei providentia hominum confusione*[EN217] the unalterable essence of the community of Jesus Christ persists even in Churches of this kind and therefore in Basel, continually pointing us in quite a different direction. But we cannot conceal the fact that a Church is in error, that it is not loyal but disloyal to its unalterable essence, if it thinks that it can and should manifest and express itself in this way, with this reversal of its true priorities.

A contrary example which ought to put us to shame is that of the decisive statements on the Church in the confession of the Protestant Batak-Church of Sumatra (which was drawn up without any Western participation at a synod held at Sipoholon in November 1951):

"We believe and confess: The Church is the congregation of those who believe in Jesus Christ and are called, gathered, sanctified and maintained by God through the Holy Spirit.

"We believe and confess: The Church is holy. The Church is not holy because of the holiness of its members themselves, but because Christ the Head is holy. Therefore the Church is holy because Christ has sanctified them and God sees them to be holy. Because the Church is holy, it is called the 'holy people,' 'the temple of the Holy Ghost' and the 'dwelling-place of God.'

"We believe and confess: The Church is a universal Church. The universal Church is the gathering of all the saints who already participate in the Lord Jesus Christ and His gifts, in the Gospel, in the Holy Spirit, in faith and love and hope. (The Church comes ...) from all lands and peoples and races and tribes and tongues, although their customs and laws are different.

"We believe and confess: There is one Church. It is based on what we are told in Eph. 4^4, 1 Cor. 12^{20}. For there is one body which is the Church. Although the members are many, the body is one. The unity of the Church mentioned here differs from what is usually meant by worldly unity. For it is a spiritual unity."

Lk. 13^{29-30}!

What does it mean: *credo catholicam ecclesiam?*[EN218] Gathering together what we have worked out in these four dimensions we can say: I believe that the Christian community is one and the same in essence in all places, in all ages, within all societies, and in relation to all its members. I believe that it can be the Christian community only in this identity, and therefore that it is its task to maintain itself in this identity, and therefore in this identity to will to be, and

---

[EN217] in the providence of God, and in the confusion of men
[EN218] I believe the catholic Church

2. *The Being of the Community*

continually to become and to remain, the Christian community, and nothing else, and therefore the true Church in all these dimensions. This has to be believed because, in fact, it is continually threatened in this identity at every point and in all these dimensions. It has to be believed because in all its visible existence it is a focal point of conflict between the true Church and the false. It is, in fact, always in danger. And the most serious danger which threatens it is always to become a community of a different essence and therefore a-catholic—it may be by reason of differences of locality, it may be by reason of unavoidable temporal change, it may be by reason of the influence of other human societies, it may be by reason of the variety of its individual members, and often enough and perhaps always in a concurrence of all these moments, which are the necessary elements of its earthly-historical existence. There is no Church which is not in fact open to attack in respect of its catholicity, its true character, and therefore its Christianity. There is hardly a Church which in this respect has not been seriously, perhaps very seriously, damaged and even destroyed on the one side or the other (and possibly on all of them together). For this reason it never has been, and never is, visible in practice as the true Church "the temple of God" (1 Cor. 3^{16}), the "habitation of God in the Spirit" (Eph. 2^{22}), the "bride without spot or wrinkle" (Eph. 5^{27}), the "pillar and ground of truth" (1 Tim. 3^{15}). It has never been visible as such to outsiders who could and can be amused or irritated with it in terms of Lessing's parable of the three rings, nor has it ever been visible as such to itself and its members in relation to what they see. Because this is the case with its catholicity, we have to say at every point: *credo catholicam ecclesiam*[EN219]. Just as without faith we cannot see its unity or holiness, so without faith we cannot see its catholicity. Conversely, it can be asserted as a negative criterion of catholicity—measured by which the Churches which most emphasise that they are "catholic" will not stand—that where a Church thinks it cannot and should not merely believe its catholicity but should be able—in its own form—to see and maintain it, then in its arrogance and unreadiness to repent this Church shows itself to be a-catholic. A real Church cannot possibly fail to see that it is only a theatre of conflict between the true Church and the false, and that in the battle which has to be fought out in this respect it is no less threatened than any others. A true Church is humbly content to be thrown back entirely upon faith in respect of its truth, and confidently to exist in this faith as the true community of Jesus Christ.

Is it superfluous at this point to refer particularly to a specific form of the supposed perception of the catholicity of the Church—superfluous because at first sight the error responsible seems so banal as almost to be unworthy of serious consideration?

The view is simply this: that if a Church or communion has a big, even a very big membership, then that is a pointer or prejudice in favour of the truth being on its side, whereas a tiny Church or group in a corner comes at once under the suspicion that it is a sect simply

---

[EN219] I believe the catholic Church

§ 62. The Holy Spirit and the Gathering of the Christian Community

because it seems that in it we have to do only with a very few people. This sounds dreadfully banal, because so obviously it does not look beyond the surface. It is comforting to think that the good God likes to be on the side of the big battalions, so that we have only to look to these to find traces of the true Church. Certainly great membership rolls and good attendance and full churches and halls (and even lecture rooms) are facts which naturally impress us—who can fail to be impressed by them?—but what do they really have to do with the truth? It was again the *Scots Confession* of 1560 which rightly pointed out that the Scribes and Pharisees were certainly in a majority against Jesus and His disciples, and yet they were wrong. And even Romanist dogmatics (B. Bartmann 2, 199) explains that the predicate *catholica*[EN220] must not be understood mechanically and quantitatively, but spiritually and qualitatively—as a divine claim of the Church which cannot be based on numbers but only on the actual superiority of the truth. This is prettily illustrated by the fact (*op. cit.*, p. 161) that in his necessary ratification of the decree of a council the Pope is not bound by the decision of the majority, but if he believes it to be right he can take up and definitively justify the *pars minor et sanior*[EN221]. To elect and vote in the Church is always a doubtful matter. It may decide what seems most opportune in the community in any given situation. But it certainly cannot decide what is the truth whether it is opportune or not. In the primitive Church an attempt was usually made to avoid it. Voting was replaced by decisions *per acclamationem*[EN222]. But it may be asked whether this is any better or more free from problems. The *veritas catholica*[EN223] may undoubtedly lie with the minority. It may occasionally lie with the tiniest of minorities, in a veritable corner. It may lie only with the two or three gathered together (as in Mt. 18^{20}) in the name of Jesus Christ. That they number several millions is of no avail to those who are not gathered in His name. The whole legitimacy of the Reformation rests upon this possibility. There are some who go further and boldly affirm that the *veritas catholica*[EN224] will very likely, indeed will fairly (or most) certainly, be found within the minority. An empty Church is regarded as a comforting indication and prejudice in favour of the fact that the pure Gospel is proclaimed in it. Is there not something strangely and in its way impressively pathetic about the existence of a small Church or group? In certain circumstances does it not involve a genuine pleasure and exaltation to be in a minority—perhaps the tiniest of minorities: the little flock to which it is the Father's good-pleasure to give the kingdom, which is therefore a kind of advance guard of God? In Schiller's words: "What is majority? Majority is folly." Good sense is never found but with the few.

But here again we must be careful. There have been minorities whose resistance to the majority has not been legitimate because their cause has had nothing whatever to do with the *veritas catholica*[EN225], because in them we are dealing only with manifestations of an utterly a-catholic individualism—in the garb of particularism and sectarianism. In the history of the Church both before and after the 16th century there have been far too many little movements of reform instigated by men who appealed readily to the fact that a majority proves nothing, that truth and the good God are more likely to be on the side of the small and even the smallest battalions, and yet in the long run they proved to be no more lasting than a kind of carnival procession. Conversely, the evangelical record itself tells us, not morosely but with joy (Mk. 3$^{7f.}$), that a great multitude (πολὺ πλῆθος) followed Jesus of Nazareth and that when they heard what He did a great multitude came to Him from Judaea and Jerusalem and Transjordania and even the districts around Tyre and Sidon. This is not

---

[EN220] catholic
[EN221] smaller and healthier part
[EN222] by acclamation
[EN223] catholic truth
[EN224] catholic truth
[EN225] catholic truth

2. *The Being of the Community*

noted as a proof of the Messiahship of Jesus or the coming of God's kingdom amongst men, but as a fact which is in its own way significant. Again the 3,000 and later the 5,000 who, according to Ac. 2^{41} and 4^4, received the Word and were baptised after the events of the day of Pentecost were not by any means negligible and did not appear so either to Luke or to Theophilus. We have also to consider that in the long run every minority, however content it may be as such, however proud of itself, has all the same a concealed or open tendency to become the majority, and that this has, in fact, often been the case. The transition is undoubtedly a dangerous one and sometimes fatal. There was something very far wrong when barely 300 years later the little flock of Lk. 12 became the imperial world-Church of Constantine, and many a minority in the Church has lost more than it has gained by becoming a majority, or a big Church instead of a small. But it is not fundamentally the case that when the few become many the truth also becomes error. Many a victory for catholic truth may be won by such transitions. Again, the truth may in the first instance have been with the majority. Why not? If the greater number is not always a guarantee of the truth, it does not need always to be against the truth. It can be a witness which those who find themselves in the minority may do well to hear. They may well have gone too far forward or lagged too far behind. The *pars maior*[EN226] may be to them the *pars sanior*[EN227], representing genuine continuity and therefore the genuine *semper reformari*[EN228]. In any case it is a very serious and responsible thing for a minority to oppose the majority in the community—a risk which no one ought to undertake too easily. For if a smaller number does not mean that catholic truth is not on this side, it certainly does not mean that it is.

[710]

The matter may seem banal, but it can be very misleading in practice, both on the one side and on the other. For that reason it is as well to state expressly that in this sense, too, there can be no perception of the catholicity of a Church, whether by small numbers or by great. As a spiritual and qualitative predicate, as the promise given to it, in its visible and historical expression either in the many or in the few, catholicity can only be believed.

But that means that objectively it is exactly the same with the catholicity and therefore the truth of the Christianity of a Church as it is with its unity and holiness: the Church has no control over it. Its being as *ecclesia catholica*[EN229], the fact that everywhere and at all times and in relation to all other societies and to all its individual members it is one and the same, is actual in the fact that it is the body, the earthly-historical form of the existence of Jesus Christ. Therefore catholicity as its own actuality is grounded in Him as its Head. It falls upon it as the reflection of the light which gives light in Him. It comes to it in the event of His living Word and work by the Holy Spirit, in its visitation by and encounter with Him. He is the man who maintains His sovereign identity both here and there, yesterday and to-day, within and on behalf of all historical forms, in face of all individual Christians. The community is catholic as He lives and speaks and acts in His community. But this means that in this respect, too, it is made responsible and called to obedience and questioned concerning its obedience by Him. Of Him it lacks nothing to enable it to rejoice in this identity of its being even in its concrete historical form in all these dimensions.

[EN226] greater part
[EN227] healthier part
[EN228] 'always to be reformed'
[EN229] catholic Church

§ 62. *The Holy Spirit and the Gathering of the Christian Community*

But in this concrete form it lives as His body in this world. It is spiritual by nature, but it exists in terms of this world. Therefore there is always something lacking in its expression of itself. It may be one thing here, another there. Indeed, in the strict sense it is everything everywhere. Its expression in terms of this world is always a compromising, and obscuring and denying of its spiritual nature. It acts like the sleeping disciples in the Garden of Gethsemane. It is like Peter who at first was so self-confident, and then struck so recklessly and finally denied so blatantly. It is even like Judas Iscariot. As the true Church it would always die and perish if He did not speak to it, if it did not hear His voice, summoning it to watch and pray: to watch over its being in all its dimensions, in its preaching and doctrine and theology, but also in its constitution and order and various ministries, and even in its actions and attitudes in face of the problems of the world around it; and to pray that in all these things it may remain with Him and in love to Him, "that we may seek no other Lord, but Jesus in a true faith, trusting in Him with all our might." For what is the good of all its watching if it does not pray that this may take place, that it may, therefore, be or be again a Christian community? What is the good of it if this does not take place with the hearing of its prayer? It is to pray that it should watch—or, rather, all its watching, and its related action and activity, should be a prayerful watching. As long as it is in the world and therefore itself worldly, even in all its watching and its watchful activity, it can never of itself secure that it should remain with its Head as His living body. This time in the words of Zwingli: "O Lord, raise up thine own chariot, Or all our ways will perish." Zwingli did not allow either his heart or his hand to sink when he thought and prayed in this way. Those who are slack in obedience are the ones who will not think and pray in this way. But the community will think and pray in this way when it is brisk and ready to obey, when it does not throw over the reins, when it is in practical earnest to protect itself against all the threatened invasions. It will not avoid the care and effort and labour and inward and outward conflict which it costs sincerely to build only on the Son of God who gathers and protects and maintains it as His community. It will be energetic to know as an event a deeper perception, a purer confession, a fuller uniting of its members in love to Him, a more confident and yet more humble, an objectively more relevant and subjectively more practical attestation to the world around of His lordship as the obedient servant of God. And when it does not spare any efforts, when it does not shun any inward or outward tension, when, in the words of 1 Cor. 16^{13}, it stands fast in the faith and is manly and strong, when, in the words of Heb. 12^4, it resists unto blood, then it will see clearly that it is not itself or anything resulting from its labour and conflict which makes it the true Christian community, but He alone, the Son of God who gathers and protects and maintains it, His work and His Spirit.

In unity with Him it will persist in its contradistinction to Him. It will therefore know that its work and the results of that work are one thing, but quite another is the attaining and achieving and possessing (καταντᾶν) of the unity of its faith in the Son of God (Eph. 4$^{13f.}$),

2. *The Being of the Community*

that being of the full-grown man in the fulness in which Christ Himself is a full-grown man. It can only be summoned and warned and directed, to leave the state of νήπιοι^{EN230}, not to be tossed to and fro and carried about with every wind of doctrine by the sleight of men, not to be deceived by cunning craftiness, but ἀληθεύοντες ἐν ἀγάπῃ^{EN231} to grow up in its whole being (τὰ πάντα^{EN232}) to Him which is the Head. To this summons, warning and direction alone can it give its attention and obedience. [712]

And if in anything at all, then in this clear knowledge of its limit it will be catholic—in its satisfaction with Jesus Christ Himself, in the fact that it will not give to its activity any other character than that of a diaconate or witness in His service, that it will be zealous and loyal in this character, that it will not invest it with any kind of mysterious importance or magic or thaumaturgy or supernatural legality or authoritative claim, that, in the words of 1 Thess. 5^{17}, it will simply prove it by praying without ceasing. He, the living Son of God, is Himself its identical and continuing and universal essence, maintaining and asserting itself in all dimensions. He is the source and norm of its identity: the *veritas catholica*^{EN233}. He constitutes the community the true Church and as such marks it off from the false. He is the man by whose irenics and polemics it lives, without whose judgment executed in His Word and by His Spirit, without whose uniting and excluding, it can only be an obscure sect even in its supposedly most perfect forms. As He makes it one and holy, so He makes it universal. And therefore faith in Him, which can never cease to be a busy faith, is the only effective and not really passive but supremely active realisation of the *credo catholicam ecclesiam*^{EN234}.

Credo apostolicam ecclesiam^{EN235}. It is excellent that in the creed of 381 after *una, sancta, catholica*^{EN236} there appeared for the first time a fourth predicate which has since become a firm constituent of the liturgy of at least the Roman and Eastern Catholic Churches: *apostolica*^{EN237}. All four predicates describe the one being of the Christian community. But we can and should read and understand them as mounting to a climax. *Una*^{EN238} describes its singularity. *Sancta*^{EN239} describes the particularity which underlies this singularity. *Catholica*^{EN240} describes the essence in which it manifests and maintains itself in this particularity and singularity. And finally, *apostolica*^{EN241} does not say anything new, in relation to these three definitions, but describes with remarkable

---

^{EN230} babes
^{EN231} speaking the truth in love
^{EN232} all things
^{EN233} catholic truth
^{EN234} I believe the catholic Church
^{EN235} I believe the apostolic Church
^{EN236} one, holy, catholic
^{EN237} apostolic
^{EN238} one
^{EN239} holy
^{EN240} catholic
^{EN241} apostolic

§ 62. *The Holy Spirit and the Gathering of the Christian Community*

precision the concrete spiritual criterion which enables us to answer the question whether and to what extent in this or that case we have or have not to do with the one holy catholic Church. The criterion is not sociological or juridical or psychological, but spiritual. The word *credo*[EN242] is still in front, and must not be forgotten. Even the criterion that the Church is apostolic, with all that that involves, can be known only in faith, and cannot be seen except in faith.

There is no doubt that, according to the ecclesiology of the Roman Catholic Church, the predicate *apostolica*[EN243], and with it the other three predicates, all need the decisive interpretation given by the term *Romana*[EN244]. It is the Roman Church, i.e., the Church which stands in unity with the bishop of Rome and under his teaching authority and jurisdiction, which is the apostolic and therefore the one holy universal Church. More recent Roman Catholic theology certainly reckons with the possibility that there might be a kind of *una, sancta, catholica et apostolica ecclesia*[EN245] even outside the visible bastions of the Roman Church. It can even consider the question whether the better part of it, or the best elements of truth, which it has itself neglected, may not be found to-day outside rather than inside that Church. But it cannot do this without the proviso that this Church outside, so far as it may be *una, sancta, catholica et apostolica*[EN246], is even in spite of its own ignorance and contrary will objectively, invisibly and actually the Roman Church, united with the bishop of Rome, pledged to him as its overlord and destined to return to him as the *vicarius Christi*[EN247]. Beyond this line even the most magnanimous interpretation of the Church cannot go. All the same—and this is one of the merits of the inviolability of an ancient liturgy—the word *Romana*[EN248] has not succeeded in penetrating into it. "Roman" would, of course, be a sociological and juridical criterion of what is apostolic. When we equate it with Roman, apostolic gives us a moment in the idea of the Church which can be seen and established neutrally by every man. And from this standpoint the unity and holiness and catholicity of the Church become qualities which can be seen and established neutrally, thus escaping the *fide solum intelligimus*[EN249] of the *Cat. Rom.* There were inner reasons why the Creed could not be expanded in this way. We can be clear that on the basis of the ecumenical creed when we speak of the Church as apostolic—even though on the other side a powerful "Roman" stands behind it—we have to do with a criterion which is spiritual.

It is, however, a concrete criterion. In this it differs from the moments in the idea of the Church which we have considered hitherto. In attempting to fill out the first three terms we could point only to Jesus Christ as the Head of the community which is His body, and therefore to the work of the Holy Spirit. Even in relation to the last term "catholic" Jesus Christ alone is the *veritas catholica*[EN250], and it is He who makes the Church the catholic Church, His Church, the true, Christian Church, and therefore, as we have seen, the one holy Church. The question may rightly be asked whether in saying this we have

---

[EN242] I believe
[EN243] apostolic
[EN244] Roman
[EN245] one, holy, catholic and apostolic Church
[EN246] one, holy, catholic and apostolic
[EN247] vicar of Christ
[EN248] Roman
[EN249] we can understand only by faith
[EN250] catholic truth

2. The Being of the Community

not said too much because we have said too little for faith, for the faith which asks after knowledge, *fides quaerens intellectum*[EN251]. In respect of catholic can we not make some concrete statement, not a sociological and juridical but a spiritual statement and therefore one which can be made and grasped only in faith, yet a concrete statement in relation to that controlling relationship of Jesus Christ as the Head to the community as His body which underlies the truth and therefore the unity and holiness of the Church?

> It was Cyril of Jerusalem who in his *Catechetical Lectures* (18, 26) gave to Christians travelling abroad this advice: "When you come into a city, do not simply ask: Where is the house of the Lord? for the godless heretics are bold to call their dens the house of the Lord. Do not simply ask: Where is the Church? but: Where is the catholic Church?" But supposing modern heretics dare to call their "den" the catholic Church? Supposing the Christian stranger hears them speak as heretics always love to do—not going outside the tradition—with particular emphasis and warmth of Jesus Christ? Supposing he hears them appeal to the Holy Spirit—perhaps with the saying in 2 Cor. 3^{17}: "Where the Spirit of the Lord is, there is liberty"—and is conscious of a very highly spiritual being? It is not at all a matter of distinguishing absolutely between the true and the false, the catholic and the heretical. For the most part the distinction will be between the greater or lesser clarity and distinctness of the catholic, or the greater or lesser proximity of the heretical. To some extent, therefore, it will be made in the half-light of a middle sphere. What is the position when an Evangelical Christian attends a Roman Catholic mass or an assembly of Protestant individualists which has more or less the character of a sect, or when he reads the dogmatics of a Tersteegen or a Biedermann, or in short whenever he encounters any kind of Christianity and he cannot withhold a certain Yes, a certain understanding which unites him, but at bottom he cannot either understand or approve or accept it, but for the most part and therefore for himself is forced to say a very exclusive No? What is really the position in one of the ecumenical conferences when one day we have to take part in, or to be ready to accept, the morning worship of Swedish-Lutherans, the next that of American Baptists, and the day after perhaps that of Eastern Catholics which seems to us incredibly antiquated and probably almost pagan in its demands: singing *Cantate Domino* in all kinds of tongues, some of which we trust, some of which are definitely outlandish and suspicious? In such situations we cannot escape some kind of distinction, even though it may be more comforting to let ourselves be reminded by the constantly recurring name of Jesus Christ that it all seems to have to do with the one centre. But the question is with what clarity and distinctness, and this question cannot be settled by the "We all believe in one God" of our male-voice choirs. What is the real ground of our predominant No—or sometimes of our participating and to some extent understanding Yes—if both are not simply to be the expression of an emotional attraction or aversion but are based on real perception? Above all, what is the standard by which we can be certain of our own cause, our own standing in the true Church, our preference for this or that place in the true Church? What is the standard by which, with equal decision on the left hand and on the right, and with a good conscience, we can publicly take our stand in this place and not in that?

[714]

It is here that the predicate "apostolic" comes in. It gives us a concrete criterion, the one and only *nota ecclesiae*[EN252], not in competition with the decisive

---

[EN251] faith seeking understanding
[EN252] mark of the Church

§ 62. The Holy Spirit and the Gathering of the Christian Community

determination of the Church by the existence and work of its living Lord, but as the true and authentic interpretation of this basic determination. It is truly helpful, of course, only when we do not try to deprive it of its character as a spiritual criterion.

Apostolic means in the discipleship, in the school, under the normative authority, instruction and direction of the apostles, in agreement with them, because listening to them and accepting their message. The Church is the true Church and therefore the one holy Church in the fact and to the extent that it is apostolic in this sense, and by this fact it can and should be known as such and distinguished from the false Church. Even the predicate apostolic, and especially this predicate, describes the being of the community as an event. This mutual relationship to the apostles is obviously something which can take place only in a history between them. And for good or evil the man who wants to see and recognise it as the apostolic community must himself take part in this history. He cannot be a neutral and decide its apostolicity from outside. He must be a living member, and as such must know its basis in the apostles, himself standing in their discipleship, in their school, under their authority [715] and direction, himself hearing their witness, himself being taught and questioned by them. He must be put by them in a definite movement, in the movement in which they found themselves, in which they still find themselves to-day—for in the New Testament they are still before us in living speech and action. To be in the community of Jesus Christ means to take part in this movement. And it is and is known as the true Church by the fact that where it exists as such it finds itself in this movement. This movement is a very concrete but a spiritual process. It is definitely distinguished from other such movements. It is the work of the Holy Spirit, and as such it can be known in its concrete distinction only by the Holy Spirit and therefore in faith.

Thus the apostolicity of the Church cannot and must not be sought on historical and juridical grounds. The particular temptation in this respect is the equivocal notion of the "apostolic succession." It is a temptation when it is understood on the presupposition of a supernatural jurisprudence which can be supported by historical proof—that by the rite of laying on of hands there is a technical inheritance or transmission of the apostolic authority and teaching office and ministry, in which in some sense it flows over from a supreme officebearer in the Church, e.g., from a bishop, to his successor, and from this successor to the inferior ministers who will be ordained by him. This is found where the list of the predecessors of the bishop who ordains to-day can demonstrably be traced back without a break through the centuries to a first bishop of the place in question who was one of the twelve apostles ordained by Christ Himself. To stand in the apostolic succession in this sense is to be in a Church which is proved to be a true Church by the fact that its ministers are attached to this line and therefore to the stream guaranteed by it, that they have a part in the apostolic grace of office which, through the centuries, has passed from one hand to another. Thus, on the one hand, apostolicity and the true Church

2. *The Being of the Community*

are a matter which we can know by reference to a transmitted list of bishops, which we can prove by the historico-critical investigation of this list, and which in favourable circumstances we can establish beyond doubt by digging up some apostolic remains. It is obvious that neither the Holy Spirit nor faith is necessary for this purpose, but only an uncritical or critical archaeological knowledge of the lists. And, on the other hand, apostolicity and therefore the true Church are an understanding and acceptance of the system in consequence of which apostolicity is like the sovereignty of a hereditary ruler or even a farm handed down from father to son. By means of the laying on of hands it passes from one bishop to a second, who is then empowered to ordain and will transmit it to a third as the successor of the first. At every stage it has a desired result for the lower clergy who take part in it, and through them for the rest of the community, the laity. Once again, it is clear that to accept this system does not need either the Holy Spirit or faith but only a definite idea of law. We may or may not be convinced of the rightness of this without either acceptance or rejection of the *credo ecclesiam*[EN253]. All that is needed is to recognise and assess the fact that—whatever else may be said—this is the law and practice of the Church. [716]

For our part we can only note that there are whole Churches, especially the Roman Catholic, but also the Eastern Orthodox, and the Anglican not far behind, who not only regard the apostolicity grounded in this kind of apostolic succession as a particular adornment of their particular estate, but, insisting more or less emphatically upon it, deduce and claim from it their character as the catholic and therefore the true Church.

In this respect the Lutheran Church of Sweden is an exception. It seems to have particularly good evidence that the apostolic succession of its archbishops and bishops was maintained without a break at the time of the Reformation. But it expressly refrains from ascribing to this fact any dogmatic significance, treating it only as a welcome adornment of its constitution as a Church. In this respect it does not meet with the approval of the stricter Anglicans, who cannot have the same historical certainty in view of what took place under Henry VIII, but who attach to the matter a supreme doctrinal importance. There is no doubt that the bishops who suddenly appeared in Lutheran Germany some twenty or thirty years ago cannot have the "succession" in view of the great disruption of it in the 16th century. It may well be suspected of them that they would like to have it. The idea seems to have been considered of acquiring it by way of the Swedes who are more fortunate and so indifferent in the matter. The latest development is that even in the Reformed sphere (e.g., Holland) there are individual ministers who feel most unhappy that they do not stand in the legitimate line of succession in their administration of preaching, baptism and the Lord's Supper, and they are casting uncertain glances here, there and everywhere to try to secure it in some concealed way from someone who already has it. Who knows what wonderful things we may not see in relation to this question!

All that we can do, perhaps, is just to—wonder. It is only one difficulty that when we understand the apostolic succession in this way, then as a historical

---

[EN253] I believe the Church

§ 62. The Holy Spirit and the Gathering of the Christian Community

and juridical hypothesis it ceases to be part of the *credo ecclesiam*[EN254]. The question also arises what is this "apostolicity" which a man who is a bishop can transfer institutionally and ritually to another man so that he becomes a bishop, and can then pass it on institutionally and ritually to the inferior clergy? Is it actually the Holy Spirit, whom the apostles received from the Lord, and in whose power they preached? If this is the doctrine of the succession, then it means that the grace of office legitimately passed from one man to another by means of a fixed rite is nothing more or less than the Holy Spirit Himself in the form of a particular gift which is decisively important for the being of the community. But in that case, who and what is the Holy Spirit? Is He the sovereign God, who as Spirit moves where He will, awakening the hearts of men to the unity of the faith and their lips to attest it?—or is He something quite different? When we speak of Him, and of the existence and continuance of the Christian community in the world as founded by Him, are we speaking of the result of the free act of grace in which God the Father continually attests Himself through the Son, and the Son to the glory of the Father even in this time between the resurrection and the return, manifesting Himself as present and active, as the Lord of the world?—or are we speaking of a peculiar supra-natural substance which once came into human history and has now passed—like a newly discovered force of nature—into the hands and control of certain men who are competent in this matter and who can use and apply it? It is at this point that the decision is made. If He is the Spirit who moves as He will, if the history of the community in the world is the result of His free acts of grace, then this does not exclude His ability to give Himself from a higher minister of the Church to a lower. But why only or preferably from a higher? On what ground do we know or hold that His work and gift are preferably—and for the rest of the Church decisively—a matter for bishops and other clergy? We will leave that point for the moment, however, and grant that it is certainly not excluded that He Himself and, therefore, apostolic authority and power and mission may be imparted by the witness of a bishop to another man—remembering always, of course, that He moves where He will, *ubi et quando Deo visum est*[EN255]. And why should it not be by the laying on of hands, as in the case of Saul in Ac. 9^{17} at the hands of Ananias (who was not, of course, a bishop but simply a disciple who dwelt in Damascus), and as attested in 1 Tim. 4^{14}, 2 Tim. 1^6 and Heb. 6^2? It is the very essence of the foundation and continuance of the apostolic community that what took place between the apostles and the first three and five thousand in Jerusalem can take place again and has, in fact, taken place again. But the question is whether there is an institution, and in the sphere of that institution a rite of ordination, in fulfilment of which the Holy Spirit has to pass from one man to another, so that He can be controlled and His presence and action confined? Of course,

---

[EN254] I believe the Church
[EN255] where and when God decides

2. *The Being of the Community*

the practical powers and legal authority of a bishop can be transferred institutionally and ritually from one man to another, like the staff and mitre and ring which symbolise them. But how can apostolic authority and power and mission, how can the Holy Spirit be transferred, when obviously apostolicity is His work and gift?—as though the Holy Spirit were a legal or technical or symbolical It, a property in the hands of one or many exalted members of the community which, without further ado, can be transferred by them into the power of others—simply because it has been institutionally arranged in this way, and simply because it takes place with due legality and ritual.

> Is it possible to think of the canalisation of the transference from one member of the community to another (if there is any such transference) of the *charisma*[EN256] described in 1 Cor. 12 and Rom. 12? Certainly we must calmly consider and accept the fact that Mt. 16$^{18f.}$ does speak of an absolutely extraordinary authority, power and mission of the apostles, and of its ultimate concentration specifically on Peter. But in this passage there is no mention at all of any institutionally guaranteed continuance of the authority, power and mission even of Peter, in another person appointed by him, of a *successor Petri*[EN257] in that sense. And if in the Pastoral Epistles and Acts we can discover or suspect traces of an incipient or developed "primitive catholicism," there is no doubt that apostolic succession in this sense, as an institutional and ritual mediation and transference of the Holy Spirit and therefore of apostolicity, is not a constituent part of these texts.

[718]

No, just as Jesus Christ is a free subject when it takes place that the apostles become apostles, it is again an event in which Jesus Christ is a free subject and His Spirit moves where He wills when the apostolic community comes into being and exists as such, when there is an apostolic succession in the true sense in which this overburdened expression can be understood.

In what, then, does the apostolicity of the Church consist as a criterion of its catholicity, holiness and unity? One thing is clear, that it belongs together with its character as the body, the earthly-historical form of the existence of Jesus Christ in this interim period. If, apart from His hidden being at the right hand of the Father, in which He is the Head of His body, He also exists in this interim period in earthly-historical form in His community in the world, then it belongs to this that He gives Himself to be known in this earthly-historical form to it and to the world through it.

But the earthly-historical medium of His self-manifestation is those in whose midst He has lived on earth, in history, as the Word of God made flesh, those who have seen and heard and handled Him in the servant-form of His flesh, but also in His glory. These are the apostles. It is He Himself who has chosen and called and ordained and sent them out for this purpose and as such. Now since they—and they alone—are His direct witnesses, they belong together with Him in a unique and special way, with Peter at their head in all his weakness. They are shown in Him to have both positively and negatively an exemplary significance. They share in His peculiar earthly-historical position. In

---

[EN256] gift of grace
[EN257] successor to Peter

§ 62. *The Holy Spirit and the Gathering of the Christian Community*

this position they are the rock on which He willed to build His Church, on which He has built it and still builds it: with the witness to Him which is peculiarly their own, which can only be heard and independently accepted and reproduced, but not augmented or in any way replaced, by the community which receives it, which in all the being and upbuilding and life and work of the community must always be maintained and confirmed as their apostolic witness. For in it it receives His own witness to Himself. Accepting the word of the apostles, it allows Him to speak. Being led by them, it is led by Him. His Holy Spirit acts and works in the concrete form of the power and truth of their word.

They are not in any sense the lords of the community, nor do they play any autonomous role in relation to it. Jesus Christ makes use of them. Their authority, power and mission consists in the fact that He does this. In this they are the rock on which He builds His Church. They are this only in this relationship of His to them, only as He Himself qualifies them. Without Him they would only be a pile of sand. And it is not they who build His community but He who builds it as He makes use of them. They are only His servants. Only in this way is there any correspondence to His own being in which He has manifested Himself to them, and therefore to the content of their preaching. For what is He Himself but the servant of God and man, and as such the Lord? How could they try to be lords in His name? The warning against this possibility sounds out unmistakably in the Gospels. Obviously witnesses of the One who Himself only served can only be those who for their part will only serve the Lord who Himself served and therefore their fellow-men. For this they are chosen and called and ordained by Him.

And it is this serving which in relation to the community gives them their exemplary, their normative significance, their greatness. In this they are the holy apostles. It is actually the case that He speaks through them. The man who hears them hears Him. The man who does not hear them does not hear Him. The "keys of the kingdom of heaven" are actually in their hands (Mt. 16^{19}). If they open it to a man, it is open. If they close it, it is closed. He uses them as His servants beside whom He has no other servants of the same kind. To that extent there devolves on them the whole responsibility in relation to the community and the world. There is no way to Him which does not lead past them. The hidden glory at the right hand of the Father in which He is manifest to the Father and to Himself has no other earthly-historical complement than that of their witness. The awakening power of His Holy Spirit has no other earthly-historical form than that of the power of their witness. The community is present and present only when their witness is sounded out and received and accepted and reproduced.

Thus the existence of His community is always its history in its encounter with this witness—the history in which it is faithful or unfaithful to it in its exposition and application. There is, therefore, a legitimate apostolic succession, the existence of a Church in the following of the apostles, only when it

2. The Being of the Community

takes place in this history that the apostolic witness finds in a community discipleship, hearing, obedience, respect and observance. But it is in the fact that they serve that the apostles follow the Lord Himself and precede the community. It would, therefore, be very strange if the community for its part tried to follow them in any other authority, power and mission than that of their service, if, for example, it tried to follow them in an institutional possession of and control over the high mystery of the free Holy Spirit, in the power to over-rule His work and gift, as though it were a matter of money or property or of the legal regulation of certain human demands and interests. In this attitude of glad possession and control, how alien it would be not only to the apostles but to the servant of God who is the Lord of the apostles and its Lord! How alien it would be if it tried to be great by ruling in the name of the apostles and in His name, which would be to rule over Him and them! In this matter there is only one true succession, and even on the part of the Church it is the succession of service. If the community is really to find itself and to act in line with Jesus Christ and His apostles, there is only one attitude, and that is the attitude of subjection and obedience.

[720]

It is a matter of the *ministerium Verbi*[EN258], of the *Verbum incarnatum*[EN259], Jesus Christ Himself. But this would necessarily be abused and corrupted and changed into a *dominium*[EN260] even by those who wish to be serious Christians if the relationship of the Church to its Lord were unformed because immediate, if it had control of His earthly-historical form. The relationship is not unformed, however, but formed. It is not immediate but mediate. And its mediacy or form is the relationship of the Church to the apostles, or, more exactly, the relationship of the apostles to the Church, the loud or quiet declaration of their witness. It has not to subject itself, nor does it owe obedience, to their witness, but to Jesus Christ, who is the Lord over all things, whom even they can only serve with their witness. But through their witness He speaks to His community. And if in the community it is a matter of His service, the *ministerium Verbi incarnati*[EN261], this means that the Church finds itself in the school of the apostles, that in this school it learns the meaning of obedience and practises obedience, making after them the movement of service which it sees them make—after them because they know immediately what it is all about, what is the meaning of service in this particular case. If the Church learns and exercises its *ministerium*[EN262] in this school, then it will certainly be kept from corrupting and transforming it into a *dominium*[EN263]. There can be no supposed human control over the Holy Spirit. But in the measure that it does learn and practise it in this school the Church acquires and has the true

---

[EN258] ministry of the Word
[EN259] Word incarnate
[EN260] mastery
[EN261] ministry of the Word incarnate
[EN262] ministry
[EN263] mastery

§ 62. *The Holy Spirit and the Gathering of the Christian Community*

power which in exemplary form is effective and visible in the apostles as the servants of Jesus Christ, and therefore something of the power of the one great servant of God the attesting of whom has taught them obedience, who Himself is the man who instructs and guides and corrects and qualifies them in this school. It will never regret it if it enters this apostolic succession, if it remains in it, if it does not desire anything better, if it takes part in it with a modesty and humility and yet also an attention and zeal which continually increase, if it becomes an apostolic community in this sense.

Potestas ecclesiastica[EN264] means *ministerium ecclesiasticum*[EN265]. Assuming that this is grasped and taken to heart, we can then reverse the statement: *ministerium ecclesiasticum*[EN266] means *potestas ecclesiastica*[EN267]. But it is advisable simply to accept and not to state it as reversed in this way. For when it is reversed it is only too easily the case that it is not grasped and taken to heart in its original form.

[721] It will be seen that in this matter we really have to do with a history which—beginning in Jesus Christ Himself, continuing in His apostles and completing itself in His community—has already taken place and constantly has to take place again. Of what avail are institutions if this history does not take place? But it takes place where Jesus Christ lives as the Lord of His body, and therefore in conformity with the earthly-historical form of His existence, in the witness of the apostles. The Church is in this school and it is the *ecclesia apostolica*[EN268] as by the ministry of the apostles He speaks in it and to it and it accepts Him as the One who speaks in it and to it. If we want to know where is the true Church, the one holy catholic Church, and how it can be distinguished from the false or doubtful Church, then we must try to see where it exists as the apostolic community in this sense. Where and to the extent that we meet it in this character, there and to that extent we can know it with certainty to be the true Church. But the blind cannot pronounce on colours or the deaf on music. To be competent for this knowledge, we have ourselves to take part in this history, to learn and practise in this school as living members of the community. The process by which the Church becomes and is apostolic and therefore the true Church is a spiritual process. In the same way the knowledge of it can only be a spiritual knowledge.

All the same, as we have seen, it is a concrete knowledge. For all the care that is needed, it is actually possible on one side to make even more concrete the line which we have drawn in the preceding paragraphs.

What we have learned to know as apostolicity and therefore as the mark of the true Church is quite naturally identical in substance with the term which in a very different dogmatic context has been used to describe the authority of

---

[EN264] ecclesiastical power
[EN265] ecclesiastical ministry
[EN266] ecclesiastical ministry
[EN267] ecclesiastical power
[EN268] apostolic church

2. *The Being of the Community*

the Bible as the source and norm of the existence and doctrine and order of the Church—the "Scripture principle."

In the first instance the apostles are the original disciples of the evangelical records. They were selected and brought together as the twelve in correspondence with the traditional twelve tribes of Israel. As such they represent primarily the inseparable connexion of the new people of God with the old, the sprouting of the new from the old as from a root. In the first instance, therefore, they are a remarkable confirmation of the authority of the Old Testament. In their person the community—even the Gentile community—is from the very first and definitively confronted with the Law and the prophets and the writings of the book of *Yahweh* as the attestation of the One who was already the meaning and hope of the existence and history of Israel, and who in the fulness of time was revealed as the Head of His body as it already existed in that form, in which it is given to the Christian Church of every age to see itself as in a glass.

It is worth noting that the creed of 381 did not adopt this relationship with the Old Testament in its definition of the Church but in its description of the Holy Spirit who is the basis of the Church: *qui locutus est per sanctos prophetas*[EN269]. [722]

At the same time, however, the twelve were in exemplary fashion the authentic eye-witnesses of that revelation of the Head, the Messiah of Israel who, as such, was the Saviour of the world. They were chosen by Him to carry the recollection of Him, and, as such, they were representative of the authority of the New Testament. From this point of view the importance of the number recedes. It is significantly breached, indeed we can and must say that it is burst wide open, by the apostasy of Judas. Among the authors of the New Testament Matthew, Peter, John, James and the other Judas are those who still count to tradition as apostles in the original sense, but there is no news of the other members of that first circle. There has now been forcefully added to them, or rather there stands over against them as the great apostle, Paul—the apostle to the Gentiles, a Benjaminite and a Pharisee. According to the picture given in the Acts, it is he who *de facto*[EN270] if not *de iure*[EN271] has replaced Iscariot. "Apostolic" now has the comprehensive sense of the witness of those who had direct personal knowledge of Jesus Christ as the Crucified and Risen—and in the special case of Paul only as the Crucified who was risen, only as the One who was alive from the dead. And what showed and declared itself to be apostolic in this sense has been plainly recognised with the Old Testament as the canonical Scripture of the New Testament.

Thus the apostolic community means concretely the community which hears the apostolic witness of the New Testament, which implies that of the Old, and recognises and puts this witness into effect as the source and norm of

---

[EN269] the one who has spoken through the prophets
[EN270] as a matter of fact
[EN271] as a matter of right

§ 62. *The Holy Spirit and the Gathering of the Christian Community*

its existence. The apostolic Church is the Church which accepts and reads the Scriptures in their specific character as the direct attestation of Jesus Christ alive yesterday and to-day, respecting them as the canon and following their direction. It was in the Reformation of the 16th century that the Scriptures were rediscovered and given their proper place, and together with them the being of the Church as described in this fourth predicate—apostolicity as the criterion of its being as the one true universal Church. The Evangelical Church recognises and confesses something that was hidden and forgotten and even denied for centuries: that the truth of the Christian community in its apostolic verification consists in its history in the concrete encounter with the concrete biblical witness; that in this witness its truth is given to it, but also given over to it, once and for all; that it is present, but has to be continually sought and found and considered, in this encounter with the witness of Scripture, in its exposition and application. The Church is apostolic and therefore catholic when it exists on the basis of Scripture and in conformity with it, i.e., in the orientation which it accepts when it looks only in the direction indicated by the witness which speaks to it in Scripture, with no glances aside in any other direction. The Bible itself cannot do this merely as a sacred but closed book. As such it belongs to the very constitution of all supposed or actual, more or less Christian Churches. But this does not of itself make them true Churches. What counts is that the Bible speaks and is heard. Again, the Bible cannot do it merely as the book of the law of the Church's faith and order. To the degree that it is treated as such, it is, in fact, controlled. Like the apostles, it does not will to rule but to serve. And it is where it is allowed to serve that it really rules; that it is not betrayed to any human control. It is not a prescript either for doctrine or for life. It is a witness, and as such it demands attention, respect and obedience—the obedience of the heart, the free and only genuine obedience. What it wants from the Church, what it impels the Church towards—and it is the Holy Spirit moving in it who does this—is agreement with the direction in which it looks itself. And the direction in which it looks is to the living Jesus Christ. As Scripture stirs up and invites and summons and impels the Church to look in this same direction there takes place the work of the Spirit of Scripture who is the Holy Spirit. Scripture then works in the service of its Lord, and the Church becomes and is apostolic and therefore the true Church.

> We cannot go into details, but I will indicate certain lines of approach which need to be considered. The Church is apostolic and therefore the true Church where its external order—what is called Church government—is made so loose by respect for the direction of Scripture that all encroachment on the lordship of the One who is alone the Lord is either avoided or so suppressed and eliminated in practice that there is place for His rule. Whether this will be better done by a monarchical or an aristocratic or a democratic form of constitution is a question which has to be considered, but it is only secondary. All these forms have their own dangers. The lordship of Jesus Christ can be attacked equally by individuals, by a group and by the totality of Christians in the Church. And it is difficult to claim that any one

2. *The Being of the Community*

of these forms has absolutely and in all circumstances to be set up and put into effect as that which is based on the Bible and in loyalty to the One whom it attests. In the obedience to Him which Scripture attests to be necessary, His community may prefer this or that form, but as it does so it will always be aware that it is only He who has the right and the power to govern the Church, not any man or men, even as His representatives. According to the witness of Scripture, He is not absent but present in the midst. He may be represented, i.e., attested, by one or many, but He does not need any vicar, either in the form of individuals, or in that of a group, or in that of the totality or the majority of the community. He needs Christians who will be only His servants. The order of the true apostolic Church and its administration can always be recognised by the fact that this is taken into account.

Again, the Church is apostolic and therefore the true Church where its regard for the direction of Scripture always gives to its preaching, doctrine, instruction and theology a strict concentration on the recognition of Jesus Christ alone, of Jesus Christ as God revealed and speaking and acting, of His death and resurrection, of the salvation which appeared in Him as the only salvation of men and the world, of the kingdom which has drawn near in Him, of the hope of His coming, of faith in Him—all under this sign, all with reference to this reality, all thinking from and thinking back to this point. This has nothing whatever to do with any kind of orthodoxy. Orthodoxy has usually done far too little than too much in [724] this direction. There are many forms in which this can be recognised and many tongues in which it can be confessed. But it will always be the business of a Church orientated by Scripture to recognise and confess it. It will always have to clarify and purify its word in respect of the possible admixture of alien elements from all kinds of neighbouring centres and truths and priorities and directions. It will always focus its thinking and word on the one thing which it has been charged to speak by the one person. As a teaching Church it will always be, and will always have to be, a listening Church—listening to that one person. We can recognise it as the Church of the true Gospel by the fact that it is caught up in this endeavour and does not grow weary of it.

Again, it is apostolic and therefore true where the faith and, we may say at once, the piety of its members, as they all take notice of the direction of Scripture, is not centred in itself, in the human experience, insight and will without which it cannot, of course, subsist, but is a piety which is held from above, from without, being maintained in that peace of God which is higher than reason, not in any depth of Christian feeling or power of thought or activity, but in the peace which is enclosed and which consists in Jesus Christ. Of course, it will then be a living and visible piety in the sphere of reason in all its dimensions, in every kind of experience and insight and will. But in the true Church what makes a man a true Christian is that he does not put any part of his confidence in any respect upon himself, his own vitality, but that his heart is elsewhere, above, in blessedness, with the Lord, and that he is held and guided by Him. Where the members of the community are Christians with this direction, because they are guided and brought up in it, we shall have no difficulty in recognising them as the true community.

And now, finally, we can put the question and answer it from a very different standpoint. The direction which was peculiar to the apostles and which we find in Scripture involved for them a particular and highly individual human attitude and way of existence which we can only describe as one of supreme realism. For them their discipleship, apostolate, authority, power and mission was not an end in itself. From first to last—at this point we are forced back to our key thought—it was absolutely a matter of their service, their ministry as heralds. As their distinctive title "apostle" shows us, they were sent out to preach the Gospel in the world, a light which had been kindled to give light to all that are in the house (Mt. 5^{15})—nothing more. The character given to them is not great or significant in itself. Not even in the highest conceivable sense is it a matter of their own good or ill, of their own honour, or

§ 62. *The Holy Spirit and the Gathering of the Christian Community*

even of the self-reposing structural importance and dignity of the work which they have to accomplish in this character. Their being and their work both point beyond themselves. Their field is the world, and they are only sowers who pass over it. They renounce any self-grounded or self-reposing lightness or importance of their distinctive being and activity. It is the special direction in which they look, to the One who has made them His and whom they have recognised as theirs, which forces them to make this renunciation. It cannot be otherwise than that even in this renunciation they should be a normative pattern to the community gathered by their ministry. As an apostolic Church the Church can never in any respect be an end in itself, but, following the existence of the apostles, it exists only as it exercises the ministry of a herald. It builds up itself and its members in the common hearing of the Word of God which is always new, in common prayer, in baptism and the Lord's Supper, in the practice of its inner fellowship, in theology. But it cannot forget that it cannot do these things simply for its own sake, but only in the course of its commission—only in an implicit and explicit outward movement to the world with which Jesus Christ and in His person God accepted solidarity, for which He died, and in which He rose again in indication of the great revelation of the inversion accomplished in Him. For this reason the Church can never be satisfied with what it can be and do as such. As His community it points beyond itself. At bottom it can never consider its own security, let alone its appearance. As His community it is always free from itself. In its deepest and most proper tendency it is not churchly, but worldly—the Church with open doors and great windows, behind which it does better not to close itself in upon itself again by putting in pious stained-glass windows. It is holy in its openness to the street and even the alley, in its turning to the profanity of all human life—the holiness which, according to Rom. 12^5, does not scorn to rejoice with them that do rejoice and to weep with them that weep. Its mission is not additional to its being. It is, as it is sent and active in its mission. It builds up itself for the sake of its mission and in relation to it. It does it seriously and actively as it is aware of its mission and in the freedom from itself which this gives. If it is the apostolic Church determined by Scripture and therefore by the direction of the apostles, it cannot fail to exist in this freedom and therefore in a strict realism more especially in relation to itself. And when it does this it cannot fail to be recognisable and recognised as apostolic and therefore as the true Church.

3. THE TIME OF THE COMMUNITY

The time of the community is the time between the first *parousia*^{EN272} of Jesus Christ and the second. "*Parousia*^{EN273}" means the immediate visible presence and action of the living Jesus Christ Himself. His first immediate visible presence and action was that in which He encountered the disciples in the forty days after Easter as the Judge who was judged for the unjust. His second presence and action will be His final coming in His revelation as the Judge of the quick and the dead. The community exists between His coming then as the risen One and this final coming. Its time is, therefore, this time between. Its movement is from direct vision to direct vision; and in this movement by His Holy Spirit He Himself is invisibly present as the living Head in the midst of it as His body.

---

^{EN272} coming
^{EN273} coming

3. *The Time of the Community*

That it lives in this time and movement is both the weakness of the community and its strength. We will first speak of its strength, then of its weakness.

Its strength consists in the fact that it comes from Easter. It has in its ears the message of those who then saw Him face to face. By the awakening power of the Holy Spirit it is gathered in the unity of the faith to this message, i.e., to the One who, according to this message, is the living Lord. For in faith in this message it can recognise the One of whom it speaks, the Judge who was judged for the unjust, as its Lord who is also the Lord of the world. In faith in this message it can hear the verdict of God executed in His death and proclaimed in His resurrection—the justification of sinful man. In faith in this message it can receive and accept this verdict, beginning to live in recognition of it. Above all, it can itself proclaim this message, representing the truth of it to the world by its word and by its existence. It can itself attest the One of whom this message speaks: not in its own strength, on its own responsibility, or at its own risk; not from a standpoint or in an enterprise which it has itself selected and [726] made its own, and for which it must, therefore, bear the responsibility, which it must excuse and justify; but in the power of its secured and promised being as the one holy universal apostolic Church, in which it is wholly dependent upon its Lord and is wholly sustained by Him.

This is its strength. From this standpoint, from behind, from its origin in the resurrection of Jesus Christ, in all the groupings of history there is none which is so strong and durable, none which has such impetus, which can be so sure of its cause and its future, as the Christian community, even in its most modest and questionable forms. It exists in the light of Easter Day. Its day is one of the days of work which follow this first day, this Sunday.

But at the same time it looks forwards. It has the message of the resurrection of Jesus Christ in its ears. It lives with it and by it. It reproduces it. But this message as such is only of a First, a beginning. Of course, it is a beginning—this is what makes it so powerful—which includes in itself and indicates the end and the whole. The First is the first-fruits, who, risen again from the dead, is the Judge of the quick and the dead (the Judge who was judged for them as their Substitute). It is as the One who had become this in the power of His death that He appeared to that first group, the twelve and those around them, and to Saul who became Paul. He is proclaimed as such by the message from which the community comes and with and by which it lives. And yet as the message of the revelation of the One He is it is only a beginning—the message of His first *parousia*[FN274] which, as such, is aimed and pointed at His second, His relation to all those whom it concerns, to all those whom He judged in His death by allowing Himself to be judged in their place. In this revelation even the community which first believes in Him will see Him as the disciples saw Him on Easter Day, but they will see Him definitively, whereas the disciples then saw Him only transitorily. The community which has this beginning

---

[EN274] coming

§ 62. The Holy Spirit and the Gathering of the Christian Community

behind it, which comes from Easter, has this end and goal, this consummation before it. This is what constitutes the particular dynamic of its existence and situation. This is what constitutes the direction which it receives from the Lord living and ruling invisibly in the midst. It comes from Him as the First, to look and move towards Him as the Last. It waits for Him. It hastens towards Him. And that means towards His revelation as the One He is for all in His visibility for all. It waits for the seeing of that which, receiving the message, it can now believe, for the definitive seeing by itself and all men of Him who has changed and turned the whole human situation, turning it back to God. As it is awakened to faith in the Easter message it hears and knows and understands it already as the verdict of God on all sinful humanity which has been executed and declared and is therefore valid and effective. It knows already that which others do not know. It knows it in faith. It does not yet see it—any more than others—but it knows it. It lives in this knowing of faith. In this knowing of its faith and in its life by it, it is the one holy universal apostolic Church, the community of Jesus Christ. In this knowing of faith it is stronger than the world and overcomes it—not in scorn and enmity, but in confidence and hope, looking to the end and goal to which it moves, and to which, without knowing it, the world moves with it. The community knows that it is the world which God has already reconciled to Himself in Jesus Christ. It knows that the judgment upon it has already been executed. It knows its justification accomplished on the cross of Golgotha. By and in this faith in it it lives. In the oneness of this faith it is gathered as the Christian community. In this faith it is in the world, itself worldly. In this faith it is led and carried as on eagles' wings to the glory of the second and final *parousia*^{EN275} of Jesus Christ; that is, to the universal direct and definitive revelation and vision of the Judge who justifies sinful humanity and of the sinful humanity justified by Him.

This teleological direction of its existence which is the consequence of its origin constitutes its strength. There are, of course, other societies which have a teleological direction, which look forward to the future with all kinds of promises and expectations. But the Christian community has the advantage that in its beginning it already has behind it the end which it awaits. To that extent it proceeds from the fulfilment of its hope. Its hope is not the expression of a longing and striving. It is the expression of the impetus by which it exists. It also has the advantage that the end which it awaits is universal and not particular, uniting and not dividing, a goal of peace and not a party goal. It has again the advantage that as it waits for it and looks and hastens towards it, it is engaged in a conflict, but in a conflict in which it is not against any one but for everyone, in the one conflict that the eyes of all—in the first instance the eyes of faith—may be opened to what has already taken place for them, for their justification as already accomplished and proclaimed by God. Its strength consists in the fact that in the unity of the faith it is gathered in every age, from

---

EN275 coming

3. *The Time of the Community*

many peoples and tribes, to be a provisional representation of all humanity as justified in Jesus Christ. This is what gives to its existence in the world its incomparable meaning and significance and power, at all times and in all circumstances, and again even in its most modest and questionable forms.

In short, it is strong because it knows what time is—time which begins and ends, but for that reason the filled-out present of every time, between every yesterday and to-morrow. It is strong because for it Easter stands behind every yesterday, the first *parousia*[EN276] of the One who is its Lord, but who as the great Servant of God is also the Lord of the whole world, of all men. It is strong because for it His coming in glory is proclaimed and present beyond every morning—His second and final *parousia*[EN277]. It knows what time is because it knows that it is this time between, and because in this knowledge it is held and impelled and directed both behind and before. [728]

But we must also perceive and state that its weakness, too, consists in that in which it is strong. All that we have to say of its weakness in its time, this time between, can be summarised in a statement based on 2 Cor. 5^7: that it is only in faith—in a faith which does not have its possibility or basis or support in any form of sight—that it can be strong and therefore "walk," pursuing its way in this time. If it is not awakened to faith and made strong in it by the Holy Spirit, this weakness will be fatal. But even in the strength of its faith it is weak in the fact that its faith is not sight, that it must be content to move in faith and without any kind of sight from the first to the second and last *parousia*[EN278] of Jesus Christ. It will be seen that its weakness, too, is to some extent ontologically grounded in the nature of its time, the time between. For it is the time between His first and second presence and action in immediate visibility. It is no longer the time of Easter, and it is not yet the time, i.e., the moment of His return. The community moves from the one point to the other like a ship—a constantly recurring picture—sailing over an ocean a thousand fathoms deep. The Lord Himself is in the midst, but He is also at the one point and the other, as the One who has come and the One who comes, concealed as the author and finisher of its faith (Heb. 12^2) both in its beginning, in the event of which the Easter message speaks, and also in its end, to which this event and its own beginning refers it.

This event of the beginning, the resurrection of Jesus Christ from the dead, is not a factor of "history" which it can see as such and to which it can cling in another way than faith. The living Lord did not encounter at all the men of the Sanhedrin, or Pilate and his people, or the folk of Jerusalem and Galilee, let alone the wider circles of the then population of the world, but only His disciples, and even His disciples in such a way that, although they could see Him directly, they were placed in the decision of faith or lack of faith, so that they

---

[EN276] coming
[EN277] coming
[EN278] coming

§ 62. *The Holy Spirit and the Gathering of the Christian Community*

first had to make the decision of faith, or, at any rate, they all did make that decision without exception. Again He encountered His disciples only transitorily at that time, in the forty days which found their definitive conclusion in the final event described as His ascension, so that even they—although with the recollection of those days—were thrown back wholly and utterly upon the Holy Spirit of the living Lord, and therefore wholly and utterly upon faith in Him. The message which is the basis of the community spoke of this event which did not have an open but an esoteric and more than that a transitory character. And if it could not be accepted by those who were the witnesses of it except by the Holy Spirit and therefore in faith, if even for them it could not retain its impressiveness in any other way, how much more is this the case for the community which is thrown back on their message, which is founded by

[729] them and in effect only by them! How much more is it the case for the many of later ages to which we also belong, who have not seen Him and have not been able to see Him in that event! They, we, have only been able to hear of the event of His revelation as the living Lord and therefore of His existence as such. We have only been able to hear of it as mediated through the message of these first witnesses, to be awakened to faith as the hearers of this message. That is how it is with the beginning of the community in its time, the time between. In relation to the character of the Easter event itself, and in relation to the slender thread by which the news of it is mediated to the community, this beginning is wrapped in a concealment which can be penetrated only by the living Lord Himself in the work of His Holy Spirit, or from the point of view of the community only by faith in Him.

But there is more to be said in relation to this beginning. Supposing the event of Easter had quite a different character from that which it actually has according to the New Testament accounts. Supposing it had the open character of an act of human "history." Supposing the news of it had the nature of a report which is basically plausible to every man. We have still to explain how it could have for those who received the report and even for its direct witnesses the meaning and character in which it is the basis of the Christian community, the meaning and character of the revelation of that which took place in the death of Jesus Christ; how that event came and comes to be a declaration concerning the end of the history of sinful humanity, the alteration, the turning of its situation, its conversion to God. The Christian community believes that this has taken place in the death of Jesus Christ because it has been proclaimed by God Himself in His resurrection from the dead—the reconciliation of the world with God. But in face of the event of His resurrection, or because it hears of this event, it can only believe as it is revealed to it by the Holy Spirit in this event and in its hearing of the account of it. That which is the real point of this event and the account of it would in any case be wrapped in the concealment of revelation and faith: the proclamation of the justification of sinful man which has taken place in it. In this sense it was hidden even from the direct witnesses of this event, to the extent that in the forty days the life of the cruci-

3. *The Time of the Community*

fied and risen Jesus Christ could be seen by them only as His life, but was concealed from them as their own life and that of all men, and therefore as the justification of themselves and all men in His life from death, a life which they confront as mortal men, as those who die (every day according to 1 Cor. 15³¹), because they are still sinners, a life which they can only hope and expect to receive from Him as their own life and therefore as their own justification. "Hid with Christ in God" (Col. 3³), this life and therefore their reconciliation, the reconciliation of the world with God, could not be seen but only believed by them even in the forty days (and more particularly afterwards). Even in these days their corruptible had not put on incorruption, their mortal immortality. Even in these days and in the light of these days, in the hearing of the divine verdict pronounced in this event, if they were not wrapped in complete obscurity in relation to their altered situation and that of the world, they could not do more than see in a glass darkly (1 Cor. 13¹²), they were thrown back on the knowledge of faith. They had not yet reached the stage of being "like" Him (1 Jn. 3²). Nor has this stage been reached by any means in the community founded by their message. The event of reconciliation proclaimed in the resurrection of Jesus Christ, the justification of sinful man, can and will always be found and known in Him, in the person of its Head, but for the time being it will be found and known only in Him—in Him as it has taken place for it and for all men, yet not with reference to its common life and that of its members (even the best of them), but only as it looks to Him and holds to Him and in its proclamation of the good news of this event points to Him, in faith in Him, therefore, and in the call to faith in Him. This is the other aspect of the great hiddenness of the beginning from which the community comes. If He who lives invisibly in the midst did not disclose to it what it means for it and for the whole world that He has risen again from the dead, what this tells us of the power of His death to renew both it and the world, if His Holy Spirit did not utter in the midst the verdict proclaimed in His resurrection, of what avail would it be to come from this beginning, however great and wonderful it may be? It would be quite dumb. It would not be the word by which it can feed and live. Even on this basis it can be made strong only by Jesus Christ Himself. Therefore it cannot recognise and confess too strictly that even on this basis it will stumble, indeed it will lie quite helpless, without Him. It has of itself no kind of power over this beginning—either over the Easter event in itself and as such, or over that which is proclaimed in it and with it. It has no hold over it. It can only be the case that this event as such, and in it the proclamation of the atonement made in the death of Jesus Christ, has taken place, that the community has actually come under the grip and is in the power of this event, and that it actually realises in faith that this is so. On the basis of this beginning it can be strong in faith. It can be strong to overcome all difficulties and obstacles. But without faith, if it were a matter of some kind of seeing, it can only be weak, and mortally so.

[730]

§ 62. *The Holy Spirit and the Gathering of the Christian Community*

[731]

This is even more true in relation to the goal of its way. If we accept that on the basis of this beginning it is strong in faith, this means that from that point, from the resurrection of Jesus Christ, we are referred to an end in which He will be just as visible to it and the world as the One He is, the One in whom God has reconciled it and the world to Himself, as He was to the disciples in the forty days, an end in which the world will therefore be visible to the community and itself as the world reconciled to God in Him, the world in which (Phil. 2^{11}) "every tongue shall confess that He is Lord, to the glory of God the Father." But how does the community know this goal and end of its way? It knows it only in the form of its beginning. It knows the returning Lord only in the form in which He came then according to the record. That the goal and end of its way is enclosed in this beginning, that the future form of its Lord, in which He comes to it and it can expect Him, is enclosed in this form, is something which it cannot see but can only believe as it looks back to Easter. It can believe it because He Himself says it who is alive in the midst by His Holy Spirit, because He Himself discloses Himself to it as the One who has not only come but will come again, and come again in a way which is quite different. What at very best (as disclosed in faith) it sees in the light of this beginning is only an individual event in the midst of the times. And with this event what does it see and know of the final event which proclaims itself in this one event, which terminates time and includes all times, in which before its very eyes and the eyes of the whole world all past time will in a single moment, the moment of eternity, become present? If in faith in that account of the beginning Jesus Christ is before it as the first-fruits of the dead, it does not in any sense see the host of the dead, as the first-fruits of which He has risen, and which will then be gathered around Him as a host of the living. If in faith in Him it hears the proclamation, made then in His resurrection from the dead, of the justification of all sinful humanity which took place in His death, it does not know anything at all of the method or extent of its actual accomplishment, or what kind of a reality is the justified humanity which is finally to be revealed as such. Even assuming that it (or its members) knows this reality in its own life in faith in Him, what does it know not merely of the individual but of the universal character of the atonement made in Him, of the justification of all men as it took place in Him, even of those with whom it does not find itself united in the unity of faith in Him? And, above all, if it knows, if Christians know in faith that they are reconciled to God, justified, in His person, in Him as their Head, what do they really know of themselves, i.e., of their being with Him, of the form of their being in which there will be no more contradiction between their being from above in faith and their being from below as poor lost sinners, in which they will be no longer on the march from their wrong to their right, from their death to their life, but already at the goal, absolutely in the right and in life? In virtue of their beginning their faith includes all this as faith in Jesus Christ as risen again from the dead. Christians, the Christian community is summoned from this beginning to hope for all this, to expect it, to hasten towards it. But obviously in such

3. *The Time of the Community*

a way that from this beginning its faith must take a sharp turn and become hope, continually renewing and revealing itself as faith directed to this goal and end, as faith in the Lord who comes again in this glory. What in virtue of this beginning it knows in faith is not at all self-evidently the knowledge of what faith has to know to be living and strong as faith directed to this goal and end. Even from this standpoint it has to be the gift and event of faith. There can be no question of seeing, even with a forward reference to the second *parousia* of Jesus Christ. What would the community be, and in what mortal weakness would it lie, if it were not awakened to faith by its Lord through His Holy Spirit, if it were not led "from faith to faith" (Rom. 1^{17}), and thus made strong forwards as well as backwards, if it did not receive of His fulness "grace for grace" (Jn. 1^{16})? It is indeed voyaging over a sea a thousand fathoms deep.

[732]

And we must not neglect to consider its actual condition at every moment and in every momentary situation between the beginning and the end, between the resurrection of Jesus Christ and His return. In the present context we are leaving aside all the complaints and accusations which arise from the fact that Church history is from first to last a history of continual human failure and defeat, that what is called Christianity is a very doubtful concern, that what are called Christians are a type of men who have always been exposed to many criticisms. In the last resort, it is not this which concerns us, but what we may call the ontological weakness of the Christian community as such, the weakness by which it is oppressed even in its best times and forms and achievements, because its time is this time, the time between.

There is this point to consider on the one hand. It is the community of the God who wills (1 Tim. 2^4) that all men should be saved and come to a knowledge of the truth. It has its faith, and, knowing in faith for all others, it knows what it has to say to all others. But it is so alone in the world. It has gained whole masses of adherents both in the past and to-day, but in spite of that it has no illusions. It is such a small minority side by side with and in the midst of all other human societies. In relation to them and to the world it can only be a very small and modest light in this world. How this contradicts its beginning in the resurrection of Jesus Christ, its commission: "Go and make disciples of all nations" (Mt. 28^{19}), and its end, that "at the name of Jesus every knee should bow, of things in heaven, and things in earth, and things under the earth" (Phil. 2^{11})! What is the Christian faith in the midst of so much unbelief and error and superstition, and, above all, such a sea of ignorance that a decision has to be made between it and its different negations? What is Church history in the human history which flows round it and over it? The Christian community can answer these questions, but not with a knowledge which is divorced from faith and grounded and supported from without, not with an anthropology and philosophy of history, not with a knowledge of the ways of God both behind and before, only with its very being, only with the faithfulness in which both outwardly and inwardly it actually is what it is. But this means again, only as it believes, and, because it can have faith only as it receives it, only as He who

[733]

§ 62. *The Holy Spirit and the Gathering of the Christian Community*

is its Lord awakens it to faith and keeps it watchful in faith. "If it had not been the Lord who was on our side, now may Israel say, if it had not been the Lord who was on our side, when men rose up against us, then they had swallowed us up quick" (Ps. 124$^{1f.}$). "Our help is in the name of the Lord, who made heaven and earth" (Ps. 124^8). It is because this is so that it is strong, stronger than all others. If it were not so, it would be weaker than all others, fatally weak. It is called upon to believe that it is so.

The second point to consider is that it can be sure of itself only in faith, and therefore it is made sure only in the awakening and sustaining of its faith by One who is able to do this. We have seen that it is the community of Jesus Christ, the one holy catholic apostolic Church. This is its being concealed in its visible form. This can be seen and confessed only under the *credo*^{EN279} or not at all. For "the spirit truly is ready, but the flesh is weak" (Mk. 14^{38}). The Christian community exists at every point in an unbroken concealment, in the weakness of the flesh. Where is it palpable even to itself, let alone to the world, that it comes from the resurrection of Jesus Christ and moves to His return, and that He Himself is present in its midst as its Head? It is only the Spirit who is truly "ready." He comes to our aid. He intercedes for the saints according to the will of God (Rom. 8$^{26f.}$). But He is the Spirit of faith, who bears witness to us that we are the children of God by the fact that we may cry, "Abba, Father," and that at bottom we cannot cry anything else (Rom. 8$^{15f.}$). He is the Spirit in obedience to whom the community (Rom. 8$^{19f.}$) and all creation can only groan for its redemption from the bondage of corruption and therefore for liberty in the glory of the children of God. As it obeys Him and does this it is strong; it can and must say this *credo*^{EN280} with confidence and joy even in relation to its own existence. And as it does that it can be absolutely certain of itself and its cause. But only as it does this. Only as it does not deny the weakness in which it is what it is. Only as it knows the thousand fathom depth on which it sails, but is not afraid. In the time which is its time, the time between, from the very beginning of the way to the end, and especially in the midst, there is no point without this Nevertheless.

But this time, which in its delimitation both behind and before is the basis of the peculiar strength and weakness of the Christian community, is in a supremely qualified sense *its* time, the time which is spared and appointed for the sake of the gathering and existence and mission of the community, the time which is given to it, the time which it has to recognise according to its true meaning, the time which it has to buy up (Col. 4^5, Eph. 5^{16}), turning it to profitable account. The community is and has the answer which has to be given to the question of the good and gracious purpose of God in the puzzling distance between the first *parousia*^{EN281} of Jesus Christ and the second, the

---

^{EN279} 'I believe'
^{EN280} 'I believe'
^{EN281} coming

3. The Time of the Community

question of the time between, in which with the world it is held, as it were, suspended between the provisional and transitory and particular revelation of its reconciliation with God in Jesus Christ and the perfect and definitive and universal revelation of it in His final coming. The life of the community shows us with what we have to do in this time between. It is the true fulness of it. To that extent it is its time.

It might have been quite different. The time which is our time might not have been at all, because there was no time at all, because all time had long since come to its end. The first *parousia*[EN282] of Jesus Christ might immediately have been His last. In a moment, in the twinkling of an eye, the event of Easter morning might have been the sounding of the last trumpet (1 Cor. 15^{52}), the event of the final revelation, presence and action of the Judge who was judged for sinful men, and therefore the event of the last day, the final judgment. In a certain sense it is this. Its content is unquestionably one and the same—the proclamation of the One who was judged on Golgotha as the Judge of the quick and the dead, and with Him the irruption of redemption, of the consummation. The only thing is that on Easter Day it all had only this provisional and transitory and particular form, a penultimate character. It really was the end—in this penultimate character. The Lord who will come again in glory is the One who with the empty tomb behind Him already encountered the disciples in the forty days and Saul on the outskirts of Damascus. God had already pronounced His decision on sinful man, the Word of grace and judgment, the final "Let there be light." Human history was actually terminated at this point. The resurrection of all the dead had already been indicated. Enclosed in the life of this One, their eternal life had already become an event. This is the point of the well-known sayings of Jesus concerning His imminent coming, the imminent redemption and consummation. Even in this form it did not lack anything in intensive power and scope. It might have had the intensive and extensive power and scope and therefore the form which it will have in the second and last *parousia*[EN283] of Jesus Christ. All time might have terminated then.

But this did not happen. It is better not to say that time continued, but rather than a further time, a new time commenced. This is already proclaimed by the fact that according to the tradition there was not simply one Easter event, but an Easter history in an Easter time. All that the tradition reports is a sequence of days and happenings in which the coming again of the Lord in glory was constantly reaffirmed. And the end and climax of this Easter time, described as the ascension, points forward unmistakably to a future of this new and further time which is limited, but the end of which cannot for the moment be seen. His first *parousia*[EN284] is over. There has begun an interval of time of

[735]

[EN282] coming
[EN283] coming
[EN284] coming

§ 62. *The Holy Spirit and the Gathering of the Christian Community*

uncertain duration. A distance in time separates the first *parousia*[EN285] from the second and the second from the first as though it were arrested by an invisible hand. What might have been a single happening, what we might almost have thought would have to be a single happening, divides into two. Not that the connexion is lost. In both cases it is one and the same. And in the person of the One who acts it not only hangs together, but both on the one side and on the other, in its Whence and also in its Whither, it is actually the same event. "Lo, I am with you alway, even unto the end of the world" (Mt. 28[20]). Yet it cannot be seen in this connexion, in this unity. Its "then" and its "one day," its whence and its whither, are distinct from one another. The two characters of the event are distinct from one another. In the one case it appears in its provisional and transitory and particular form, in the other in its perfect and final and universal. Between the two there opens up the new and further space of time, that of all the days to the end of the world: the time between, which is more properly called the end-time, because in both those forms it is the end—the end of all the ways of God—which it has before it and yet already behind it. This end-time is our time.

Let us imagine for a moment that there were no such end-time. In that case God would not have caused any new and further time to begin. Without interposing this interval He would have wound up all time and the existence of heaven and earth and everything within them in the way that as their Creator He caused them all to begin and as one day He will in fact bring them to an end. He would have reconciled the world to Himself in Jesus Christ, and the resurrection of Jesus Christ, like the seventh day of the story of creation, but far surpassing it, or rather fulfilling its prophetic meaning, would have been the beginning of His rest from all His works, and therefore the beginning of the eternal Sabbath. In this case God would have renounced any further activity in and with the world beyond what He accomplished and revealed in Jesus Christ. He would simply have contemplated the totality of what He had done to it and in it (as He did His work of creation), and He would have found it well done, and therefore not in need of any continuation. But this means that He would have been satisfied with the existence of the generations *ante Christum natum*[EN286] and with their history, i.e., with what He had done for them as Creator and Reconciler. He would not have needed any further generations and their history. He would not have expected any further human response to what He accomplished and revealed in Jesus Christ, to the execution of His judgment and to the proclamation of the verdict operative in His judgment.

Note that in this case the fulfilment of the covenant, the reconciliation of the world with Him, would have been a kind of unilateral decision and exercise of force, the revelation of it a dictatorial declaration of will, and the whole a sovereign overpowering of humanity to His own glory and its own continu-

---

[EN285] coming
[EN286] before the birth of Christ

3. *The Time of the Community*

ance, but still an overpowering, a sovereign act of grace in which He wanted no thanks and did not expect to receive any. Why should this not have been His resolve and will and act? When He sacrificed Himself in the death of His Son for man, when He declared His severity and mercy to him in His resurrection from the dead, did He not do something supreme and final which renders quite superfluous any correspondence on the part of man, or the continuance of humanity, and therefore further generations and their history, and therefore all further time (e.g., ourselves and the fact that we still have time)? And when we again consider the two thousand years of history and culture *post Christum*[EN287], and even that which appears within it as the history of the Church, we may well be tempted to ask whether there was any real value in postponing the second *parousia*[EN288] of Jesus Christ, and therefore allowing a new and further time to commence and to continue even to this present, this puzzling time of ours, the time between. Would it not have better served both the glory of God and the salvation of man if all that has happened since had not happened, if that eternal Sabbath had in fact begun? For after all there was no real need of this afterwards. Indeed this afterwards can only obscure and compromise the turning which was made in Jesus Christ. Often enough it has, in fact, obscured and compromised it.

What does it mean, then, that God—whose thoughts in this matter, too, are higher than our thoughts—quite obviously did not will and think in this way, that this interval did begin and does continue, that we have behind us as a promise and an admonition and a warning the temporal sabbath of the resurrection of Jesus Christ, the penultimate end, but that the dawning of the eternal Sabbath of His second *parousia*[EN289] is still before us? What does it mean that God still has a time for humanity, for us? In the first instance, of course, it means that even after He has done and spoken that supreme and final thing, even after He has set and revealed—in that penultimate form—its goal and end, His activity in and with the world and humanity created by Him has not in fact ended. That the world is still there and that this new and further time has begun carries with it as a final presupposition the fact that God is still at work as its Lord. Strangely enough, for what more can God will and work when everything has already been accomplished? But that is how it is. And if that is how it is, it is obvious that He still has a goal and goals, that He still expects something in the world and humanity created and preserved by Him. He has spoken His final Word, but He has not yet finished speaking it. The last hour has struck, but it is still striking. And this means that there is still space for humanity, and in that space it can still exist—surplus space, and a surplus existence, but still a possibility of being, and actual being. It can still develop. There

---

[EN287] after Christ
[EN288] coming
[EN289] coming

§ 62. *The Holy Spirit and the Gathering of the Christian Community*

[737] is still a history. A history which is a postscript, but a real history, and therefore more generations, more opportunities for human existence from God and before God and to God, more opportunities of fellowship, of psycho-physical life, more spans of life—and all within the great and astonishing span which has still been allotted to the world as a whole. It has to have this great span, this end-time.

Negatively, this results from the fact that—however final was that which was done in the death of Jesus Christ and revealed in His resurrection—it was not a unilateral decision of force or a dictatorial declaration of will or a sovereign overpowering. God did not will to act and He did not act in this way in Jesus Christ. This is not the aspect of what He did for His own glory and our good, of the act of grace in which He confirmed Himself as the Creator of man and the Lord of the covenant for which He elected him, of His conflict with the pride and fall of man, and the conversion of man to Himself—although this is indeed His last and supreme achievement. And note that it is not He, the God of Abraham, Isaac and Jacob, the Father of Jesus Christ, the God of all mercy and comfort, who would have thought and acted in this way. We may think that this would have contributed to His glory or been of great benefit for the world, but it would have been the act of an abstract and godless grace, not His own grace, not the divine grace addressed to man in Jesus Christ, but a faithfulness full of unfaithfulness, just because it is a unilateral decision which over-rides man, eliminating and ignoring him. Grace which does not want any response, any thanks? Grace which does not yearn for any correspondence on the part of man? No eternal glory of the world consummated in this way could alter the fact that an act of this kind is unfriendly to man, that it is at bottom an ungracious act. No sovereignty of which man might boast in the exercise of such grace can alter the fact that it is brutal grace—grace as brutal man might conceive it, but not the grace of the true and living God, who is Father, Son and Holy Spirit. The fact that between the first end which has already come and the future final end there is interposed our time, the end-time, shows us first of all that we have to rid our minds completely of all thought of a god or a grace of this kind.

What is the purpose of the space which is still given to man, of his actual existence in this new and further time after the reconciliation of the world with God as already seen and proclaimed in Jesus Christ? We can now give the positive answer. Its purpose is obviously this—that God will not allow His last Word to be fully spoken or the consummation determined and accomplished and proclaimed by Him to take place in its final form until He has first heard a human response to it, a human Yes; until His grace has found its correspondence in a voice of human thanks from the depths of the world reconciled with Himself; until here and now, before the dawning of His eternal Sabbath, He [738] has received praise from the heart of His human creation. That is the greatness of His grace. That is the reach of His condescension. That is the seriousness of the solidarity to which He has committed Himself with us men in the

3. *The Time of the Community*

person of His Son. He does not will to be without man, to have become his Reconciler and to become his Redeemer over the head of man. He does not will the isolation of His Son, the blindness, the deafness, the exclusion of the others for whom He died. He wills a body, an earthly-historical form of the existence of this Head. He wills open eyes and ears for what took place in His death, and therefore for the turning from wrong to right, from death to life, which came about in the human situation. He wills human hearts which see this turning, and human tongues which confess it. He wills not only that the justification which has taken place in Jesus Christ should have taken place, but that the news of it should be sounded out and should meet with faith. In order that this may happen, He still gives to the world space, time and existence, He allows the end-time to commence and continue. It is the sphere in which there can be this correspondence.

He did not need it. He might have done without it. But it is a further dimension of His friendliness to man (Tit. 3^4) that He willed not to do without it, not to forgo man's Yes to His action, his praise and thanks, not to have reconciled him, not to redeem and perfect him, without summoning him to this response and giving him the opportunity for it. Of course it is always deficient. Even as a response to the grace of God it stands always in need of grace. Not all will believe and know and confess. Those who do so will be a minority in all the generation even of this end-time. They will, of course, not only be unable to neglect but they will be irresistibly constrained to call others to their faith, to participate in what they know and confess. But they will not be surprised if they always find themselves in a minority, if with their faith and knowledge and confession they have to go their way representatively for the others. Thus the response which God expects will always in fact be a modest one even externally. And more particularly internally, from the point of view of the quality of the faith and knowledge and confession even of this minority. It is provided that they always have this treasure in very earthen vessels (2 Cor. 4^7), that their thanks are always very equivocal, that their faith is smaller than a grain of mustard seed, that their knowledge is wrapped in obscurity, that their confession is an impotent stammering. It is provided that their praise of God will always be that "poor praise on earth" in which ultimately they can only pray that it will be received in grace, in the hope that "it will be better in heaven when I am in the choirs of the blessed." There is no perfection in it, only the deep and radical imperfection of the cry, "Abba, Father." Even the voice of this minority is only the voice of the sinful humanity justified only in Jesus Christ, which can only believe in its right as established in Him. It certainly cannot escape a wonderful similarity with its Lord who became a servant. When we consider its situation, it is not in any sense arbitrary to think of the night and day and other night of His burial. [739]

Nevertheless, and for this very reason, for the sake of what takes place in the world in and through this people of those who believe and know and confess,

§ 62. *The Holy Spirit and the Gathering of the Christian Community*

the second *parousia*[EN290] of Jesus Christ is postponed. That this may take place there is still time even though the last hour has struck: time for the work of the Holy Spirit and for the prayer for Him; time for faith and repentance; time for preaching the Gospel throughout the world; time for the Christian community, and in this sense the time of grace. God does expect its "poor praise on earth." He is divinely good and gracious in the fact that He will actually receive it. And in this sense the end-time is the time of the community. It does not have it and its existence in it merely for its own sake. As we have seen, it cannot be an end in itself. It has it for God, who is so very much for us men that He will not have it otherwise than that before He has finished speaking His last Word some, and even many, should already be for Him. And it has it for the world in order that as a provisional representation of the justification which has taken place in Jesus Christ it may be the sign which is set up in it, which is given to it, which summons it, in order that it may be to it a shining light—a feeble and defective but still a shining light—until the dawning of the great light which will be the end of all time and therefore of this end-time, the coming Jerusalem in which Rev. 21^{22} tells us there will be no more temple because the Almighty God will Himself be its temple. The Christian community will then have rendered its service. Its time will end with all time. But there is still time. And the time which is now is its time, and the time of its service. It renders it in the strength and weakness which both have their basis in the nature of this time. But in strength or in weakness it can render it gladly because it knows why we still have time, and it can do the decisive thing which gives meaning, real meaning, to the time which is given us.

[EN290] coming

§ 63

[740]

THE HOLY SPIRIT AND CHRISTIAN FAITH

The Holy Spirit is the awakening power in which Jesus Christ summons a sinful man to His community and therefore as a Christian to believe in Him: to acknowledge and know and confess Him as the Lord who for him became a servant; to be sorry both on his own behalf and on that of the world in face of the victory over his pride and fall which has taken place in Him; and again on his own behalf and therefore on that of the world to be confident in face of the establishment of his new right and life which has taken place in Him.

1. FAITH AND ITS OBJECT

We must now speak of that which makes a man a Christian, of the basis of the Christian existence of the individual, and therefore of faith. It is a matter of the faith of the Christian community which, as such, is that of its individual human members, those who are called Christians and who may perhaps be serious Christians.

In the modern period there have been massive theological structures which have begun at the very point where we now end. They started with the presupposition that, whatever may be the attitude to it, Christian faith as such is a fact and phenomenon which is generally known and which can, as such, be explained to everybody; or rather more cautiously, that a generally plausible account can be given of it because the possibility of it can be demonstrated and explained in the light of general anthropology. According to this type of structure the task of dogmatics is the description of Christian faith as such (the *fides qua creditur*[EN1]) and the enumeration, exposition and explanation of its characteristic expressions (the *fides quae creditur*[EN2]). And all on the further underlying presupposition that the really interesting and vital problem of the Christian is the one which is nearest to hand, that is to say, himself, his existence as a Christian, and therefore the fact and phenomenon of his faith. Dogmatics, therefore, is the "doctrine of faith."

The following comments may be made on this view. It is certainly true that at every point Church dogmatics has to bring out and describe the content of the knowledge and confession of Christian faith. To that extent it is not absolutely impossible that it should be understood and called the doctrine of faith. If it does not do this it is because its leading concept is that of the right knowledge and confession of Christian faith, and as the essence of this that of dogma—not the dogma laid down by the Church, but the dogma which is authoritative and normative for the Church. Christian faith itself and as such belongs to the content of the

---

[EN1] faith by which it is believed
[EN2] faith which is believed

§ 63. The Holy Spirit and Christian Faith

right knowledge and confession of Christian faith implied in the doctrine of the Holy Spirit and therefore in the third article of the Creed. It belongs to that of which the right knowledge and confession has to be sought in dogmatics. But for that very reason the basic presupposition of these modern structures is called in question. Christian faith is not in any sense a fact and phenomenon which is generally known and which can as such be explained to everybody. The Christian religion is a fact and phenomenon of this kind. As such it can be considered and estimated historically, psychologically, sociologically and perhaps even philosophically. But the Christian religion is not as such Christian faith. Christian faith is something concealed in the Christian religion (like the true Church in its visibility). As such it can only be believed. It can be known and confessed only in faith. For the same reason we must question the other version of the presupposition, that the possibility of it can be demonstrated and explained in the light of general anthropology. A human self-understanding which includes the possibility of faith can itself be only that of an anthropology which for its part derives from the actuality of faith, which is a specific form of that knowledge and confession, whereas the possibilities which can be demonstrated and explained in the light of anthropology may perhaps be religious, but they are not those of Christian faith. If faith itself belongs to the content of the knowledge and confession of Christian faith, we have to note that although it knows and confesses itself it cannot in any sense think of itself as grounded in itself. As *fides qua creditur*^{EN3} it cannot regard itself as a primary datum (δός μοι ποῦ στῶ^{EN4}) and therefore as the author of its so-called "expressions," the *fides quae creditur*^{EN5}. It can think of itself only as a last thing which follows, and can only follow, a fourth, a third, a second—and, above all, and supremely a first, so that it needs a whole series of bases and finally, or first of all, its new basis in which all the intermediate bases are themselves grounded. Christian faith knows and confesses that it is this last thing. In no case can its knowledge and confession begin with itself. It knows and confesses first its one basis which includes all the others. It knows and confesses itself only as referred wholly and utterly to this first thing, only as the consequence of it. That is why in this first part of the doctrine of reconciliation we had to speak first of all (implying all that follows and therefore this last thing) of Jesus Christ Himself, the Lord who became a servant, the Judge who was Himself judged for us. Then, of course, we had to speak at once of man, but of man in his antagonism to Jesus Christ—the man of sin. Then in the doctrine of justification we had to expound the divine Nevertheless pronounced to man in Jesus Christ. Then at last, in the first form of ecclesiology, we had to come to the underlying form of the subjective realisation of this whole being and occurrence as fulfilled by man too. The other form of it, Christian faith, or concretely, the Christian who knows this whole being and occurrence in faith, has accompanied us as a presupposition all along our way. But it is only now that he can properly become for a short time an independent theme.

The objection against the underlying but all the more powerful presupposition of those modern doctrines of faith is in moral categories an objection against their arrogance. They rest on the fact that in the last centuries (on the broad way which leads from the older Pietism to the present-day theological existentialism inspired by Kierkegaard) the Christian has begun to take himself seriously in a way which is not at all commensurate with the seriousness of Christianity. They represent Christian truth as though its supreme glory is to rotate around the individual Christian with his puny faith, so that there is cause for gratification if they do not regard him as its lord and creator. From the bottom up we can neither approve nor make common cause with this procedure of modern doctrines of faith. We shall

---

^{EN3} faith with which one believes
^{EN4} grant me a place to stand
^{EN5} faith which one believes

1. *Faith and its Object*

give to the individual Christian and his faith the attention which he demands, but it must be at this point—not at the beginning of our way, but very briefly at the end.

We will begin by considering the relationship of Christian faith to its object. Faith is a human activity which cannot be compared with any other in spontaneity and native freedom. But it is in a relationship. It is in relationship to its object, to something which confronts the believer, which is distinct from him, which cannot be exhausted in his faith, which cannot be absorbed by his believing existence, let alone only consist in it and proceed from it and stand or fall with it. The very opposite is true, that faith stands or falls with its object. It is a subjective realisation. That is, as a human activity it consists in the subjectivisation of an objective *res* which in its existence and essence and dignity and significance and scope takes precedence of this subjectivisation and therefore of the human subject active in it, being independent of and superior to this subject and what he does or does not do. It does not owe anything at all to this human subject and his activity, his faith. What takes place in faith is simply that in a specific activity, which in this sense it to some extent expects, this objective *res* finds existence and essence and dignity and significance and scope, creating respect for itself and actually being respected in the presence of this activity—but only as it was already the object of this subject, only as it had all these things, existence, essence, dignity, significance and scope even for this subject, and without his activity and faith and respect. Faith is simply following, following its object. Faith is going a way which is marked out and prepared. Faith does not realise anything new. It does not invent anything. It simply finds that which is already there for the believer and also for the unbeliever. It is simply man's active decision for it, his acceptance of it, his active participation in it. This constitutes the Christian. In believing, the Christian owes everything to the object of his faith: the incomprehensible fact that he may not only be in relation to this object, but may be active in this being. The great advantage which he has over all others, and which he can never prize too highly, is that this object is not only there for him but that he for his part can be there for this object. It does not remain only a matter of its relationship with him. He himself enters into a relationship with it. This distinguishes the Christian from the non-Christian. The object is like a circle enclosing all men and every individual man. In the case of the Christian this circle closes with the fact that he believes. In the case of non Christians it is still open at the point where he ought to believe but does not yet believe, or no longer believes. The unbeliever has not accepted the relationship to that which is in relationship to him. He is abnormal in this respect. Faith is the normalising of the relationship between man and this object. It is the act in which man does that which this object demands, that which is proper to him in face of this object—the fulfilment of the correspondence to what this object is and means of itself for every man.

[742]

§ 63. The Holy Spirit and Christian Faith

But enough of this formal description of the problem. The "object" of faith, the objective *res* subjectivised in faith, is Jesus Christ, in whom God has accomplished the reconciliation of the world, of all men with Himself—the living Jesus Christ Himself, in whom this occurrence, this fulfilment, this restoration of the broken covenant between God and man, is not an event of the past, not a theoretical truth and doctrine, but for all humanity and all men (irrespective of their attitude to Him) a personal present, no, a present person. He, the living Jesus Christ, is the circle enclosing all men and every man and closed in Christian faith—the circle of divine judgment and divine grace. The great abnormality of unbelief consists in the perversion of the relationship to Him. The normalisation of the human relationship to him is the concern of faith as the human activity in which not all men but Christians are engaged. In the second section we will describe it as this activity. In the present section—because this is what determines it as activity—we will describe it as activity in this relationship of the Christian to Christ.

A first thing which characterises the Christian in this respect is the fact that it consists in the orientation of man on Jesus Christ. It is faith in Him. The man who believes looks to Him, holds to Him and depends on Him. He renounces all self-determination in His favour. To the fact that the circle objectively drawn around man closes in faith there corresponds the further fact that the closed circle of man's being is opened in faith whereas it remains closed in unbelief. In faith man ceases to be in control. He can be this only when he is not orientated on Jesus Christ, at any rate decisively, at the very centre of his being, with what the Bible calls his "heart." To describe this relationship we have already thought in terms of the "eccentric." In faith man is no longer in control at his centre. Or rather, at his centre, he is outside himself and therefore in control. The orientation on Jesus Christ which takes place in faith is not external and occasional. It is not one of the orientations in which he may find himself in his relationship with other things and persons. If he believes, this means that he can no longer fix his "heart" on other things (even the most important) or on other persons (even the dearest and most indispensable). At the centre of his being he is no longer here or there, but at this very definite place outside himself which cannot be exchanged for any other. His mind is then set (Col. 3^2) on "things above, not on things on the earth." "Things above" are not simply the other world generally. They are defined in Col. 3^1: "where Christ sitteth on the right hand of God." All other seeking or orientation is subordinate to this, in which it has its measure and law. All human striving for the beyond is exhausted in this. Man sees that it is an illusion that he can himself be in control at this centre, or that outside himself he can be in any other place, in other things or persons, or even in some other beyond. He is lifted above himself, but in the only direction in which this can take place. If a man believes, this means that he has found in Jesus Christ an object which does not merely concern him and concern him urgently, which does not

1. *Faith and its Object*

merely call him to itself and therefore out of himself, which does not merely claim him, but which is the one true object, which concerns him necessarily and not incidentally, centrally and not casually. It means that he has found in Him the true centre of himself which is outside himself. It means that he must now cling to Him, and depend on Him, that he finds that he belongs to Him.

We can say the same thing in another way. Faith is the human activity which is present and future, which is there, in the presence of the living Jesus Christ and of what has taken place in Him, with a profound spontaneity and a native freedom, but also with an inevitability in face of His actuality. The reverse is equally true: with an inevitability, but with a native freedom. "In the face of" means with eyes open for His actuality as it is before the eyes of all men. "We all with open face mirror the glory of the Lord" (2 Cor. 3^{18}). How can the mirror be a mirror if it does not reflect that which faces it? Again, how can it reflect it if it is covered? Again, what is there of its own in that which is reflected by it? If it is not covered, what can it reflect but that which faces it? This reflecting of the glory of the Lord is made possible by the uncovering of the human face, by the seeing which is the result of this uncovering, by the fact that in this seeing man becomes the mirror of that which faces him, the "glory of the Lord," and, above all, by the "glory of the Lord" itself. It is the free but necessary work of faith which is completely bound to its object, which stands or falls with it and with its existence, essence, dignity, significance and scope. In this work man himself is nothing. He is not in control. He simply finds himself in that orientation. He accepts it. In it he sees and reaches out and grows beyond himself. In it he is for the first time faithful to himself. For as the doer of this work he loses his own life to find it again as he loses it (Mk. 8^{35}). This work can hardly be described as anything but renunciation in favour of the living Lord Jesus Christ. But as he does it, he does a genuine and free work, his own proper work. That is the first thing. Faith is in Jesus Christ. It is the action of the Christian in the face of this His Lord, in direct responsibility to Him, in renunciation in His favour.

The second thing that we have to say of faith in its relationship to Jesus Christ as its object is that, as it is related to, it is also based upon it.

We do not compromise its character as a free human act if we say that as a free human act—more genuinely free than any other—it has its origin in the very point on which it is also orientated. It is also the work of Jesus Christ who is its object. It is the will and decision and achievement of Jesus Christ the Son of God that it takes place as a free human act, that man is of himself ready and willing and actually begins to believe in Him. The two things are not a contradiction but belong together. If the Son makes us free, we are free indeed (Jn. 8^{36}). The Son makes a man free to believe in Him. Therefore faith in Him is the act of a right freedom, not although but just because it is the work of the Son.

§ 63. *The Holy Spirit and Christian Faith*

A man does not have this freedom unless the Son makes him free. The Christian is a sinful man like all others. In his proud heart, in consequence of the proud thoughts and words and acts which proceed from that heart, he is not ready and willing to accept that orientation on Jesus Christ. He is not free for the faith in which everything depends on renouncing. He is not prepared to lose his life in order to gain it. There is a great gulf between him and faith. It did not need to be so. It belongs basically and decisively to the good nature of man as God created it that he should be able to believe. Believing might have been more natural to him than breathing. He was created to be the covenant-partner of God and therefore for God. The gulf between him and faith is something contrary to nature. It is created only by his being in the act of pride. But it is there. And seeing that we are all radically involved in this act of pride, no one has ever surmounted it. Even the believing Christian has not done so. He knows that he ought not even to try. He knows that with all other men he is concluded in disobedience (Rom. 11^{32}), that it is the supreme pride and therefore the supreme fall of man if he undertakes to believe of himself, as though he could do so, as though he could make himself do it and move to do it. He may make the laborious and profoundly dishonest attempt to regard as true something which he cannot regard as true because it is too high for him. He may even make the further and still more painful effort to persuade himself that this convulsive acceptance is redemptive. But a self-fabricated faith is the climax of unbelief. Whatever a man may do in this way he never comes any nearer to faith. Indeed, he moves away from it. For in faith it is not a matter of this or that truth or this or that redemption, but of the person who is Himself truth and redemption. And in relation to this person it is not a matter of proposing and doing something for ourselves, but of following Him, of repeating His decision. But how can any man do that? The Christian knows—and the non-Christian experiences it in practice—that he can make nothing of this person in his own strength, that He remains always as inaccessible to him as sinful man as He is inimitable, that "in his own reason and strength he can neither believe in Him nor come to Him," that in his own reason and strength he will move instead in the very opposite direction. Whenever faith takes place in a man, it will always mean a swimming against this current—a counter-movement which is not undertaken in his own reason and strength. We do not forget that it is the counter-movement of a free human act. But the freedom of it is not the evil freedom which man in his pride has made for himself and which he thinks he can possess for himself and use for himself. As a genuine freedom for this counter-movement it is completely alien to the personal reason and power of proud man entangled in his pride. It is a new freedom and therefore his true freedom. How can he procure it for himself when in his proud heart and the proud being determined by it he is not the one who can have it or win it or even know about it? How can he jump over his own shadow, which is to break free from himself as the one who casts this shadow? In other

1. Faith and its Object

words, how can sinful man—there is an obvious *contradictio in adiecto*^{EN6}—believe?

If we tried to give an answer to the question as put, to posit some supreme possibility of faith, our answer would be mistaken from the very outset. Seeing we have to do with sinful man, the mere "possibility" of faith would obviously be confronted by the other possibility which is the only true possibility, that of the man who in his own reason and strength simply goes with the current in the opposite direction. Who is to choose between them? Who is the man who will choose aright and therefore choose the possibility of faith? The only man who enters into the picture at all is the man who not only can go in the opposite direction, but actually does go in that direction, who not only has the possibility of choosing the sin of pride, but is a proud sinner from the crown of his head to the sole of his foot. The possibility of faith may be very wonderful and it may be held out in a very attractive way, but what does it mean to him? In the rivalry between a possible faith and actual sin, faith will always come off second best. The rivalry will have ended in favour of sin even before it has begun. The whole idea of a possibility of faith confronted by that of unbelief, the whole conception of man as a Hercules at the crossroads able to choose between faith and sin (and therefore unbelief), is a pure illusion. Whatever may be the possibility of faith, this Hercules has always already chosen unbelief.

But there is a necessity of faith, and it is as we point to this that we shall give a sound answer to our question. Faith does not stand or hover somewhere in face of the possibility of unbelief (which is not a possibility but the solid actuality of sinful man). It is not itself a mere possibility, grand and attractive but impotent and useless like all mere possibilities. It has itself the character of an actuality, an actuality which is absolutely superior to that other actuality. In this superiority it is not a mere alternative to unbelief. It is not a mere chance, or proposition. It is not for man to choose first whether he himself will decide (what an illusion!) for faith or for unbelief. Faith makes the solid actuality of unbelief an impossibility. It sweeps it away. It replaces it by itself. It does not build a bridge over the gulf. It closes it. It has already closed it. This takes place in the necessity of faith in the strength of which the only act which remains for a man is the genuinely free act of faith. This is its foundation. It is because this is its foundation that it is both negatively and positively so vigorous as the human act as which we still have to describe it. And it is because it is grounded in this necessity that when it takes place as a human act it has the adamantine, unquestioning and joyful certainty which characterises it and in which it cannot be compared even remotely with the certainty of any other human action. [747]

But this necessity of faith does not lie in man. It does not lie even in the good nature of man as created for God, let alone in his being as the sinner who in denial and perversion of his good nature has turned away from God and in so

---

^{EN6} contradiction in terms

§ 63. *The Holy Spirit and Christian Faith*

doing deprived himself already of the possibility of faith. It does not even lie in faith in itself and as such. It is to be found rather in the object of faith. It is this object which forces itself necessarily on man and is in that way the basis of his faith. This object is the living Lord Jesus Christ, in whom it took place, in whom it has taken place for every man, in whom it confronts man as an absolutely superior actuality, that his sin, and he himself as the actual sinner he is, and with his sin the possibility of his unbelief, is rejected, destroyed and set aside, that he is born again as a new man of obedience, who now has the freedom for faith, and only in that faith his future. In this destroying and renewing of man as it took place in Jesus Christ there consists the necessity of faith, because beyond this destroying and renewing there remains for sinful man only faith in the One in whom it has taken place. In the death of Jesus Christ both the destroying and the renewing have taken place for all men, and the fact that they have taken place has been revealed as valid for all men in His resurrection from the dead. Therefore objectively, really, ontologically, there is a necessity of faith for them all. This object of faith is, in fact, the circle which encloses them all, and which has to be closed by every man in the act of his faith. Jesus Christ is not simply one alternative or chance which is offered to man, one proposition which is made to him. He is not put there for man's choice, *à prendre ou à laisser*^{EN7}. The other alternative is, in fact, swept away in Him.

> With Max v. Schenkendorf: "Arise, thou morning light, / Gone is the ancient night, / Which daily comes again." For, "The devil's claim of old, / On all our human fold, / Is forfeited and lost." And with Ambrosius Lobwasser: "For God's salvation everywhere, / From Heaven is sprinkled down, / That is, He has His own dear Son, / Sent down from heaven's highest throne, / That everything on earth, / In Him may have new birth."

With the divine No and Yes spoken in Jesus Christ the root of human unbelief, the man of sin, is pulled out. In its place there is put the root of faith, the new man of obedience. For this reason unbelief has become an objective, real and ontological impossibility and faith an objective, real and ontological necessity for all men and for every man. In the justification of the sinner which has taken place in Jesus Christ these have both become an event which comprehends all men.

[748] And it is the awakening power of the Holy Spirit that this impossibility as such and this necessity as such so confront a man and illuminate him that he does the only objective, real and ontological thing which he can do, not omitting or suppressing or withholding but necessarily speaking the Yes of the free act which corresponds to it, choosing that for which he is already chosen by the divine decision, and beside which he has no other choice, that is to say, faith. How can he have faith if not in this way? The divine decision is not made and cannot be made in him, in his spirit. It can only be repeated. For how can he destroy himself as the old man, posit himself as the new, and therefore free

---

^{EN7} to take or leave

1. *Faith and its Object*

himself for the true freedom in which he can believe? But, again, how can he have anything else in that way but the freedom to believe? Of himself he may have many other things, very many: "Lord, I believe; help thou mine unbelief." But not in that way. In that way he can have only the freedom to believe. And how can the fact that he believes be anything meaner or weaker or more doubtful than an absolute necessity, his most proper and inward necessity, to obey which is not something strange but self-evident? No other human action is self-evident. But the action of faith is the doing of the self-evident—just because it takes place in the free choice beside which man has no other choice, so that it is his genuinely free choice. The Holy Spirit is the power in which Jesus Christ the Son of God makes a man free, makes him genuinely free for this choice and therefore for faith. He is the power in which the object of faith is also its origin and basis, so that faith can know and confess itself only as His work and gift, as the human decision for this object, the human participation in it which he makes in his own free act but which he can only receive, which he can understand only as something which is received, which he can continually look for as something which is received again and which has to be confirmed in a new act. It is not that he is strong when he believes. But the One in whom he believes shows Himself to be strong over him when he believes—strong as the One who is raised again from the dead to awaken him first from the death of unbelief to the life of faith. Faith means to be awake on the basis of this awakening: to be awake to the strong One who awakens him and who alone can awaken him; to be awake to the necessity with which He does this, a necessity which excludes all pseudo-freedoms; to be awake to the self-evident nature of the arising which, on the part of man, will directly follow his awakening. Faith is at once the most wonderful and the simplest of things. In it a man opens his eyes and sees and accepts everything as it—objectively, really and ontologically—is. Faith is the simple discovery of the child which finds itself in the father's house and on the mother's lap. But this simple thing is also the mystery of faith because only in Jesus Christ is it true and actual that things are as man discovers them, and because man's own discovery can itself be an event only in the fact that man is again awakened by Him to see and accept everything as it is: that the night has passed and the day dawned; that there is peace between God and sinful man, revealed truth, full and present salvation. This simple thing, and this mystery, constitute the being of the Christian, his being by the One in whom he believes. [749]

We now come to a third and decisive thing. Indeed, in the narrower context in which we are now speaking, it can also be the final thing. This is that in the twofold relationship of faith to Jesus Christ, as faith is orientated and based on Him as its object, there takes place in it the constitution of the Christian subject. At a later stage we shall have to understand faith as the particular human action of this subject. And we do not forget that it becomes and is this subject only in this action: not on the basis of a creaturely character of this action as such, but in virtue of the fact that as it is orientated so it is also based on Jesus

§ 63. The Holy Spirit and Christian Faith

Christ. Yet it is also true, and we must say it expressly, that in this action there begins and takes place a new and particular being of man.

"But of him are ye in Christ Jesus" (1 Cor. 1^{30}). "For we are his workmanship (ποίημα), created (κτισθέντες) in Christ Jesus unto good works" (Eph. 2^{10}). "Blessed be the God and Father of our Lord Jesus Christ, which according to his abundant mercy hath begotten us again" (ἀναγεννήσας ἡμᾶς, 1 Pet. 1^3)—an expression which is expounded in 1^{23}: "not of corruptible seed, but of incorruptible, by the word of God, which liveth and abideth for ever." New being, new creation (Gal. 6^{15}, 2 Cor. 5^{17}), new birth—they are all predicates which are ascribed only to the Christian, and they are all too strong to be taken only as figurative expressions to describe the changed feelings and self-understanding of Christians. Christians do not lose their character as members of the race which God created good and which fell from Him. But in these predicates they are addressed as something other than those with whom in other respects they are still bound in the twofold solidarity of creatureliness and sin. We read in Ac. 11^{26} that they were first called Χριστιανοί^{EN8} in Syrian Antioch, a name of which we read in 1 Pet. 4^{16} that it pledged them to glorify God. That to be a bearer of this name involves a real change of the form of human existence seems to come out in Agrippa's ironical words to Paul as reported in Ac. 26^{28}: "Almost thou persuadest me to be made (ποιῆσαι) a Christian." It is not without theological significance that this name—that the fact that these folk are adherents of Christ—should have prevailed. And it is not only in Acts and the Pastoral Epistles that what distinguishes them as adherents is described by the term πιστοί^{EN9}. We find the same in 2 Cor. 6^{15}, where they are contrasted with the ἄπιστοι of their heathen environment, under whose yoke they are not to submit, with whom they can have no μετοχή^{EN10}, no κοινωνία^{EN11}, no συμφώνησις^{EN12}, no μερίς^{EN13}. Being themselves ἐκ πίστεως^{EN14}, they have a part in the blessing of πιστὸς Ἀβραάμ^{EN15} (Gal. 3^9). πιστός^{EN16} can be used either as a substantive or as an adjective. In 2 Cor. 6^{15} it is absolute. In Col. 1^1, Eph. 1^1, 1 Pet. 1^{21} and Ac. 16^{15} it is related to Christ or to the God who raised Him from the dead. In Col. 1^1 and Eph. 1^1 it is set in juxtaposition with the term ἅγιοι^{EN17}, clearly emphasising that which marks off subjectively those who are described in this way. That it is an abbreviation for πιστεύοντες^{EN18} or ὄντες ἐκ πίστεως^{EN19} is evident from Jn. 20^{27}: μὴ γίνου ἄπιστος, ἀλλὰ πιστός^{EN20}. The translation "faithful" seems unavoidable. If only it did not carry the suggestion of a psychological consistency which is not conveyed in the very least by πιστός^{EN21}! This does, of course, speak of a being of those who are described in this way, of the being of which they are participants as they are πιστεύοντες, but of the being of which they are real and objective participants in the fulfilment of this act and as the subjects of it. Just as the sinful man is what he does as such, so he is what he does when as a sinful man he is awakened to faith and can live by it.

EN 8 Christians
EN 9 believers
EN10 fellowship
EN11 partnership
EN12 agreement
EN13 part
EN14 from faith
EN15 faithful Abraham
EN16 faithful
EN17 saints
EN18 those who believe
EN19 those from faith
EN20 do not be unfaithful, but faithful
EN21 faithful

1. *Faith and its Object*

We recall that the creaturely subject constituted in the being and work of Jesus Christ is seriously and definitively the new man himself as he is brought into peace with God from his struggle against Him, and is therefore a partaker of the salvation allotted to him. It is the world as it is loved by God and reconciled by Him to Himself in Jesus Christ. The faith which has Jesus Christ for its object is therefore faith in this being and action of His for the world, for all men and for every man. And those who can believe in Him—in Paul's phrase, those who are of faith (of faith in Him)—are the first-fruits and representatives of the humanity and the world to which God has addressed Himself in Jesus Christ. It is their business to give to the God who has done this, to "the living God who is the Saviour of all men" (1 Tim. 4^{10}), the glory which the others do not give Him, and in so doing to attest to them that which they do not know although it avails for them. What Christians have in and for themselves in the sharply differentiated particularity of their being they have as the bearers and representatives of a specially qualified and emphasised solidarity with all other men.

That the living God of 1 Tim. 4^{10} is "specially" ($\mu\acute{\alpha}\lambda\iota\sigma\tau\alpha$ EN22) the Saviour of those that believe means that in the first instance—in His activity to and with them as the spearhead of the whole cosmos, concretely revealed to them and concretely known by them, demanding their concrete service—He is a Saviour for them.

We recollect further that the creaturely subject awakened in this special sense by God through the power of the Holy Spirit is the Christian community in the world: the "We" who pray the Lord's Prayer or simply cry "Abba, Father," the "You" who are reminded in the apostolic message of their origin and nature, the people drawn from both Jews and Gentiles which is, as such, the body whose Head is Jesus Christ, the people in which His truth is known in obedience, and acknowledged in humility and confessed in thankfulness, the people which lives and builds up itself to be a light shining in the world (Phil. 2^{15}) in reflection of His glory. This people as such is the provisional representation of the justification which has taken place in Jesus Christ. The faith which has Him as its object is as such faith in Him as the Creator and Lord of the fellowship of the saints. It is faith as it lives by and for and in and with this fellowship—the faith of this fellowship and as such the faith of individual Christians. Just as a man would not be a man in and for himself, in isolation from his fellow-men, so a Christian would not be a Christian in and for himself, separated from the fellowship of the saints. With his personal faith he is a member of this body of Christ. In the New Testament sense of the term this does not involve any deficiency in his own being and having in relation to that of the whole. It does not involve any limitation of his responsibility by that of the whole or of the others who are in this whole with him. It does not involve, therefore, any diminution of the freedom of his faith. As a member of this

[751]

EN22 those who believe

§ 63. The Holy Spirit and Christian Faith

body he is in direct touch with its Head. As he believes in and with the community—he does it as a whole, for it is only as a whole that he is a member—the whole with its gift and commission is his whole, and he believes with a royal freedom. What it does involve is that he can believe only in and with the community, only in the sphere and context of it, only in the limitation and determination set by its basis and goal. The royal freedom of his faith is the freedom to stand in it as a brother or a sister, to stand with other brothers and sisters in the possession granted to it and the service laid upon it. If faith is outside the Church it is outside the world, and therefore a-Christian. It does not have as its object "the Saviour of all men, and specially of them that believe."

But when all that is said and considered, we have to add at once that the creaturely subject constituted in the being and work of Jesus Christ and awakened as such by the power of the Holy Spirit is in the last resort the individual Christian in the act of his personal faith. The humanity and world loved by God, fallen from Him and reconciled by Him to Himself, lives in individual men and their particular creatureliness and sin. And the community founded and preserved and ruled by Jesus Christ in the world lives in individual Christians and the multifarious but unitary activity of their faith. There are no saints without the fellowship, but there is no fellowship without the saints. If there is no Christian I and Thou and He outside the twofold, Christ-centred circle of the We and You and They of the race and the community, then the general no less than the particular is an abstraction, not to say an illusion, since it does not become event in the Christian I and Thou and He, in the personal faith of the members of the body of Christ. It is of this event that we must now speak.

As a human act it consists in a definite acknowledgment, recognition and confession. As this human act it has no creative but only a cognitive character. It does not alter anything. As a human act it is simply the confirmation of a change which has already taken place, the change in the whole human situation which took place in the death of Jesus Christ and was revealed in His resurrection and attested by the Christian community. But it obviously belongs to the alteration of the human situation which Christian faith can only confirm, that it does find this confirmation, that there are men who do recognise and acknowledge and confess it, who can be the witnesses of it—in other words, that there are individual Christian subjects. It is not their faithfulness which makes them this (not even when it is understood as the act of their believing). That would simply mean that they could do it and have done it of themselves. By their faithfulness (as the doers of this act of believing) they simply confirm without knowing it—and it is to be hoped without boasting about it—that they are the subjects who in some astonishing way are capable of and willing and ready for this act and therefore for this acknowledgment, recognition and confession. How has this happened? How do they come to be qualified to do this? They obviously cannot be, and will not be, as the sinful men they are like all other men. If they are all the same, since the faith and therefore the acknowledgment, recognition and confession are their act, it is

1. Faith and its Object

evident that the event of their faith (while it has no creative aspect as their act) is more than cognitive in character. From the point of view of the presupposition at work in their act, from the point of view of the men as its doers, it is clearly the positing of a new being, the occurrence of a new creation, a new birth of these men. In their act these sinful men confirm that they are the witnesses of the alteration of the human situation which has taken place in Jesus Christ: not the men who are altered in it—for as such they cannot so far be seen—but certainly, and this is the astonishing thing—as those for whom it has happened and not not happened, as the witnesses of it. It belongs to the alteration of the human situation as it has taken place in Jesus Christ that it now has at least the confirmation of its witness in certain human subjects. Not because they believe, not in the power in which they do believe, but as they do actually believe (in strength or weakness), as they do it and are in a position to do it, they become and are Christians in the midst of all other men—men with this particular characteristic as men. To this extent we cannot deny to the event of their faith a certain creative character.

But how does it acquire this character, which it can have only on the presupposition of what man himself does in it, but which on this presupposition it cannot derive from sinful man? It is here that we must obviously try to think seriously of the object of faith and therefore of Jesus Christ as its starting-point. Christian faith is both orientated and based on Him. The believer is enclosed by Him both before and behind: he is encircled by Him. He owes it to Him that he can believe at all, and that he does believe. He believes as one who is confronted and apprehended by Him (Phil. 3^{12}), as the one in face of whom He is the stronger and has proved Himself to be the stronger. In face of him He is the stronger in virtue of what He has done for all men and therefore for him in His death, and of the fact that God has manifested Him for all men and therefore for him as the One who has done this in His resurrection from the dead. And in face of him He proves Himself to be the stronger by the irresistible awakening power of His Holy Spirit. In this strength and in this proof He calls him to faith. And in so doing He creates the presupposition on the basis of which the sinful man can and actually does believe. He introduces him as a new subject which is capable of and willing and ready for this act, as a witness of His act and revelation, as a Christian. Because the faith of this sinful man is directed on Him and effected by Him, the event of his faith is not merely cognitive as a human act but it is also creative in character. The new being effective and revealed in it, the new creation, the new birth—they are all the mystery of the One in whom he believes and whom he can acknowledge and recognise and confess in faith. When it is this One who closes the circle around him, a man can and must do that which he does in faith.

It remains to ask how we have to think of this closing of the circle and therefore of the creative mystery of the Christian existence. On the one hand we are dealing with the being and action of Jesus Christ, on the other with the particular, the most particular, fact of the existence of the individual man. For this

[753]

§ 63. *The Holy Spirit and Christian Faith*

reason we have to seek our answer in the form of the being and action of Jesus Christ in which it encloses within itself His being and action in a special relationship between Him and this particular man. His being and action has this form. He confronts all men. He confronts His community. But in so doing He also confronts the individual as such. He confronts thee and me, this one and that one. His act and revelation took place for the world and the fellowship of the saints, but they also took place for thee and for me, for this one and that one. As the Mediator, the Saviour and the Lord, He lives not only in the outer but also in this inner circle, and therefore as thy Mediator, Saviour and Lord, and mine. "Jesus lives"—and I with Him—which means that from all eternity God has thought of me, elected me, acted for me in Him, called me to Himself in Him as His Word. This is—in general terms—the form of His being and activity in which He Himself is the mystery in the event of faith, in which He gives to this event a creative as well as a cognitive character. For when I, as the sinful man I still am, recognise and acknowledge and confess Him in this way, taking my place in the Christian community, this means that I also am reached and found and seized by Him—by His being and activity, and therefore that I discover and confirm myself as the subject also intended and envisaged in His being and activity, as a man whom His existence as the Saviour of the world and the Head of His community also concerns, who is also bound and committed to Him as the Saviour and Head. If I discover myself as this subject, what can I do but confirm myself as such? What can I do, therefore, but that which is proper to this subject as a member of the world reconciled and the community founded by Him, that is to say, believe?

[754] But in saying "also" we have said too little and not been sufficiently clear. When a man can and must believe, it is not merely a matter of an "also," of his attachment as an individual to the general being and activity of the race and the community as determined by Jesus Christ. In all the common life of that outer and inner circle he is still himself. He is uniquely this man and no other. He cannot be repeated or represented. He is incomparable. He is this in his relationship with God and also in his relationship with his fellows. He is this soul of this body, existing in the span of this time of his. He is this sinful man with his own particular pride and in his own special case. For all his common life he is alone in this particularity. It is not simply that he also can and must believe, but that just he can and must believe. And if the being and activity of Jesus Christ Himself is the mystery of the event in which he actually does so, then we must put it even more strongly and precisely: that in this event it takes place that Jesus Christ lives not only "also" but "just" as his Mediator and Saviour and Lord, and that He shows Himself just to him as this living One. He became a servant just for him. It was just his place that He took, the place which is not the place of any other. In this place He died just for him, for his sin. And, again, in his place He was raised again from the dead. Therefore the Yes which God the Father spoke to Him as His Son in the resurrection is spoken not only also but just to him, this man. In Him it was just his pride, his

1. Faith and its Object

fall which was overcome. In Him it is just his new right which has been set up, his new life which has appeared. And in Him it is just he who is called to new responsibility, who is newly claimed. It is just he who is not forgotten by Him, not passed over, not allowed to fall, not set aside or abandoned. It is just he— and this is the work of the Holy Spirit—who has been sought out, and reached, and found by Him, just he whom He has associated with Himself and Himself with him. God did not will to be God without being just his God. Jesus did not will to be Jesus without being just his Jesus. The world was not to be reconciled with God without just this man as an isolated individual being a man—this man—reconciled with God. The community was not to be the living body of Christ without just this man being a living member of it. The whole occurrence of salvation was not to take place but just for him, as the judgment executed just on him, the grace addressed in this judgment just to him, just his justification, just his conversion to God. The gift and commission of the community of Jesus Christ is personally just his gift and commission. And all this not merely incidentally, among other things, or only in part for him, but altogether, in its whole length and breadth and height and depth just for him, because Jesus Christ, in whom all this is given to the world and the community, in whom God Himself has sacrificed Himself for it, is Jesus, the Christ, just for him. That this shines out in a sinful man is the mystery, the creative fact, in the event of faith in which he becomes and is a Christian, so that he can and must acknowledge and recognise and confess as such what is proper to him as this subject. [755]

What do I acknowledge and recognise and confess as this subject? That Jesus Christ Himself is *pro me*[EN23], just for me. But it is not the first thing to acknowledge and recognise and confess this. The first thing is that Jesus Christ is, in fact, just for me, that I myself am just the subject for whom He is. That is the point. That is the newness of being, the new creation, the new birth of the Christian. Everything else follows from this, especially the fact that, whatever may be the force of the basis and validity of the *pro me*[EN24], it can never be a *pro me*[EN25] in the abstract, but includes in itself and is enclosed by the communal *pro nobis*[EN26] and the even wider *propter nos homines*[EN27]. We can and should give it all its own weight as *pro me*[EN28]. It carries the *pro nobis*[EN29] and the *propter nos homines*[EN30], just as it is carried by them. There is no *pro nobis*[EN31] or *propter nos homines*[EN32] which does not include in itself and is not enclosed by the *pro*

[EN23] for me
[EN24] for me
[EN25] for me
[EN26] for us
[EN27] for us men
[EN28] for me
[EN29] for us
[EN30] for us men
[EN31] for us
[EN32] for us men

§ 63. The Holy Spirit and Christian Faith

me^{EN33}. In its connexion, its unity with this, it has its own dignity and truth and actuality, which, if it is not greater, is certainly not less—the dignity, truth and actuality which is proper to the individual Christian subject, just to me and to thee, to this one and that one, who are believers in Jesus Christ.

In saying this we have made the statement or statements which bring us to the high-water mark of our serious agreement with one line of Luther's thinking, with that of Pietism old and new, with that of Kierkegaard, with that of a theology like W. Herrmann's, and with that of the theological existentialism of our own day (so far as it can be seriously regarded as theological). In this respect they all were and are right: that the question of the individual Christian subject has to be put, and that it has to be answered with the *pro me*^{EN34} of faith. Without the *pro me*^{EN35} of the individual Christian there is no legitimate *pro nobis*^{EN36} of the faith of the Christian community and no legitimate *propter nos homines* of its representative faith for the non-believing world. The being and activity of Jesus Christ has essentially and necessarily the form in which He addresses Himself, not only also, but just to the individual man, to thee and to me, to this man and that man, in which He makes common cause with the individual in his very isolation, in which His Holy Spirit speaks just to his spirit.

It has been an unfortunate necessity in recent years to criticise the I-hymns which came into our hymn-books with the transition from the 16th to the 17th century (cf. *C.D.* I, 2, 252 f.), and the I-piety which underlies them. Such criticism is a counterblast to the general subjectivist trend of modern Protestantism, and in face of this aberration it will constantly have to be made. But as is obvious from the presence of the I-Psalms in the Bible, it can only be a relative and not an absolute criticism. It cannot try to eliminate or suppress altogether either the I-hymns or I-piety. It must be content with a limited objective. Not only is it impossible to reject as such the glance at the *pro me*^{EN37}, but this glance is actually necessary and commanded in connexion and unity with what the Christian faith is beyond this. It acts as a kind of catalysator in which every *pro nobis*^{EN38} and beyond that every *propter pro homines*^{EN39} has to show whether those who confess it are competent subjects, or whether what they seem to confess is only an abstract theory which cannot have in their mouth the power of witness but only the nature of myth. But there is more to it than that. *Credo*^{EN40} as a baptismal confession is said in the first person singular, and it is not accidental that in this form it is the confession of the Christian Church and is made representatively for the unbelieving world and as proclamation to it. When the community says *credo*^{EN41}, then in its members on the one hand and proleptically with men of the world on the other, it gathers itself into a single person, just as Jesus Christ its Head is an individual who represents many individuals and unites them with Himself, and according to the biblical view Adam was also a representative individual and the prototype of Jesus Christ (Rom. 5^{14}). In the light of this we cannot deny, but are forced to maintain, that each individual as such—not in identity with Adam or even with Jesus Christ, but in analogy with Adam by virtue of his creatureliness, and with Jesus Christ by virtue of his justification—stands in the place of many, of all, uniting and representing in himself as this man the whole race, and in himself as this Christian the community. In

---

^{EN33} for me
^{EN34} for me
^{EN35} for me
^{EN36} for us
^{EN37} for me
^{EN38} for us
^{EN39} for us men
^{EN40} I believe
^{EN41} 'I believe'

1. *Faith and its Object*

his existence as an individual he is not a particle or a sample or a specimen. He is the one who is and has and does and signifies the whole and everything. He is the one who is responsible for all and everything. His life in all the narrowness of its limits is the theatre of the whole action of loss and salvation. In all its pettiness it is the object of the whole judgment and grace of God. From and to all eternity the eye of God is wholly directed upon it and His almighty hand wholly occupied with it. In all the work of God, in what God does and says as Creator, Reconciler and Redeemer, he is not merely envisaged in general, or together with others. He is not only also but just the object of God's love and wrath and mercy. He is not only also but just the temple of His Holy Spirit. What God does is all of it done just for him, just for thee and me. What God wills is all expected just of him, just of thee and me. Is there any I-hymn which can express this strongly enough? Is not the confession of faith itself necessarily the strongest I-hymn of all? For what would faith be if it were not the event in which it suddenly flashes on a man that everything that God does and wills is with reference to him, that it is therefore *pro me*[EN42]?

But having said that, we have to point out at once what must never happen in this respect. The *pro me*[EN43] must never be systematised and itself made a systematic principle and applied as such. Its nerve and meaning is in the fact that Jesus Christ is *pro me*[EN44]. Therefore the I-hymn can be composed and sung and sounded forth legitimately only as a hymn to Christ. This is what Zinzendorf perceived in contrast to the Pietism of his day, and this is what he taught and practised in his own baroque but not incorrect fashion. What has to be seen and understood and said—this is the canon of the criticism we have to make—is what Jesus Christ is just for thee and me, for the individual as such, and what Jesus Christ expects just of him.

When this is observed, the *pro nobis* and the even more comprehensive *propter nos homines*[EN45] will not be submerged and disappear in the *pro me*[EN46], but in and with the *pro me*[EN47] they will necessarily be given the same degree of honour. The existence of the community and its gift and mission, the existence of the world and the salvation of God allotted and addressed to it, cannot then be mere (if possible facultative) consequences of the Christian existence of the individual, mere peripheral phenomena and incidental determinations of his personal salvation. In and with the *pro me*[EN48], Jesus Christ the Lord of the community and the Saviour of the world will assert Himself as the subject of the *pro me*[EN49]. Only in the light of its object can the faith in which the individual becomes aware and certain of his own justification be the faith of the community and a faith which is open and addressed to the world. It will therefore be prevented from becoming a morose or humdrum or sentimental or Bohemian private enterprise. In this light, in the light of its object, it will always be enclosed by, as it encloses, that twofold We-faith. In it it will have its catalysator, as it is itself its catalysator. It will necessarily be preserved from the subtle egoism which would be proper to it as an abstract I-faith. But only in the light of its object! In the words of M. Gerhardt: "In me and in my living, / Is nothing on this earth, / What Christ to me hath given, / Of love alone is worth."

[EN42] for me
[EN43] for me
[EN44] for me
[EN45] for us men
[EN46] for me
[EN47] for me
[EN48] for me
[EN49] for me

§ 63. The Holy Spirit and Christian Faith

Again, it cannot happen that the *pro me*[EN50], the relationship of the activity and will of God to the individual, is made as such the basis and measure of all things, as though at bottom we were dealing with the relationship of the individual to the activity and will of God, as though the value, truth and actuality of God were to be found only in what thou and I, the individual sees to be of value, truth and actuality for him, only in what he acknowledges and confesses to be "existentially" relevant to him. In respect of what can be *pro me*[EN51], of what can be "existentially" relevant, we have to refrain from interpreting it in the light of any kind of anthropology or ontology or pre-understanding, into the framework of which the God who is *pro me*[EN52] in Jesus Christ can be fitted and to the measure of which He can be cut as in a bed of Procrustes. Jesus Christ will be to the man who believes in Him something more, something other, than an obscure point of contact, or a mere exponent or cipher of his I-faith. He will be allowed to proclaim Himself as the One He is as the object and origin of his I-faith. And it will be left to Him to decide the fact and extent that He is *pro me*[EN53], that He is existentially relevant to thee and to me. Every anthropology and ontology will have its norm and law in Him, not *vice versa*[EN54]. The usurping invasion of theology by a subjectivist philosophy—and it was no accident that this coincided with the rise of Pietism—will then be checked, although, of course, there will be a true appraisal of the problem of the individual Christian subject. It will be acknowledged that Christian faith is an "existential" happening, that it is from first to last I-faith, which can and should be sung in I-hymns. But there will take place the necessary "de-mythologisation" of the "I" which Paul carried through in Gal. 2[20]: "I live, yet not I, but Christ liveth in me."

We remember all this only in passing. The genuine "interests" of Christian individualism will be asserted when we learn to jerk ourselves free—and do, in fact, jerk ourselves free—from the abstractions which have been so kindly received in modern Protestantism.

2. THE ACT OF FAITH

We have now said and considered what we had to say concerning the object of faith, its origin, and finally and above all the basis of the Christian subject, and therefore the coming into being and the being of the Christian. In what follows we must always keep this in mind as the presupposition, but we must turn no less resolutely to the other aspect of the problem. Christian faith is a free human act.

From this particular standpoint it is *the* act of the Christian life. Of course, the same may be said of love and hope as well as faith. But in line with our first main consideration and attempted understanding of reconciliation, the being and work of Jesus Christ as the Lord who became a servant for us (§ 59), its counterpart in human sin in the form of pride (§ 60), the justification of sinful man in Him (§ 61), and the gathering and foundation of the Christian community by Him (§ 62), this act of the Christian life has the form of faith. Like

---

[EN50] for me
[EN51] for me
[EN52] for me
[EN53] for me
[EN54] the other way around

2. The Act of Faith

love and hope from other aspects, faith is *the* act of the Christian life to the extent that in all the activity and individual acts of a man it is the most inward and central and decisive act of his heart, the one which—if it takes place—characterises them all as Christian, as expressions and confirmations of his Christian freedom, his Christian responsibility, his Christian obedience. On whether or not this act takes place depends whether these acts are rightly done from the Christian standpoint. If a man does them in faith, if in doing them he first performs the basic act of faith, then he does them as a Christian, he does them rightly from the Christian standpoint. As against that (Rom. 14^{23}), whatsoever is not of faith, is not done of and in this basic act of faith, is sin. By what we have called in the title the act of faith we mean the basic Christian act which, when it takes place, is *the* act of the Christian life, the Christian act which embraces and controls all individual acts and activities, permeating and determining them like the leaven of Mt. 13^{33}. We must now describe faith as this act.

[758]

We will try to do this by developing it under three mutually related terms. It is an acknowledgment, a recognition and a confession. As all these terms indicate, it is a knowledge.* And as the object and basis is the same in every case, so in every case it is an active knowledge. Why a knowledge? As we have seen, underlying it there is the presupposition of a creative event—the being and activity of Jesus Christ in the power of His Holy Spirit awakening man to faith. As the event of a human act on this basis, faith is a cognitive event, the simple taking cognisance of the preceding being and work of Jesus Christ. But we are not dealing with an automatic reflection, with a stone lit up by the sun, or wood kindled by a fire, or a leaf blown by the wind. We are dealing with man. It is, therefore, a spontaneous, a free, an active event. This active aspect is expressed in the three terms: acknowledgment, recognition and confession.

Christian faith is an acknowledgment. In our description of that taking cognisance this must come first. It might be objected that acknowledgment includes and presupposes recognition, so that the latter ought to be treated first. This may be true enough in other cases, but when it is the taking cognisance of Christian faith the reverse is true. The recognition is certainly included in the acknowledgment, but it can only follow it. Acknowledging is a taking cognisance which is obedient and compliant, which yields and subordinates itself. This obedience and compliance is not an incidental and subsequent characteristic of the act of faith, but primary, basic and decisive. It is not preceded by any other kind of knowledge, either recognition or confession. The recognition and confession of faith are included in and follow from the fact that they are originally and properly an acknowledgment, the free act of obedience.

---

* In the German the three terms are *Anerkennen*, *Erkennen* and *Bekennen*: three different forms of *Kennen*.—Trans.

§ 63. *The Holy Spirit and Christian Faith*

In the older dogmatics the classical definition of faith was that it takes place in the three acts of *notitia, assensus*^EN55 and *fiducia*^EN56. This seems evident enough, for cognisance of a thing implies a prior acquaintance. But what does *notitia*^EN57 mean in this case? Calvin makes this his starting point and he fills it out at once and quite correctly in this way: faith is the *notitia divinae erga nos voluntatis ex eius verbo percepta*^EN58 (*Instit.* III, 2, 6). But how can there be an acquaintance with the will of God for us taken from His word except in that act of acknowledgment and therefore of obedience and compliance? Calvin's more precise definition of faith (*l.c.* 2, 7) is that it is the *divinae erga nos benevolentiae firma certaque cognitio*^EN59. But concerning the term *cognitio*^EN60 or *intelligentia*^EN61 Calvin had already remarked at the beginning of his work (I, 6, 2) that it is basically present only *ubi reverenter amplectimur, quod de se testari Deus voluit. Neque enim perfecta solum, vel numeris suis completa fides, sed omnis recta Dei cognitio ab oboedientia nascitur*^EN62. For this reason Paul described it as the task of his apostolate to call to the ὑπακοή^EN63 (Rom. 1⁵) or the λειτουργία τῆς πίστεως^EN64 (Phil. 2¹⁷). If we were to use the terminology of the older dogmatics, we should have to speak first of *assensus*^EN65 and only then of *notitia*^EN66—although this would have sounded very strange to its authors with their concern for formal logic. The only thing is that acknowledgment is much more than *assensus*^EN67 and recognition than *notitia*^EN68.

In our exposition of this basic acknowledgment, we will start with the fact that the calling of sinful man to faith in Jesus Christ is identical with his calling to the community of Jesus Christ built on the foundation of the apostles and prophets, the community which is His body, the earthly-historical form of His existence. On the level of an earthly-historical event—of which we are now speaking—his encounter with this object of his faith will therefore be in some form his encounter with the Christian community, a direct or indirect encounter with its ministry or proclamation or one of its activities. And what he will experience in this encounter if he comes to faith will be this, that the relative authority and freedom in which the Christian community exists in the world and in which he experiences its existence will confront him, not in some kind of non-obligatory way, but with such compulsion that he must not only accept and respect it but submit to its law and desire to associate himself with it and join it. Why? Not because of what the community is and represents and does in the world and as a worldly phenomenon. It always was and is the more than doubtful Christians who are impressed by the phenomenon of the Church as

---

EN55 knowledge, assent
EN56 trust
EN57 knowledge
EN58 knowledge of God's will towards us, perceived from his word
EN59 sure and certain knowledge of God's goodness to us
EN60 knowledge
EN61 understanding
EN62 where we embrace reverently that which God wills to declare about himself. For it is not only a perfect and complete faith, but all true knowledge of God which is born from obedience
EN63 obedience
EN64 service of faith
EN65 assent
EN66 knowledge
EN67 assent
EN68 knowledge

2. *The Act of Faith*

such and won by it to submit to it and join it. And woe to the Church which loves and is out to try to impress men as such! For what has this kind of impressing to do with Christian faith and its acknowledging, or even with an introduction to it? If a man comes to Christian faith, this means that in the encounter with the community of Jesus Christ he encounters Jesus Christ Himself, that in its relative authority and freedom he encounters His absolute authority and freedom, the law to which the community itself is subject, and therefore a law which is superior to him and binds him. If he comes to faith, then this means that through its ministry and proclamation he does not submit to it but to its law and therefore to the Lord Jesus Christ Himself, and that in so doing he will necessarily desire to associate with it and join it. It is not the Church which has won him for itself, but—by the ministry and proclamation of the Church—Jesus Christ has won him for Himself, bringing him to the [760] point where he can freely acknowledge Him (and with Him the community which represents Him), where he can show himself obedient and compliant to Him (and therefore to it), where he can put to Him (and therefore to himself and the community) the question of Ac. 8^{36}: "What doth hinder me to be baptised?"

Acknowledgment as the basic moment in the act of Christian faith has reference to Jesus Christ Himself—presupposing, of course, the mediatorial ministry of the Christian community which is His body and the consequence of an active acknowledgment of its existence and the desire to be a member of it. It has reference to the fact which the community represents in the world, to the person by whom it is constituted and who is its living law.

At this point we must clear away certain misunderstandings. The active acknowledgment of Christian faith, in which recognition and confession are included and from which they result, does not have reference to any doctrine, theory or theology represented by or in the community. It does not have reference to any creed or dogma formulated and championed by the community, not even the most ancient and universal. Even less does it have reference to the dogmatics which gathers together and expounds that dogma, not even the most churchly of dogmatics. Nor does it have reference—as the Reformers so sharply emphasised—to the histories of the Old and the New Testaments, to the prophetic and apostolic theology as such on whose witness the proclamation of the community is founded. At its root as this acknowledgment Christian faith is not the subservient acceptance of any reports or propositions, irrespective of whether they are biblical or churchly or modern. At this root it is indeed an obedient acceptance. But the object of it is the One whom the Bible attests and the Church as taught by the Bible proclaims, the living Jesus Christ Himself, none other. He is the Lord. He is sovereign. He is the Master, who cannot be replaced by the prophets and apostles with their word about Him, whom they only desire to serve with their word, who cannot be replaced by the Church with its word of proclamation, whom it, too, can only desire to serve. It is Jesus Christ who is acknowledged by Christian faith. Of course—we

§ 63. The Holy Spirit and Christian Faith

will return to this in a moment—not Jesus Christ as portrayed according to the measure and capacity of imagination, metaphysics or history, but as attested by Holy Scripture and proclaimed by the community. Yet Jesus Christ Himself, not a biblical text which attests Him or a biblical or churchly thesis which proclaims Him. That "Jesus Christ is my Lord" (Luther) is what Christian faith maintains when in this acknowledgment it begins to accept "this" as true. It does so in obedience to the Bible's witness to it and in indebtedness to the Church's proclamation of it. But in so far as this act is a basic acknowledging it accepts only "this" as true. And "this" is more than a "this." It is superior to every "this." It is the basis and fulfilment of every "this." It is He Himself, the living Jesus Christ, the Head of the Church, the Lord of Scripture. It is most important to maintain this expressly and in face of all false orthodoxy because this is the point which decides whether we will understand faith rightly: that it is the work of human insight, resolve and action; but that as this human work it is real Christian faith only directly in the encounter with its object, only as the gift of the Holy Spirit of Jesus Christ Himself, only as the work of the obedience which is pledged to Him and the freedom which is given by Him. This truth is either denied or hopelessly obscured in a conception of faith which involves as its basic act the acceptance of certain statements which attest and proclaim Him, which does not, therefore, consist in simple obedience to Himself.

> Are we in agreement at this point with W. Herrmann and our contemporary R. Bultmann? In the result it might appear so, but perhaps only in relation to the negative element in this result, our opposition to a false orthodoxy, our refusal to ground the act of faith in the acceptance of the texts of the Bible or the propositions of the Church. If only there were an obvious unity on the positive element, that the living Lord Jesus Christ attested by the Bible and proclaimed by the Church is the One who must be accepted and acknowledged at the basis of the act of faith, and therefore that the negation must be made only on this ground (and not on the ground merely of certain ethico-anthropological propositions)! To the extent that this is not clear, and so long as it is not clear, it is better to leave open the question of this agreement. For it is much to be feared that in what we are now going to say we shall have the support neither of Herrmann nor of Bultmann.

Christian faith is a recognition. That is how we have to continue. This statement can only be secondary. Recognition is not of itself and as such the basic act of faith, which consists in that obedient and compliant taking cognisance. Faith is a recognition only to the extent that a recognition is included in that obedient and compliant taking cognisance. When we say this, we say that it is only the statement which is secondary. For that which proceeds from the acknowledgment as a second thing is already included in it as the first. If we may, and must, understand and formulate positively the definition given by Calvin—"All true knowledge of God (*omnis recta Dei cognitio*) is born of obedience"—then as the basic act of faith this obedience is not an obedience without knowledge, a blind obedience without insight or understanding, an obedience which is rendered only as an emotion or an act of will. How could a

2. *The Act of Faith*

recognition proceed from it or in any way follow it if it were not already contained in this first thing as a second?

It was Calvin again who, at the beginning of his great tractate on faith (*Instit.* III, 2, 2) hastened to rebut as sharply as he could the scholastic conception of a *fides implicita*^{EN69}, a readiness to subject reason to the teaching of the Church. This was a *commentum*^{EN70} which would not merely bury true faith but completely destroy it. *Non in ignorantia, sed in cognitione sita est fides*^{EN71}: and not in a bare knowledge of God, but in the knowledge of His concrete and revealed will with us. How can we lay hold of our salvation in faith if it is not an *explicita divinae bonitatis agnitio, in qua consistit nostra iustitia*^{EN72}: the knowledge that God is our gracious Father in the atonement made by Christ? [762]

But there is a recognition in the basic act of that obedience, of that acknowledgment (we must now continue) because the living Jesus Christ who is the object of that acknowledgment, to whom man subjects himself in the obedience of faith, is Himself not without form, but is the Jesus Christ attested in Holy Scripture and proclaimed by the community. In faith we have to do with Him and only with Him, but with Him as attested by Scripture and proclaimed by the community. But when as the One who is attested by Scripture and proclaimed by the community He encounters man and calls him to faith, and presents Himself to him as his Lord, He does not do so in a featureless way which is at the mercy of every possible conception and interpretation, but He does so as a genuine object with a very definite form which cannot be exchanged or mistaken for any other form, which is determined by His own being and His own revelation of His being, which is His authentic form. It is in this authentic form that from the very first, with the very first step, He becomes to everyone who comes to faith, and is obedient to Him, the object of his recognition. By what particular features of this form, to what extent, and with what distinctness or indistinctness, He is first recognised is a secondary question—that of the subjective fulfilment of the knowledge of Jesus Christ proffered to him. What is decisive is the objective truth that in and with the fact that he is called by Him to the obedience of faith he is given ground and cause to recognise Him in His authentic form, and therefore rightly. He would not obey Him if at the same time he did not begin in some way to see and understand Him, if of his obedience there were not born in outline a *recta cognitio*^{EN73}. Not any *cognitio*^{EN74}, but in outline, in what is at first a very primitive and rudimentary and even at best a very imperfect form, a *recta cognitio*^{EN75}. It is a right recognition in so far as it is in the form determined by His own being and His own revelation of His being that He encounters man in

---

^{EN69} implicit faith
^{EN70} falsehood
^{EN71} faith is located not in ignorance, but in knowledge
^{EN72} explicit acknowledgement of God's goodness, in which our righteousness consists
^{EN73} true knowledge
^{EN74} knowledge
^{EN75} true knowledge

§ 63. *The Holy Spirit and Christian Faith*

the witness of Scripture and the proclamation of the community; in so far, therefore, as the subjective fulfilment of the knowledge objectively proffered to man is limited and controlled by the fact that it always takes place in the sphere of Holy Scripture which attests Him and the community which proclaims Him in obedience to Scripture.

This sphere is a wide one, which leaves open to the believer many and different possibilities of seeing and understanding Jesus Christ and therefore of the subjective fulfilment of the right knowledge proffered to him.

> We have considered the general definition of Calvin, that it is a matter of the recognition: *Deum nobis esse propitium patrem, reconciliatione per Christum facta*^{EN76}. This is the very compressed insight of Calvin. It is not indefinite but very definite because it has obviously arisen and been formed in this sphere. Against it we may set the rather more express statement which Luther offered as his knowledge of Jesus Christ in the passage of the Catechism already mentioned. The decisive (and of itself very explicit) declaration is: "I believe, that Jesus Christ ... is my Lord." But obviously he could not and would not make this in the void, so he added to the name of Jesus Christ: "very God, eternally begotten of the Father, and very man, born of the Virgin Mary," and to the words "my Lord": "who has redeemed and purchased and loosed me, lost and sinful man, from all sin, from death and from the power of the devil, not with gold or silver, but with His own sacred and precious blood, with His innocent death and passion, that I may be His, and live under Him in His kingdom, and serve Him in eternal righteousness, innocence and felicity, as He is raised from the dead, and lives and reigns to all eternity." This is a more developed, but again a particular and selective, description of the knowledge of the One who is acknowledged as Lord. It is Luther's own description, but it is not for that reason arbitrary or strange or indefinite. It is obviously made in the sphere of Scripture and the community and to that extent it is most definite. The description in the well-known answer to the first question of the *Heidelberg Catechism* takes a different turn, but again it has this in common with those of Luther and Calvin, that it is made in that sphere, and with the responsibility which that involves, so that for all its peculiarity it is both definite and in order—as *recta cognitio*^{EN77}.

The recognition of Christian faith can and should be varied. The reason for this is as follows. Although its object, the Jesus Christ attested in Scripture and proclaimed by the community, is single, unitary, consistent and free from contradiction, yet for all His singularity and unity His form is inexhaustibly rich, so that it is not merely legitimate but obligatory that believers should continually see and understand it in new lights and aspects. For He Himself does not present Himself to them in one form but in many—indeed, He is not in Himself uniform but multiform. How can it be otherwise when He is the true Son of the God who is eternally rich? Of course, all knowledge of Jesus Christ will have not merely its basis but its limit and standard in the witness of Scripture and the proclamation of the Church. It is possible only within this definite sphere. It is only in this sphere that Jesus Christ has a form for us men, that He can therefore be an object of our knowledge and known by us. Again, it is a wide sphere with many possibilities. But in correspondence with the unique-

---

^{EN76} that with reconciliation accomplished through Christ, God our Father is favourable to us
^{EN77} true knowledge

2. *The Act of Faith*

ness and unity of Jesus Christ Himself it is a sphere with limits, and these limits are always the criterion in the question whether what we regard as the knowledge of faith in Jesus Christ is true knowledge, whether indeed it can be seriously called knowledge or not. Outside this sphere, Jesus Christ has no form for us; He is not an object of our knowledge and He cannot be known by us. The believer whom He has definitely encountered in this sphere and not elsewhere will not even try to seek Him outside this sphere. If he did, both Jesus Christ and his faith would dissolve into nothingness. The problem of the knowledge of faith in Jesus Christ is, therefore, absolutely tied up with the existence of this sphere, as is the answering of the problem with respect for this sphere. [764] This knowledge is nourished by the witness of Scripture and its exposition and application in the proclamation of the community. It cannot refuse to accept this as its norm, and to be criticised and corrected by it as it listens to the exposition and application of it in the fellowship of the saints.

Here in the question of the knowledge of faith is the place where the biblical texts, and in their subordinate place the propositions and confession and dogma of the Church, and in their proper degree and dignity the teaching and theory and theology advocated by and in the community, all have their own functions. If to believe means *eo ipso*[EN78] to associate and attach oneself to the community, then the knowledge of faith necessarily consists in the fact that a man enrols and continues in the school in which the community has always found and from which it can never remove itself, that of the witness of Scripture, in which he cannot help but learn with the community and therefore listen as well to the voice and word of the community. In the measure that it takes place in this context, the knowledge of faith is genuine knowledge—and the question of its range and form and particular direction, although it is serious, is only secondary. What matters is that it is a knowledge which is qualified by the context in which alone it can take place. And since we all have to have this qualification, it may well be that those who are first in respect of the range and form and particular direction of their knowledge of faith are really the last, and that those who seem to be insignificant and uninteresting are really the first. It is a matter of recognising in this context the Lord whom we acknowledge. We must all see to it that in our recognition we accept our particular responsibility to Him. As He is the object and origin of faith in general, He is also of the recognition of faith. And He is the ultimate Judge who they are that truly recognise Him when they acknowledge Him.

But we have not yet explained what we really mean by recognition. We must not allow ourselves to be persuaded by any anti-intellectualism that there is not a definite element of knowing—of which the existence of this sphere of Scripture and the Church is the basis and limit and norm. If we believe, then (whatever may be the range and form and particular direction) we know in whom we believe. There may be many things which as believers in Him we should and

---

[EN78] by definition

§ 63. *The Holy Spirit and Christian Faith*

could know (and perhaps need to know), but we are never complete ignoramuses, who cannot distinguish and think and speak. If we do not know, we do not recognise, and if we do not recognise, it will be a poor look-out for the basis of our faith, the primary acknowledgment and obedience in which faith in Jesus Christ has its root. At bottom, we shall not believe at all. Of course, faith and its knowing will always be an initial faith and knowing. But without an initial knowing there can be no initial faith, for faith takes place only in that sphere of Scripture and the community in which Jesus Christ has a form and is an object of knowledge and can be known, in which, therefore, everyone in his own measure can know something concerning Him. Not outside this sphere, not outside faith and recognition, but in this sphere, in faith and its recognition, everyone can know something, everyone can know what he needs to know. We can even dare to say that every Christian—in however primitive and rudimentary a way—can and must be a theologian, and that no matter how primitive and rudimentary he can and must be a good theologian, having a true vision of the One in whom he believes, having true thoughts concerning Him and finding the right words to express those thoughts. Of course, if what he feels and wants is something without form, then he is not a theologian, but he is also not a Christian. For Jesus Christ is not without form, but in the sphere in which he encounters Him He is both form and object—and in the same sphere in which he listens to the word of Scripture and to that of the community (and therefore to Himself) he can know Him. Theological scholarship in the narrower sense can only develop with a particular responsibility, and according to a method which has to be continually sought out and clarified, enduring with coherent form, that which in this sphere can be known and is actually known by every real Christian.

Of course, the knowing of faith and its recognition can never be an abstract knowing.

> It is to be feared that when our older dogmaticians found the beginning of faith in *notitia*[EN79] they were thinking of an abstract knowledge of all kinds of truths of faith as formulated in the Bible or dogmatics, the sort of knowledge which a man may amass and enjoy without its having any further relevance to him. They then thought it necessary to proceed to the *assensus*[EN80] in which a man decides to accept these truths for himself, to make them his own, until finally he attains to *fiducia*[EN81] in them and penetrates to their true meaning and flavour. We have seen why this is impossible from the very outset. In all the so-called truths of faith we have to do with the being and activity of the living God towards us, with Jesus Christ Himself, whom faith cannot encounter with a basic neutrality, but only in the decision of obedience. The idea of an abstract knowledge of this object—we might almost say the idea of a theologian abstracted from the fact that he is a Christian—is one which has no substance.

But positively the knowing of faith cannot be an abstract knowledge because

---

[EN79] knowledge
[EN80] assent
[EN81] trust

2. *The Act of Faith*

it is only one element in the active recognition of faith. It is an indispensable element. It is an integral element. It decides its meaning and direction. It shows us what must be the object and origin of the recognition of faith. But it is only one element. Taken alone, as an abstract knowledge of God and the world and even of Jesus Christ, it can only be described as unimportant and even, as Jas. 2^{19} tells us, negative, a possibility or impossibility of demonic being.

The knowing of faith is, of course, a true and genuine knowing. It is related to its object. It is an objective and, as such, a theoretical knowing. We can say this quite calmly, and it must not be denied. But, as such, it is at once a practical knowing. It both knows and recognises. It is this to the extent that as a knowing about Jesus Christ it includes in itself from the very first a knowing about the believer himself. It is already included in the root of faith as the acknowledgment of Jesus Christ, it is born of that obedience as cognition, that the One in whom I believe and about whom I can know when I believe in Him, that this One—we now come to the final proposition of our second section—is what He is and does what He does for me, *pro me*^{EN82}; that He is "my Lord," as Luther so rightly emphasised in a formula which unfolded so much objective knowledge; that He is my Lord and therefore my Saviour and Mediator, my Redeemer from sin and death and the devil, my hope of service in righteousness, innocence and felicity, because He died for me and rose again for me. This is just what He is in the form which is determined and limited by the witness of Scripture and the proclamation of the community. This is just what He is as He has always been understood by every normative confession and dogma, by every healthy teaching and theology. This is just what He is as alone He can be perceived and understood in the sphere in which He may be known and is known. This is what Christian faith knows concerning Him. And in knowing this, the believer knows of himself that he himself is the man for whom Jesus Christ is, for whom, in whose place, He acts and rules, in short, with whom He deals as an all-powerful and all-loving human lord—if there were such a thing—would have to deal with a man who is utterly attached and subject to him. He knows that he himself is the man who is the possession of this Lord. But if this is what he knows concerning Jesus Christ and therefore himself, it is not an abstract or dead or neutral, but a concrete and living and—do we need to say it?—a supremely and profoundly implicated knowledge. Let us say it for once, it is his existential knowledge, his knowledge in the active recognition of his faith.

[766]

But we have still to take a further step. We have not yet done sufficient justice to the active character of the recognition of Christian faith. The fact that it is active is based on what we have just described as the believer's knowledge concerning Jesus Christ and therefore himself. But if it is an active recognition—a recognition in the full sense of this important word—then necessarily

---

^{EN82} for me

§ 63. The Holy Spirit and Christian Faith

it reaches out from that knowledge to the awareness, the self-understanding and self-apprehension, of the whole man, thus becoming an action and decision of the whole man. What does it mean when I know that it is true, that it is actually the case, that Jesus Christ is for me, that He takes my place, that I am the possession which He controls, which He has controlled from all eternity, that He has died and risen again for me? What follows from this? Does nothing follow? Can I simply know that this is so, although with a concrete and living and implicated knowledge? From this knowledge, from the recognition characterised by this knowledge, does there not necessarily follow a total disturbance of my being, a radical decision in relation to my situation *vis à vis*[EN83] myself and the world? Does not this recognition—without ceasing to be recognition, but becoming recognition in the deepest sense—necessarily take on the form of a free act which is characterised as a basic act by the fact that it is—we must not say only, but just—the act of my heart?

Here we must halt for a moment. We have come to a point in our discussion which is not entirely free from danger. We have referred to a total but not an absolute disturbance, a radical but not an eschatological decision, a free act of man, of the human heart, grounded in the act of God, but not the act of God itself and as such. Therefore even at this climax of our exposition of the recognition of faith we are speaking of most important penultimate things, but not of ultimate things.

> One description of what is involved in the believer's knowledge concerning Jesus Christ and himself is as follows. The real event of faith in Jesus Christ consists in the fact that the event of salvation as it took place in Jesus Christ is made present or re-enacted in it. Ths history of Jesus Christ, His death and resurrection, becomes the history of the believer. The whole significance of what has taken place in Jesus Christ ἐφ' ἅπαξ[EN84] consists in the offer that it be repeated in the existence of those who receive the *kerygma* concerning it. The truth and power of faith consist in the fact that man avails himself of this offer, takes up his cross, and dies with Christ to himself and the world, that he may be open for the future of his life. If this is a true description, we have been speaking already not merely of the penultimate but of the ultimate things, of the absolute disturbance, of the eschatological decision, of the act of God in itself and as such, as these take place in faith.
>
> There have been many attempts to make the history of Jesus Christ coincident with that of the believer, and *vice versa*[EN85]. The theology of the younger Luther (up to 1519) was nothing but a powerful move in this direction. But we can approve and make common cause with it neither in its earlier forms nor in that authoritatively represented to-day by R. Bultmann. The real presentation (*repraesentatio*[EN86]) of the history of Jesus Christ is that which He Himself accomplishes in the work of His Holy Spirit when He makes Himself the object and origin of faith. Christian faith takes note of this, and clings to it and responds to it, without itself being the thing which accomplishes it, without any identity between the redemptive act of God and faith as the free act of man. Jesus Christ and His death and resurrection do not cease to be its object and origin. It is always grounded in the fact that Jesus Christ becomes

---

[EN83] in relation to
[EN84] once for all
[EN85] the other way around
[EN86] representation

2. *The Act of Faith*

and is and remains its object and origin. What takes place in the recognition of the *pro me*[EN87] of Christian faith is not the redemptive act of God itself, not the death and resurrection of Jesus Christ, not the presentation and repetition of His obedience and sacrifice and victory. What is Bultmann's conception but an existentialist translation of the sacramentalist teaching of the Roman Church, according to which, at the climax of the mass, with the transubstantiation of the elements—in metaphysical identity with what took place then and there—there is a "bloodless repetition" of the sacrifice of Christ on Golgotha? Those who regard this doctrine of the mass as basically untenable will find it impossible to make what took place ἐφ' ἅπαξ[EN88] in Jesus Christ coincident with what takes place in faith. With the later Luther they will understand faith as a recognition and apprehension (*comprehendere*) of Jesus Christ as the One who died and rose again for us men and in our place, but they will not confuse it with the dying and rising again of Jesus Christ, nor will they confuse the dying and rising again of Jesus Christ with what takes place in faith. Therefore when they speak of what takes place in faith, they will not speak of an absolute disturbance or an eschatological decision or the redemptive act of God.

[768]

When I say this I am not looking only at Bultmann. I am also looking in quite a different direction (of which I am reminded by the closeness of his thesis to the Roman theory of the sacrifice of the mass). In modern Roman Catholic theology there is a promising but, of course, unofficial movement which is apparently aiming in the direction of what we might call a christological renaissance. I am not thinking only of the well-known book which Hans Urs von Balthasar addressed to me, in which I find an understanding of the concentration on Jesus Christ attempted in *C.D.*, and the implied Christian concept of reality, which is incomparably more powerful than that of most of the books which have clustered around me. For H. U. v. Balthasar has with him and under him quite a chorus of German and especially French friends who in different ways and with varying emphases all seem to wish to look again to the centre, to the "author and finisher of our faith" (Heb. 12²), who alone can make possible either theology itself or any attempt at ecumenical agreement. And more recently H. U. v. Balthasar himself has written a small series of other notable books, on Theresa of Lisieux, Elisabeth of Dijon and Reinhold Schneider. And if I understand aright their theological content, it seems plain to me that he too (like Bultmann, but with infinitely richer material) sees from that centre which he has grasped so clearly and finely a whole field of possible and actual representations of the history of Jesus Christ, the repetitions or re-enactments of His being and activity by the saints or by those who achieve some measure of sanctity. And as the author sees and represents them these have taken place and do take place in history *post Christum*[EN89] and in our own time with such significance, such positive and stimulating force, that the One whose being and activity is supposedly reproduced obviously fades into the background as compared with His saints. I now have an inkling of something which at first I could not understand: what is meant by the "christological constriction" which my expositor and critic urged against me in terms of mild rebuke. But we must bring against him the counter-question, whether in all the spiritual splendour of the saints who are supposed to represent and repeat Him Jesus Christ has not ceased—not in theory but in practice—to be the object and origin of Christian faith. I do not know sufficiently whether the "christological renaissance" in the sphere of Roman Catholicism is developing in the same way in the case of its other representatives. If so, it unfortunately means that this promising new beginning in Roman Catholic theology is in danger of returning to, or it may be has never left, the well-worn track on which the doctrine of justification is absorbed into that

---

[EN87] for me
[EN88] once for all
[EN89] after Christ

§ 63. The Holy Spirit and Christian Faith

of sanctification—understood as the pious work of self-sanctification which man can undertake and accomplish in his own strength. My concern is whether this is perhaps the case. For the doctrine of the sacrifice of the mass, the archetype of the whole idea of representation, is still unshaken. If I were a Roman Catholic theologian, I would begin my attempt at reconsideration and cautious amendment at the point where the Roman Catholic Church has in practice its christological centre, perhaps reaching out from there to an appraisal of the saints which would be more subdued—and probably less impressive, but all the more truthful because it gives more honour to the Holy One. If only we were agreed—and this applies to my neighbour on the left as well as on the right—that the ultimate and the penultimate things, the redemptive act of God and that which passes for our response to it, are not the same. Everything is jeopardised if there is confusion in this respect.

That is the danger which threatens at this point and which we must here avoid. And we must see to it that we do not fall into it again by way of certain theories of baptism which are current even in Protestantism. Faith is the free act of man, and is wonderful enough in relationship to Jesus Christ as its object and origin. It is a recognition and apprehension of His being and activity for man. But it is not the repetition of it. The being and activity of Jesus Christ needs no repetition. It is present and active in its own truth and power.

Faith is the free act of man. If this is secure, we cannot speak too strongly of what takes place in it as the recognition and apprehension of Jesus Christ, as the subjective realisation of the *pro me*[EN90]. There is no doubt that in it as this recognition there is a comprehensive disturbance and decision, an act of the human heart which carries with it, and after it, a total change in man's whole situation. There can also be no doubt that this act and this disturbance and decision do stand in a very direct and intimate relationship to the object and origin of that apprehension, to Jesus Christ and therefore to His death and resurrection. The concept which forces itself upon us is that which says neither too much nor too little, the concept of analogy. What follows from the fact that the recognition of faith is a knowing of the believer—an active knowledge about Jesus Christ which is personal and moves him—is obviously this, that he has to shape his existence, or, more exactly, his understanding and apprehension of his existence, his attitude to himself and the world, in a way which is in some sense parallel to the One who as his Lord took his place, that he has to model himself in conformity with the One in whom he believes, that he can and will be man only in the likeness of Jesus Christ as the One who died and rose again for him. If there are those to whom this seems to be saying too little, let them be careful that in attempting to do better they do not do worse. Is not this the greatest thing we can say of man, of what he can will and do and be in faith? Not the final thing, certainly. Here and now, short of the end of the ways of God, the final thing can be said only with reference to the man Jesus. But it is the greatest penultimate thing, the greatest thing concerning the man who with God is on the way to this end, the greatest and most wonderful thing concerning the man who, as the sinful man of the world that he is, can still believe and be a Christian. He expresses himself as a Christian in the fact that he is able and willing to be only in the likeness of Jesus Christ and His death

---

[EN90] for me

2. *The Act of Faith*

and resurrection, in both an inward *mortificatio*[EN91] and an inward *vivificatio*[EN92]. We must now develop this in relation to the active recognition of faith.

If it is the case that I can clearly recognise in faith that what took place in the death of Jesus Christ and was revealed in His resurrection took place for me and was revealed as efficacious for me, then that immediately carries with it a very definite practical self-recognition: Not, of course, a fantastic notion that I am a kind of second Christ. That would lead me out of faith and its knowledge, in which He has for me the form of another, in which He is object, and there would be no solid ground under my feet. And the notion could only be an illusion. I am not the Lord who became a servant. I am not the Son who in obedience to the Father allowed Himself to be judged as my Judge and the Judge of all men. The glory of God has not been revealed in me as in His resurrection. Far from being a Saviour, I am only a proud man like all other men, and as such I have fallen a prey to eternal death and perdition. I can only believe in Him as the One who is also, who is just, my Saviour. And I cannot do this in my own reason and strength, but only as He encounters me in the witness of Scripture and the proclamation of His community, only as He awakens me to it by the power of His Holy Spirit. But this faith in Him, this recognition of Jesus Christ, carries with it ineluctably a recognition of myself—and in this recognition a real estimate, an understanding and apprehension of myself—in which, without even remotely being or becoming like Him, I see myself as the man I am irresistibly determined by Him, unmistakably stamped by Him, clearly set in His light from the depth, the lowest depth, in which I find myself in relation to Him. Faith in Him necessarily calls me to the recognition of myself in the power of which—and this is the real act of the heart in faith—I can only wish to be the man determined and stamped by Him and set in His light.

[770]

But what is this determining and stamping and enlightening of the believer in Jesus Christ, the Christian? In accordance with what we have tried to make clear concerning faith within the context of the doctrine of justification, we must distinguish two great aspects and try briefly to indicate the peculiar characteristics of each. They correspond to the positive and negative character of the substitutionary being and activity of Jesus Christ Himself (as the *analogans*[EN93]), and they mark the beginning and end of the way on which the life of the Christian—the one who recognises Jesus Christ in faith—will become and be the *analogatum*[EN94], the parallel, the likeness—no more but no less—of His justifying being and activity. What is this *analogans*[EN95]? What do I

[EN91] mortification
[EN92] vivification
[EN93] basis of analogy
[EN94] analogy drawn
[EN95] basis of analogy

§ 63. *The Holy Spirit and Christian Faith*

know in faith as that which has taken place and been revealed in Jesus Christ for me?

We recall the first thing—the overcoming, we do not say now of the pride and fall of man in general but of my pride and my fall in particular. It is the overcoming of that which I myself had not overcome and could not overcome. I myself, the man of sin, who has not and will not overcome himself, am the one who finds that he is overcome in Him. My proud heart is vanquished. My proud thoughts and words and works as they flow from that heart are vanquished. The plight of my imprisonment, to which I had betrayed myself in my pride, and in which I could only languish in my pride, is vanquished. The man of sin is vanquished. Vanquished means removed, destroyed, put to death. That is the substitutionary being and activity of Jesus Christ on its negative side. That is what He has done for me in His death, and what, again for me, is shown to be done in His resurrection. If I recognise Him in faith, that means that I find that I am the one to whom this has happened in Him. What follows from this? It cannot be denied that something very necessary and direct must follow for my self-understanding and self-apprehension, for my whole attitude to myself. But what?

Caution is demanded. We say too much if we try to deduce from the overcoming which has come to me in Jesus Christ that it has taken place in me, that I have to understand and conceive of myself as the man who has it behind him. For although that removing and destruction and putting to death has come to me it has not taken place in me. When I believe in Jesus Christ and see what has come to me in Him, I still find in myself my pride and fall. In this respect there is no sense in trying to imagine that my history coincides with that of Jesus Christ and that therefore sin and death in me have no further power over me. In relation to my being in Jesus Christ, I can and must maintain this, but better not in relation to myself. I have overcome in Him, but not in myself, not even remotely. It is a poor theology that grasps at equality with Jesus Christ—a perfectionism which will not accept any distinction between me and Him.

But we say too little if we allow and accept the overcoming of my pride and fall which has taken place in Him, but are then acquiescent and content that it should not take place in me, that the old Adam, as more than one example shows, should be cheerfully alive with all his qualities and impossible possibilities, that he should be permitted to carry on just as before, my consolation being that he is overcome in Jesus Christ, and the reflection that I still cannot overcome him being the excuse for granting him this permission. It is a poor theology that persists in the inequality between me and Jesus Christ—a pious cushion which is content to maintain the distinction from Him.

What, then, is the alternative? What is it that really follows from the recognition that my pride and fall are vanquished in the death of Jesus Christ and that this is manifest in His resurrection? It follows that I am seriously alarmed at myself, that I am radically and heartily sorry for my condition, that I can no longer boast of myself and my thoughts and words and works and especially my

2. *The Act of Faith*

heart, but can only be ashamed of them, that I can think of myself and my acts only with remorse and penitence. Of myself—and we must add at once, of the world, the world of men to which I belong, which in the strict sense, although in my own individual way, I resemble in all these things, which is my mirror and of which I myself am the mirror. What is to become of this world which is my world, and of myself who belong to it from the crown of my head to the sole of my foot? To what must I see both it, and myself with it, roll and fall and plunge to destruction?—not, of course, because it is my own (perhaps rather too pessimistic) view that both it and myself are not in the best of ways, but because I recognise that both it and myself are vanquished, i.e., removed and destroyed and put to death, in Jesus Christ, because I have to see that in Him an end has [772] been made of both it and myself. That is the total disturbance which I have to accept, which I cannot spare myself, when I know Jesus Christ and myself in Him.

This is what the older theologians called *mortificatio*[EN96], the *mortificatio*[EN97] which does not come to a Christian and which he does not have to effect once only, but continually, which does not determine his attitude only occasionally, but is everywhere present as a muffled undertone. It is the Christian attitude on its negative side. The knowledge of faith involves no less than this. This heartfelt act of penitence cannot be avoided by anyone who knows Jesus Christ as his Saviour and is determined and stamped and enlightened by Him. It is not more than this. We are not dealing with the ultimate things, with the absolute disturbance. No one must imagine that in what may take place as his heartfelt act of penitence or sorrow or remorse, of *mortificatio*[EN98], it is all up with himself and the world, the world and himself are really brought to an end. "Putting off the world"? There is no such thing. Certainly, we are not dealing with anything less than penitence: a break, a tear, the sharp piercing of the two-edged sword of the Word of God (Heb. 4^{12}), which will necessarily cut through the old Adam in so far as he is as a believer, a new subject in the knowledge of faith (different from when he did not believe); a wound, a pain from which he can never again be free, which from the heart, the affected centre of his existence, will continually accompany and penetrate all his thoughts and words and works, which will constantly thwart and disturb him in his pride, which will not allow him to give himself up to his evil cause and to himself and the world. Not a loud, but at any rate a small: "I dismiss you," will be his response to what has come to him—not in himself but in Jesus Christ— as this overcoming, to what in faith in Him he can and must recognise to be his overcoming. And to this extent he will exist in analogy with Him. For all the unlikeness there will be a likeness. For all the similarity there will be a parallelism, a correspondence. In his own modest way he offers a likeness of His being

---

[EN96] mortification
[EN97] mortification
[EN98] mortification

§ 63. *The Holy Spirit and Christian Faith*

and activity. The publican in the temple in Lk. 18$^{9f.}$ and the prodigal son of Lk. 15$^{11f.}$ are a likeness of the One who as the Lamb of God took away the sin of the world: no more, but no less. And the man who believes in this One and knows himself in Him can and must and will unreservedly place himself at least alongside the publican and the prodigal—we have in them the minimum—and with them be the likeness, the *analogatum*^{EN99}, of what Jesus Christ has been and done, and is and does, for him.

But the second thing which I recognise as having taken place and been revealed for me in Jesus Christ is the restoration, we do not say now of the right and life of man in general, but of my right and life. This is the positive side which I as little create or can create as the negative. I myself have denied and forfeited my right. I have hazarded my life and lost it. But this right and life have been restored in the act of obedience in which Jesus Christ sacrificed Himself for me, and manifested in His resurrection from the dead. He stands in my place as my righteousness and life. If I know Him and myself in Him—and that is the knowledge of faith—this means that I see myself as the one to whom that right and life are given, as the one to whom He has given Himself as righteous and alive for me. But, again, and from this positive standpoint, what follows from this?

Caution is again demanded. We say too much if we try to deduce from my restoration as it has taken place in Jesus Christ that it has taken place in me, that before God and man and myself I can boast of a right which is under my own name, which has come into my own possession, and of a life which I can live and enjoy as my own life. On this side, too, there is no sense in imagining that my history coincides with that of Jesus Christ. That triumphant restoration has not really taken place in my heart, in my activities and attitudes. Nothing has taken place or can be perceived in me of the glory of that right and life. To what can I cling in myself? What can I show to God and man, and in my own conscience to myself? In relation to Jesus Christ I can know and boast that my right stands like the mountains, and that I shall not die but live, and proclaim the works of the Lord. But what am I in myself? What can I know in relation to myself? Where and how can I find in myself anything but imaginary assurances in and with which I shall then have to live? It is a bad theology that maintains an exact similarity with Jesus Christ, a false because arbitrary assurance of salvation, in which man wants everything to be different and thinks that he can have everything different.

But, again, we say too little if we conceive the idea that, although ultimately Jesus Christ has ordered everything positively in my favour, yet I myself am so far removed from Him that for the moment I do not have anything of it at all, that I am still accused of my old and recurrent wrong, that I can only accuse myself in respect of it, that I must still fear death as the wages of my sin—just as though nothing had happened. And the certain result is, of course, that

---

^{EN99} analogy drawn

2. *The Act of Faith*

although my right and life as restored in Jesus Christ are my consolation as a profound and supreme truth, yet they are, as it were, in cold storage, they are for the moment of no practical value, and therefore a dangerous consolation. For the moment it is the case in practice that as concerns my restoration I am thrown back on myself; I must provide and answer for my own right, or make myself worthy of it; I must earn and attain my own life. For the moment it is my own affair in practice to set myself at rights with God and man and my own conscience, and it is my own affair to live in the peace which is attained in this way. It is a bad theology which has no assurance of salvation, which persists in dissimilarity with Jesus Christ, which looks away from Him to a situation of man which He has not altered, which falls back on some pride or subtle form of the righteousness of works, thus evading the one thing which is necessary even on this side. This, too, is obviously quite incompatible with the knowledge of faith. [774]

What, then, is the alternative? What is it that really follows from the recognition that my right and life have been restored once and for all in the death of Jesus Christ and manifested once and for all in His resurrection? It follows that although there is no escape from the accusation of my wrong and the threat of judgment and death which it involves, I can still have a complete and assured, and because assured, a comforted and strong and joyful confidence. I can rely on that which has taken place for me. I can regard myself as secure in my heart. I can think my few thoughts in peace, say my few words in peace, do my few works in peace. I can look forward from myself as I am, and from the things of myself as they are and as they are done. To what? Certainly not to the void of a better future, but to the fulfilment of the promise given to me in Jesus Christ, to the revelation of the verdict pronounced in Him which ascribes to me right and life. I can trust. On this positive side faith is simply trust—that is why the older theologians talked of *fiducia*[EN100]. Not an arbitrary trust, but a trust which responds to the Word of God spoken to me. Not an indefinite trust, but a trust which is grounded in the knowledge of faith as the knowledge of Jesus Christ. And we must add that in this responsive and well-grounded trust we have to do not only with myself but with the community and the world. That which took place and was manifested positively in Jesus Christ took place and was manifested for the world—and therefore also and just for me. When, as a member of the community, I confidently recognise that it took place and was manifested for me, I must at once relate it as well to the community and the world. In it, in the world reconciled with God in Jesus Christ, I recognise as in a mirror myself as a reconciled man. And I, for my part, have to recognise and understand and conduct myself as the mirror of its reconciliation. It would be a strange Christian confidence if I were to have a sure trust for myself but to give up for lost the Church and the surrounding world to which I belong both in evil and in good; if I were to succeed in despairing not of myself

---

[EN100] trust

§ 63. *The Holy Spirit and Christian Faith*

but of the Church and the world. If I know my right and my life in Jesus Christ, then I must hold to the fact, and act by it, that in Him my right and life are promised to them, not, of course, in any optimistic misjudgment of their nature and ways, but in view of the salvation which has come and the hope which is given both to them and to me. That I have confidence is the radical decision which I cannot avoid but have to make when I know Jesus Christ and myself in Him.

This is what the older theologians called *vivificatio*[EN101], the *vivificatio*[EN102] which does not come to a Christian once only but continually, which does not determine his attitude only occasionally, but is everywhere present—this time as a clear overtone. Again we must say that the knowledge of faith involves no less than this. When a man knows in Jesus Christ his Saviour and that of the world, when, therefore, he is determined and stamped and enlightened by Him, this heartfelt act cannot be omitted. On this side, too, there is nothing more: no ultimate things, no eschatological decision. No one must imagine that in and with what he experiences and practises as his *vivificatio*[EN103] the new heaven and the new earth has dawned even for himself, let alone for the Church and the world. But there can be nothing less than this confidence—a confidence on the old earth and under the old heaven but resolutely grasped. And in the light of it little renovations and provisional sanctifications and reassurances and elucidations will necessarily penetrate the whole man, who in the knowledge of faith has undoubtedly become a new subject. At this point we are already peeping into the sphere of the second part of the doctrine of reconciliation, which, as far as the anthropological material is concerned, will be discussed under the titles sanctification and love. In the present context a few very brief indications must suffice. It cannot be otherwise than that, when a man believes, then, in spite of all the limitations in which he still exists, in the knowledge of the restoration of his right and life as it has taken place in Jesus Christ, he will become a free man, i.e., a man who is no longer a simple servant and victim of his pride, but who is called away from it to the obedience of humility, for which he is also both ready and willing. As he bears that deep wound and accepts that bitter pain of penitence, he will hope for the grace of God and in that hope he will be at bottom a cheerful man. And although on his journey from the beginning of his way to the end he will often enough be assaulted and he will have to fight and he will often be thrown down, but will always rise up again and continue, yet in his relationship with God and man and himself he will be seriously and finally a peaceful man, peaceful because held by the One in whom he is already restored, in whom he is already the righteous and protected covenant-partner of God. He is, of course, exposed to all kinds of questions, and for that reason he has no claim. But he is such a

---

[EN101] vivification
[EN102] vivification
[EN103] vivification

2. *The Act of Faith*

man. He is the response to that which has taken place and been revealed, not in him, but in Jesus Christ for him. And in this attitude he is a copy, a parallel, a likeness of His being and activity for him. In all his imperfection He is a reflection of His perfection, a little light in His great light. He exists, then, in his petty thankfulness for the demonstration of His almighty grace.

To sum up: In the power of faith in Jesus Christ there can take place no more and no less, and it must and will take place with a supreme reality (in the sphere of the penultimate things), that as the Christian knows the overcoming of his pride and fall and the restoration of his right and life in Christ, in the light of this happening he can be with Christ in penitence but also in confidence. This takes place in the power of faith as it is an active recognition of Jesus Christ. And it is this that makes faith an event in its character as recognition. It is not the event of the redemptive act of God. It can only follow this. It is subsequent and at the deepest possible level subordinate to it. But it has this in common with it, that it, too, is an event—in the sphere and context of the awakening of the Christian who can be and remain for ever a living member of it. [776]

Christian faith is a confession. At the very first we called it generally an act of taking cognisance. We described this as basically an act of acknowledgment in which we then saw an act of recognition from which this proceeded. In this limited and definite sense Christian faith is man's taking cognisance of Jesus Christ. Now that we have seen how it is filled out we must return to the general concept as such.

Is it just a taking cognisance? As we are using the concept, most definitely not. The taking is accompanied by giving, the acknowledgment and recognition by confession. A Christian who simply acknowledges and recognises without confessing is not a Christian. Even in his supposed acknowledgment and recognition of Jesus Christ he is deceiving himself and others. But he cannot deceive Jesus Christ, who as Himself the truth knows that he neither acknowledges nor recognises Him. The goal of the freedom in which He makes a man genuinely free—free to believe in Him—is the freedom to be His witness. And so the goal of faith as the free act of man is the act of his witness and therefore of his confession. What is acknowledged and recognised by man in faith is the radiance of God, His *qabod*, δόξα, *gloria*[EN104], glory, honour, self-manifestation in the being and activity of Jesus Christ. But this radiance cannot be stopped in and by the one who acknowledges and recognises it. It breaks through and lights up the man himself. The man on whom it falls cannot help but be lit up by it. "A city that is set on a hill cannot be hid" (Mt. $5^{14f.}$). To light a candle and put it under a bushel is nonsense: it belongs to the candlestick. The man who believes in Jesus Christ is, as such, the lighted candle which belongs *per se*[EN105] to the candlestick. His taking cognisance is also a giving.

[EN104] glory
[EN105] by definition

§ 63. *The Holy Spirit and Christian Faith*

There is nothing concealed which shall not be revealed, nothing hid which shall not be made known. What is told to the disciple by his Lord in darkness, he speaks out in light; what he hears from Him in the ear, he preaches upon the house-tops (Mt. $10^{26f.}$). The consequence is irresistible that where anyone believes as a Christian a history is enacted: a history of the heart, which, as such, is audible and visible in world-history; an individual history which, as such, calls for impartation and communication; a secret history which, as such, has a public character and claim; a history which is not apparent—for what does it matter that a man finds himself summoned to that obedience and compliance in relation to Jesus Christ, and resolved upon it in his own freedom, and what is the little penitence and confidence in which this is revealed in his attitude?—but a history of immeasurable dynamic because it takes place in the light of the great history of God. The fire and the sword which Jesus came to bring on earth (Lk. 12^{49}, Mt. 10^{34}) are shown to be effective in it. It may be that the Christian does not desire at all but is opposed to the idea of putting himself at the disposal of this dynamic, of being a witness and confessor. But he is not asked concerning his own wishes or aversions. When he believes in Jesus Christ he is at the disposal of this dynamic. Whether he wills it or not—and if he does not will it, perhaps only the less so—the free act of his faith is as such the free act of his confession. He cannot be a Christian without bearing this fire and sword.

What does confessing mean? This is not the place to develop the concept in its full reach and especially in relation to the substantive "confession." We will simply sketch some of the main outlines which are indispensable to an understanding of it as an integral moment in the concept—the act—of faith.

In general terms, confessing is the moment in the act of faith in which the believer stands to his faith, or, rather, to the One in whom he believes, the One whom he acknowledges and recognises, the living Jesus Christ; and does so outwardly, again in general terms, in face of men. Confessing as the act of faith in Jesus Christ means "to confess him before men" (Mt. 10^{32}), not to conceal the fact that we belong to Him, and the involved alteration of our attitude, which would be to deny Him, but, since both negatively and positively it is a matter of the attitude of the whole man, to be that altered man who belongs to Him in our whole being and therefore outwardly as well. To that extent confessing is not a special action of the Christian. All that is demanded is that he should be what he is. And what he is, or what he does as the free act of his faith, is not, as we have seen, something absolutely different and new in relation to what others do or can do. It is not action in the *eschaton*. When he is penitent and confident, he is only relatively different from others. He is absolutely different only in the mystery of his existence as grounded in Jesus Christ, not in what he himself is and does on this basis. His confessing is striking and extraordinary and surprising and spectacular and aggressive, both in itself and in its effects, only in the eyes and ears of those who lack categories to understand what he is and does on this basis. But—without concealing this from their eyes

2. *The Act of Faith*

and ears—he simply stands to what he is. If he stands out in this respect, if his action acquires the character of a venture, if he does something which is perhaps annoying to others and dangerous to himself, if he accepts the risk of a collision with their action, if he provokes unfriendly or even hostile reactions on their part, if, as a confessor, he has to suffer in some way, it is not because he intends all this. It proceeds from his action, but he himself does not impart to it the quality to provoke it. It has this from the object and origin of his faith. It has it from the mystery of his existence which he himself cannot control. Because he is little light reflecting the great light, his action stands out from that of others, he becomes a witness of the great light, without especially willing to do so, and without in any way helping to do so. His task is that he should not cease to be that little light reflecting the great light. His task is that he should not place that little light under a bushel. If he sees to this, he does the act of confessing which is required of him, the confession of faith. [778]

It is required of him by the very fact that in accordance with creation and by nature humanity means fellowship. This is equally true, indeed it is genuinely true, only of the humanity of the Christian. Since faith is his free human act, he cannot perform it without his neighbours, without communication with them. He cannot try to keep it concealed from them. Whatever may be their attitude to him, he owes this to them. To exist privately is to be a robber. And things would have come to a pretty pass if in faith in Jesus Christ anyone tried to be a robber. This is all the less possible in so far as what is required is not an act of particular heroism, but simply that in the sight and audience of his fellows he should stand to his faith, i.e., to the One in whom he believes and to what his attachment to Him involves for himself, that he should not be unbelieving, but believing.

Above all, the necessary summons to confession is concretely given by the existence of others who, according to their confession in the world, are likewise caught up in the act of faith by the existence of the Christian community. It is not on the basis of his own discovery and private revelation, but by the mediatorial ministry of the community which is itself in the school of the prophets and apostles, that a man comes under the awakening power of the Holy Spirit and therefore to faith. This is his starting-point in the act of faith, and to what other goal will he return? He can as little deny it as a child its mother. He needs it, just as he needs the awakening power of the Holy Spirit and that school if he is to stand and continue in that faith to which he has come, to live by his faith. And it needs him, for its ministry is not concluded but must go on, and it is not an easy ministry, but calls for the assistance of the witness of every believer, and in a given situation a great deal, indeed everything, may depend upon the assistance of his witness. He can never escape the communion of the saints; he can never leave it in the lurch. If he did he would be denying himself and his own faith which is the faith of the community. For good or evil, he has to confess it, he has to be with Jesus Christ and to repent and to have confidence together with it. He has to confess his attachment to it

§ 63. *The Holy Spirit and Christian Faith*

and to its Head publicly to the world. He will therefore desire baptism. And by the fact that he is baptised, and is known as one who is baptised, he has to make it plain that he is one for whom Jesus Christ has overcome, and whose right and life Jesus Christ has restored. As a living member of His body he will concretely show himself to be thankful in this basic act of all confession.

But finally the world around him is itself and as such no less concrete—the world which does not confess Jesus Christ because it obviously does not acknowledge and recognise Him. He is surrounded by men who seem to know nothing of what has taken place and been revealed for them too in Him, of the judgment which has been executed on them and the verdict which has been proclaimed over them in Him, who seem to be very far removed from anything that could seriously be called either repentance or confidence, who seem to know nothing of what faith is, because they do not know the One in whom to believe, let alone do what it is open for them to do. What is the significance of the existence of this world for the one to whom it is given to believe within this world? For in everything else he belongs to it. He finds the fashion of it in himself. He has a full part in its sin and death. He can understand better than it can itself its opposition or indifference to faith. He knows more radically than it does both the fact, and the reason for it, that no man of himself can either come to faith or live by his faith. He knows who and what is needed for this to come about in the life of a man. Above all, in the midst of other men he is the one who knows the decisive fact—who knows it in this active knowledge of himself—that Jesus Christ died and rose again not only for him but for them, that it is the world which God has reconciled to Himself in Him. And this being the case, can he keep this knowledge to himself, can he refrain from confessing his faith, when even the very stones would cry out to impart the knowledge which he has received, when it is actually the case that not the stones only but all the creatures of God proclaim: "God was in Christ reconciling the world to himself"? It is his task to make this known in human language for human ears, and with the act of his human life before human eyes—yet again, not in great deeds, but in the mere fact that he is who he is, and that as such he says what he has to say and does what he has to do and makes open use of the freedom which is given him to do this. If it is not possible for a man of the world who has come to faith and can live by faith to deny himself, then in face of the world—his world—he can only be, very humbly but very courageously, a confessing Christian in the confessing community.

INDEX OF SCRIPTURE REFERENCES

OLD TESTAMENT

GENESIS
3,20	155
15,6	101, 103

JOB
5,17	25
42,1f	58
42,5	56
42,7f	56, 58

PSALMS
1,3	56
1,5f	23
5,4	23
5,12	56
7,8f	56
9,4	56
11,7	18
16,5f	92
17,6f	93
18,1f	93
18,23f	56
23	94, 95, 117
25,10f	92
26,1f	56
30,5	25
32	62, 64, 91
34,16	23
36,6	18
37,20	23
38,2f	23
48,10	18
50,1–6	23
51	62, 64, 65, 66, 91
62,12	25
64,10	56
66,10f	25
73,1	57
73,13f	56
73,21f	93
78	57, 91
85	93
90,7f	23
92,12f	56
102,13	25
106	57, 91
116,5f	91
118,14f	92
118,18	25
119	76
124,1f	222
124,8	222
130	92
130,6f	94
136	91
142,5	93
142,7	93
143,1f	92
145	94
119,142	18

PROVERBS
3,11f	25

ISAIAH
26,2f	92
48,22	27
53,2	122
54,8	25
57,21	27

JONAH
1,3	28

Index of Scripture References

MALACHI
4,2   53

NEW TESTAMENT
MATTHEW
5,14   156
5,14f   265
5,15   213
5,16   179
6,24   75
10,26f   266
10,32   266
10,34   266
13,24f   186
13,33   247
13,47f   186
16,18   179
16,18f   207
16,19   187, 208
18,20   155, 168, 198
23,8   152
25,40   154
25,45   154
28,19   221
28,20   224

MARK
3,7f   198
8,35   233
9,24   102
14,38   222
15,34   52, 76

LUKE
1,34   136
12   199
12,49   266
13,29–30   196
14,10   172
15,11f   262
15,32   31
17,10   190
18,9f   262
20,38   157
22,31f   179
22,61   62

JOHN
1,11   158
1,14   20
1,16   221
3,8   135, 136
4,42   153
8,12   156
8,36   233
14,6   44
15,5   152
17,15   179
17,19   175
17,21–23   166
19,23   165
19,40   155
20,22   135
20,27   238

ACTS
2,1f   136
2,41   199
4,4   199
8,36   249
9,4   154
9,17   206
11,26   238
15   161
16,15   238
26,28   238

ROMANS
1,5   248
1–8   10
1,17   221
1,18   23
2,13–15   68
3,3   20, 101
3–8   67
3,21   68
3,24   19
3,26   19, 47
3,28   108
4,3f   101
4,11   100
4,13   100
4,15   71
4,25   42
5,1   25
5,5   19
5,12   72
5,13   71
5,13–14   72
5,14   244
5,20   71, 72
6   114
6,4   42
6,6   67

Index of Scripture References

6,8	67	1,9	20
6,11	67	1,30	238
7	66, 67, 68, 76, 91, 95	2,4	137
7,1–6	68, 69	2,9	154
7,2	69	2,14	154
7,2f	69	3	161, 171
7,3	68	3,6	161
7,4	151	3,11	123
7,7–13	71	3,12f	170
7,7–25	69	3,16	197
7,9b-10	71	4,2f	57
7,24	151	4,7	117
7,24–25	67	8,5	134
8	91, 95	9,21	68
8,1	68, 69	10,16	152
8,1–2	67	10,17	152
8,1f	69	11,26	152
8,2	68, 69, 73, 138	12	207
8,4	68	12,3	154
8,9	183	12,4–31	150, 155, 156
8,14	19	12,7	154
8,15	86	12,9	100
8,15f	222	12,12	150, 153
8,16	86	12,13	154
8,17	90	12,20	196
8,19f	222	12,27	150, 151, 153
8,26f	222	13,9f	6
8,29	155	13,12	219
8,30	65	14,33	17
8,30f	57	15,10	117
9,4–5	159	15,21f	152
9–11	159	15,31	219
9,30	100	15,44	151
10,3	19	15,45	152
10,4	19	15,45f	152
10,5	19	15,52	223
10,6	100	16,13	199
11,26	159		
11,32	6, 234	**2 CORINTHIANS**	
11,33f	6	1,18	20
12	207	1,19	20
12,3–8	156	1,24	162
12,5	151, 214	3,17	201
12,6	154	3,18	233
12,8	162	4,7	227
13,8	68	5,7	217
13,10	68	5,17	238
14,23	247	5,18	162
		5,19	83
1 CORINTHIANS		5,20	133, 162
1	161	5,21	89
1,2	188	6,9	25

Index of Scripture References

6,14	23	5,3	126
6,15	238	5,4	128
8,9	121	5,5	128
8–9	161	5,6	108, 126, 128
		5,7	125, 127
GALATIANS		5,8	128
1,1	124, 162	5,9	126
1,3	8	5,10	125, 127
1,4	124, 128	5,11	126, 128
1,6	125	5,13	125, 126
1,8–9	125	5,14	68
1,8f	112	5,24	125
1,10	125	6,1	125
1,12	7, 124	6,2	68
1,13–14	124	6,12	128
1,15f	124	6,13	126
2	91	6,14	124
2,4	126	6,15	126, 127, 238
2,12	6	6,16	126, 159
2,16	112, 124, 125, 126	6,17	124
2,17	126, 128		
2,19	7, 124	EPHESIANS	
2,20	9, 124, 246	1,1	238
2,21	19, 128	1,4	151, 155
3,1	125	1,9f	153
3,1f	127	1,13f	154
3,3	127	1,23	153
3,6	101	2,1	71
3,9	238	2,10	238
3,13	126	2,16	151
3,14	126	2,22	197
3,15	125	4	163
3,21	19, 68	4,1–7	156
3,22	126	4,1f	162
3,26	125	4,4	196
3,27	125	4,12	151
3,28	151	4,13f	199
3,29	125, 126	5,1	121
4,3f	127	5,16	222
4,4f	126	5,23	151
4,6	86	5,27	197
4,6f	126	5,30	151, 153
4,10	126		
4,11	125	PHILIPPIANS	
4,12	125	1,1	162
4,14	125	1,23	157
4,19	121, 125	2,3f	121
4,26	148	2,5	121
4,31	125	2,7–8	122
5,1	126	2,10f	149
5,2	128	2,11	220, 221

Index of Scripture References

2,15	239	**HEBREWS**	
2,17	248	4,12	261
3,9	19, 100	6,2	206
3,12	241	12,2	123, 214, 217, 257
		12,4	199
COLOSSIANS		12,7f	25
1,1	238	12,11	25
1,12	90		
1,18	151, 153	**JAMES**	
1,22	151	1,13	155
1,24	153	1,17	17
2,3	15	1,18	156
2,11	151	1,22	141
2,17	150	2,19	255
2,19	151	2,26	151
2,23	105		
3,1	232	**1 PETER**	
3,2	232	1,3	86, 90, 238
3,3	219	1,21	238
3,15	151	1,23	180, 238
4,5	222	2,9	156
		2,24	151
1 THESSALONIANS		4,16	238
5,17	201		
		1 JOHN	
1 TIMOTHY		2,2	152
2,4	221	3,2	86, 219
2,5	152	4,14	153
3,15	165, 197	5,4	115
4,10	239		
4,14	206	**JUDE**	
		5,31	52
2 TIMOTHY			
1,6	206	**REVELATION**	
		2–3	160
TITUS		3,19	25
3,4	227	18,13	150
		21,22	228

INDEX OF SUBJECTS

acknowledgment of faith   247–50, 251
Anglican Church   165, 205
Anglicanism   191
anthropology   230
Antichrist   144
apostolic Church   201–7, 210, 212–13
apostolicity   207–8, 210–11
apostolic succession   204–9
ascension   132
atheism   96
atonement   123
   Holy Spirit and   132
   proclamation of   219
   realization of   130–1

baptism   154, 181, 183, 184–5
Baptist Church   164, 203
Batak-Church of Sumatra   196
Buddhism   164

calling   7
categorical imperative   51
catholic   190–5, 197, 199, 201–2
catholicism
   of Church   197, 199
   primitive   207
catholic truth   198, 201–2
Christian community   140–1
   beginning of   215, 217–19
   being of   137–214, 148
   as body of Christ   149–51, 154–6, 176, 186, 200
   concealment of   222
   faith and   222, 239–40
   gathering of   159–60
   goal of   220–1
   holiness of   173–4, 178, 182–3, 185, 189–90
   Holy Spirit and   130–4
   Holy Spirit calling into being   142
   Holy Spirit gathering   163
   Jesus Christ as head of   148–9, 176
   justification as basis of   4–6
   mystery of   152
   obedience of   189–90
   proclamation and   137, 248–9, 253, 255, 259
   strength of   215–17
   teleological direction of   216–17
   time of   214–28
   unity of   159–63
   weakness of   217, 221
Christian religion, faith and   230
Christology   123, 130–1, 170
Church *see also specific churches*
   apostolic   201–7, 210, 212–13
   belief in holy   173–4, 179
   catholocity of   197, 199
   confession of belief in   143–5, 147, 149, 205–6
   confession of belief in one   166–8, 171–3
   criticizing   180–1
   disunity of   165–72, 195
   divisions of   164
   external views of   142–3
   heretical   191
   holiness of   173–5, 189
   Holy Spirit and   139–41
   invisible   139–42, 144, 146, 156–7
   Israel and   11, 158–9
   justification of   169
   militant   157
   national   195
   origins of word   138–9
   plurality of   160, 162–6, 169–70, 181, 191
   salvation and   177
   start of   140
   triumphant   157

Index of Subjects

unity of 162, 163
visible 139–42, 144, 156–7
when of 137–9
Word of God and 140–1
Church discipline 187
Church militant 157
Church triumphant 157
circumcision 107
colloquy of Ratisbon 110
confession
  of belief in Church 143–5, 147, 149, 205–6
  of belief in one Church 166–8, 171–3
  of belief in resurrection 141
  of faith 229–30, 247, 265–8
  of Jesus Christ 15
  of sin 64–5, 80
conversion 170
Council of Trent 110, 112
covenant, fulfillment of 224
credo apostolicam ecclesiam 201
credo catholicam ecclesiam 190–1, 196–7, 201
credo ecclesiam 143–5, 147, 149, 205–6
credo sanctam ecclesiam 173–4
credo unam ecclesiam 166–8, 171–3

determined future 81
discipleship 204, 211
divine judgement 1–2, 16–60
divine sentence 100, 104
  execution of 1–4, 6, 27
  justification and 78–80, 88
  on man 54
  pardon and 54–6, 58–61, 63, 83, 89
  promise of God and 90–1
  resurrection revealing 1–3
  wrong of man and 82
Docetism 140–1
dogmatics
  as doctrine of faith 229
  justification and 7–8
  of Roman Catholic Church 198
dualism of man 30–2, 35

Easter 215, 218, 223
Eastern Catholic Church 201, 203
ecumenism 192
the Enlightenment 9, 10
eschatology, realized 84
Evangelical Church 165, 203, 212

evangelical records 211
Evangelical theology
  justification and 8–10
  justification by faith and 101
  Roman Catholic opposition to 191

faith
  acknowledgment of 247–50, 251
  act of 246–68
  as act of Christian life 246–7
  calling to 248–9
  Christian community and 222, 239–40
  Christian religion and 230
  confession of 229–30, 247, 265–8
  defining 103–4, 247–8
  dogmatics as doctrine of 229
  Evangelical theology and 101
  free act of 258
  freedom in 236–7, 264
  Holy Spirit and confession of 230
  as human act 240–1, 246, 258
  human activity of 231, 233
  humility of 99–100, 104–6, 113–14
  in Jesus Christ 118–20
  Jesus Christ as event of 256
  Jesus Christ as starting-point of 241
  justification by 94–129
  knowledge of 247, 253–6, 261, 264
  Law v. 107, 110
  necessity of 235–6
  negative form of 114–15, 117
  obedience and recognition of 251
  as obedient humility 106, 113, 121–3
  object of 229–46
  positive form of 115–17, 119
  possibility of 235
  pride overcome in 260
  recognition of 247, 250–6, 259–63
  reconciliation and 5
  Reformation and justification by 101, 106–7, 113, 128
  relationship of Jesus Christ to 237–8
  righteousness and 100–1
  vain-glory v. 104
forgiveness of sins 82–5
freedom 40–1, 64–5, 126
  in faith 236–7, 264
  Jesus Christ and 233–4
  Law and 68–9

275

Index of Subjects

Galatian Churches 125–8
God *see also* Word of God
  creative work of 59–60
  future determined by 81
  grace of 24–6, 226
  immutability of 47
  judgement of 1–2, 16–60
  jurisdiction of 22–3
  justification as creative work
    of 59–60
  justification as turning to 43
  justification maintaining right of 20–1,
    31–2
  living being of 48
  loving-kindness of 18
  positive relationship with 16
  promise of 84, 90–1
  reconciliation of world with 218–19,
    224, 226, 232
  right as Creator of man 48–50
  right as Father 50–3
  righteousness of 16–17, 19, 24–6,
    28–31, 36
  right given by 3–4
  right of 16–18, 20, 21, 23–4, 27,
    47–53
  role in justification of man 4, 18,
    31–2
  rule of 22–5
  self-attestation of 133
  self-determination of 22
  self-justification of 47–8, 53–4,
    102, 128
  self-manifestation of 207
  sentence of 1–4, 6, 27, 54–6, 58–61,
    63, 78–80, 82, 83, 88–91, 100, 104
  time for humanity given by 225–8
  turning to 43
  will of 78–9
  work of, in Jesus Christ 50
  wrath of 26–7
Gospel
  justification as Word of 8–10
  law of 138
grace
  of God 24–6, 226
  God's righteousness hiding 26
  of justification 111–12
  misunderstandings of 10
  pardon and 60–1
  reconciliation and 60

Holy Spirit
  atonement and 132
  awakening power of 215, 236
  as awakening power of Jesus Christ 140
  Christian community and 130–4
  Christian community called into being
    by 142
  Christian community gathered by 163
  Church and 139–41
  confession of faith and 230
  Jesus Christ and 135
  reconciliation and 177
  work of 130–7, 139–41, 177
hope, justification and 87–8, 91–2
human beings
  divine sonship of 86–7
  dualism of 30–2, 35
  faith as act of 240–1, 246, 258
  God giving time for 225–8
  God's right over 24
  God's role in justification of 4, 18,
    31–2
  old v. new 54–5, 69, 80–1, 236–7, 239
  pardon of 54–94
  participation in reconciliation
    of 130–2, 178
  relationship with Jesus Christ of 232
  righteousness of God over 28–31
  righteousness of justified 80–1, 85, 89
  self-contradiction of sinful 74
  self-demonstration of justified 97–9,
    115–16
  self-understanding of 230
  sentence of God on 54
  as subject of justification 94–7
  turning to God 43
  vain-glory of 104
  wrong of 21, 22, 26–7, 35, 43, 82
humanism 95, 110
humility
  of faith 99–100, 104–6, 113–14
  obedience of 113, 121–3

individualism 95
inheritance 58, 81, 90, 92, 153
invisible Church 139–42, 144, 146, 156–7
Islam 164
Israel
  Church and 11, 158–9
  election of 18
  Law and 72–3, 108–9

Index of Subjects

Jesus Christ
  action of   39, 50-1
  awakening power of   140
  call to faith by   248-9
  Christian community as body
    of   149-51, 154-6, 176, 186, 200
  confession of   15
  death of   1-2, 41-2, 50, 124
  divine obedience in   2, 41
  earthly-historical form of   207
  election of   155
  as event of faith   256
  faith in   118-20
  freedom and   126, 233-4
  God's right as Father of   50-3
  as head of Christian community   148-9, 176
  history of   131
  holiness of   178, 182-3, 189
  Holy Spirit and   135
  humiliation of   2
  innocence of   42
  isolation of   118-19
  judgement of God executed on   1-2
  justification in   37-8, 41, 43, 50, 116-17
  man's relationship with   232
  as Mediator   152-3
  mystery of   155
  parousia of   214, 215, 217, 221, 222-5, 228
  pride overcome in   260
  proclamation of   36, 177
  relationship of faith to   237-8
  as Representative   51-2
  resurrection of   2-3, 42-5, 50-4, 215, 217-21, 259-63
  righteousness of   36
  right restored in   262-3, 265
  as starting-point of faith   241
  as subject of justification   41-2
  work of God in   50
judgement
  execution of God's   1-2
  of God   1-2, 16-60
  justification and   3, 45
jurisdiction of God   22-3
justification
  as basis of Christian community   4-6
  beginning of   61, 62, 66-7
  of Church   169

  as creative work of God   59-60
  development of   11-13
  dialectic of   78
  divine sonship and   86-7
  dogmatics and   7-8
  Evangelical theology and   8-10
  experience of   33
  as expression of God's right as Creator   48-50
  by faith alone   94-129
  genuineness of   4-5
  God's role in   4, 18, 31-2
  grace of   111-12
  history of   32-5
  hope and   87-8, 91-2
  human wrong destroyed through   43
  in Jesus Christ   37-8, 41, 43, 50, 116-17
  Jesus Christ as subject of   41-2
  judgement and   3, 45
  knowledge of   77
  negation and   106-7
  pardon and   54-5, 58-61, 94
  presupposition of   4-5, 16-17
  primacy of   8-10
  problem of   1-16, 18, 67
  proclamation of   67, 218
  promise of   81-2, 85
  reconciliation and   7, 60
  Reformation and   101, 106-7, 113, 128
  resurrection and   50-3, 116
  righteousness of man in   80-1, 85, 89
  right of God and   20-1, 31-2
  Roman Catholic Church and   110-13, 257-8
  sanctification and   12-14, 123, 257-8
  self   47-8, 53-4, 102, 128
  self-demonstration of man in   97-9, 115-16
  subject of   94-7
  theological difficulty of   6, 7
  turning to God in   43
  as Word of Gospel   8-10

knowledge
  apolosticity and   210
  of faith   247, 253-6, 261, 264
  genuineness of   79
  of justification   79
  self   69, 73, 77
  of sin   77, 79, 80

Index of Subjects

latent sin   71
Law
  faith v.   107, 110
  freedom and   68–9
  of Israel   72–3, 108–9
  sin v.   70–5
law of gospel   138
law of sin   70–5
Liberalism   193
Lord's Prayer   82
Lord's Supper   154, 164, 170, 181, 183
Lutheran Church   203, 205
Lutheranism   9, 165, 168, 170

man *see* human beings
Methodist Church   168, 170
modern positivism   193
modern Protestantism   195, 244, 246
modern theology   193
moral categories   230
mystical body   146

National Socialism   192
neo-Lutheranism   10, 12
neo-Protestantism   193

obedience
  of Christian community   189–90
  faith and   106, 113, 121–3
  of humility   113, 121–3
  of Jesus Christ   2, 41
  recognition of faith in   251
Orthodox Church   164

pardon
  absoluteness of   55–6
  as affirmation   78–9
  divine sentence and   54–6, 58–61, 63, 83, 89
  grace and   60–1
  justification and   54–5, 58–61, 94
  of man   54–94
  receiving   55
  resurrection and   54
  unconditional   59
Peace of Westphalia   165
penitence   56, 61, 80, 83, 118, 122, 164, 172
Pentecost   132, 136, 154, 158, 199
Pharisaism   102

Pietism   230, 244
positivism   193
primitive catholicism   207
proclamation
  of atonement   219
  Christian community and   137, 248–9, 253, 255, 259
  of Jesus Christ   36, 177
  of justification   67, 218
Protestantism, modern   195, 244, 246

recognition of faith   247, 250–6, 259–63
reconciliation   131, 224
  credo ecclesiam and   147
  faith and   5
  final goal of   85
  grace and   60
  justification and   7, 60
  man's active participation in   130–2, 178
  message of   10
  work of Holy Spirit and   177
  of world with God   218–19, 224, 226, 232
Reformation   10, 12, 193, 196, 205, 212
  justification by faith and   101, 106–7, 113, 128
  Roman Catholic opposition to   191
Reformed Church   12, 164, 165, 170, 205
resurrection
  as beginning   42–3, 217–21
  confession of belief in   141
  divine judgement and   43–5
  innocence of Jesus Christ and   42
  justification and   50–3, 116
  pardon and   54
  recognition of faith and   259–63
  sentence of God revealed in   1–3
revelation   224
right
  of God   16–18, 20, 21, 23–4, 27, 31–2, 47–53
  of God as Creator of man   48–50
  of God as Father   50–3
  God giving   3–4
  of God over man   24
  restoration of   262–3, 265
  sin v.   16
  of sonship   86–7

278

Index of Subjects

righteousness
   faith and 100–1
   of God 16–17, 19, 24–6, 28–31, 36
   grace hidden by 26
   of justified man 80–1, 85, 89
   in Psalms 56–8
Roman Catholic Church 164, 168, 201, 203
   christological renaissance in 257
   dogmatics of 198
   ecclesiology of 202
   Evangelical theology opposed by 191
   justification and 110–13, 257–8
   mass of 170
   redemptive system of 107, 111
   Reformation opposed by 191
   sanctification and 258

sacrifice 257
salvation, Church and 177
sanctification 7
   justification and 12–14, 123, 257–8
   Roman Catholic Church and 258
Scripture principle 211
self-attestation of God 22
self-demonstration 97–9, 115–16
self-determination 22
self-justification 47–8, 53–4, 102, 128
self-knowledge 69, 73, 77
self-manifestation of God 207
self-understanding 34, 230

sin
   confession of 64–5, 80
   forgiveness of 82–5
   knowledge of 77, 79, 80
   latent 71
   law of 70–5
   right v. 16
   self-contradiction of 74
skepticism 95
sonship, right of 86–7

theology
   difficulty of justification in 6, 7
   Evangelical 8–10, 101, 191
   modern 193
totalitarianism 15, 95, 165
Tridentinum 111–12

unconditional pardon 59
unitarian movements 170

vain-glory 104, 105, 119
veritas catholica 198, 201–2
visible Church 139–42, 145, 156–7

Whitsunday 137
Word of God
   Church and 140–1
   made flesh 207
work of Holy Spirit 130–7, 139–41, 177

INDEX OF NAMES

Alexander VI 195
Augustine 132

Baier, J. W. 9
Balthasar, H. U. von 147, 257
Bartmann, B. 198
Biedermann, A. E. 203
Bjornson, B. 95
Böhl, E. 12
Buddeus, J. F. 9
Bultmann, R. 250, 256, 257

Calvin, J. 12, 13, 14, 103, 110, 114, 175, 177, 178, 183, 248, 250, 251, 252
Contarini, C. 110
Cullmann, O. 162
Cyril of Jerusalem 203

Dostoievski, F. M. 95

Elisabeth of Dijon 257

Gerhardt, M. 245
Gyllenkrok, A. 13

Heer, F. 147
Henry VIII 205
Herder, J. G. 146
Herrmann, W. 244, 250
Hirsch, E. 165
Hollaz, D. 9

Ibsen, H. 95

Kähler, M. 10, 175
Keller, G. 64
Kierkegaard, S. 95, 177, 230, 244
Kohlbrügge, H. F. 12

Lucius, S. 9
Luther, M. 6, 7, 8, 9, 10, 11, 12, 13, 14, 91, 106, 108, 109, 110, 113, 114, 132, 140, 145, 179, 181, 182, 244, 250, 255, 256, 257

Marcion 109
Mauthner, F. 96
Melanchthon, P. 11, 110

Nietzsche, F. 95

Osiander, A. 12

Pelagius 10
Pius XII 146

Reuter, H. 96

Schenkendorf, M. von 236
Schiller, J. C. F. von 198
Schleiermacher, F. E. D. 143
Schneider, R. 257
Schopenhauer, A. 95
Schweitzer, A. 11
Strindberg, (J.) A. 95

Tersteegen, G. 203
Tertullian 132
Theresa of Lisieux 257
Tolstoy, L. 95

Wesley, J. 9
Wolf, Ernst 8
Wrede, W. 11

Zinzendorf, N. L. Graf von 9, 114, 171, 245
Zwingli, H. 12, 110, 140, 200

CPSIA information can be obtained
at www.ICGtesting.com
Printed in the USA
LVHW022358260722
724418LV00004B/142